Tudor Government

Tudor Government

Structures of Authority in the Sixteenth Century

DAVID LOADES

Copyright © David Loades 1997

The right of David Loades to be identified as author of this work has been asserted in accordance with the Copyright, Designs and Patents Act 1988.

First published 1997

2 4 6 8 10 9 7 5 3 1

DA
315
.L578
1997

Blackwell Publishers Ltd
108 Cowley Road
Oxford OX4 1JF
UK

Blackwell Publishers Inc.
Commerce Place
350 Main Street
Malden, Massachusetts 02148
USA

All rights reserved. Except for the quotation of short passages for the purposes of criticism and review, no part of this publication may be reproduced, stored in a retrieval system, or transmitted, in any form or by any means, electronic, mechanical, photocopying, recording or otherwise, without the prior permission of the publisher.

Except in the United States of America, this book is sold subject to the condition that it shall not, by way of trade or otherwise, be lent, resold, hired out, or otherwise circulated without the publisher's prior consent in any form of binding or cover other than that in which it is published and without a similar condition including this condition being imposed on the subsequent purchaser.

British Library Cataloguing in Publication Data

A CIP catalogue record for this book is available from the British Library.

Library of Congress Cataloging-in-Publication Data

Loades, D. M.
    Tudor government : structures of authority in the sixteenth century / David Loades.
    p.   cm.
    Includes bibliographical references (p.) and index.
    ISBN 0–631–19156–9 (acid-free paper). — ISBN 0–631–19157–7 (pbk. : acid-free paper)
    1. Great Britain—Politics and government—1485–1603. 2. Power (Social sciences)—England—History—16th century. 3. Church and state—England—History—16th century. 4. Authority—History—16th century. I. Title.
    DA315.L578   1997
    320.942'09'031—dc21   96–54621
                                                                              CIP

Typeset in 10.5 on 12pt Plantin
by Grahame and Grahame Editorial
Printed in Great Britain by T. J. Press International Limited, Padstow, Cornwall

This book is printed on acid-free paper

Contents

Maps

Preface

Constitutional history has been out of fashion for a generation. It is now fifteen years since the publication of the second edition of Sir Geoffrey Elton's *Tudor Constitution*, and recent political history has paid little attention to the skeleton of government. There has been excellent work upon particular regions, specific social groups, individuals, and social and economic trends, but little upon institutions, with the exception of parliament. When Sir Geoffrey's influence was at its height, his research students were working on the Royal court, upon Requests, Star Chamber, Augmentations, the Privy Council, and every part of the central machinery. However, even then sheriffs, coroners and escheators, to say nothing of deans, archdeacons and petty constables, were underserved by scholarship. Even the *Tudor Constitution* itself contains only twenty pages upon local government, apart from the regional councils. The diligent scholar supported by a good library, has no difficulty in finding works on the administration of justice, or upon the clerical profession, or upon the changing roles of gentry and nobility. However, it is difficult for the student to find a general work which provides a structural map of the offices and institutions of Tudor England, or any guidance as to how they related to each other. Penry Williams's admirable *The Tudor Regime* is a study of a society in motion, more concerned with dynamics than with statics, and the same could be said of Stephen Gunn's more recent *Early Tudor Government, 1485–1558*. That is the best approach for an understanding of political events and developments, but it leaves a gap. This survey consequently makes no claims to originality of either content or method, but aims to provide the student with an accessible guide to official and institutional relationships at all levels. Tudor society treated status with immense seriousness, and status became increasingly linked to office. That is the progressive theme of the work – the thesis – but without the framework it makes little sense. The literature of this subject is potentially enormous, and a bibliography of some of the more important work is appended, together with a glossary of terms which may be unfamiliar or require accurate definition.

Tudor government was in many respects pragmatic. Like politicians in any age, Henry VII, his son and his grandchildren were concerned with the art of the possible. Only Edward VI and Mary could be said to have followed ideological agendas, and the special circumstances of a minority mean that the latter enjoys the unique distinction of being the only Tudor to act consistently out of conviction rather than opportunism. However, that did not mean that there was no ideological framework, and it is essential to understand contemporary ideas of law, and of the Divine authority, in order to make sense of what was done – and not done. Medieval and early modern man always started with God, who was the source of all legitimate power. That power could be devolved in numerous ways. The papacy had long claimed to be a unique channel, through which the divine will could be mediated to emperors and kings as well as to patriarchs and bishops. Such claims had been challenged from their inception, not only by successive Holy Roman emperors, who also claimed a unique mandate, but also by other kings and independent rulers. By the time of the renaissance it was generally accepted that the papacy (with or without the partnership of General Councils) exercised spiritual authority, while the temporal 'sword' remained with the secular rulers. This was a rough and ready solution, which left plenty of scope for skirmishing along the jurisdictional boundaries, and a good deal of room for ambitious princes like Henry VIII to develop their positions before they reached the toleration limits of the existing structure.

There were also some entirely different ideas about how God's authority was mediated: via the collegiality of Christian bishops; directly to all territorial lords; or even to the *populus,* which then elected its magistrates and rulers. The first of these had appeared in the Conciliar movement of the fifteenth century, and was of little relevance to Tudor England; but elements of the second can be found in the concept of 'the lord in his country', and of the third in the massive complexities of the common law. It is therefore essential to grasp the theories which were accepted by the Tudors and their subjects, and the extent to which they were challenged. That is why a study which is primarily about structures starts with a chapter on ideas. To anyone brought up in the context of twentieth-century liberal democracy, some of these ideas will seem strange, but it is essential to realize that the utilitarian principle that the purpose of society is 'the greatest happiness of the greatest number' was a product of the eighteenth-century enlightenment. Sixteenth-century rulers, or magistrates, certainly believed that it was their duty to safeguard the well-being of those whom God had entrusted to their care, but that had little to do with happiness, and nothing to do with numbers. All the Tudors started from their relationship with God, even if Henry VIII did have a propensity to create a deity in his own likeness. My intention, therefore, in offering this book is to provide a guide to structures both intellectual and institutional, because without the one the other often makes little sense.

As I have struggled with numerous distractions to complete it, I have incurred the usual debts of gratitude: to Tessa Harvey at Blackwell for her patience; to my wife Judith for her constant support; and above all to the late Sir Geoffrey Elton, who sadly died while the book was in preparation. I hope he would have regarded it as a modest supplement to the *Tudor Constitution*.

David Loades
Oxford

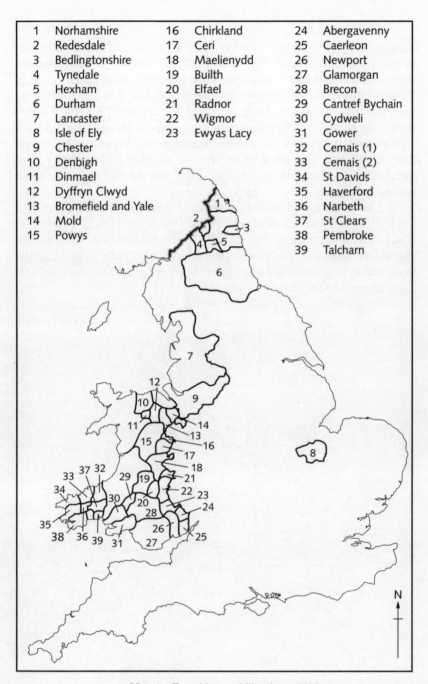

1	Norhamshire	16	Chirkland	24	Abergavenny
2	Redesdale	17	Ceri	25	Caerleon
3	Bedlingtonshire	18	Maelienydd	26	Newport
4	Tynedale	19	Builth	27	Glamorgan
5	Hexham	20	Elfael	28	Brecon
6	Durham	21	Radnor	29	Cantref Bychain
7	Lancaster	22	Wigmor	30	Cydweli
8	Isle of Ely	23	Ewyas Lacy	31	Gower
9	Chester			32	Cemais (1)
10	Denbigh			33	Cemais (2)
11	Dinmael			34	St Davids
12	Dyffryn Clwyd			35	Haverford
13	Bromefield and Yale			36	Narbeth
14	Mold			37	St Clears
15	Powys			38	Pembroke
				39	Talcharn

Map 1 Franchises and liberties *c.* 1490

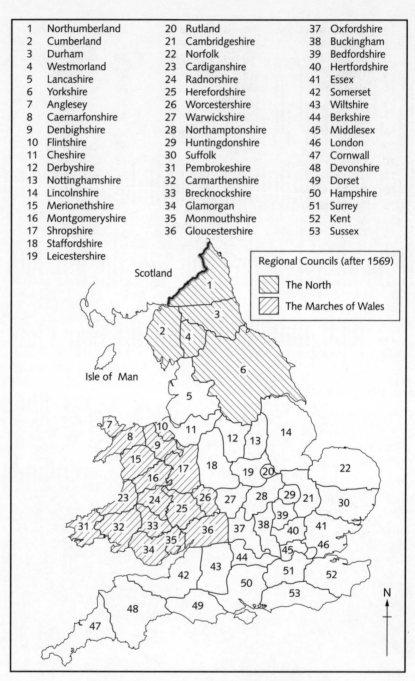

1	Northumberland	20	Rutland	37	Oxfordshire
2	Cumberland	21	Cambridgeshire	38	Buckingham
3	Durham	22	Norfolk	39	Bedfordshire
4	Westmorland	23	Cardiganshire	40	Hertfordshire
5	Lancashire	24	Radnorshire	41	Essex
6	Yorkshire	25	Herefordshire	42	Somerset
7	Anglesey	26	Worcestershire	43	Wiltshire
8	Caernarfonshire	27	Warwickshire	44	Berkshire
9	Denbighshire	28	Northamptonshire	45	Middlesex
10	Flintshire	29	Huntingdonshire	46	London
11	Cheshire	30	Suffolk	47	Cornwall
12	Derbyshire	31	Pembrokeshire	48	Devonshire
13	Nottinghamshire	32	Carmarthenshire	49	Dorset
14	Lincolnshire	33	Brecknockshire	50	Hampshire
15	Merionethshire	34	Glamorgan	51	Surrey
16	Montgomeryshire	35	Monmouthshire	52	Kent
17	Shropshire	36	Gloucestershire	53	Sussex
18	Staffordshire				
19	Leicestershire				

Regional Councils (after 1569)

The North

The Marches of Wales

Scotland

Isle of Man

N

Map 2   The counties of England and Wales *c.* 1600

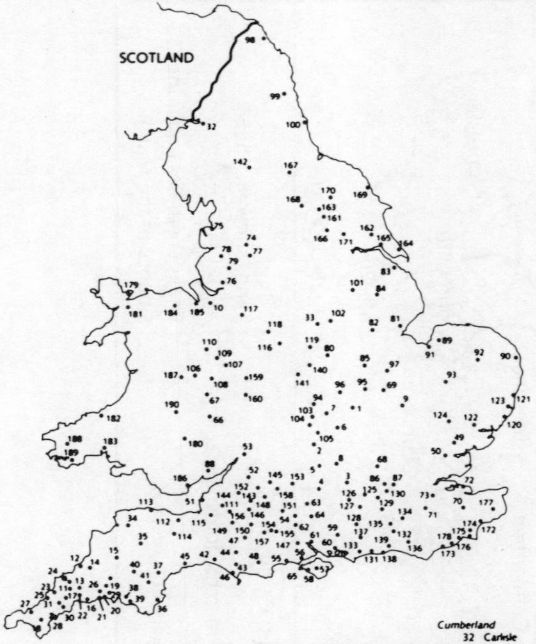

Map 3 Parliamentary boroughs c. 1600

ENGLAND

Bedfordshire
1 Bedford

Berkshire
2 Abingdon
3 New Windsor
4 Reading
5 Wallingford

Buckinghamshire
6 Aylesbury
7 Buckingham
8 Chipping Wycombe

Cambridgeshire
9 Cambridge

Cheshire
10 Chester

Cornwall
11 Bodmin
12 Bossiney
13 Camelford
14 Callington
15 Dunheved (Launceston)
16 Fowey
17 Grampound
18 Helston
19 Liskeard
20 East Looe
21 West Looe
22 Lostwithiel
23 Mitchell
24 Newport
25 Penryn
26 St Germans
27 St Ives
28 St Mawes
29 Saltash
30 Tregony
31 Truro

Cumberland
32 Carlisle

Derbyshire
33 Derby

Devon
34 Barnstaple
35 Beer Alston
36 Dartmouth
37 Exeter
38 Plymouth
39 Plympton
40 Tavistock
41 Totnes

Dorset
42 Bridport

43 Corfe Castle
44 Dorchester
45 Lyme Regis
46 Melcombe Regis (Weymouth)
47 Shaftesbury
48 Wareham

Essex
49 Colchester
50 Maldon

Gloucestershire
51 Bristol
52 Cirencester
53 Gloucester

Hampshire
54 Andover
55 Christchurch
56 Lymington
57 Newport Isle of Wight
58 Newtown Isle of Wight
59 Petersfield
60 Portsmouth
61 Southampton
62 Stockbridge
63 Whitchurch
64 Winchester
65 Yarmouth Isle of Wight

Herefordshire
66 Hereford
67 Leominster

Hertfordshire
68 St Albans

Huntingdonshire
69 Huntingdon

Kent
70 Canterbury
71 Maidstone
72 Queenborough
73 Rochester

Lancashire
74 Clitheroe
75 Lancaster
76 Liverpool
77 Newton
78 Preston
79 Wigan

Leicestershire
80 Leicester

Lincolnshire
81 Boston
82 Grantham
83 Grimsby
84 Lincoln
85 Stamford

Middlesex
86 London
87 Westminster

Monmouthshire
88 Monmouth Borough

Norfolk
89 Castle Rising
90 Great Yarmouth
91 Kings Lynn
92 Norwich
93 Thetford

Northamptonshire
94 Brackley
95 Higham Ferrers
96 Northampton
97 Peterborough

Northumberland
98 Berwick-on-Tweed
99 Morpeth
100 Newcastle upon Tyne

Nottinghamshire
101 East Retford
102 Nottingham

Oxfordshire
103 Banbury
104 New Woodstock
105 Oxford

Rutland

Shropshire
106 Bishop's Castle
107 Bridgnorth
108 Ludlow
109 Much Wenlock
110 Shrewsbury

Somerset
111 Bath
112 Bridgwater
113 Minehead
114 Taunton
115 Wells

Staffordshire
116 Lichfield
117 Newcastle under Lyme
118 Stafford
119 Tamworth

Suffolk
120 Aldeburgh
121 Dunwich
122 Ipswich
123 Orford
124 Sudbury

Surrey
125 Bletchingley
126 Gatton
127 Guildford
128 Haslemere
129 Reigate
130 Southwark

Sussex
131 Arundel
132 Bramber

133 Chichester
134 East Grinstead
135 Horsham
136 Lewes
137 Midhurst
138 New Shoreham
139 Steyning

Warwickshire
140 Coventry
141 Warwick

Westmorland
142 Appleby

Wiltshire
143 Calne
144 Chippenham
145 Cricklade
146 Devizes
147 Downton
148 Great Bedwyn
149 Heytesbury
150 Hindon
151 Ludgershall
152 Malmesbury
153 Marlborough
154 Old Sarum
155 Salisbury
156 Westbury
157 Wilton
158 Wootton Bassett

Worcestershire
159 Droitwich
160 Worcester

Yorkshire
161 Aldborough
162 Beverley
163 Boroughbridge
164 Hedon
165 Kingston upon Hull
166 Knaresborough
167 Richmond
168 Ripon
169 Scarborough
170 Thirsk
171 York

Cinque Ports
172 Dover
173 Hastings
174 Hythe
175 New Romney
176 Rye
177 Sandwich
178 Winchelsea

WALES

Anglesey
179 Beaumaris

Brecknockshire
180 Brecon Borough

Caernarfonshire
181 Caernarfon Borough

Cardiganshire
182 Cardigan Borough

Carmarthenshire
183 Carmarthen Borough

Denbighshire
184 Denbigh Borough

Flintshire
185 Flint Borough

Glamorganshire
186 Cardiff Borough

Merionethshire

Montgomeryshire
187 Montgomery Borough

Pembrokeshire
188 Haverford West
189 Pembroke Borough

Radnorshire
190 New Radnor Borough

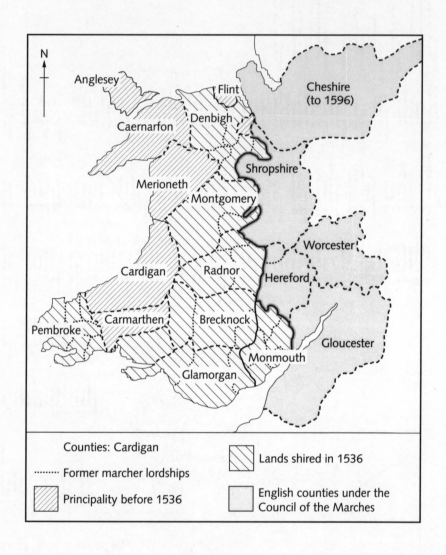

N

Anglesey

Flint

Cheshire
(to 1596)

Caernarfon

Denbigh

Shropshire

Merioneth

Montgomery

Worcester

Cardigan

Radnor

Hereford

Carmarthen

Brecknock

Pembroke

Gloucester

Monmouth

Glamorgan

Counties: Cardigan

Lands shired in 1536

········ Former marcher lordships

Principality before 1536

English counties under the
Council of the Marches

Map 4 Wales and the Acts of Union

N

O'Donnell

O'Neill

O'Rourke

Burke

Ulster

Louth

Dublin

O'Flaherty

Connaught

Meath

The Pale

Burke

O'Brien

Kerry

Tipperary

Limerick

Kilkenny

Cork

Wexford

Waterford

O'Brien	Gaelic overlords
Wexford	Counties
▨	The obedient lands

Map 5 Ireland *c.* 1530

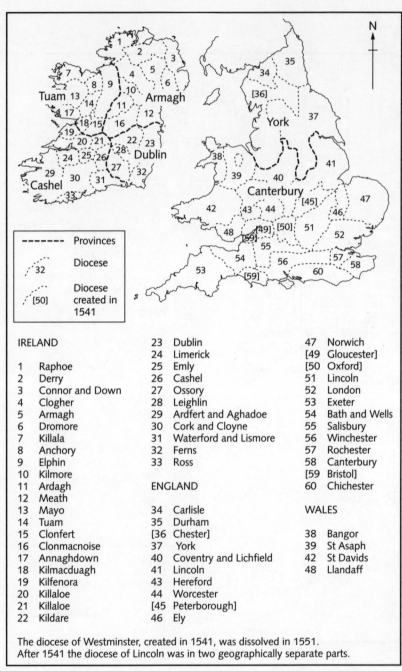

Map 6 The dioceses of England, Wales and Ireland *c.* 1600

N

-------	Provinces
32	Diocese
[50]	Diocese created in 1541

IRELAND

1 Raphoe
2 Derry
3 Connor and Down
4 Clogher
5 Armagh
6 Dromore
7 Killala
8 Anchory
9 Elphin
10 Kilmore
11 Ardagh
12 Meath
13 Mayo
14 Tuam
15 Clonfert
16 Clonmacnoise
17 Annaghdown
18 Kilmacduagh
19 Kilfenora
20 Killaloe
21 Killaloe
22 Kildare

23 Dublin
24 Limerick
25 Emly
26 Cashel
27 Ossory
28 Leighlin
29 Ardfert and Aghadoe
30 Cork and Cloyne
31 Waterford and Lismore
32 Ferns
33 Ross

ENGLAND

34 Carlisle
35 Durham
[36 Chester]
37 York
40 Coventry and Lichfield
41 Lincoln
43 Hereford
44 Worcester
[45 Peterborough]
46 Ely

47 Norwich
[49 Gloucester]
[50 Oxford]
51 Lincoln
52 London
53 Exeter
54 Bath and Wells
55 Salisbury
56 Winchester
57 Rochester
58 Canterbury
[59 Bristol]
60 Chichester

WALES

38 Bangor
39 St Asaph
42 St Davids
48 Llandaff

The diocese of Westminster, created in 1541, was dissolved in 1551.
After 1541 the diocese of Lincoln was in two geographically separate parts.

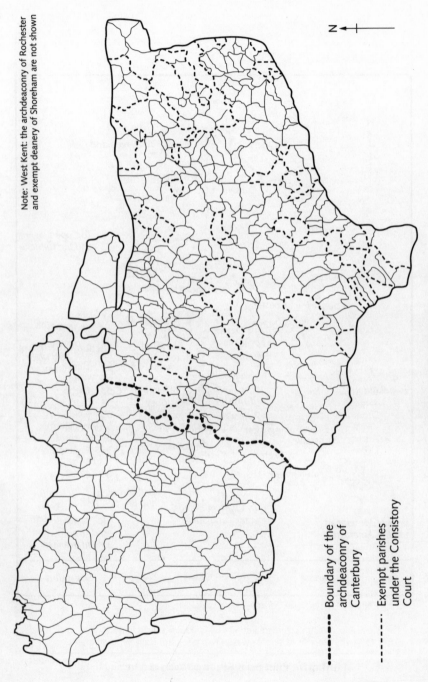

Note: West Kent: the archdeaconry of Rochester and exempt deanery of Shoreham are not shown

N

Boundary of the archdeaconry of Canterbury

Exempt parishes under the Consistory Court

Map 7 The Parishes of Kent pre-1830

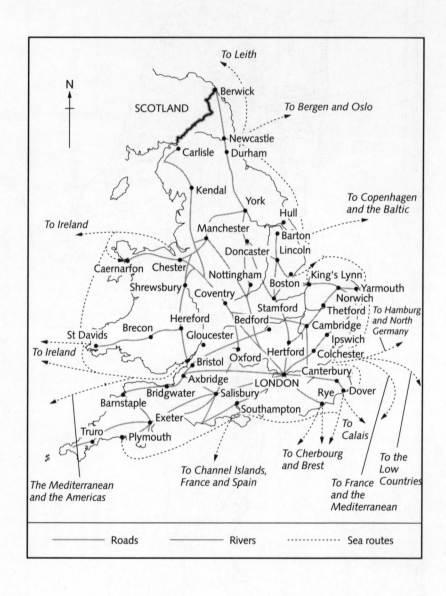

Map 8 Principal roads, rivers and sea routes *c.* 1600

Map 9a London c. 1600

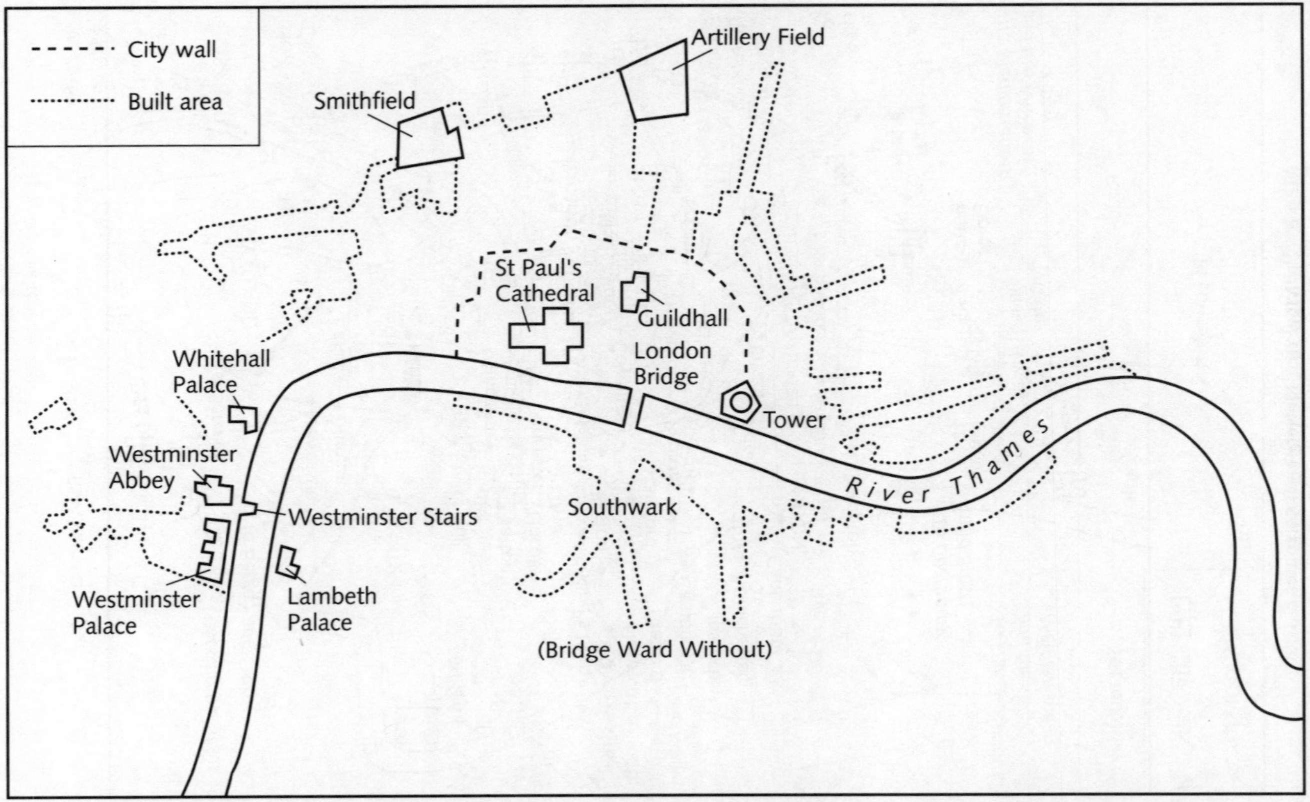

Legend:
- - - - City wall
.... Built area

Westminster Palace
Westminster Abbey
Westminster Palace
Whitehall Palace
Lambeth Palace
Westminster Stairs
Smithfield
St Paul's Cathedral
Guildhall
London Bridge
Artillery Field
Southwark
Tower
(Bridge Ward Without)
River Thames

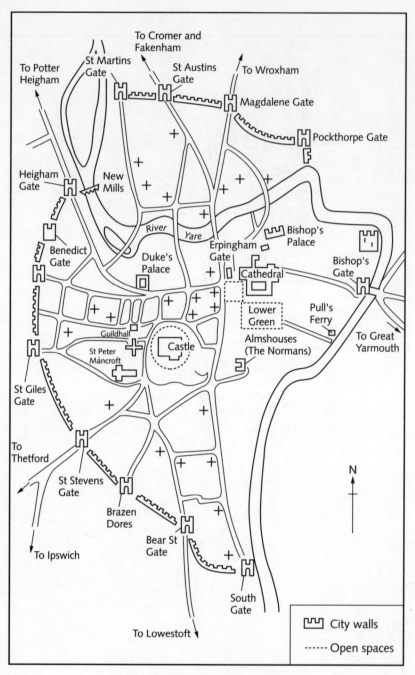

Map 9b Norwich *c.* 1550

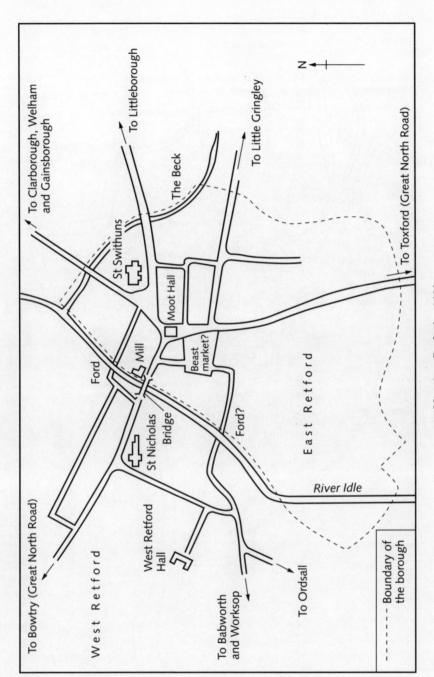

Map 9c Retford *c.* 1600

To Littleborough

To Clarborough, Welham
and Gainsborough

The Beck

To Little Gringley

N

St Swithuns

Moot Hall

To Toxford (Great North Road)

Ford

Mill

Beast
market?

East Retford

St Nicholas
Bridge

Ford?

River Idle

West Retford
Hall

To Bowtry (Great North Road)

West Retford

To Babworth
and Worksop

To Ordsall

- - - - - Boundary of
the borough

Introduction

Theories of Authority

Sixteenth-century England had no concept of sovereignty.[1] What is usually called the sovereignty of the Tudor state was a unilateral declaration of independence from the papacy, which did not embrace any theory of accountability. As Jean Bodin, the contemporary French theorist, pointed out in chapter 8 of his first book, it is meaningless to describe as sovereign any person or institution which is subject to constraint or limitation.[2] A sovereign must by definition be immune from any lawful resistance whatsoever, for the person in whom sovereignty rests is required 'to give account to none but to the immortal God alone'. English writers from Sir John Fortescue to Sir Thomas Smith spoke of 'most high and absolute power', but they were thinking within a context of medieval law. When Henry Bracton had written that the king should be 'under God and the law' he had not been using a polite figure of speech but declaring a contractual theory of monarchy. Monarchs were officers who derived their authority from God, and were answerable to him, but their office had been created for a purpose, and others had a legitimate interest in the way in which it was exercised. Hence the critical importance of consent. 'That which touches all must be approved by all' had been a commonplace of the canon law, much emphasized by the Thomists, and picked up during the Reformation period by Francisco de Vitoria. That consent had traditionally been given substance in two ways. In

1   I use the term 'England' to mean 'the realm of England', that is all the posses-sions of the English crown. Where the word is used in the more limited sense of England as distinct from Wales or Ireland, this is usually apparent from the context. 'The counties of England', for example, does not include Wales (which had no counties until 1536) or Ireland (where counties were rather different). After 1541 Ireland was a separate kingdom, and therefore not part of the 'realm of England'.
2   Jean Bodin, *Six Books of the Commonwealth*, ed. M.J. Tooley (1967), pp. 25–36.

the first place the feudal contract bound monarchs and their vassals in a mutually recognized system of rights and obligations, and second, customary codes of law were not seen as the products of identifiable legislative wills. Consequently to say that the king was 'under the law' meant that he was obliged to act within the framework prescribed by the customs of his realm. How such an obligation could be enforced, or its neglect properly identified, were subjects of fierce controversy. The feudal contract was the more tangible, and its defenders were swift to appear. In England it had been the nobility who had put an end to the absolutist pretensions of John, of Edward II and of Richard II, although in each case violations of the law beyond the feudal contract had been alleged. By the 1470s, when Sir John Fortescue was writing *De Laudibus Legum Angliae* (*Concerning the Laws of the Realm of England*), it was self evident that the monarch exercised authority within a firmly established network of constraints. The *dominium politicum et regale* was not so much a theory as an observation.

Fortescue's pragmatism was shared by his Tudor successors, who were less concerned with political philosophy than with the need to justify the twists and turns of royal policy. Stephen Gardiner's *De Vera Obedientia Oratio* (*An Oration concerning the Obedience*) was a defence of the break with Rome, and Sir Thomas Smith's *De Republica Anglorum* (*Concerning the Government of England*) a constitutional analysis of the position which had been reached as a result of the upheavals of the previous thirty years.[3] The only people who approached a principled discussion of the proper uses of political power were the Protestants challenged by Mary's restoration of the papal obedience. Christopher Goodman, in *How Superior Powers Ought to be Obeyed,* expanded upon the familiar idea that kings are God's lieutenants to conclude that only the godly might exercise legitimate authority. At the same time he returned to an ancient gloss upon the responsibility of kings to their subjects, assuming rather than declaring that all kingship should be elective. Putting these two ideas together, he urged that true monarchy should be a kind of populist theoracy: 'The Word giveth us these notes to know whether he be of God or not whom we would choose for our king.'[4] The people thus became in some undefined sense not only the arbiters of what their rulers did,

---

3 Stephen Gardiner, *De Vera Obedientia Oratio*, trans. and ed. P. Janelle, *Obedience in Church and State* (1930); Sir Thomas Smith, *De Republica Anglorum*, ed. Mary Dewar (1982).
4 Christopher Goodman, *How Superior Powers Ought to be Obeyed* (1558), p. 50.

but of who those rulers should be. It is not surprising that after Mary's death Goodman found himself in a political wilderness, but he had none the less addressed fundamental issues which mainstream Tudor writers had shirked. In one sense Elizabeth's accession gave Goodman what he wanted, but at the same time it made debate of the kind which he had encouraged extremely dangerous. No doubt if they had been asked to vote in November 1558 the people of England would have chosen Henry VIII's only surviving child as their queen, but that was not the ground upon which she claimed the throne. Elizabeth's title depended upon an Act of Parliament – her father's last Succession Act of 1543 – because by no stretch of legal imagination could both Henry's daughters be legitimate, and Mary had been accepted as the lawful heir.[5] Whether she liked it or not, Elizabeth was therefore a 'constitutional' monarch, and all talk of indefeasible hereditary right was designed to press the claim of Mary Stuart, the legitimacy of whose descent from Henry VII was unchallengeable. This delicate situation, and the political stability which depended upon it, put an effective dampener upon all speculation concerning the nature of the monarchy for the next thirty years.

It was only after Mary's execution in 1587, and the devolution of her claim upon her Protestant son James VI, that debate of a sort could resume. Although the queen could not be brought to admit it, and discouraged all such speculation to the very best of her power, James was the obvious candidate. However, his mother had been excluded from the Succession Act of 1543, and the basis of his claim was therefore the opposite of Elizabeth's. Consequently we find by the 1590s what might loosely be described as 'divine right' arguments appearing for the first time in England, while a 'constitutional' position was being adopted by the Jesuit Robert Parsons, who would have preferred to see the Spanish Infanta on the throne.[6] This led to some tortuous and illogical reasoning, because the English were very reluctant to abandon the supremacy of statute, and yet found themselves forced into arguing that Henry's last Succession Act was *ultra vires* – an extremely dangerous proposition as long as Elizabeth was alive. Both Sir John Hayward and Sir Thomas Craig argued that no human

5 At the time of their father's death both Mary and Elizabeth had been declared illegitimate by statute, in spite of being included in the succession. Mary's legitimacy had been affirmed after her accession.
6 Parsons, using the pseudonym 'R. Doleman', published *A Conference about the Next Succession* in 1595, arguing against James's right mainly on the grounds that he was a heretic.

authority could abrogate any part of the Law of God, which was
deemed to include the principle of hereditary succession:

> To begin then with the Law of God, I can scarcely think that any man
> can be so brutish as to imagine that any Mortal can derogate from the
> Laws of God or Divine Right. And that process of Henry VIII against
> his wife Queen Katherine, which was confirmed by the opinions and
> suffrages of so manie universities, expressly affirms that no man of what
> Degree, Estate or Condition he be, the Pope himself not excepted (tho
> these Jesuits think he can do any thing) hath power to dispense with
> God's law.[7]

Both also argued for what they called the 'sovereignty' of the prince,
but neither included in their definition of sovereignty the power to
make law. Both accepted that that function remained with the
monarch in parliament, and consequently failed to identify a sovereign power in England which would have satisfied Bodin's criteria.
Political reality is seldom logical, and the circumstances of 1603
required a divine right theory of the succession, coupled with a constitutional definition of how the royal power should be exercised. It is
not surprising that King James, with his passion for intellectual defi-
nitions, should have found the situation incomprehensible.

Without a sovereign will in Bodin's sense, there was no means of
cutting through the tangle of laws, but this was more a problem of
theory than of practice. In the Protestant polity which had emerged
by 1600, the law of God was effectively the scriptures as interpreted
by the most authoritative reformers, particularly John Calvin and the
authors of the Edwardian prayer books. This definition had the great
advantage of not being associated with any visible legislator. Although
the crown in parliament had in effect taken over the role of the pope
and the General Council in interpreting the will of God to
Englishmen, no one was prepared to accept the implications of that.
It was universally asserted that a valid statute must be consistent with
the law of God, and nobody attempted to justify the fact that parliament had created three conflicting religious settlements between 1549
and 1559. The same applied to the law of nature. In theory the law of
nature was implanted in all men, not only in Christians, and was not,
therefore, dependent upon revelation. Its consistency with the law of
God was assumed because the almighty was the originator of both,

7   Sir Thomas Craig, *Concerning the Right of Succession* (written about 1603 but
not published until 1703), p. 120.

but the law of the Bible was far more detailed and prescriptive than that of nature. Sir John Hayward was not a great thinker, but his definition of natural law is the more useful for that reason, in that it expresses little more than the accepted consensus:

> God in the creation of man imprinted certain rules within his soule, to direct him in all the actions of his life; which rules, because wee take them when we take our being, are commonly called the primarie lawe of Nature; of which sort the canons accompt these precepts following: To worship God; to obey parents and gouvenours and thereby to conserve the common society; lawful conjunction of man and woman; succession of children; education of children; acquisition of things which pertain to no man; equall libertie of all; to communicate commodities; to repel force; to hurte no man; and generally to do to another as he would be done unto, which is the sum and substance of the second book of the decalogue.[8]

Hayward was perfectly well aware that the whole of this catalogue was based upon the scriptures, and unconcerned about that, since his purpose was to assert the primacy of both natural and divine law over human law. A slightly earlier and even more undistinguished author, Charles Merbury, summed up the theoretical dilemma with unintentional clarity:

> But some will aske, if this great Monarche of ours shall not be subjecte unto the Lawes, Customs and privileges of the Contrey where he governeth; unto the othe which he taketh at his entrance; unto such covenantes and promises as he maketh unto his people. Unto whom we answer that our Prince is subject unto lawes both civill and common, to customs, privileges, covenantes and all kinds of Promises, so farre forth as they are agreeable unto the Lawe of God.[9]

So the prince was subject to law, but not to any human authority, a position which depended for its validity upon having no identifiable legislator.

This position could be maintained in England because the common law, which was the principal form of positive law in use, was customary in its origin. Not only did its early form long predate the appearance of parliament, but its first codification and application to

8   Sir John Hayward, *An Answer to the First Part of a Certain Conference* (1603), p. 46.
9   Charles Merbury, *A Briefe Discourse of Royall Monarchie* (1581), p. 44.

the purposes of unified royal government also went back to the reign
of Henry II. Consequently no one could argue that either the king or
the parliament had created the common law. This was certainly not
divine right monarchy as Bodin, or even King James, understood it,
but it was not constitutional monarchy in any modern sense either.
Sir Edward Coke appears to have believed that the common law itself
was sovereign, but his attempts to embody that law in the judiciary
failed totally when confronted with the fact that only the monarch
could appoint or dismiss judges.[10] It could be argued that the political theory of England at the end of the sixteenth century was an
illogical shambles, but it would be more realistic to understand that
the country was still living in a world of medieval pluralism, where
numerous laws and authorities interlocked, without a tidy hierarchy
and without any identifiable sovereign. In practice this situation did
not much inhibit the processes of government, any more than it had
undermined the effectiveness of such kings as Edward I or Edward
III. After 1535 the Tudor state was sovereign in the face of the outside
world, but its internal order depended upon a *de facto* concordat or
understanding between the monarch and the political nation. Such
concordats had existed before, and indeed constituted the normal
political situation, but because of developments which owed far more
to expediency than to principle, the political nation had become
increasingly identified with parliament. So much was this so that as
early as 1565 Sir Thomas Smith could declare 'The most high and
absolute power of the realme of Englande is in the Parliament.',
because the parliament embodied the concept of consent: 'For everie
Englishman is entended to bee there present, either in person or by
procuration and attornies, of what preheminence, state, dignitie or
quality soever he be, from the Prince (be he King or Queen) to the
lowest person of Englande. And the consent of the Parliament is
taken to be everie mans consent.'[11] Consequently for most practical
purposes parliament was sovereign, and its legislative instruments, or
statutes, of unchallengeable authority. Statute amended or interpreted the common law, controlled custom and contract, and
declared how the public worship of the church should be conducted.
However, parliament was a composite institution. It did not corres-

10 Coke was dismissed in November 1616 for his 'perpetual turbulent
carriage'. See J.S. Cockburn, *A History of the English Assizes, 1558–1714* (1972),
pp. 227–9.
11 Smith, *De Republica Anglorum*, p. 79.

pond to any of the classical categories so beloved of renaissance political thinkers, and continued to belong to the world of the *dominium
politicum et regale*.

So also did that much vaguer limitation upon the prince's freedom
of action known as 'good lordship'. Good lordship originated in the
feudal contract, whereby a vassal was required to serve his lord in arms
on specified terms, and to aid him with counsel, in return for the land
which he held. When disputes arose between the king's vassals,. they
naturally turned to him as arbitrator, not because he was the king, but
because he was their lord. Tenants in chief were not exempt from the
normal processes of law, but they did enjoy a privileged position
because the king was bound by his own side of the contract to protect
their interests and to listen to their advice. This was an arrangement
of mutual convenience which lay at the heart of the medieval state.
Because a vassal was bound to serve his lord in peace as well as war,
a king could use his tenants as executive agents to enforce his laws and
policies, not only upon their own dependents, but upon his subjects
at large. They could do this effectively because he had granted them
the necessary resources. As no feudal monarch enjoyed the revenues
necessary to support a full-scale professional bureaucracy, some such
arrangement was abolutely essential. The English situation, however,
differed from that appertaining in most of western Europe in that the
king did not use his vassals as judicial agents. Their enforcement of
the laws did not extend to the hearing of pleas, which remained in the
hands of justices directly answerable to the king.[12] By the fifteenth
century also the early and relatively simple structure had evolved in a
number of ways. A distinction had developed between tenancy in chief
and the status of nobility. It had always been accepted that only the
king could confer the title of earl, and this also applied to the titles of
viscount, marquis and duke as these were introduced. However, the
idea that anyone who held an honour directly of the king could be
styled a baron was only gradually displaced. The use of the title to
describe officers of the Exchequer and magistrates of the Cinque Ports
continued to reflect the earlier usage, although by 1440 it had become
established that only a barony created by royal patent entitled the
holder to an individual writ of summons to the parliament. When
Richard III chartered the College of Heralds in 1484, he was setting

12   All feudal lords heard the customary pleas in their honour and manor courts,
but pleas of the crown, which covered all issues of real property, felony and
treason, were heard exclusively in the king's courts. See below, pp. 70–9.

the seal on over a century of steady progress whereby the crown had established complete control over the award of titular honours.[13]

By the beginning of the Tudor period that control gave the king a powerful strategic advantage in dealing with a peerage which, because it was hereditary, had frequently been able to exploit periods of royal weakness. Similarly the feudal right of wardship, whereby the lord controlled both the person and the estate of any heir to a tenancy who entered as a minor, encouraged powerful families to acknowledge their dependent status. Nevertheless 'good lordship' remained a limitation, not least because it was imprecise. Henry VI lost his crown because he alienated too many of his nobles at the same time, and because he was not perceived to be dealing justly with those who served him. Henry VIII could deal ruthlessly with individual nobles who displeased him, such as the duke of Buckingham, but he was a generous patron to the peerage as a whole, and respected its military ambitions. When he declared in the aftermath of the Pilgrimage of Grace that he would not be bound to be served by lords in the north of his kingdom, but by whoever, of whatever status, he should see fit to appoint, he was articulating an ambition which was beyond his reach. Both Henry VII and Henry VIII broadened the basis of their lordship by employing and patronizing many men of lesser status – the knights and gentlemen who made up the elite of every county society – but that did not remove the contractual nature of the relationship. Henry VIII also created many 'service peers' from among his administrators and the kindred of his various wives. Just over half the peers alive at the time of his death in 1547 owed their titles to him, by way of either creation or promotion.[14] By the second half of the sixteenth century great magnates with virtually independent resources no longer offered a challenge to the monarch, but the collective political weight of the nobility had not greatly declined. What had changed was the extent to which the *nobilitas major* could control, as distinct from influencing, the *nobilitas minor*. Not only did the clientage systems of the Elizabethan peerage resemble the political networks of the eighteenth century more closely than they did the private armies of the fifteenth, but the monarch's own clientage had greatly increased in both quality and scale. As a result of these changes, 'good lordship' had become detached from its feudal roots, and had become a much

13   *Calendar of the Patent Rolls, Edward IV, Edward V and Richard III (1476–1485)* (1901), p. 422.
14   Helen Miller, *Henry VIII and the English Nobility* (1986), pp. 259–63.

wider *entente*. Elizabeth knew perfectly well that she could neither make nor enforce laws against the concerted opposition of the English aristocracy, and that whatever policy she wished to pursue had to be acceptable to most of them, most of the time.

This limitation was none the less real for being unexpressed. There was no theory of 'good lordship'. By the sixteenth century it had passed beyond the competence of feudal law and become a matter of custom and common sense. The theory which permitted this was not specific but general, or distributive. All authority was of divine origin, not only that of monarchs in their realms or bishops over their flocks, but also that of the lord in his 'country', the father over his family, or the master over his pupils. The right to property, the sanctity of inheritance, even the right to resist constituted authority in defence of contract or obligation, were all divine in origin. In practice most of the authority to which people were subjected in their daily lives derived by delegation from the prince, and that was particularly true in England where there was no independent *sacerdotium*, but this did not mean that the prince was the sole channel through which the authority of God was deployed. The conventional imagery of the state strove to express this reality. The commonest image was that of the natural body, of which the ruler constituted the head, the nobility the hands, and the peasantry the feet. This could be developed to elaborate lengths, and was frequently used to justify a hierarchy of subordination, but it did not constitute a theory of sovereignty. A classic example can be found in Thomas Starkey's *Dialogue between Pole and Lupset*:

> First, this is certain; that like as in every man there is a body and also a soul, in whose flourishing and prosperous state both together standeth the weal and felicity of man; so likewise there is in every commonalty, city and country as it were a politic body, and another thing also resembling the soul of man, in whose flourishing both together resteth also the true common weal. This body is nothing else but the multitude of people, the number of citizens, in every commonalty, city or country. The thing which is resembled to the soul is civil order and politic law, administered by officers and rulers. For like as the body in every man receiveth his life by the virtue of the soul, and is governed thereby, so doth the multitude of people in every country receive, as it were, civil life by laws well administered.[15]

15 Thomas Starkey, *A Dialogue between Pole and Lupset*, ed. T.F. Mayer (Camden Fourth Series, 37, 1989), p. 31.

Such a body politic was immutable, and the purpose of its existence was unspecified. It was assumed rather than stated that God had created such entities to further his own purposes for the redemption of mankind. The human body was the usual medieval metaphor, but it did not cope very well with the changes which renaissance politics was engendering. An alternative model was also to hand in classical antiquity – that of the state as artefact. Starting from Aristotle's proposition that man is by nature a political animal, the state became a set of institutions crafted by men to serve their own purposes, which were, or should have been, directed towards the provision of justice. Because each state had been created by human hands, it could be altered in the same way, and therefore the relationship between ends and means became critical. The most celebrated example of the artefact metaphor was the ship of state.[16] Not only is a ship designed and built for a purpose, but each particular voyage has a purpose and destination as well. If a ship is proved to be unseaworthy, it can be dismantled and reconstructed. Similarly if it sails off course, remedial action can be taken. The ship became a popular image with those who were anxious to retain the importance of consent in the political process, and who were opposed to what they saw as the insidious rise of royal power. By the ancient laws of the sea the captain was bound to consult his crew before making important decisions which involved the safety of the ship, and if he became drunk, or manifestly incapable, then they were entitled to remove him and place another in his room. The safety of the vessel and the discharge of its functions were more important than the principle of obedience.[17] It is not surprising that the ship of state became a favourite device of those who opposed the personal government of Charles I, but its implications had hardly begun to be explored at the time of Elizabeth's death.

The laws of the sea had been codified in the twelfth century, and were known as the Laws of Oleron, after an island near the mouth of the Gironde. Nobody knew how, or when, they had originated, or whether any authority existed which could change them.[18] They were customary laws *par excellence*. However, new circumstances demanded new remedies, and the international mercantile com-

16   E.g. John Foxe, *The First Volume of the Ecclesiastical History . . .* (1570), sig. 4v.
17   D. Burwash, *English Merchant Shipping, 1460–1540* (1947), pp. 171–6.
18   Sir Travers Twiss, *The Black Book of the Admiralty* (Rolls Series, 1871–6).

munity of the sixteenth century could not make do with such a primitive code. It consequently adopted, and adapted, the Roman or civil law. In so far as this was an imperial code which transcended territorial boundaries, it was appropriate, but in so far as it was the product of a legislative will, it was less so. Because the will which had created it was obsolete, this *lex maritima* could only be developed by judicial interpretation, like a customary code. It also bore the imprint of the circumstances which had produced it, and which were not particularly well suited to those to which it was adapted. For example, two witnesses were required to secure a conviction for piracy, following the code of Justinian, but the habits of pirates and the nature of the mariner's trade made it almost impossible to produce such witnesses when and where they were required. Laws might derive their prestige from antiquity, but the advantages of a contemporary and responsive legislative will were overwhelming. It had been this practical need, rather than any desire for enhanced authority, which had created the ability to make new law in a number of western European societies. In France the king legislated, with the consent of the sovereign courts, or *parlements*. These were corporations of professional lawyers. They had no representative function on behalf of the community, and they were vulnerable to coercion by the crown. The king's legislative will could be impeded, but not frustrated, and it was largely for that reason that Sir John Fortescue had described France as a *dominium regale*.[19] In England the process of consent was taken more seriously, and by the end of the thirteenth century it was becoming accepted that new laws needed not only the support of the king and the assent of his peers, but also the consent of the commons. This could only be obtained in a visible and recognized manner by the convening of a parliament, and parliament therefore became the sole legislative body. Parliament was called a high court, and continued to discharge judicial functions, but it did not legislate by judicial interpretation. A statute was a formal instrument, endorsed by king, lords and Commons, and was recognized by the end of the fourteenth century as the most authoritative pronouncement of which secular government was capable. Fortescue's definition of the English polity depended largely upon the formal participation of the Lords and Commons in the legislative process.

The competence of statute, however, was circumscribed by

19 Sir John Fortescue, *The Praise of the Laws of England,* trs. and ed. S.B. Chrimes (1942).

contemporary perceptions of the nature of law. No positive law, however made, could contradict or diminish the authority of natural or divine law. This meant, in the first place, that all spiritual matters were *ultra vires*, but parliament also avoided issues of inheritance, which pertained to the common law, and matters such as war and peace, or royal marriages, which were wholly within the prerogative of the crown. The Lords and Commons petitioned vigorously against what they considered to be malpractices in government, or abuses of authority on the part of either the king or the church, but accepted that they had no power of themselves to curb either. The theoretical relationship between statute and the common law was unclear. Where the law provided no remedy, the power of parliament to supply the deficiency was unquestioned. New offences could be created, and new penalties imposed for crimes already recognized, but altering the established principles of inheritance, or removing long-recognized rights, was another matter. A good example of the kind of problem which this uncertainty created can be seen in respect of the succession to the crown. There was no clear law of the succession, only custom, and when the duke of York claimed the throne against Henry VI in 1460, he was advancing the right of the heir general against that of the heir male.[20] When appealed to, the parliament declared itself to be incompetent to adjudicate on so high a mystery of state. Consequently at the end of the fifteenth century the legislative function of the parliament did not give it a firm control even over the common law, let alone over any of the higher codes. This situation was never explicitly confronted, but when the urgent need for a solution to Henry VIII's 'Great Matter' drove the king to resort to parliament in 1532, there were soon found to be unexpected potentialities in the power to legislate.

Signs of this had been visible much earlier. During a protracted quarrel with the papacy over the latter's claim to provide to vacant benefices in England, a series of statutes had been enacted, both against that claim and against the exercise of ecclesiastical jurisdiction without the king's licence. These had culminated in the great act of

20   Henry was descended directly in the male line from John of Gaunt, Duke of Lancaster, the fourth son of Edward III. Richard, Duke of York, was descended in the male line from Edmund of Langley, the fifth son, but he was also descended in the female line from Lionel, Duke of Clarence, the third son, and that was the basis of his claim.

Provisors and Praemunire of 1393.[21] Successive popes continued to regard this statute as an infringement of their prerogatives, and consequently a breach of divine law, but the English crown refused to budge on the ground that all questions of property, and of rights over it, belonged exclusively to English law. The same was also true of secular allegiance. The duty which a subject owed to the prince, and the breaches of that duty displayed by felony or treason, could be adjudicated only in the king's courts. The exercise of ecclesiastical jurisdiction could be represented both as an issue of property, and also as an issue of allegiance, especially if a breach of the 1393 statute could be alleged. It was along these lines that the English clergy were attacked in 1531–2. The original object was probably to coerce the pope into providing a solution to Henry's matrimonial problem within the recognized jurisdictional framework. Only when that failed did a more radical course have to be contemplated. The king was by nature a conservative man, and it was a measure of his desperation in 1533 that he was prepared to sanction such an attempt. Anglo-papal relations had been amicable in the recent past, and in 1521 Leo X had granted Henry the title *Fidei Defensor* for his polemic against Luther. However, unresolved issues remained from earlier generations; not only the Act of Provisors and Praemunire, but also the fact that King John had at one point surrendered his kingdom to the pope, and had received it back as a papal fief. Technically, therefore, the king of England remained a papal vassal, which was no more than a minor issue, but confused the conflict which was shortly to break out. As early as 1529–30 Henry had been advised that it was possible to challenge papal authority on the grounds that the church had no *dominium* in temporal matters.[22] Such ideas had been developed by anti-papal writers of earlier generations, notably Marsilius of Padua, whose *Defensor Pacis* (*Maintainer of the Peace*) had originally appeared in 1324. Marsilius's thesis had been that it was the mission of the church to teach and preach the gospel, not to rule. God had given coercive authority to Christian princes, and to what he called the *legislator humanus*, which he did not precisely define. Implicitly embracing this thesis, or something very like it, the king then allowed his chief adviser,

21 16 Richard II, c. 5.
22 A manuscript of advice to the king had been offered at about that time, known as the *collectanea satis copiosa* (*adequate collection for the purpose*), and containing that suggestion, among others. G. Nicholson, 'The Act of Appeals and the English Reformation', in *Law and Government under the Tudors*, eds C. Cross, D. Loades and J. Scarisbrick (1987), pp. 19–30.

Thomas Cromwell, to draft and to steer through parliament a series of acts decreeing punishments for those who refused to accept that the traditional *potestas jurisdictionis* of the church properly belonged to the king.

These statutes did not claim to create any new situation. The critical preamble to the Act in Restraint of Appeals used arguments of history and divine law to state that the ecclesiastical supremacy in England was, and always had been, vested in the crown.[23] This had recently been obscured by a conspiracy of clergy and the complacency of kings, but henceforth the proper and ancient order of church and state must be observed. Cromwell's strategy worked. Some of the Lords and Commons supported his bills, believing that the king would be a better and more effective reformer of the church than the pope had proved to be. Many believed that they were mere expedients to get rid of Queen Catherine, and would soon be forgotten. All accepted that parliament was the proper body to decree punishments for breaking the law, and most were prepared to overlook the fact that the law in question actually represented a revolutionary departure from accepted norms. It was because he recognized this fact, and announced it loudly, by his actions if not his words, that Sir Thomas More was so dangerous. Few, however, were prepared to be martyrs for the pope, and consequently by the time that Cromwell fell in 1540 it had become accepted that statute was the proper instrument to interpret the natural and divine laws in their application to the kingdom of England. The theoretical argument used to justify this was Marsilius's concept of the *legislator humanus*. In 1535 William Marshall published what was clearly a sponsored translation of the *Defensor Pacis*, in which he slightly adapted the author's original words to suit the circumstances of the king's Great Matter: 'the lawemaker or cheyfe and propre cause effectyve of the lawe is the people or the hole multytyed of cytesans inhabytauntes or ells the byggest part of the sayde multytude, by theyr elecyon or wyll by wordes expressed in the generall congergacyon parlymente or

---

23 'Where by divers sundry old authentic histories and chronicles it is manifestly declared and expressed that this realm of England is an Empire, and so hath been accepted in the world, governed by one supreme head and king having the dignity and royal estate of the Imperial crown of the same' (24 Henry VIII, c. 12). For the meaning of 'Empire' in this context, see G.R. Elton, *The Tudor Constitution*, 2nd edn (1982), pp. 338–45; W. Ullman, 'This realm of England is an Empire', *Journal of Ecclesiastical History*, 30, 1979, pp. 175–203.

assembly of the communes.'[24] Marsilius had not used any equivalent of the word 'parliament', but Marshall's rendering is legitimate. However, he then went on to omit those passages in which the original had attributed supreme executive authority also to the *legislator humanus*. To Marshall executive authority remained vested in the king alone, and he also omitted 'as nothyng appertaynynge to this realme of Englande' the provision that the *legislator* should exercise disciplinary control over all magistrates. Marsilius had envisaged an institution which was for all practical purposes sovereign, but Marshall was not prepared to go that far. He saw parliament as a legislator unrestrained by other laws or powers, but operating within a traditional context of government. That, after all, was what he was required to demonstrate.[25]

For the remainder of the sixteenth century, English constitutional practice advanced ahead of the theories which sought to justify it. It was apparently Sir Thomas Audley, Lord Chancellor from 1533 to 1544, who declared that no act of parliament could be annulled, except by another act, thereby implying that no statute could be *ultra vires*, or at least that nobody was competent to declare it so.[26] By the same token, if there were 'fundamental laws' of the English state, similar to the Salic Law in France, then nobody other than parliament had any clearly established right to say what they were, or what sanctions could be used to enforce them. Audley's precept also meant that no parliament could bind its successors. This was demonstrated in practice by the Marian acts of repeal, which removed Henry's and Edward's religious legislation from the statute book, and caused Thomas Cranmer such agonies of conscience. However, parliaments continued to act from time to time as though this principle did not exist. For example the 1559 Act of Supremacy, in defiance of recent experience, declared that:

24 William Marshall, *The defence of peace lately translated out of laten into englysshe* (1535); *A Short Title Catalogue of books printed in England, Scotland and Ireland and of English Books printed Abroad, 1475–1640*, eds A.W. Pollard and G.R. Redgrave, rev. W.A. Jackson, F.S. Ferguson and K.F. Pantzer (London, 1976–86), 17817, f. 27v–28.
25 S. Lockwood, 'Marsilius of Padua and the case for the royal ecclesiastical supremacy', *Transactions of the Royal Historical Society*, 6th series, 1, 1991, pp. 89–119.
26 It was Stephen Gardiner who testified to this pronouncement of Audley's in 1547; *The Letters of Stephen Gardiner*, ed. J.A. Muller (1933), pp. 319–20).

no foreign prince, person, prelate, state or potentate spiritual or
temporal shall at any time after the last day of this session of parliament
use, enjoy or exercise any manner of power, jurisdiction, superiority,
authority, pre-eminence or privilege spiritual or ecclesiastical, within
this realm or within any other your Majesty's dominions or countries
that now be or hereafter shall be, but from henceforth the same shall
be clearly abolished out of this realm and all other your highness's
dominions forever; any statute, ordinance, custom, constitution or any
other manner or cause whatsoever to the contrary in any wise notwithstanding.[27]

It was not until the following century that Sir Francis Bacon finally
drew the obvious conclusion from the practice of the previous two
generations:

a supreme and absolute power cannot conclude itself, neither can that
which is in nature revocable be made fixed; no more than if a man
should appoint and declare by his will that if he made any later will it
should be void. And for the case of the act of parliament, there is a
notable precedent of it in King Henry VIII's time; who doubting he
might die in the minority of his son, procured an act to pass that no
statute made during the minority of a king should bind him or his
successors, except it were confirmed by the king under his great seal at
his full age. But the first act passed in King Edward VI's time was an
act of repeal of that former act; at which time nevertheless the king was
a minor.[28]

By 1603 the crown in parliament had achieved *de facto* sovereignty,
but the political mentality of England was still medieval. Lawyers
spoke of fundamental rights and liberties, and alluded to *Magna Carta*
as though it were a Bill of Rights. The common law still escaped
rational codification, and both the customary law of the manorial
courts and the executive prerogative of the crown remained outside
the accepted scope of legislation. There was every reason why Tudor
government should have been paralysed by the uncertainties and
contradictions which afflicted its constitutional structure. But that
was very far from being the case, and it is important to understand
why.

27   1 Elizabeth, c. 1.
28   Francis Bacon, *Works*, ed. J. Spedding (1858), VI, p. 160.

1

The Central Machinery

CROWN AND COUNCIL

'[T]he prince is the life, the head and the authority of all things that be done in the realm of England. And to no prince is done more honour and reverence than to the king and queen of England.'[1]

The Tudors may not have been sovereigns, but they were a great deal more than chief executives. Not only did these monarchs symbolize their realm, they also provided a visible point of contact with the divine. The monarchs were the Lord's anointed, whose coronation unction gave them a quasi-sacerdotal status unique among the laity. Their physical health, longevity and fertility were all intimately connected with the well-being of the realm and people, and might display coded messages of God's favour or disfavour. All secular government was conducted in the monarchs' name, wherever their writ ran. Issues of war and peace rested upon the monarchs' personal decision, and no distinction was made between their private interests and the interests of the realm. The monarchs honoured whom they chose, and rewarded their servants at their discretion. When England welcomed its first ruling queen in 1553, there were those who argued that Mary could have only a 'woman's estate' in the kingdom, and that it would pass to her husband on marriage, like a private inheritance. However, parliament declared otherwise, judging that her authority to rule was as great as that of any of 'her noble progenitours, kings of this realm', and that her husband's right in the kingdom would cease with her death.[2] Nor, in theory at least, did a royal minority create any problems. The king's authority to govern, declared Stephen Gardiner,

---

1   Thomas Smith, *De Republica Anglorum*, ed. Mary Dewar (1982), p. 88.
2   1 Mary st. 1, c.2. For a discussion of this statute and its implications, see D. M. Loades, *The Reign of Mary Tudor*, (1991), pp. 89–91; J. Loach, *Parliament and the Crown in the Reign of Mary Tudor* (1986), pp. 91–104.

with the air of one uttering a commonplace, 'never wanteth, though he were in his cradle'.[3] Neither a woman nor a child was expected to lead an army into battle, but campaigning in person had never been required of a king, depending not only upon his age, but also upon health and inclination. Henry VIII was the only Tudor to lead an army abroad in the manner of Edward III or Henry V, and once Henry VII had secured himself at the battle of Stoke in 1487, martial prowess became virtually irrelevant to the success or security of the dynasty. Both Henry VIII and Elizabeth used tournaments as part of their display behaviour, but such exercises bore little relation to real war, even in 1510, let alone in 1580. Henry was extremely proud of his imposing physique, and genuinely skilled in a variety of sports, so jousting became a branch of diplomacy, and a way of establishing a useful rapport with his young nobles. For Elizabeth, of course, the significance of such combats was quite different. By encouraging exhibitionism and competitiveness they enabled her to revive the ancient culture of courtly love in her own interest. As the mistress, eternally desirable but unattainable, she presided in splendour, driving her courtiers to feats of emulation in return for the most tenuous of favours.[4]

The monarch was the fount of honour. All public offices and dignities were directly or indirectly in his or her gift, and all offices terminated with the demise of the crown. Apart from war and peace, several other areas of policy were also reserved exclusively for the monarchs' decision: the marriages of all members of the royal kindred, the management of the coinage, and the right to suspend or dispense the application of laws, including the pardon of offenders. The monarchs were entirely at liberty to take what advice they chose, and to follow or reject it at their pleasure. On the other hand, they were bound both by custom and common sense to consult with those whose assistance was necessary to them for the conduct of government. As their prerogative did not extend to the levying of taxes *meri motis suis*, the monarchs of England did not deploy the revenues necessary to support a professional bureaucracy, and they were therefore particularly dependent upon voluntary co-operation. They consulted

3   Gardiner to Cranmer (after 12 June 1547), in *The Letters of Stephen Gardiner*, ed. J. A. Miller (1936), p. 313.
4   'She is the mighty Queen of Faerie, / Whose fair retrait I on my shield do beare, / She is the flowre of grace and chastitie, / Throughout the world renowned far and neare, / My life, my liege, my Souveraigne, my deare': E. Spenser, *Faerie Queene*, Book 2, 2, xlii. See also below, pp. 250–3.

in a number of different ways. Certain aspects, particularly the raising of taxes, were reserved for the parliament, but for the majority of regular purposes the relevant body was the council. Originally this had consisted mainly of the king's tenants in chief, both spiritual and temporal, but by the end of the fourteenth century clergy and officials of non-noble rank were also prominent. In theory the monarchs were entirely free to call whomever they chose to council, because the feudal obligation to serve in that manner was a duty to attend if called, not a right. The idea of the 'councillor born' was an invention of the duke of York and his friends in the 1450s, intended to force a reluctant Henry VI to give him access to the court. It did not work, and by the time that the ensuing strife had been appeased, the idea had been discredited.[5] It remained true, however, that a monarch who wished to govern with the assistance of the nobles would be well advised to listen to some of them at least some of the time. Political advice was always the most nebulous of the council's functions. It was seldom proferred from formal meetings, and never so recorded. When the monarchs consulted their councillors on issues of importance, they normally did so in small groups or individually. There was, consequently, very seldom a consensus, let alone unanimity. Unlike a modern cabinet, the medieval council had no collective responsibility. Each individual swore an oath to advise and assist the monarch to the best of his conscience and ability, without reference to the views of others. The Tudors took this process of consultation seriously, but for the most part welcomed conflicting advice because it contributed to their maximum freedom of action.

The other main functions of the council were executive and judicial. It carried out the monarch's policies, irrespective of whether it had had any hand in shaping them, and made large numbers of routine administrative decisions. This work was substantially carried out in formal meetings, usually recorded, and was by far the most time-consuming of the council's activities. The monarch was hardly ever present at such sessions, which were dominated by a small number of key office holders. What might broadly be described as 'police work' and the allocation of money were the most important responsibilities discharged in this fashion, but the council was omnicompetent and a wide range of business could be brought to it for resolution. The judicial work had originally been very flexible. The council was the king's personal court of equity, and dealt with all those disputes where either the

5   D. M. Loades, *Politics and the Nation, 1450–1660* (4th edn, 1992), pp. 48–55.

status of the parties or the nature of their quarrel made reference to the courts of common law inadvisable. It also dealt with grievances for which the law provided no remedy, but which for a variety of reasons might require redress. By 1530 such work was becoming confined to special sessions, known as the courts of Star Chamber and Requests, and some councillors were beginning to specialize in judicial business. The Star Chamber was normally presided over by the Lord Chancellor, who was known as 'the keeper of the king's conscience', and Requests by a minor councillor, often the Almoner. There were other equity courts, but they were not aspects of the council.[6]

Although its functions remained much the same, the council evolved in a number of ways during the Tudor period. Henry VII's policy was conventional. Some 227 councillors are recorded for his twenty-four-year reign, and there were probably about sixty or seventy at any given time. Many of these are not known to have attended any formal meetings, and no council oaths are recorded for them. Some may have been specialist advisers, who were called only when required. Others may have been primarily local officials, upon whom the title of 'councillor' was conferred to give them extra prestige. Of those who did appear, the core of regular attenders numbered no more than about twenty at any given time, and the average attendance at routine meetings seems to have been about twelve. Formal and recorded meetings were confined to the law terms, but meetings were clearly held at other times, apparently not minuted. Henry called both nobles and prelates to council, as well as lay and clerical officials of lesser rank, although there was a shift of emphasis as the reign advanced. By 1505 non-noble lay officials formed the most numerous group, a situation which probably reflects both the king's greater security after the end of the Warbeck threat, and also a cooling of relations with many of his nobles as a result of his increasingly oppressive fiscal policies. At different times Henry created a number of *ad hoc* and standing groups of councillors for particular purposes, of which the best known is the Council Learned in the Law. These were not committees, because they operated autonomously and were not required to report back to the main council. There is no tidy modern

---

6　For the early development of Star Chamber, see J.A. Guy, *The Cardinal's Court* (1977), esp. pp. 119–40. See also J.S. Leadam (ed.), *Select Cases in the Court of Star Chamber, 1477–1509* (Selden Society, 1903) and *Select Cases in the Court of Requests, 1497–1569* (Selden Society, 1898). The other principal equity court was Chancery.

way to classify groups of this kind, any more than there was an institutional distinction between the 'council attendant' and the council at Westminster. That terminology was simply used to describe those councillors who happened to be in one place or another at any given time. The king was always accompanied by councillors as he moved about, partly because he needed them for functional purposes, and partly because they were necessary for his honour. At the same time routine administration had to be carried on, so the council existed in two places simultaneously, and individuals moved between the two groups as circumstances, or the king's pleasure, dictated. Henry relied heavily upon a small number of men whom he particularly trusted, both to give him advice and also to make decisions on his behalf. John Morton, bishop of Ely and subsequently cardinal archbishop of Canterbury, was the greatest of these, and after his death in 1500 the chief part was played by Sir Reginald Bray. It was these men, and a few others such as Sir Henry Wyatt and Edmund Dudley, who formed the core of the council and were the most regular attenders. They did not, however, constitute a settled 'inner council' which could be distinguished in any way from the body as a whole. Like any other medieval king, Henry deployed his councillors at his discretion, and bestowed his trust upon people, and not upon offices. His most influential adviser, who held no office and who outlived him by only a few months, was probably his mother. Her role was generally recognized at the time, and should warn us not to place too much emphasis upon institutional structures.[7] Henry also consulted from time to time a body known rather confusingly as the Great Council. This was quite distinct from the king's council proper, which was a standing body, and can best be described as the House of Lords meeting without the Commons. The Great Council had no clearly defined function, but each of the five meetings during this reign was connected with precautions against war or rebellion. The last such assembly was in 1537, and it did not convene again until 1641, by which time no one remembered how it ought to operate.[8]

Henry VIII succeeded a few days short of his eighteenth birthday, and although there was no question of a minority, the role of the

---

7 M.K. Jones and M.G. Underwood, *The King's Mother: Margaret Beaufort, Countess of Richmond and Derby* (1992), discusses her role at length.
8 P.J. Holmes, 'The Great Council in the reign of Henry VII', *English Historical Review*, 101, 1986, pp. 840–62; P.J. Holmes, 'The last Tudor Great Councils', *Hisrorical Journal*, 33, 1990, pp. 1–22.

council naturally changed. Henry had the good sense to retain most of his father's experienced servants, particularly Richard Fox and William Warham, and was at first guided largely by their advice. However, it was also necessary to signal a change of direction in fiscal policy, and to make the change of regime appear rather more dramatic than it was. This was done by sacrificing the unpopular *judices fiscales*, Sir Richard Empson and Edmund Dudley. Henry also began to show early signs of adolescent bellicosity, talking loudly about recovering his 'ancient rights' in France. Instead of an elderly and diligent king whose application to business was something of an obsession, England now had a glittering renaissance prince, whose mind was on tilting, masques and war. The responsibility of the council for decision making consequently increased, and although it was never wise to presume upon the king's disinterest, in fact he played little part in the regular processes of government. In November 1511 Henry joined the Holy League of Cognac, and committed himself to war with France in the following year, to the deep chagrin of those who had been trying to advise him. Although it was inspired by personal ambition, this decision also solved a problem which had been growing steadily for over a decade. A new generation of aristocrats had grown up, loyal to their traditional code of military honour, but deprived of any opportunity to serve their king in arms. Henry's ageing ecclesiastical councillors were ill equipped to see the danger in that situation, and were to that extent less wise than their young master.

The old council governed, largely undisturbed, until the end of the war in 1514. There were some indications that the king was listening to his courtiers, and even to his wife, in preference to his official advisers, but he was perfectly entitled to do that. It was not until the management of the campaigns themselves turned up a new administrator of enormous energy and ability that the situation began to change. Thomas Wolsey was not a particularly young man. He was nearly 40 when he became Henry's almoner in the autumn of 1509; a father rather than a companion to the young king. However, he quickly made his mark in the new reign, and by the time he was entrusted with the management of the campaign of 1512 he was already (according to his biographer George Cavendish) Henry's right-hand man.[9] It was his skill and driving force which made the

9 George Cavendish, *The Life and Death of Cardinal Wolsey*, ed. R.S. Sylvester (1959). See also Peter Gwyn, *The King's Cardinal: the rise and fall of Thomas Wolsey* (1990), pp. 15–16.

successes of that summer and of 1513 possible, and the rewards soon began to accumulate. Between March 1514 and December 1515 he became in rapid succession bishop of Lincoln, archbishop of York, cardinal and lord chancellor. His advent marked the end of the 'old' council, and established a new pattern of government which was to remain in place until his own fall fourteen years later. Wolsey became a 'councillor sole', so much so that some contemporaries described him as *alter rex*, or even as the true king of England. Such perceptions were greatly distorted. No one knew better than Wolsey himself that Henry always remained master in his own house, and that a minister's confidence had to be worked for. Nevertheless his ascendency was so great that for a decade it appeared that the king would listen to no one else on issues of policy, and that all the crown's patronage was passing through Wolsey's hands. The executive functions of the council were also substantially diminished, not intentionally but simply because Wolsey undertook so much work himself, and regularly used his own servants and agents to carry out his wishes. The king connived at this, because it was obviously effective, and Wolsey was careful to keep him informed, even when he could not be bothered to read the papers. Instead of urging Henry to apply himself to business, as his older councillors had done, Wolsey was happy to encourage his master's pastimes, and tackle the work himself. This gave him a comprehensive grasp of what was afoot, and that knowledge was the basis of his ascendency.

At the same time he refocused the judicial work of the council, formalizing the existing special sessions into what soon became known as 'the Cardinal's court'. This was his proper function as chancellor, but his energy was unprecedented.[10] The suspicion that he may have done this to keep some of his fellow councillors usefully employed as Star Chamber judges may well be unworthy, but he certainly increased the flow of equity business. This aroused the hostility of the common lawyers, who felt that business, and consequently fees, were being poached from their own jurisdiction. Wolsey had no training in the common law, and was contemptuous of its quiddities, but there is no reason to suppose that he was deliberately encroaching. The popularity of Star Chamber was simply a reflection of its speed and efficiency. Nevertheless by 1526 the king was becoming discontented. Attendance at formal council meetings had dwindled, not surprisingly, and Henry could be heard complaining that he was bereft of

10   Guy, *Cardinal's Court*, pp. 23–51.

counsel, and that this was not conducive to his honour. Perhaps Wolsey had become complacent, or perhaps the king's confidence had been shaken by the fiasco of the 'amicable grant' in 1525.[11] Whatever the cause, Wolsey was quick to respond to the symptoms, and early in 1526 drew up a new code of practice, known as the Eltham Ordinances. Ostensibly these regulations, which also included a sweeping programme for the reform of the household, reduced the amorphous and extremely flexible council which had hitherto existed to a hard core of twenty, all but four of whom held state or household offices. The nominal role of this council was preceded by the statement: 'it is ordered and appointed by his Highness that a good number of honourable, virtuous, sad, wise, expert and discreet persons of his Council shall give their attendance upon his most royal person, whose names hereafter follow'.[12] However, this plan was so riddled with exceptions and provisos that it ended by requiring only two councillors of lesser rank to be constantly in attendance. Wolsey had no incentive to create a new and more effective council, and the ordinances give only a very superficial impression of doing that. What they did was to point to the virtual disappearance of that large penumbra of occasional councillors who had been such a feature of the late fifteenth century. In the short term the ordinances made very little difference, because Henry's concentration span was short, and he had many other things on his mind. He did not return to the theme again before Wolsey's fall in the autumn of 1529.

That seismic event restored the political influence of such senior councillors as the duke of Norfolk and the earl of Wiltshire, and returned many executive functions to the council as a whole. For about three years the cardinal's numerous activities were picked up by about half a dozen different officers, and the king himself was constrained to participate more regularly. Henry may have found this uncongenial, or recognized its relative ineffectiveness, because he was quick to identify and employ a new administrative genius who entered his service in 1531. By the end of 1532 Thomas Cromwell was high in the king's confidence, and by the end of 1533 he was supreme. Just as Wolsey had won his spurs by masterminding the

11   For a full examination of this episode and its implications, see G.W. Bernard, *War, Taxation and Rebellion in Early Tudor England* (1986); also G.W. Bernard and R. Hoyle, 'The Instructions for the levying of the Amicable Grant, March 1525', in *Historical Journal*, 67, 1994, pp. 190–202.
12   *Ordinances for the Royal Household* (1790), pp. 159–60.

capture of Tournai, so Cromwell won his by converting the king's confused aspirations to ecclesiastical autonomy into a workable programme of legislation. Although he did not invent any of the ideas which he employed, by putting them together in a new way Cromwell resolved the king's Great Matter.[13] For about seven years thereafter he was as unchallengable in Henry's confidence as Wolsey had once been. Unlike the Cardinal, however, he worked through the council rather than nudging it aside. In April 1534 he became the king's principal secretary, and in June 1536 lord privy seal. In both these capacities his office became the central clearing house for all business, except for those delicate matters which Henry reserved for himself. Cromwell ran the council, and worked it hard, but did not distract himself with judicial business. That remained in the hands of the lord chancellors – first Sir Thomas More and then Sir Thomas Audley – and became increasingly separate. At some point between 1535 and 1537 the council was also reformed and reorganized. The plan outlined in the Eltham Ordinances was finally implemented, and in place of a body of some fifty or sixty men, varying enormously in status and input, the council became a group of about twenty office holders and senior courtiers, most of whom were expected to attend most of the time. By 1540 it was normally and properly known as the Privy Council, a title which it thereafter retained.[14]

Sir Geoffrey Elton believed that this reorganization was a deliberate policy on Cromwell's part to make the government more efficient, but other scholars have recently pointed out that it was no more in Cromwell's political interest to make the council more efficient than it had been in Wolsey's. Far from being the secretary's idea, they argue, this plan originated with the king, probably remembering the abortive scheme of ten years earlier and seeing its advantages in the new situation. Cromwell's compliance – because it was he who had to make the policy work – arose partly from his perception that

13   All the ideas which Cromwell used in the creation of the Act in Restraint of Appeals were present in a *consulta* presented to the king in 1530. His contribution lay mainly in devising a form of statute to give those ideas effect. G. Nicholson, 'The Act of Appeals and the English Reformation', in *Law and Government under the Tudors*, eds. C. Cross, D. Loades and J. Scarisbrick (1987), pp. 19–30.
14   G.R. Elton, *The Tudor Constitution*, 2nd edn (1982), pp. 91–2. For a different point of view, see J.A. Guy, 'The king's council and political participation', in *Reassessing the Henrician Age*, Alistair Fox and J.A. Guy, (1986), pp. 121–50.

Henry was in earnest this time, and partly from the fact that it could be used to reduce his profile at a time when he was almost uniquely unpopular, both at court and in the country. Consequently, although Cromwell's fall in the summer of 1540 brought his personal system of administration to an end, its main effect upon the council was to consolidate a development which had already taken place.[15] On 10th August that year, Henry decided:

> 'by the advice of his . . . Privy Council . . . That there should be a clerk attendant upon the said Council to write, enter and register all such decrees, determinations, letters and other such things as he should be appointed to enter in a book, to remain always as a ledger, as well for the discharge of the said councillors touching such things as they should pass from time to time, as also for a memorial unto them of their own proceedings.'[16]

There was already a council clerk, but his duties were henceforth to be confined to the Court of Star Chamber, and although minutes of meetings had been kept earlier, it was at this point that the *Acts of the Privy Council* were born. Thereafter, although there are gaps caused by accidents of survival, a day-by-day record of the council's business was kept, to become one of the most valuable archive sources for English administrative history.

In the last few years of Henry's reign the Privy Council met almost daily, and almost invariably at the court, wherever that happened to be. Between a dozen and fifteen councillors were regular attenders. The council was a focus of political intrigue and rivalry, although nothing of that appears in the *Acts*, probably because the clerk was excluded when any sensitive issues were under discussion. Financial matters and police work dominated the recorded agenda. Instructions were issued to local officials, and the delinquent were summoned, sometimes to be admonished, sometimes imprisoned, and sometimes kept in frustrating and expensive attendance. Participating in such meetings, and carrying out their decisions, must have occupied a large part of the working lives of most councillors. Membership conferred honour and power, but it was burdensome, and only for those who were making a full-time career in the royal service. It is therefore not surprising that only about ten of the fifty or so adult peers then alive

15　Guy, 'King's council'.
16　N.H. Nicolas, *Proceedings and Ordinances of the Privy Council of England* (London Record Commission, 1837), VII, pp. 3–4.

were members of the Privy Council in 1546. A political career at the highest level was now a question of diligent application and talent rather than of lineage and great estates. The duke of Norfolk was almost the last of the old-style magnates to hold high office, and he fell with a resounding crash in the last days of the king's life. By 1547 men were obtaining lands and titles because they held offices, not the other way round, and that reversal of emphasis was one of the most important developments in Tudor government during the first half of the sixteenth century.

After 1547 many things changed. First there was a six-year royal minority, and then two ruling queens who occupied the throne until 1603. Edward's Privy Council originated as the executors of his father's will, a curious and probably unworkable arrangement which was quickly abandoned in favour of a more orthodox approach. Deciding that they needed a single person at the head of the government, in February 1547 the council appointed the king's maternal uncle Edward Seymour, earl of Hertford, to be protector of the realm and governor of the king's person. Seymour, who became duke of Somerset at the same time, was at first constrained by the terms of his appointment to consult his council colleagues over every important decision, and was given no authority to appoint new councillors. As Edward was only 9 years old, however, and almost a decade of minority government was in prospect, this was clearly unsatisfactory. It was not even clear what constituted an important issue, or who was authorized to decide. Consequently on 12 March the new protector was granted augmented powers by letters patent; the requirement to consult was removed and the power to create new councillors inserted. Two years later, when the protectorate was breaking down, these changes were conveniently attributed to Somerset's ambition and pride, but at the time they were freely conceded by the council, and for perfectly good reasons.[17] For several months the new arrangements worked well enough, and in December the protector's powers were confirmed. However, by the spring of 1548 things were clearly going wrong. The protector's aggressive policy in Scotland was stretching his resources, and he had failed to persuade the emperor Charles V to extend the Anglo-imperial treaty of 1543 to cover Boulogne. This meant that renewed war with France was always a possibility, and England could not afford to fight on two fronts. At the

17 *Calendar of the Patent Rolls*, Edward VI (1924–39), I, p. 97; *Acts of the Privy Council*, eds J. Dasent et al. (1890–1907) II, pp. 67–74.

same time Somerset was pursuing highly controversial policies, both
in the reform of the church and in his attempts to defuse an increasingly explosive situation in the countryside.

Opposition on both these fronts was inevitable, and opposition
brought out the worst in Somerset, exposing all his limitations as a
head of government. Irritated by the criticisms of his colleagues, he,
began to bypass the council, using his own servants to carry out his
decisions. Ostensibly the Privy Council continued to meet as before,
and to deal with the same range of business, but close scrutiny of the
records has revealed that they were sometimes falsified, with dates and
attendances being filled in later. When Somerset did meet his advisers,
he became increasingly brusque and autocratic in his demeanour,
causing gratuitous offence to men whose support and co-operation he
needed. In short, the protector began to behave as though he was the
king, and to forget the duties of stewardship. The summer of 1548
saw an ominous escalation of agrarian violence, including a particularly serious incident in Cornwall, and some clear evidence that these
outbreaks were linked to the eclosure commissions by which Somerset
set such store. In August the protector's Scottish policy, for which he
had sacrificed so much, collapsed in ruins when the Scots signed the
treaty of Haddington with France, and sent their young queen over to
Brittany to be betrothed to the Dauphin.[18] A wise man would have
reconsidered his priorities on both fronts, but Somerset did his best
to ignore the setbacks, issuing fresh enclosure commissions in the
spring of 1549, and planning another major campaign in Scotland for
the summer. Sir William Paget, his closest confidant in the early days
of the protectorate, became increasingly alarmed. In May 1549,
following a particularly abrasive council meeting, he took the
protector sharply to task: 'I am forced to say that unless you show your
pleasure more quietly in debate with others, and graciously hear their
opinions when you require them, there will be sorry consequences and
you will be the first to repent . . . You have lately been very angry when
contradicted', he went on. 'A king who discourages men from saying
their opinions frankly imperils his realm', [19] and a lord protector who
does the same thing puts himself in great danger as well. Paget's words
were prophetic. Either Somerset paid no heed, or it was already too
late. In July riots and more serious disturbances erupted right across

18   M.L. Bush, *The Government Policy of Protector Somerset* (1975), pp. 9–10. BL
MS Harley 523 f. 28b.
19   PRO SP10/7, no. 5.

the south of England, and early in August the French declared war. By September, when domestic order had been restored, the majority of the council had decided that the protector was a liability, and would have to be removed.

The *coup* by which this was achieved in October 1549 lies outside the scope of this discussion, but it resulted in the restoration of a form of collective responsibility. The king was still only 12, but the office of protector was abolished. After several months of uncertainty, and a sharp power struggle, by the beginning of 1550 John Dudley, earl of Warwick, had emerged as the new leader of the council. For the next three and a half years Dudley (who became duke of Northumberland in November 1551) ran the country as lord president. He gradually reshaped the council to his own purposes, removing religious conservatives, such as the earls of Arundel and Southampton, and potential rivals like Paget. In their place he appointed staunch Protestants such as Thomas Goodrich, bishop of Ely, and personal friends and followers like the marquis of Dorset and Sir John Gates. He had every incentive to use the council fully, and deliberately used the resources of its individual members to supplement his security arrangements in and around the court. His policies were never popular, even with the aristocracy whose interests they generally supported, but he enjoyed one great advantage. Both nobles and gentry were so fearful of another 'camping summer' that they were prepared to support a strong leader like Dudley in order to preserve a common front. The last thing they could afford was for strife within the council, or overt dissent among the ruling class, to open the door to a renewal of civil strife. In the circumstances of a minority, and at first of a dangerous foreign war, disunity would have been fatal. It was his failure to appreciate this mood which tempted the duke of Somerset to his doom. Stripped of his office, but restored to the council, he could not resist the temptation to challenge Warwick's leadership, and the latter destroyed him in December 1551, with the full support of a council only too aware of the danger which he represented.[20] During the period of his presidency, Dudley expanded the council somewhat, from twenty-five to thirty-two, and several attempts were made to improve efficiency by drawing up guidelines for the handling of business. In 1550 Paget went back to an earlier idea, and suggested that there should always be a 'core council' of six members attendant upon the king, and that different days should be

20   D.M. Loades, *John Dudley, Duke of Northumberland* (1996), pp. 181–9.

set aside for different kinds of work. These ideas seem to have appealed to Edward, who loved schemes and lists, but how far they were implemented is not clear. The *Acts of the Privy Council* reveal no obvious changes of procedure. Early in 1553 a further memorandum of the same kind was drawn up, ostensibly by the king himself, and although again the implementation is uncertain, the effective management of council business was obviously a recognized political priority.

Dudley's strategy was long term. His objective was to secure his own supremacy, and that of his family, in the councils of King Edward when the latter came of age in 1555. To this end his programme of political education for the apprentice king was thorough, including specially staged council meetings as 'practice sessions', and a series of 'position papers' on issues of principle and practice, written by the clerk of the council, William Thomas. He was repaid with complete confidence. According to one contemporary observer, Edward 'revered him as if he were himself one of his subjects – so much so that the things which he knew to be desired by Northumberland he himself decreed in order to please the Duke'.[21] This should be treated with scepticism, but Dudley's handling of the young king's precocious talent was skilful and effective. It was also futile, because in the early weeks of 1553 Edward became ill, and on 6 July he died, without ever attaining his majority. The succession crisis which followed was totally unnecessary, because a lawful order had been laid down in Henry VIII's will, in accordance with the terms of his last Succession Act of 1543. However, the designated heir was the king's elder sister, Mary, a staunch religious conservative, and illegitimate by English law. Some months before his death, Edward had resolved that she must not succeed, and later decided to replace her with his Protestant cousin Jane Dudley, the grandaughter of his father's sister Mary. After he died the council, so solid over the previous three years, split under the pressure of this crisis. Northumberland and a small number of his closest adherents endeavoured to carry out the king's wishes, but the majority rallied to Mary as the lawful heir. By so doing they upheld the newly extended authority of statute, and preserved the Tudor dynasty, but they also presented their new mistress with a number of taxing problems which she was not well equipped to resolve.

During the crisis itself Mary had done the only thing which was required of her: proclaimed her own right to the throne and

21 Bibliothèque Nationale MS Ancien Saint-Germain Français, 15888, fols. 214b–215b; D. Hoak, *The King's Council in the Reign of Edward VI* (1976), p. 123.

summoned her subjects to her assistance. However, while the outcome was still in the balance she had, perforce, begun to assemble a council. Among her existing servants, and those who first joined her, there was no one of political weight and experience – naturally, as she had been *persona non grata* with the previous regime. Consequently the 'Framlingham council', as it became known from its original place of assembly, was a lightweight body, commended only by its strong personal loyalty. It was only after 19 July, when the defectors began to arrive from London, that the queen could begin to assemble a credible administration. Considering her lack of relevant experience, Mary reacted to this situation with commendable sagacity. The first arrivals, who were also those who had been least associated with Northumberland, such as Lord Paget and the earl of Arundel, were welcomed and swiftly employed. The less nimble, notably Lord Treasurer Winchester, were allowed to sweat for a while before being reinstated, while those whose change of heart had clearly followed the resolution rather than preceeding it, like Northumberland himself, were consigned to the Tower.[22] About a third of Edward's final council was retained, and several former servants of Henry VIII, notably the duke of Norfolk and Stephen Gardiner, the bishop of Winchester, were reinstated. The result was a large body, numbering over forty, with a very wide range of talent and experience. It was more like the pre-1535 council than the Privy Council of the 1540s. Mary accepted this, perhaps more readily than she need have done, and the council continued to grow slowly in size, numbering about fifty by the time that she died five years later. 'Numbers', complained Simon Renard, the imperial ambassador, 'cause great problems', and King Philip's personal envoy, the Count of Feria, later expressed the same view.[23]

There was some justice in what they said. So large a body gave ample room for parties and factions to develop, and Mary's council was notoriously divided upon just about every issue of importance. As an advisory body it was consequently confused and ineffective, but Renard and Feria were really looking for excuses for Mary's failure to

22   J.G. Nichols (ed.), *The Chronicle of Queen Jane and of the first two years of Mary* (Camden Society 48, 1850), pp. 10–11; D. MacCulloch (ed.), '"The Vita Mariae Angliae" of Robert Wingfield' (Camden Miscellany 28, 1984), pp. 184, 188.
23   Loades, *Reign of Mary*, pp. 34–8. A. Weikel, 'The Marian Council revisited', in *The Mid-Tudor Polity, 1540–1560*, eds J. Loach and R. Tittler (1980), pp. 53–73.

respond to their masters' expectations. The political weakness of the council was caused by the queen herself. In spite of her sensible initial policy she never really trusted many of those whom she called to serve her. Inevitably any man of political experience must have served her brother or her father in the execution of policies which she regarded as immoral and unacceptable. Less wise than her grandfather in a similar situation, she could not put that out of her mind. For that reason she did not consult her council either over her marriage or over her decision to seek the restoration of papal authority. On the first issue her adviser was Simon Renard, and on the second her cousin, Cardinal Reginald Pole. These were prerogative matters, particularly the former, so it could not be claimed that she had acted improperly, but her conduct nevertheless caused understandable resentment among those who believed that it was their function to be consulted. Mary did not know how to deal with her council. She seems to have expected the councillors to give her unanimous advice, and when they inevitably failed to do so, she became unjustifiably suspicious of their loyalty. At one point she claimed that she spent all her time shouting at them, to no effect.[24] Nor did they know how to deal with her. There were no guidelines for a ruling queen. Mary's councillors expected her to be irresolute, and anxious to leave most of the business of government to them. To their surprise they found her obstinate beyond measure on issues of conscience, diligent in her application to business, and unwilling to deal with them collectively on any issue of importance. After Philip's arrival, in the autumn of 1554, one of his servants declared that the English council 'ruled everything', and were the absolute lords of the kingdom, but they did not see it that way. Lack of trust increased the friction between councillors, and led to the kind of situation which arose in the parliament of 1554 when Gardiner, the lord chancellor, introduced a bill into the House of Lords with the queen's knowledge and approval, but without informing his fellow councillors. A group of them, led by Lord Paget, combined to defeat his intention, and then found that they were in disgrace. For a while Mary was convinced that Paget was conspiring with the French, and allowed Renard to intercept his mail. She seems to have been incapable of grasping the fact that differences of opinion within the council were legitimate, and did not imply disloyalty.

Philip, who assumed the title of king of England when he married Mary in July 1554, seems to have managed the council better, in spite

24   D. Loades, *Mary Tudor: a life* (1989), pp. 315–20.

of not speaking the language. This was partly because he did not seek a very active role in the government, and partly because he understood the nature of political animals much better than did his rather innocent wife. He was responsible for Paget's rehabilitation and promotion to the office of lord privy seal, and for negotiating the settlement with Rome. He shut out the officious Renard, and did not allow Pole undue influence. Before he departed in August 1555 he also established a 'select council' or Council of State. There had been talk of doing this for two years, but the obstacles had always appeared insurmountable. Philip simply ignored objections and vested interests, believing, quite correctly, that the format of the council was a prerogative matter. However, his creation did not long survive his departure, and may have existed only for his benefit.[25] It conducted a Latin correspondence with him on English affairs, but seems to have kept no minutes of its own, and was totally ignored in the records of the main Privy Council. By the time that Philip returned to England briefly in 1557, it had disappeared.

In spite of these political limitations, as an executive instrument Mary's council was just as effective as its predecessors. Attendance at routine meetings averaged ten to fifteen, hardly, if at all, higher than in the previous reign. A number of earlier practices were, however, restored. Council committees and special working groups reappeared, notably in February 1554 when no fewer than eleven such groups were set up for a variety of purposes, from the calling in of debts to the examination of prisoners. At the same time it was provided that there should always be a 'standing council' at Westminster, no matter where the court might be, as had been the case in the early years of the century.[26] Certain councillors who seldom, if ever, attended meetings were nevertheless used regularly on committees, and even more on commissions set up to deal with specific local problems. A few 'councillors at large' were even appointed, who were not required to take the council oath, and were not therefore members of the Privy Council at all. Although the Marian system has an antique look about it, it worked because it was driven by a small team of dedicated and efficient royal servants, led by Lord Paget. Paget's political influence was negligible after Philip's departure, but he was the key man in maintaining the momentum of council activity in the last three

25   D. Loades, 'Philip II as king of England', in *Law and Government under the Tudors*, eds C. Cross, D. Loades and J. Scarisbrick (1987), pp. 177–94.
26   *Acts of the Privy Council*, IV, pp. 397–9.

years of the reign. In 1556 the Privy Council acquired its own seal, which perhaps indicates an aspiration to greater autonomy in administrative matters; but if that was the case it came to nothing, and was quietly forgotten after Mary's death. Whatever her personal and political failures, the queen was well served by her council, and in November 1558 the country was as well governed as it had been at any time since 1485.

Unlike her half-sister five years earlier, Elizabeth had a shadow council waiting in the wings. The circumstances of her accession were quite different, and she was under no pressure to appoint councillors who were not entirely to her taste. Nevertheless, and in spite of her determination to reverse many of her sister's policies, Elizabeth appointed half her initial council from among those who had served Mary in the same capacity. Some of these, notably the marquis of Winchester, represented continuity and experience in office; others, such as the earls of Arundel, Shrewsbury and Pembroke, were magnates whose support the young queen judged to be particularly important. The whole council numbered only twenty, half the size of her predecessor's, and reverting to the Cromwellian practice of 1536–40. The remaining ten places were filled by her 'shadow' councillors, of whom the most important was Sir William Cecil, who had been principal secretary under the duke of Northumberland. The balance was obviously calculated: ten who might broadly be classified as conservative Erastians, and ten reformers, most of whom were clearly Protestants. Elizabeth was not giving herself an easy ride, but she was proclaiming her willingness to listen to more than one point of view. Like Henry VII she judged that consensus was critical, and that competence and loyalty to herself were of greater importance than former allegiance. Cardinal Pole saved the new queen a lot of trouble by dying on the same day as Mary, and the most conspicuous casualties of the new regime were the former chancellor, Nicholas Heath, and Lord William Paget. Heath's principled refusal to abandon the papacy made him unacceptable both as a bishop and as an officer of state, while Paget had been too closely associated with Philip to outweigh his distinguished services as an administrator. The most surprising omission from the new council was Matthew Parker, the archbishop of Canterbury. Parker was the queen's personal choice for his most sensitive and difficult post, and yet he was not accorded a status which had always hitherto been regarded as *ex officio*. Elizabeth was never very fond of clergy, and was particularly averse to married clergy, but it is unlikely that Parker's exclusion was the result of a personal fad. It was probably intended to signal the reduced status which the church could expect under its new supreme governor.

The relationship between the queen and her council over the next forty-five years was complex and full of stresses, but on balance both dynamic and successful. Divided counsels did not worry Elizabeth; they helped her to procrastinate and to weave her own webs. Unanimity worried her far more, because it created pressures which she found it hard to avoid. Unlike Mary, she did not take refuge in the dictates of an inflexible conscience. Every decision was political, and taken reluctantly because her keen intelligence made her only too aware of the possible consequences of every course of action. For this reason she was constantly hedging, and leaving ways of retreat open from apparently committed positions, a style which exasperated her more straightforward advisers. For the first twenty years of her reign, Elizabeth's council was unanimous in its opinion that she should marry, although divided as to the identity of the potential husband.[27] By every accepted standard of political wisdom they were right, but the queen evaded their pressures, playing off one group against another. She did this not out of any settled determination to avoid matrimony, and certainly not because she was gifted with prophetic vision, but from a shifting mixture of personal and political motives. The judgement of Maitland of Lethington, that she had 'an high stomach' and would brook no master, was probably the most consistent truth; and yet she was herself responsible for initiating negotiations with both Henry and Francis, successively dukes of Anjou. If she ever wanted to marry any man, it was probably Lord Robert Dudley, and yet in that case she showed herself responsive to political pressure because it was applied by men whose judgement she trusted, particularly William Cecil. Instead she made Dudley earl of Leicester and appointed him to the council in 1565, converting him from a loose cannon into an orthodox politician. Thereafter his rivalry with the Secretary could be conducted in a normal and containable manner. Elizabeth was constantly at loggerheads with some or all of her council; at first over marriage and the succession, then over the fate of Mary, Queen of Scots, and later over the conduct of the war against Spain. As Sir John Davies said, the politics of the court was

27   Wallace MacCaffrey, *Elizabeth I* (1993), pp. 82–102. For a full consideration of all these negotiations, see Susan Doran, *Monarchy and Matrimony* (1996), pp. 13–153.

like a complex dance. But Elizabeth knew better than to call the loyalty of her councillors in question. She had chosen them, and remained confident that it was their devotion to her service and the well-being of the realm which caused them to disagree so vehemently. In spite of their undeniable private agendas, she was on balance right. Political disagreements were about means rather than ends.

Elizabeth was, nevertheless, a baffling and infuriating mistress in ways which Mary had never been. Her councillors were never for a moment allowed to be unaware that they were dealing with a woman. They perceived her as devious, and she exploited her sexuality, never attempting to disguise herself as a king. On their side, her councillors were tempted to take political liberties which they would never have risked with her father. It was the council, led by Lord Burghley, which introduced into the parliament of 1572 that bill for the execution of Mary Stuart which the queen subsequently vetoed.[28] As recent research has demonstrated, Thomas Norton, the council's principal 'man of business' in the House of Commons, was so often involved in the promotion of matters which attracted the queen's disapproval that he was long regarded by historians as a classical example of parliamentary opposition. After twice returning to the charge, the council eventually had its way over Mary, although Elizabeth could hardly have conceded with a worse grace, and insisted on making William Davidson, her principal secretary and a chief manager of council business, the scapegoat for her displeasure. As she grew older, the queen's indecisiveness became more pronounced, and as the war with Spain dragged on her instinctive parsimony became oppressive. She hesitated for nearly a decade before appointing Sir Robert Cecil to the important post of secretary in 1596, and the Great Seal was in commission, or in the hands of a lord keeper, for all but twelve years of the reign. In 1603 the peerage had become depleted by natural wastage in spite of Lord Burghley's promptings, the queen's unwillingness to make grants of land compounded by uncertainties over the merits of possible candidates. It was this general situation, rather than any deliberate policy, which caused the Privy Council gradually to shrink in size. Elizabeth became less and less willing to accord the degree of confidence necessary for new appointments, and by the time of her death it numbered no more than a dozen.

This wastage did not imply any diminution in the power or import-

28   M.A.R. Graves, *Thomas Norton, the Parliament Man* (1994), pp. 192–4.

ance of the council, rather the reverse. That minority of councillors who were primarily honorific, still present in the 1560s, had disappeared by the end of the century. Council membership in 1600 meant a full-time political and administrative grind. The range of business had changed somewhat, but not sufficiently to change the nature of the meetings. The Court of Star Chamber was now entirely detatched from the Privy Council, and ecclesiastical business had diminished with the development of High Commission. Whatever representative nature the council may once have had was long since gone, and the carefully constructed balance of Elizabeth's first council had become unnecessary with the passage of time. The long reign of the last Tudor settled many issues. Those who did not believe that ecclesiastical jurisdiction could be exercised by a layman – let alone a woman – had been reduced to an identifiable minority. The religion of the country had become firmly, even aggressively, Protestant. England no longer hankered after Calais, and was beginning to think instead about colonies in the New World. Above all, the *de facto* sovereignty of parliament had become accepted. So much was this the case that Privy Councillors were using the House of Commons to put pressure on the monarch over policy issues. Elizabeth knew that this was happening, and in a sense condoned it, but it was a dangerous development. When Gardiner and Paget had taken their rivalry to the House of Lords in 1554, it had caused Mary serious embarrassment. When Cranfield and Coke engineered the impeachment of Sir Francis Bacon in 1621, the authority of the crown was compromised.[29] Elizabeth's highly personal method of dealing with her council had subtly changed the nature of the relationship, and exposed James to ambush in an institution which should have been simply an instrument of his own will.

THE PARLIAMENT

Parliament had arisen out of the king's occasional need for consultation and a show of support. Early assemblies, when they first appeared at the beginning of the thirteenth century, usually consisted of the lay and ecclesiastical tenants in chief. For half a century or more the terms 'parliament' and 'Great Council' were interchangeable.

29 Loades, *Reign of Mary*, pp. 90–1. Loach, *Parliament and the Crown*; M. Prestwich, *Cranfield: politics and profits under the early Stuarts* (1966).

Such meetings were always held for a particular purpose, and were convened wherever the king deemed to be most convenient. After 1250 other representative assemblies also began to appear on an occasional basis. Four knights were summoned from each shire in October 1258, and again in June 1264.[30] These meetings were not connected with the Great Council, which was meeting on average about twice a year, and seem to have been of short duration. However, in January 1265 the prelates and magnates were joined at Westminster by two knights from each shire and two burgesses from each of a limited selection of boroughs, in what was clearly a single consultation. Although Great Councils and other selective meetings continued to be held quite frequently, by the end of the thirteenth century the term 'parliament' normally implied at least the presence of prelates, peers and knights. On a number of occasions between 1295 and 1335 not only were representative burgesses summoned, but also clergy from each diocese. It was not until the middle of the fourteenth century that these occasional assemblies finally acquired the form which they were to take at the beginning of the Tudor period. Very unusually among European estates, the bishops, mitred abbots and secular lords met together in a single house, while the knights and burgesses also convened together in a separate chamber. The lower clergy were eventually excluded on the grounds that their proper representation was through the Convocations, and there was consequently no house of clergy. By the end of the fourteenth century the parliament thus constituted had acquired the customary right to approve all grants of direct taxation, and to legislate, at least in the sense of providing the most authoritative interpretation of the law.[31] For both these processes, and for the creation of any parliamentary act, the consent of both houses and the monarch was required. It was at about that time also that the finer points of membership were resolved. The Lords had always been summoned by individual writ, but it was only in the early fifteenth century that the limits of the king's discretion in issuing such writs was determined. It was then accepted that every bishop, and every lay peer of full age and recognized creation, was entitled to a summons. The king could excuse attendance at his discretion, and withold a writ from any peer who was insane, of inadequate substance, or an unpardoned felon. Only in the case of the

30 *Handbook of British Chronology*, eds. E.B. Fryde, D.E. Greenway, S. Porter and I. Roy (1986), pp. 539–41.
31   M.A.R. Graves, *Early Tudor Parliaments, 1485–1558* (1990), p. 2.

abbots was a degree of flexibility retained. Some great houses, such as Glastonbury and St Albans, were always represented, but the number varied from a dozen to nearly thirty.

In the House of Commons the county representation was settled at two knights from every English shire, with the exception of Durham and Chester, which were counties palatine. Burgess representation was similarly two from every enfranchised borough, except for the great City of London, which was accorded four. During the fourteenth century the king had summoned towns according to his whim, sometimes as few as twenty, sometimes as many as a hundred. By the middle of the fifteenth century, however, it had become accepted that a defined list of towns was entitled to representation, and although the king could enfranchise boroughs at his pleasure, once granted the privilege could only be withdrawn for good reason. By 1485, 37 counties and 110 towns sent members to the House of Commons, making it one of the largest such houses in Europe.[32] In theory the knights represented the whole county community, and it was laid down by statute in 1406 that every freeman holding freehold land to the value of forty shillings a year was entitled to attend the county court, and to vote for his representative. This was based on the assumption that the voters would be keener to exercise their rights than the members were to serve, and was never very realistic. By the middle of the century membership was sought after, and competed for by leading gentry families. Freeholders were regularly bribed or intimidated, and elections were determined sometimes by royal or magnate influence, and sometimes by pacts or feuds among the gentry families themselves. Borough franchises varied considerably, in accordance with the terms of the charters of creation, and it was decreed in 1413 that only residents might be elected to serve. The purpose of this was clearly to ensure a genuine burgess presence, but it was a dead letter within twenty years. Gentry families squeezed out of the county competitions began to intrigue and struggle to obtain borough places. By 1440 about 30 percent of borough seats had been captured in this way, and the proportion steadily increased over the next century and a half.[33]

Parliament was not a regular institution of government, because the

---

32 A.G.R. Smith, *The Emergence of a Nation State: 1529–1660* (1984), p. 387. A.R. Myers, 'Parliament 1422–1509', in *The English Parliament in the Middle Ages*, eds R.G. Davies and J.H. Denton (1981), p. 166.

33 Myers, 'Parliament 1422–1509'; Elton, *Tudor Constitution*, p. 249.

king was under no obligation to convene it. On the other hand he did so with surprising frequency. Between 1272 and 1399 there were almost 200 meetings, more than one a year, although a number of these were really Great Councils rather than parliaments proper, because the commons were not summoned. A better comparison with later practice is provided by the period 1399 to 1485, when there were more than fifty meetings, all of them full parliaments. Most of these sessions were very short, and a number were dissolved as soon as they had made a financial grant. Nevertheless the legislative programme steadily developed in range and usefulness, and procedural devices, such as three readings of a bill in each house, began to appear. The political troubles of the 1440s and 1450s also gave parliament a new role. One of the main functions of the House of Commons had by that time become the collection and presentation of petitions for the redress of grievances. As discontent with the government of Henry VI mounted, these becamne increasingly concerned with abuses of the judicial system, and with the breakdown of civil order. In 1450 the Commons initiated an impeachment against the duke of Suffolk on the grounds of misgovernment and abuse of the king's confidence. The Lords judged him guilty, and Henry was forced much against his will to dismiss his favourite into exile. The parliament itself played no part in the ensuing struggle, but duly registered each turn of the political wheel. In theory only a lawful king could convene a valid parliament, but Edward IV made no attempt to annul his predecessor's legislation on those grounds. Only the re-adeption parliament of 1470 was not subsequently recognized. Throughout the fifteenth century the Parliament Roll provides not only a complete record of legislation, but also an informative account of the proceedings. That situation changed in the solitary parliament of Richard III in 1484. Thereafter the roll became merely a record of statutes, and apart from a few notes kept by the clerk of the House of Lords, we have no further information about proceedings until the Lords Journals begin as a continuous sequence in 1509.[34] On the other hand, 1484 also saw the beginning of the sessional printing of statutes. This was a very rapid deployment of a new technology, and indicates not only the perceived importance of statutes, but also the need for lawyers to have access to accurate texts.

In its early days the parliament had met in a variety of places to suit

34   G.R. Elton, 'The early journals of the House of Lords', *English Historical Review*, 89, 1974, pp. 481 ff.

the king's convenience, but after 1340 sessions outside Westminster became very rare, the last being at Coventry in 1459. The Reformation parliament of 1529 was originally summoned to Blackfriars, and Mary's second parliament in 1554 to Oxford, but both eventually met at Westminster. In the autumn of 1545 there was plague in the London area, and both Reading and Windsor were considered as venues, but in the event the start was held back to late November, and Westminster used as usual. There was nothing to prevent the king from changing this, but custom was reinforced by convenience, because the members regularly used their visits to the capital to discharge other business, particularly in the courts of law. Significantly, the leaders of the Pilgrimage of Grace in 1536 pressed Henry to convene a parliament at York, claiming both that the north was under represented (which was true), and also that the usual venue gave the meetings a southern viewpoint and preoccupation.[35] The Lords had their own meeting room in the Old Palace, which also housed most of the institutions of central government, and there was suitable accommodation for the much larger House of Commons as well, although not always in the same place. It was not until 1547 that St Stephen's chapel was finally designated as the Commons chamber. The limitations of the chapel seating, in terms of both capacity and arrangement, were not without influence on Commons procedure, but the symbolic recognition accorded by the grant more than outweighed the inconveniences.[36] It was probably no coincidence that the Commons Journals commenced at the same time. Thereafter both houses were keeping a day-by-day record of their business, which more than compensated for the loss of the old Parliament Roll. All such business was strictly confidential, being part of the *arcana imperii*, and members could be reprimanded or punished for discussing 'parliament matters' with outsiders. It was perhaps for this reason that parliamentary diaries, which were to be such useful sources for the study of the Commons in the seventeenth century, did not begin to appear until the latter part of Elizabeth's reign. Sir Simonds D'Ewes's unofficial *Journals* commenced in 1559, but they contain little beyond extracts from the official records until 1571. The official journal is missing from 1584 until 1603, and D'Ewes provides the only record for those years, but there is no reason to suppose that his work was

35 *Letters and Papers of the Reign of Henry VIII*, eds J.S. Brewer et al. (1862–1932), XI, 504.
36 J. Loach, *Parliament under the Tudors* (1991), p. 43.

made available to outsiders at the time. The same preoccupation caused strangers to be very strictly excluded from the premises. In 1571 two gentlemen who entered without authorization were committed to ward, and in 1593 one Matthew Jones, 'being found sitting in this House and no member of the same', was arraigned at the bar, where his plea of ignorance was accepted, and 'seeming to be a simple old man' he was discharged.[37] Security could never be tight in such a rambling building, and even disorderly serving men could only be effectively excluded by posting watchmen at the door in the manner of nightclub bouncers.

Before 1529 there was nothing to suggest that the parliaments of the Tudors would be in any way different from those of their immediate predecessors. Henry VII called six meetings in the first twelve years of his reign. He needed recognition, he needed money, and he needed the maximum authority for attainders, forfeitures and restorations. A modest legislative programme included navigation acts designed to protect English commerce, and restrictions upon benefit of clergy and rights of sanctuary. These latter could have been contentious, but they were in accordance with precedent and Henry's relations with the church were generally good. There were fierce arguments about money, and the king did not always get exactly what he wanted, but there was nothing unusual about that. The only straw in the wind was a statute of 1497 which incorporated the liberties of Tynedale and Redesdale into the county of Northumberland. This was not a major matter in itself, but it had not been customary for franchises to be either created or discontinued by that means. After 1497 Henry convened only one more parliament, in 1504, which suggests that he saw no further need for extensive consultation, and did not regard regular legislation as a necessary feature of good government. When money could be obtained by other means, there was also no incentive to risk the political storms engendered by demands for taxation. In 1509 an observer could well have been forgiven for thinking that the great days of parliamentary activity were past, and that if the monarchy continued to be strong, parliament would gradually become an irrelevance. There were no recorded protests at the king's failure to convene a parliament in the last five years of his reign, although there were plenty of complaints about other matters. Henry VIII called parliaments in 1510, 1512 and 1515,

37 Sir Simonds D'Ewes, *The Journals of all the Parliaments during the reign of Queen Elizabeth* (1682), pp. 511–12.

which suggests that his 'old' councillors may have had a higher opinion of their usefulness than their late master. But during the fourteen years of Wolsey's ascendency there was only one meeting, in 1523, and the chancellor made such a mess of it that his reluctance to meet another is understandable. However, by 1529 the king was desperately in need of new ideas, and anxious to mobilize the support of his subjects, in his battle with the pope.

There was nothing unusual about the composition of what came to be known as the Reformation parliament, and no hint at first that any dramatic developments were in the offing. Lay anti-clericalism, which could always be aroused in the Commons by issues of money and jurisdiction, was gratified with bills against the collection of probate and mortuary fees, but by comparison with the heated exchanges of 1515 it all seemed very low key. What could have been the main issue, the fate of Wolsey, was resolved by his death in 1530, and it was not for another two years that the king's Great Matter was explicitly reflected in the parliamentary agenda. In 1532 the House of Commons, heavily prompted and guided by Thomas Cromwell, but probably not unwilling, drew up a list of anti-clerical grievances known as the 'Supplication against the Ordinaries'. This Henry then used to force the clergy into a surrender of their jurisdictional autonomy, a surrender which was eventually confirmed by statute in 1534. At the same time parliament authorized the king to withold papal taxation, if he should see fit to do so. The lord chancellor, Sir Thomas More, resigned in protest against such blatant illegality. The clergy had no right to surrender their autonomy, and parliament had no right to legislate on the subject of ecclesiastical taxation. In principle he was right, but given the precedent of Provisors and Praemunire it is unlikely that many members of the parliament felt that they had exceeded their traditional powers. However that was soon to change as Cromwell, utilizing ideas from Marsilius of Padua and other imperial theorists of the past, constructed a strategy for enabling the king to bypass the authority of the papacy altogether. The Act in Restraint of Appeals was prompted by the fact that in January 1533 Anne Boleyn was discovered to be carrying Henry's child. Few people had any liking for Anne, and sympathy for the rejected queen, Catherine, was widespread and vocal. However the succession was a real and urgent problem, and there was no doubt about the king's wishes in the matter. Nor did the papacy itself command much loyalty. Consequently parliament used its own authority to sever the jurisdictional link entirely, and followed this up with a series of statutes recognizing and implementing the king's ecclesiastical supremacy. The illegality of Henry's first marriage was confirmed, and the succession to the crown settled upon his issue by Anne Boleyn.[38]

By 1536 there was no doubt that the Reformation parliament had trespassed upon hitherto forbidden ground. Why so conservative a body should have leant itself to a revolutionary programme of action requires some explanation, because the whole subsequent course of English government was altered by the events of these years. The habit of obedience was deeply engrained, and both Henry VIII and his father made effective use of the fifteenth-century wars to discourage opposition. It was also generally recognized that the king needed a male heir. Anti-clericalism in the traditional sense, and disillusionment with a papacy which had consistently failed to provided the English church with a much-needed programme of reform, also made their contribution. But the most important factor was probably a deeply rooted scepticism about the king's intentions. Once Catherine had gone and the succession issue had been resolved, no one really believed that Henry would persist with his ecclesiastical supremacy. It was a bargaining counter to bring the pope to terms, and as such needed the full backing of the kingdom's most authoritative assembly. In other words the rhetoric was not taken seriously, and neither individual lords nor members of the Commons were prepared to risk their lives and fortunes for a cause which would be restored by negotiation as soon as it suited Henry's convenience. That may even have been the king's original intention, since his own cast of mind was as conservative as any. However, by the summer of 1536 he had changed his opinion. With a capacity for self-persuasion which was typical of him, he had become convinced that the royal supremacy did indeed represent the way in which God intended his church to be run, and when both Catherine and Anne were dead, he declined to renegotiate his relations with the pope. By then it was also beginning to occur to his parliamentary accomplices that there were great possibilities for their own profit in the new situation, and by the time that Cromwell had fallen in 1540 the king's right to govern the church had been accepted by the vast majority of his subjects. In doing that they sanctioned the new role which parliament had adopted in the affairs of the kingdom.

38   25 Henry VIII, c. 20 (Restraint of Annates); 25 Henry VIII, c. 21 (Dispensations); 25 Henry VIII, c. 22 (Succession).

In 1565 Sir Thomas Smith summarized parliament's functions in sweeping terms:

> The Parliament abrogateth old laws, maketh new, giveth orders for things past, and for things hereafter to be followed, changeth rights and possessions of private men, legitimateth bastards, establisheth forms of religion, altereth weights and measures, giveth forms of succession to the Crown, defineth of doubtful rights whereof is no law already made, appointeth subsidies, tallies, taxes and impositions, giveth most free pardons and absolutions, restoreth in blood and name as the highest court, condemneth or absolveth them whom the prince will put to that trial. And, to be short, all that ever the people of Rome might do either in *Centuriatis comitiis* or *tributis*, the same may be done by the Parliament of England.[39]

From being a specialized instrument, used for a limited number of purposes, statute had become the standard means of authorization for all types of business. In 1536 statute abolished the ancient franchises of the Welsh marches, reduced Wales to shire ground, and conferred parliamentary representation upon the new counties. In the same year all religious houses worth less than £200 per annum were delivered into the king's hand, and in 1539 the Act of Six Articles laid down a standard of orthodoxy for the English church. A decade earlier none of these things could have been done. Had a Succession Act been a viable option in 1527, the king's Great Matter might never have come about. By the time he died Henry had rearranged the succession three times by that means, and in 1571 parliament was to declare it to be high treason to deny the authority of statute to determine the identity of the next ruler. In 1549 an Act of Uniformity converted the doctrinal basis of the church to Protestantism, the Act of Six Articles having already been repealed. When Mary came to the throne in 1553, she was advised by her kinsman Reginald Pole that it would be unnecessary to repeal either her brother's or her father's religious legislation, as all such statutes were invalid as *ultra vires*; but her legal advisers persuaded her otherwise, and she accorded parliament the ultimate compliment of creating her new catholic establishment by statute, as had been done for its predecessors.[40]

39 Smith, *De Republica Anglorum*, p. 78.
40 Loades, *Reign of Mary*, pp. 104–5. Loach, *Parliament and the Crown*, pp. 74–90. Pole disagreed strongly with this course of action: Pole to the Cardinal of Imola, September 1553, *Calendar of State Papers, Venetian*, eds. Rawdon Brown et al. (1864–98), V, pp. 409–10.

What was true for matters of high policy was equally valid for more routine affairs. The volume of legislation produced by the Reformation parliament was unprecedented. All sorts of business, from the making of hats and caps, or hunting in disguise to the creation of new felonies and treasons, were resolved by statute. That level of activity was not sustained, but Edward, Mary and Elizabeth all followed their father's lead in legislating for social control and welfare, while private lobbying groups took up an increasing proportion of session time. Historians have disagreed about how that change of emphasis should be interpreted. Sir John Neale virtually ignored it, concentrating upon the political debates and conflicts engendered by matters such as the queen's marriage and the further reform of the church. Sir Geoffrey Elton reversed that emphasis, arguing that 'high politics' was no more than an occasional intrusion into a business scene dominated by party issues. The designing and processing of acts became an expensive and time-consuming occupation, breeding a new school of parliamentary lawyers, and the majority of members never took their noses off that humdrum grindstone. More recently, however, the balance of interpretation has tilted back again, Michael Graves and others pointing out the extent to which Elizabeth's councillors used parliament, and particularly the House of Commons, to promote their political programmes. The Tudor Commons could be every bit as difficult as their medieval predecessors, particularly over money and over issues which affected the members' material interests. It had been fears over arbitary confiscation rather than any sympathy with the Protestants which had caused the 1555 parliament to reject the government's Exiles bill, and grievances over lost business and enhanced prices which drove the monopolies controversy at the end of Elizabeth's reign. Individuals and groups of members repeatedly expressed dissatisfaction with aspects of the monarch's policies, but the concept of 'an opposition', whether political or religious, is an anachronism. What did begin to appear, and it was portentous for the future rather than significant at the time, was the opinion that, because of their representative function, members of the House of Commons were entitled to offer their prince advice on any issue of public concern. In 1576 Peter Wentworth was outspoken in his criticism of the queen for refusing to countenance such unsolicited counsel:

'It is a dangerous thing in a prince unkindly to abuse his or her nobility and people, and it is a dangerous thing in a prince to oppose or bind herself against her nobility and people . . . And how could any prince more unkindly intreat, abuse, oppose herself against her nobility and people than her Majesty did the last Parliament?'[41]

This was a stand for which the house was not ready, and Wentworth was imprisoned for presumption by its own order. It was, however, a genuine expression of the seriousness with which the members were beginning to take their role in the formation of policy. Controversy of this kind was rare, but it certainly existed, and demonstrates that the dominance of routine business should not be overstressed.

Up to a point the Tudors were prepared to encourage independence, being confident of the general support of both houses, and of their own powers of management. It was because parliament existed to do the monarch's business that members enjoyed their various privileges. Whatever the Jacobean House of Commons might think, those privileges were of grace, and not of right. No member, and no member's servant, might be arrested on a private suit during a session; and whereas that privilege had traditionally been exercised by writ, in 1543 control was transferred, on Henry's explicit instruction, to the parliament itself. Thereafter any member of the Commons so attached could be released by 'writ of mace', thereby engendering a number of conflicts with the jurisdiction of the sheriff of London, in which the crown consistently supported the Speaker.[42] Freedom of speech also had originated in the king's need to know what his subjects really thought about an issue which had been referred to them. Until the early sixteenth century it had taken the form of a petition from the Speaker at the beginning of each session, begging leave to present the views of the Commons freely without fear of displeasure, against either himself or the house. However, long before Wentworth sought his revolutionary extension of the concept it had been interpreted to mean the freedom of any individual member to speak his mind on an issue which was before the house. It was, after all, in the monarch's interest to know what views were being canvassed, as well as the collective response upon which the house eventually agreed.

There were also a number of 'grey areas' of privilege, over which the Commons endeavoured to gain control, with varying success. Richard Cook, who tried to claim immunity from a subpoena in 1585, was overruled by the lord chancellor, but when a burgess was indicted

41 D'Ewes, *Journals*, pp. 236–40.
42 The fullest account of Ferrer's case, which established the privilege, is in R. Holinshed, *Chronicles of England, Scotland and Ireland* (1808 edn), III, pp. 824–6.

for felony in 1581 (a circumstance not covered by privilege), the chancellor refused a writ for a new election on the grounds that it was for the house itself to decide whether he continued to be a member. The queen was not entirely happy with this complaisance, and in 1586 instructed Sir Thomas Bromley that an election writ was 'a thing in truth impertinent for [the] House to deal withal, and only belonging to the charge and office of the Lord Chancellor'.[43] However, the Commons persisted, and by 1593 had established its right to adjudicate upon the validity of returns. One of the reasons for this success was the fact that the house had earlier established its right to discipline and control members. Absence from all or part of a session required the Speaker's licence, and the members could be randomly 'called' to ensure that they were attending. Similarly members who sufficiently displeased their colleagues (as Peter Wentworth did in 1576) could be imprisoned, or even expelled. The House of Commons was not, as some members appear to have believed, a court of record, but by 1603 it had established a much greater degree of autonomy in the conduct of its business than had been true half a century before.

Whatever Wentworth may have thought, Elizabeth applied direct pressure to the parliament very reluctantly, preferring an appearance of willing and spontaneous co-operation. Like her father, who had frequently inquired about the progress of debates, the queen was more anxious to know what was being said than she would willingly have admitted. In spite of grievances and disputes, it would be a mistake to read the situation of 1640, or even of 1629, back into the sixteenth century. The Speaker of the House of Commons was a royal servant, and the elaborate charade of election deceived no one. That in itself was sufficient to ensure that the council was in control of the agenda, and from the 1530s onwards extreme care was always taken to prepare the presentation of official business in advance. The lesson of Wolsey's failure in that respect in 1523 was well learned. In 1535 a memorandum, probably by Cromwell, noted: 'some way to be devised betwixt this and next session . . . for the restraint and utter extinction of the abuses of lawyers. Some reasonable way to be devised for the king's wards and primer seisin . . . That an act may be made against usury, which is cloaked by pretence of law.'[44] In February 1554 a committee of the Privy Council was set up 'to consider what

43 D'Ewes, *Journals*, p. 432.
44 *Letters and Papers*, IX, 725 ii.

laws shall be established' in the coming session, and during the reign of Elizabeth the passage of every bill was weighed and plotted, even down to the details of which councillor was to make which points in debate. It was only when such management failed, as it did in 1555 and to some extent in 1601, that serious difficulties were experienced.

It was much easier to manage business than it was to control membership. Stephen Gardiner's allegation that the Commons of the Reformation parliament had been 'packed' was mere wishful thinking. The crown did control a number of seats through conventional patronage, but Thomas Cromwell's notorious order to the sheriff and commonalty of Canterbury in 1536 to elect Robert Darknell and John Bryges was altogether exceptional. A larger number of members sat for constituencies controlled by private lords, and both Henry and Elizabeth certainly mobilized their noble servants to increase the number upon whose voices the council could rely. However, every peer had his own agenda, and members would have been pledged to their lords' interests only on specific issues. In the parliaments of Edward VI perhaps as many as seventy or eighty MPs would have belonged in some sense to a noble affinity, but this was a small minority of the whole House, and very difficult to mobilize for a coherent programme. In any case, voting was comparatively uncommon. Divisions were counted by the end of Henry VIII's reign, but the real objective of council management was not to win votes so much as to create a favourable consensus by an orchestrated campaign of argument. There are very few signs that this was resented, even in Elizabeth's reign, as most members were probably only too glad to know what the official line on any issue might be in advance of committing their own voices.

Management did not end on the floor of the house. As the agenda became more crowded, and measures began to jostle and queue for attention, bill committees became increasingly important. By the end of Henry VIII's reign it was already normal to present bills on paper rather than parchment, in order to facilitate the process of amendment, and it was in the committees that the rival interest groups locked horns over controversial measures. When a bill was of official origin, the council had to ensure that enough of its own members, or 'men of business', were named to the relevant committee to control the proceedings – and that they turned up. Pressure of business ensured that both houses met almost every morning during sessions, and with the committees occupying the afternoons, many members were tempted to defect in order to pursue their own affairs. No Speaker's licence was required to miss a committee. It was also important that the council should be adequately represented on the business committes which were set up to deal with such matters as issues of privilege, and on the numerous *ad hoc* committees which blossomed in almost every session. It used to be believed that the Committee of the Whole House, which appeared for the first time in the 1590s, was a device to get the Speaker out of the chair while members indulged their desire to criticize the queen, but it was probably unconnected with that sort of political ambition. Criticism in full debate was sufficiently obvious during the monopolies controversy, and the Committee of the Whole House was more probably intended to facilitate regular business.[45]

The Tudor House of Commons undoubtedly developed further, and more rapidly, than the House of Lords; but that should not be allowed to conceal the fact that the upper house was the more powerful and important, at least until the very end of the century. By 1610 it could be argued that it was the Commons, rather than the parliament as a whole, which spoke for the realm, because every member represented a constituency, whereas 'their lordships be but particular persons'. Moreover by then it was probably true, as was claimed, that the Commons could buy out the Lords several times over. Such claims, however, expressed a calculated ambition and did not represent the whole truth. Throughout the sixteenth century the peers had greater political experience, and far better access to the monarch than did the commoners, in addition to their superior individual status and wealth. The duke of Norfolk in Henry VIII's reign, or the earl of Leicester in Elizabeth's, might control as many as a dozen seats in the lower house, and it was very rare for the Lords to be obstructive when potential legislation was known to have the royal approval. Henry 'managed' the Lords mainly by warning those unsympathetic to his programme to stay away, but once Elizabeth had a reliable bench of bishops in place, she had no need to resort to such tactics. It was more usual for the monarch to use the upper house to put pressure on the lower when it was showing signs of recalcitrance. In 1515 the lord chancellor and a group of his fellow peers descended upon the Commons to remind them that the subsidy voted in 1512 was still largely unpaid; and in November 1558 the same tactic was employed to convince the lower house of the

45 S. Lambert, 'Procedure in the House of Commons in the early Stuart period', *English Historical Review*, 95, 1980, pp. 753–81.

need for further war taxation.[46] Financial measures were by custom initiated in the Commons, but not the exclusive concern of that house. Sometimes conferences between the two houses were arranged for similar reasons, but more often to prevent misunderstandings and crossed purposes. Whenever these meetings took place, protocol ensured that the intitiative rested with the peers. They set the agenda, played the hosts, and 'did sit there covered', while the Commons representatives stood bareheaded.[47] Eventually the erosion of their traditional affinities, and the rise of courtier and service peers at the expense of provincial magnates, was to undermine that supremacy, but it would have required a sharp eye to see that before 1590.

Eventually the changing balance of power between the two houses was a function of numbers as much as of policy. In 1504 there had been about 100 peers, spiritual and temporal, and that number stayed substantially unchanged until 1536. Henry somewhat increased the number of lay peers, from forty-two to fifty-one. However between then and 1540 the dissolution of the monasteries removed the mitred abbots, and although the king created five new sees the number of spiritual peers was halved. This not only gave the temporal peers a permanent and substantial majority, it also reduced the size of the house by about 25 percent. Elizabeth's reluctance to make any new creations in the second half of her reign led to a further slight decline, so that, allowing for minorities and other accidents, the Lords could muster no more than about seventy effectives by 1603. At the same time the Commons was expanding rapidly. In 1509, 296 members represented 37 counties and 110 boroughs. After the enfranchisement of Wales, Calais and Chester in 1536 the number of county members was 90 and of borough members 251. Thereafter the county representation remained unchanged, but enfranchised boroughs continued to multiply, particularly in the south and west of England, until by 1603 their representatives numbered 370, out of a total of 460. It is not surprising that the collective wealth of so substantial body of men was then perceived to outweigh that of a mere seventy peers, particularly as twenty-six of those were bishops in more or less reduced circumstances.[48]

---

46 *Journals of the House of Lords*, I, p. 21. PRO SP11/12, no. 31, ff. 67–67v.
47 H. Scobell, *Remembrances of some Methods, Orders and Proceedings heretofore used and observed in the House of Lords* (1657), pp. 30–31.
48 Smith, *Nation State*, p. 387.

The achievement by parliament of a new political and constitutional status was reflected in the frequency and length of its sessions. A long period of intense activity had come to an end in 1497. Between then and 1529 there were five parliaments divided into nine sessions covering some fourteen or fifteen months altogether. The next thirty years, to the beginning of Elizabeth's reign, saw twelve parliaments and twenty-six sessions, filling a total of sixty-one months. Thereafter increased stability saw a slight reduction of activity again: ten parliaments and thirteen sessions over forty-four years – thirty-eight months in all. The longest interval between parliaments in the first period was seven years and four months, from December 1515 to April 1523; in the second period thirteen months, from December 1534 to February 1536; and in the third period four years and ten months, from March 1576 to January 1581. Elizabeth frequently left two years or more between sessions, but meetings of several months' duration became much more common. The 'parliament man' was thus a creation of the middle and later years of the sixteenth century. These gentlemen, who were often lawyers, made a significant part of their public careers sitting in the House of Commons. They often served in three or more successive parliaments, and became extremely knowledgeable about the conduct of business. Experience created a demand for their services as brokers and promoters, and the increasing popularity of party legislation gave them lucrative employment. Whatever the constitutional theory, Elizabeth knew perfectly well that the parliament had become a regular and indispensable institution of government, and she was happy with that situation, because she believed – as her father had come to do – that sessions represented an excellent opportunity for the monarch to exercise her charisma upon her subjects, consolidating that bond between the crown and the gentry commonwealth which was the essential secret of the Tudor regime.

THE INSTITUTIONS OF FINANCIAL MANAGEMENT

The original royal treasury was almost literally a coffer under the king's bed, but the earliest financial office was the Exchequer. By the end of the twelfth century this had already gone 'out of court' and become an independent institution. It consisted of two departments; the Lower Exchequer, or Exchequer of Receipt, which was a treasury for the receipt and disbursement of money; and the Upper

Exchequer, or Exchequer of Account, which was an office of scrutiny and audit. Neither its structure nor its procedures changed very much over the ensuing three hundred years, and this venerable immutability gave it enormous prestige. The rules governing the passage of accounts, known as the 'course', were primarily designed to prevent fraud and to keep track of outstanding debts. In both respects they were extremely successful, but for purposes of budgeting or discovering the current state of the royal finances, the 'course' was totally useless. It was also very slow, many audits taking more than two years to complete. Consequently it was realized as early as the middle of the thirteenth century that a more flexible and responsive system was needed if the king was to enjoy ready access to his money, and full control over how it was spent. Henry III and Edward I used the Wardrobe of the Household for that purpose. While the tellers of the Exchequer continued to receive fixed revenues, such as the income from the 'ancient demesne' of the crown, which was accounted for by the sheriff in respect of each county, occasional revenues such as the proceeds of direct taxation were paid by the collectors directly into the Wardrobe, for the king's use. Edward II and Edward III used the Treasury of the Chamber in the same way. The Chamber had its own clerks and its own receivers, and was to a large extent independent of the old revenue system, although it was not uncommon for money to be transferred from the Exchequer before being disbursed. Under the Lancastrians the Exchequer officials in a large measure recovered control. Henry IV was concerned to retain the support of as many vested interests as possible, and Henry V spent almost the whole of his short reign fighting in France. As the financial situation deteriorated after 1430, this control became something of an embarrassment, because income was frequently 'assigned', or pledged in advance, and the tellers found their actual cash balances disappearing. So bad had matters become by 1455 that receivers, such as the customer of the port of London, often had backlogs of undischarged assignments, and all the Exchequer ever received was records of these transactions to discharge the account. Consequently when Edward IV reverted to a chamber system after 1460, it made less difference than might be supposed.

However, as the king's revenues recovered the Exchequer derived little benefit. Assignments continued to be used because they were convenient. There was little point in transporting the profit of the port of Newcastle all the way to London, only for it to be sent back to pay the garrison of Berwick. Customs revenue, and the profits of the sheriffs' farms, continued to be paid to the Exchequer in theory, but in practice what usually arrived was a tally of assignment. As the crown recovered land by forfeiture, escheat or judicial inquest, the profits were assigned to the chamber, and that was also the destination of such occasional windfalls as the French pension which began to be paid after the treaty of Picquingy in 1475. After a brief hesitation resulting from his inexperience, Henry VII adopted the same strategy. New land revenue, the profits of justice and administration, parliamentary grants and the income from wardships all went into the Treasury of the Chamber, which became the king's principal revenue department. As such it was the hub of Henry's famous (or notorious) fiscal policy. Like Edward, he used *ad hoc* commissions to track down his prerogative rights to lands and forfeitures, but from 1500 a standing committee was responsible for collecting fines on penal statutes, and in 1508 a new office was created with the revealing title of 'surveyor of the king's prerogative'. Similarly his *judices fiscales*, Sir Richard Empson and Edmund Dudley, set up and operated a grinding system of bonds and recognizances, designed partly to bind the king's servants to the proper discharge of their duties, and partly to provide instant sanctions against aristocratic recalcitrance. As a result of unremitting pressure from the king himself, his income from every source increased. The Duchy of Lancaster, a self-contained part of the royal demesne, paid £666 13s 4d into the Treasury of the Chamber in 1488; by 1508 the equivalent sum was £6,566. The other royal lands, worth no more than £3,765 after fixed deductions in 1491, were by 1504 producing a clear profit of nearly £25,000. Bonds and recognizances, worth about £3,000 in 1493–4, were bringing in a theoretical £35,000 ten years later. Much of this was not real income, as it represented obligations incurred rather than sums actually paid. Some of these debts were pardoned, and some defaulted, but even so there was a massive increase of revenue from that source, and the resentment it created is entirely understandable.[49] The king sat assiduously on the tail of his treasurer of the chamber, checking the accounts in person, but he knew how to spend money, as well as gain it. His court was lavish, and he spent heavily on jewels and plate, the contemporary equivalent of stocks and shares. Another appeal of the chamber system was its responsiveness to the king's spending

49   F.C. Dietz, *English Government Finance, 1485–1558* (1921), p. 33. Loades, *John Dudley*, pp. 4–5.

demands. Whereas the Exchequer would respond only to a writ under the Great or Privy Seal, the Treasurer of the Chamber would act upon a sign manual instruction, or even a verbal one.

Henry VIII executed his father's *judices fiscales*, and immediately discontinued the office of surveyor of the king's prerogative, but the core of the system, the use of the Treasury of the Chamber, continued largely unchanged. Disgruntled Exchequer officials pointed out, quite correctly, that this deprived the revenue of 'certainty', by which they meant guarantees against peculation. These had been provided by the old king's personal assiduity, but young Henry could only occasionally be troubled to inspect the accounts in person, and the opportunities for malpractice were clearly greater. At first the king responded to this criticism by appointing two general surveyors of the crown lands, with responsibility for the collection of such revenue, and for taking the accounts of other officers. In 1515 this reform was also embodied in an Act of Parliament, the preamble of which set out the background to the acquisition of responsibility by the chamber, and provided against further counter-attack from the Exchequer by giving the general surveyors authority to wind up all accounts still open from the previous reign:

And where it is considered that neither by course of the King's Exchequer nor by this present act or acts any officer or officers accountable . . . be discharged of their accounts or payments in the said Exchequer or by the said executors of this act . . . which now by experience is not possible to be accomplished forasmuch as many and most part of the said accounts, which were of long time past by the commandment of our late sovereign lord King Henry VII taken by divers several auditors thereunto appointed, which auditors be deceased and not only the said accounts allowed be broken, lost and otherwise embezzled, so that no sufficient matter may be had to make new the said accounts according to the continue and purport of the said act; and so the said officers accountable be without remedy to their extreme loss, danger and utter undoing [it is enacted that all accounts shall be quit by certificate of the General Surveyors for all sums, arrears, etc. down to Michaelmas 1508].[50]

Financial management was not Wolsey's strong suit, and little more was done to upgrade the system during his period in power. Even the

50   6 Henry VIII, c.24; *Statutes of the Realm* (eds E. Luders et al. (1810–28)), III, pp. 145–52.

general surveyors were only sanctioned from one parliament to the next, until their offices were made permanent in 1535. As long as Sir Henry Wyatt remained treasurer of the chamber, every pressure in the direction of greater complexity and formality of organization was resisted, but once he had been succeeded by Sir Brian Tuke in 1528 the treasury began to resemble a structured department. For most purposes the general surveyors were agents of the chamber, but their own accounts were ultimately passed by the Exchequer, and they continued to rely on the Privy Seal for some of their authority. In 1531, before the major changes introduced by Thomas Cromwell, all the receivers of crown revenues were answerable to one of three accounting departments: the Exchequer for the sheriffs' farms, the customs and the profits of justice; the Duchy of Lancaster for its own lands; and the general surveyors for the rest – crown lands, feudal profits, butlerage, vacant bishoprics, Calais and the Hanaper of Chancery. Although the mint remained in a sense independent, if there was any profit from its operations the general surveyors passed it on to the chamber.[51]

Cromwell began to address this situation as soon as he achieved first place in the king's confidence. His motives for so doing are debatable. Geoffrey Elton believed that he appreciated the inadequacy of the chamber system, and set out to replace it with something which would be more formal and bureaucratic, without retreating into the obsolete rigidities of the Exchequer. More recently John Guy and Christopher Coleman have argued that Cromwell was really more concerned to set up a system which he could control himself, and that his attack on the chamber was more concerned to reduce its power than to provide a better financial service. Elton's thesis is supported by the general effect of the reforms, but it also has to be born in mind that Cromwell's first step was to use his initial office, as master of the jewel house, to set up a rival to the chamber, and to begin the process of diverting revenue into it. Most of the organizational changes did not, in fact, take place until after Cromwell had fallen, but that is not a significant consideration.

The establishment of the royal supremacy provided the occasion for these changes. Not only were annates now paid to the king instead of to the pope, but the dissolution of the monasteries, which began in 1536, transferred from the church to the crown lands with a capital

---

51 *State Papers of Henry VIII*, (1830–52), vi, pp. 32–7; C.E. Challis, *The Tudor Coinage* (1978).

value well in excess of £1 million. Whether this land had been retained or sold, the administration of the process would have required a massive extension to the existing structure, and the opportunity was taken to reorganize the whole revenue management. The first step was to create a new, self-contained institution, called the Court of the Augmentation of the King's Revenues, to deal with the monastic lands. This was erected by statute in 1536, and consisted of a chancellor, treasurer, attorney and solicitor, armed with their own seals and empowered to undertake all transactions relating to the new acquisitions, including the hearing of cases arising out of disputes. Ten local auditors and sixteen 'particular receivers' were also to be appointed to deal with the relevant business on the ground, and the officers of the Exchequer were explicitly excluded from any supervisory function:

> Also . . . that all manner of process that shall be made out of the King's Exchequer to or against any persons or any farms, rents, issues or profits concerning the premises or any part thereof limited by this act to be in the survey, order or governance of the said court and the ministers thereof shall be clearly void and of no effect.[52]

The erection of this new court did not, in itself, affect any aspect of the existing revenue administration, but a stock taking of 1537 makes it clear that a precedent was intended. First fruits and tenths, which had been accounted to their own treasurer for some time, became an autonomous court of the same type in 1540, and Wards and Liveries was established at the same time to handle the feudal prerogative.[53] Finally, in 1542 the general surveyors also became a court, with jurisdiction over those lands which had been collected by the crown between 1485 and 1530. Neither the Duchy of Lancaster nor the Exchequer was directly affected by these changes, but the establishment of General Surveyors drastically reduced the function of the Chamber, returning it to the relatively minor household functions for which it had been originally intended.

The great advantage of Cromwell's system was that it made both budgeting and financial control a great deal easier. All the new courts used a modern double-entry system of accounting, which made it comparatively simple to assess the state of their balances, and thus to

52 27 Henry VIII, c. 27; *Statutes of the Realm*, III, pp. 569–74.
53 27 Henry VIII, c. 27. *State Papers of Henry VIII*, ix, pp. 106–7.

ensure that demands made could actually be met. The main disadvantages were compexity, and the multiplication of local officers and agents which the courts generated. Once Cromwell's own political agenda was no longer relevant, this diversity became increasingly apparent. The king also found that he no longer had a significant treasury responsive to his own personal needs. The Privy Purse was a 'pocket money' account, held by the chief gentleman of the privy chamber, and turning over no more than £3,000–4,000 a year. Consequently, once Cromwell was out of the way a new informal spending department was created, usually known as the King's Coffers. This was held by the keeper of the Palace of Westminster, and expended tens of thousands of pounds over the last five years of the reign, largely on building projects and on the purchase of jewels. It was fed mainly from the Court of Augmentations, and was not subject to any regular accounting procedure. In theory the keeper's account was taken by a special commission, as was still the case with the chamber, but that did not actually happen until after Henry's death. Consequently, although the informality of the household system had been in a sense overcome by the creation of the revenue courts, in another sense it had reappeared on the back stairs of the Privy Chamber.[54] The Court of General Surveyors had almost certainly been created to give the *quietus* to the Chamber as a public spending department rather than because there was any real need for it. As soon as Henry was dead, and the possibility of a Chamber revival remote, it was merged into the Court of Augmentations, giving the latter control of all royal lands except the ancient demesne.

The mint was not a spending department, and therefore stood outside the normal structure of management, but for nearly twenty years it played a central role in the crown's financial calculations. Struggling to meet a massive war expenditure of over £2 million between 1542 and 1547, Henry debased the coinage not once but several times. This produced an income of some £363,000, but destabilized the currency and triggered a sharp rise in inflation, that mysterious and unfamiliar ailment which jeopardized all the financial calculations of the period. The minority governments of Edward VI continued that policy down to 1551, and so for nearly a decade the mint was an unpredictable element in the economy, offering opportunities for both public and private corruption. After 1551

54   D.E. Hoak, 'The secret history of the Tudor court: the King's Coffers and the king's purse, 1542–1553', *Journal of British Studies*, 26, 1987, pp. 840–62.

debasement was discontinued, and the mint reverted to normal production, but as long as the base coin continued to circulate price stability remained elusive. At last, in 1561, Elizabeth's council grasped the nettle and carried out a complete recoinage. That did not end inflation, which was also fed by other factors, but it returned the mint to its normal function as a small service department, and ended the activities of bullion speculators.

The financial difficulties of Edward VI's reign have been much exaggerated, and in any case are beyond the scope of this discussion, but the reign did see a continued momentum towards organizational reform. On the one hand account was finally taken of the Privy Coffers, first under the control of Sir Anthony Denny and latterly of Peter Osborne. Not long before Edward's death the whole operation was dramatically scaled down, perhaps with a view to placing it in the king's own hands, or perhaps of discontinuing it altogether. The lord treasurer, the marquis of Winchester, seems to have been a great believer in unity of control, and the fact that the coffers were not replenished in the new reign would seem to support the latter conclusion. More importantly, Winchester also began to prepare a scheme for the reunification of the fragmented structure of public management. His original intention seems to have been to absorb all the remaining revenue courts into a revitalized Exchequer, although whether this was also intended to involve a general return to the 'ancient course' is not clear. By 1552 the Court of Augmentations was handling well over half of the crown's gross income, so it would have seemed more logical to absorb the Exchequer into Augmentations, but the status and antiquity of the older institution precluded that possibility. In March 1553 the king was empowered by statute to reorganize his revenue administration by letters patent, and guarantees of compensation were offered to all those officers of the existing institutions who stood to lose their jobs. That statute lapsed with Edward's death, but Mary's decision to continue Winchester in office also ensured the continuity of his programme. The empowering act was repeated in October 1553, and the relevant letters patent issued on 23 January following. On that day the Courts of Augmentations and of First Fruits and Tenths ceased their legal existence. Their officers were pensioned, and their assets and records transferred to the Exchequer. The Marian statute appears to be quite explicit about the next step: 'that then all things within the survey of the said Court [of Augmentations] so conveyed shall be ordered in like manner to all intents as the said Court of the Exchequer is or ought to be by the

Common laws and statutes of the realm'.[55] That should have meant
that each of the dissolved courts would survive only as a small record
office within the Exchequer; its accounting procedures would be
discontinued and its network of receivers disbanded. All crown lands
would henceforth account through the sheriffs according to the
'ancient course', something which had not been seen since the
thirteenth century. However, what actually happened was significantly different.

The lord treasurer and barons had been granted specific authority
in the letters patent to 'ammend and correct' anything in the original
schedule according to their own knowledge and experience, and what
Winchester did in the first instance was to set up the 'Office of first
fruits and tenths' as a self-contained department within the
Exchequer, managing all the business of the former court, and run by
its own remembrancer. A very much larger 'augmentations office' was
then established on the same lines, except that it did not have its own
remembrancer. This office continued to use the modern accounting
methods of the former court, and its local officers and receivers
continued to function as before. Unity of control had thus been
achieved, but not at the anticipated cost of reverting to the antiquated
accounting methods of the traditional tellers. It may have been in
order to protect the control of the Augmentations office over such
'foreign' accounts as butlerage and the Staple of Calais that the audi-
torships of the prests within the Exchequer were abolished at the same
time. It would be too simple to suggest that they went to 'make way
for' the new offices, but not entirely misleading.

From early in 1554, therefore, only the Court of Wards and
Liveries and the Duchy of Lancaster remained outside the Exchequer umberella. The Treasury of the chamber was concerned
with little beyond the payment of Chamber wages, and the Privy
Purse, held by the mistress of the robes, dealt only with the queen's
personal expenditure. While all these changes were taking place, Sir
Edmund Peckham was commissioned on a temporary basis to
receive and disburse the whole of the crown's revenue, which he did
for nearly two years, from December 1553 until the autumn of 1555.
Once the normal flow of business had been restored, the reshaped
Exchequer changed hardly at all during the remainder of the century.
The auditors of the prests were restored in 1560, and given oversight

55 1 Mary st. 2, c.10. *Statutes of the Realm*, IV, pp. 208–9. PRO C54/500 ms.
3–6.

of all those accounts outside the 'ancient course' which were not concerned with the crown lands. The work of the Office of First Fruits and Tenths, which had shrunk considerably after the restoration of the papal authority in 1555, recovered its former importance with the royal supremacy in 1559. However, stability did not guarantee efficiency, and the absence of further reform during the Elizabethan period was more due to the conservatism of the queen and her officers than to the satisfactory nature of the service which was provided. The Elizabethan Exchequer was an uneasy mixture of modern practices with entrenched rituals and habits of mind. The Lower Exchequer again dealt with cash – quite large sums of it – but continued to issue the split wooden tallies which belonged more properly to a pre-literate society. The Upper Exchequer used both ancient and modern auditing processes. At every level, entrenched vested interests had forced compromise upon those who were seeking to make the organization more appropriate to contemporary needs. The result was a lumbering dinosaur of an institution, which was less responsive to the demands which the crown made on it than either the chamber of Henry VII or the revenue courts of Cromwell. Only the qualities of the principal officers enabled it to function at all. At the top there was both efficiency and continuity. Winchester was followed as lord treasurer by Burghley, and Sir Walter Mildmay as chancellor by John Fortescue; between them these four men covered virtually the whole reign, and contrived to manage the queen's resources effectively in spite of, rather than because of, the means which they had to use.

However, no amount of institutional efficiency could have cured the endemic poverty of the English crown. Both Edward IV and Henry VII had died solvent, but both had eschewed foreign wars, and the latter became notorious in his own lifetime for the grinding oppression of his fiscal policies. At the end of his reign Henry's ordinary income was probably a little in excess of £50,000 per annum, but extraordinary receipts including taxation more than doubled that total, producing an annual surplus of between £5,000 and £10,000. His fabulous wealth was a legend, but he had probably accumulated the equivalent of one year's total income – perhaps £120,000 or £130,000.[56] Henry VIII lived on the brink of insolvency most of his life because of his addiction to war. In fact only eleven of the

---

56   Sir Francis Bacon, *History of the Reign of Henry VII* (1622), in *Works*, ed. J. Spedding (1858), vol. vi, p. 210; Dietz, *Government Finance*, pp. 86–7.

thirty-eight years of his reign were spent in that way, and not all those years saw expensive campaigns, but the level of expenditure was truly staggering. In the first ten years of the reign the normal disbursements of the chamber totalled about £60,000 a year, but in 1513 the equivalent sum was nearly £700,000, and the total for the three years of fighting in excess of £1 million. The futile campaigns of 1522–3 cost about £400,000, £352,000 of which was raised in forced loans by Wolsey, who was never scrupulous about legal niceties when it came to obtaining money. In 1523 he was constrained to approach parliament with a demand for £800,000, and obliged to settle for less than half that sum, spread over a number of years. When the golden opportunity came in 1525 to take advantage of Francis I's defeat at Pavia, Henry was in the humiliating position of not being able to afford a campaign. Wolsey's disastrous scheme for another forced loan, or 'amicable grant', produced a taxpayers' strike, and a further humiliation for both the king and the cardinal.[57] However, Wolsey did leave one positive financial legacy. The traditional parliamentary grant had been of one fifteenth on the value of land, and one tenth on the value of moveables, the assessment of which on the basis of communities had become fossilized to produce about £30,000. Without abolishing the tenth and fifteenth, Wolsey introduced a new type of tax, called the subsidy, which was assessed directly on individuals by commissioners appointed specifically for the purpose. This was recognized as being both fairer and more efficient, and the subsidy became thereafter the standard parliamentary tax.

Traditionally, direct taxation had been a wartime expedient, but taxation could be sought at other times of danger, and it is by no means clear that Cromwell's success in obtaining grants during the 1530s was innovatory.[58] Nearly fifteen years of peace, and the massive injection of about £75,000 a year from the dissolution of the monasteries, should have made the financial situation in 1540 uncommonly healthy. Moreover, the establishment of the royal supremacy had enabled the king to tax his clergy without resistance, and all benefices were reassessed in 1535. However, in 1542 Henry returned to war. In five years he spent over £2 million. Repeated subsidies contributed some £650,000 to that total, and the sale of monastic land about the

---

57   G.W. Bernard, *War, Taxation and Rebellion in Early Tudor England* (1986), passim.
58   J.D. Alsop, 'Innovation in Tudor taxation', *English Historical Review*, 99, 1984, pp. 83–93.

same. The balance was made up by loans of various kinds, and by the debasement of the coinage, as we have seen. By the time he died the French war was over, and his debts were not enormous by contemporary standards; probably about £200,000, of which a half was on short-term contracts in Antwerp at about 12 per cent. However, the bulk of the monastic land had gone, and the ordinary income of the crown was not much greater than it had been before. If Cromwell had ever entertained the ambition of making his master independent of parliamentary grants, then the chance of that disappeared with the war. Moreover the lesson was wasted upon the duke of Somerset, who ran the government as lord protector from 1547 to 1549. Pursuing an obsessive conflict with Scotland, and being forced to defend Henry's last conquest of Boulogne against renewed French threats, he spent another £800,000. Most of this was found in the same way, from subsidies, sales and debasement. Some £600,000-worth of chantry land was confiscated to replenish the dwindling supply of monastic property, and the crown debt increased to about £250,000. After Somerset's fall in October 1549 the wars were quickly brought to an end.[59] Boulogne was sold back to France for a useful £180,000, and a cautious policy of retrenchment was commenced. The English government could not afford to disarm in a Europe increasingly distracted by religious strife, nor to abandon its position in Ireland, so military expenditure remained high, but land sales continued and the debt was gradually reduced without further recourse to parliament until 1553. By skilful operations in Antwerp the exchange value of sterling, so adversely affected by debasement, was also restored, to the considerable benefit of the trading community. At the same time the City of London greatly assisted the council in supporting the government's loan negotiations with its massive credit resources, so that by the summer of 1553 the overall debt was reduced to about £180,000.

Mary's accession, and improved relations with the Low Countries, should have allowed that retrenchment to continue, but by remitting almost £50,000 of the last Edwardian subsidy, and borrowing £80,000 in Spain, Mary in fact began by allowing the debt to increase again. This political naievity did not continue, and by the end of 1554 Lord Treasurer Winchester had again brought the situation under control. Although the queen insisted upon returning ecclesiastical

59 W.K. Jordan, *Edward VI: the threshold of power* (1970), pp. 116–32. Loades, *John Dudley*, pp. 151–6.

revenues to the church, this did little harm in the short term as the obligation to pay remaining monastic pensions was returned as well. Strict economy, peace and continued land sales had probably reduced the debt again to a little more than £100,000 by the spring of 1557, with only one recourse to parliament, in the autumn of 1555. However, at that point the queen, against the almost unanimous advice of her council, decided that it was her duty to support her husband in his war against France. By comparison with Henry's efforts in 1543–6, this was war on the cheap, because Philip bore the whole cost of the English army which went to the Low Countries in 1557. Nevertheless the cost over eighteen months, down to Mary's death, was in excess of £500,000, towards which the parliament contributed £180,000 through a subsidy voted in the spring of 1558, and a Privy Seal loan another £100,000. The City of London, however, was not noticeably co-operative, and when Mary died in November 1558 the debt stood at almost £300,000.[60]

It is against this background that Elizabeth's notorious parsimony must be viewed. In the first few years of her reign she borrowed almost £700,000 on the bourse, and, with the renewed co-operation of the city, eliminated her debts by 1565. However, she knew perfectly well that, with the reserves of monastic land almost exhausted, and with debasement an economic disaster area, it was only by a massive dependence upon parliament that she could afford to wage war. The queen's relations with parliament were reasonably good, but she was extremely reluctant to press the members for money in case the political price should turn out to be too high. It was for this reason also that the subsidy assessments were allowed to slide. In Henry VIII's reign each subsidy had been freshly assessed, at least in theory, and a serious attempt had been made to pursue increasing wealth. That was done for the last time in 1555. Thereafter the assessments became fossilized, like those of the fifteenth and tenth, and whereas some reductions were made on appeals of poverty, there were no increases no matter how obviously the subjects had prospered. By 1585 a single subsidy was actually worth less in face value than it had been in 1545, and had less than half the value in real terms, because of continuing inflation. When Elizabeth was finally forced into war in 1585, the parliament was not unduly difficult. The war was recognized as necessary, if not exactly popular, and at least £1,560,000 was contributed in subsidies between 1585 and the end of the reign.

60 Loades, *Reign of Mary*, p. 357.

However, this was less than £100,000 a year, significantly less than Henry had received in the 1540s, in spite of generous-looking grants of treble and even quadruple subsidies. The fact is that, even in wartime, England was the most lightly taxed country in Europe, and the reason for that was that the assessment lay in the hands of the taxpayers themselves. In theory it was a very fair system, which fell only on those able to pay. Unlike the French *taille*, it did not exempt the nobility, and the poor were almost totally excluded, but in practice it deprived the crown of a realistic tax revenue. Imprisoned in the system of parliamentary consent, and dependent upon the co-operation of the political nation, the English monarchy was, by the end of the sixteenth century, trapped in a cycle of poverty which was seriously undermining a hundred and twenty years of remarkable political achievement.

ADMINISTRATIVE INSTITUTIONS

The oldest office of the royal administration was the Chancery. In origin the king's writing office, it had gone 'out of court' soon after the Exchequer, and by the end of the fifteenth century had the same well-established staff and inflexible routines. Unlike the Exchequer, however, it had retained its primary function. Chancery issued writs, which were essentially orders for action, and all other documents requiring the authentication of the Great Seal. Writs had long since adopted set forms, and were known by brief latin descriptions of their function: *habeas corpus*, *fieri facias*, *sub poena*, and so on. Most of them related to set legal proceedings, and might be issued on the order of a court, by instruction from the king's council, or by supplication of the litigant. Individuals suing writs were charged fees in accordance with a fixed scale, but it was also normal practice to offer rewards or inducements to the Chancery clerks in order to expedite what could otherwise be a very protracted business. Writs were central and essential to the operation of medieval English government, but they had long since lost the capacity to diversify, or to generate new forms. Neither these proceedings, nor the structure of the office which generated them, changed in any significant way during the Tudor period. However, Chancery had for centuries also discharged a less formal administrative function, issuing royal orders which did not require the authentication of the Great Seal, and enrolling them on the Close Rolls. This business had greatly diminished by the end of the fifteenth century, and disappeared altogether in the reign of Henry VIII, when the secretariat became responsible for all such matters.

Apart from servicing the judiciary, the main function of Chancery in the sixteenth century was the authentication of grants and appointments. Baronies, for example, were created by patent under the Great Seal; all major offices were granted in the same way, and commissions such as gaol delivery or oyer and terminer (see below, pp. 121–31). This procedure had become established by custom in the fourteenth century, and confirmed by a council ordinance of 1444. Grants might be initiated by a verbal order, or by a note over the sign manual, but they were then required to proceed to the signet office, whence a formal instruction would be sent to the Privy Seal office in order to activate the Great Seal. This bureaucratic elaboration was probably intended to prevent fraud or misrepresentation, but its main effect was to create fees for a relay of officials and make the whole process extremely expensive. Understandably, attempts were made to short circuit this ritual by applying to the king for an 'immediate warrant' which would directly activate the Great Seal – the only authentication legally required – but they were ended by statute in 1536. Thereafter the full passage of the seals was protected by law, and although this was one of Cromwell's measures, it did not promote either speed or efficiency of administration. What it did do was protect the vested interests of the seals' clerks. The importance of the Great Seal was such that it had to be available at all times, and this was one of the lord chancellor's most onerous responsibilities. When Wolsey went to France in 1527 and took the Great Seal with him, the king was seriously displeased and ordered its immediate return. The chancellor's own courts also used this means of authenticating their proceedings, the Chancery Court itself throughout the period and the Court of Star Chamber from the 1530s onwards. It was one of the signs of the growing status of the latter that it moved from the Privy Seal, which was used by the council, to the Great Seal.

The Chancery Court was a court of equity, that is to say it was intended to redress grievances for which the common law provided no remedy. The development of statute, which made the law more amenable to extension and reform, should logically have reduced the need for equity, but this does not seem to have been the case. Equity decisions were less sure than those of the common law, but the courts were cheaper, and their procedures less arcane. Sir Thomas Smith explained the function succinctly:

So he that putteth up his bill in the Chancery, after that he hath declared the mischief wherein he is, has relief as in the solemn *forum*. And for so much as in this case he is without remedy in the common law, and therefore he requireth the chancellor according to equity and reason to provide for him and to take such order as to good conscience shall appertain. And the Court of Chancery is called of the common people the court of conscience, because that the chancellor is not strained by rigour or form of words of law to judge but *ex aequo* and *bono*, and according to conscience, as I have said. And in this court the usual and proper form of pleading of England is not used, but the form of pleading by writing which is used in other countries according to the civil law; and the trial is not by twelve men, but by the examination of witnesses as in other courts of the civil law.[61]

He might also have added that the written proceedings were in English, and not in law French. During the fifteenth century the court of Chancery had extended the range of its business considerably by adjudicating disputes arising out of customary tenures. Such cases were heard in the first instance in the manor court of the appropriate manor, but if the lord was a party then the justice of the verdict might well be questioned. Appeal could lie to the honour court of the over-lord, if he was a mesne lord, but the same consideration would apply. Being customary, such cases were not pleadable before the king's courts of common law, and a remedy in equity was therefore both appropriate and necessary. The Court of Requests performed a similar service, as we shall see. At the same time the chancellor extended his protection to enfeoffment to use, which was an attempt to evade the common law's ban upon the devising of lands by will, and the feudal incidents due upon the death of a tenant in chief. Chancery also had the unique function of acting as the conscience of the common law. There was no concept of appeal in the modern sense, but there were procedures for dealing with acknowledged miscarriages of justice, and one of these was the 'petition of right'. As no action could lie against the crown, this was the only way to remedy an injury which the monarch might have done to a private litigant. Chancery received such petitions and requested the investigation and redress of the grievance.

The second seal office, in terms of both status and antiquity, was that of the Privy Seal. Originally, as its name suggests, the king's personal authentication, down to the middle of the fourteenth

61 Smith, *De Republica Anglorum*, pp. 93–4.

century its keeper was usually described as *secretarius regis*. By the early fifteenth century the offices of secretary and keeper were clearly distinct, and the Privy Seal office had become the main clearing house for administrative business. Regular administrative orders, such as warrants to the Exchequer for payments, or instructions to local officers, were sent out over the Privy Seal. It was also used by the council for its more official utterances until the Privy Council acquired its own seal in 1556, and by the Court of Star Chamber, as we have seen, until it was replaced by the Great Seal. Until the reign of Henry VIII the keeper was invariably a cleric. Sir Henry Marney was the first layman to hold the post, for a few months in 1523, but when Cuthbert Tunstall, the bishop of London, was replaced by the earl of Wiltshire in 1530, he was the last ecclesiastical incumbent. Thereafter the keeper was usually a peer, and was styled lord privy seal. However the increase in dignity coincided very closely with a decline in function. Thomas Cromwell, who held the office from 1536 to 1540 was the last who used it in anything like its old omnicompetent way, and its demise was very much the result of his own actions. As King's Secretary from 1533 to 1536 he had relocated the centre of administrative action in that office, and although his highly personal style of management resulted in some of that work returning to the Privy Seal when he was promoted, the change turned out to be permanent. Subsequent lords privy seal, such as Lord Paget from 1555 to 1558, were often important political figures, and in Paget's case a master of council business, but their offices never recovered the central role which they had enjoyed before 1533.

The office of king's secretary was an ancient one, but had traditionally been a household position of little status. The secretary was a clerk (in both senses of the word), who dealt with the king's personal correspondence, and had custody of the private seal, known as the signet. At a time when the council was large, and somewhat amorphous, the secretary might be a councillor, or might not; the status was certainly not *ex officio*. Richard Pace, who held the post in the 1520s, was far from being a menial servant. He was a scholar and a diplomat of some note, but he was constrained to explain to Wolsey, who had taken exception to a letter which he had written, that he was merely obeying the king's instructions:

> And when his grace had your said letters, he read the same three times, and marked such places as it pleased him to make answer unto, and commanded me to write and rehearse as liked him, and not further to

meddle with that answer. So that I herein nothing did but obeyed the King's commandment as to my duty appertaineth.[62]

When the Eltham Ordinances were drawn up in 1526 the secretary ranked with the vice chamberlain for the provision of bouge of court. Pace was a member of the council, and probably had more influence with the king than he was prepared to admit, but he was still operating within the traditional context. Thomas Cromwell was not only the first layman to hold the post when he was appointed in 1533, he was the first incumbent to have gained the king's confidence at the highest level before his appointment.

It would probably be true to say that Cromwell chose the somewhat improbable office of secretary as the vehicle for his influence, rather than being dependent upon it. If so, he deserves great credit for spotting the potentialities of regular and unchallenged access to the king's person. Over the following seven years Cromwell's unique position enabled him to channel virtually all discretionary business through the secretary's office, using his own staff of clerks, rather as Wolsey had used the much more prestigious office of chancellor. In 1539 it was decreed that the secretary, if a baron or a bishop, should have precedence over all other holders of the same rank, and even if a commoner should give place only to the major officers of state. After Cromwell's execution, the office inevitably fell back somewhat, having been divided in two in March 1540 with the appointment of Sir Thomas Wriothesley and Sir Ralph Sadler. This was partly a result of the dramatic increase in the workload, but partly also in order to have the convenience of a secretary with the king and another at Westminster. Wriothesley and Sadler did not manage the Privy Council in the way Cromwell had done, but they were *ex officio* members of it, and the household ordinances of 1544 confirm how far the office had advanced since 1526: 'The two Secretaries to sit in their own chamber, and to be served with their own servants from all offices', [63] while each enjoyed lodging at court, with provision for two servants and eight horses. Thereafter there were normally two secretaries, although Sir William Cecil acted alone from 1558 to 1572, and his

---

62 Pace to Wolsey, 29 October 1521; *State Papers of Henry VIII*, I, pp. 79–80. For a further discussion of this office, see Charles Knighton, 'The principal secretaries in the reign of Edward VI: reflections on their office and archive', in *Law and Government under the Tudors*, eds C. Cross, D. Loades and J. Scarisbrick (1987) pp. 163–76.

63 *Household Ordinances*, p. 172.

son Sir Robert from 1596 to 1600. The elder Cecil, indeed, came close to the unique political power which Cromwell had enjoyed, but his colleagues both before and after should be seen as managers and administrators rather than as statesmen.

In the reign of Elizabeth the secretaries were chief executive ministers, with particular responsibility for security and for diplomatic negotiations. They acted also as channels of communication between the queen and her council, but apart from the Cecils they were not policy advisers. After 1540 they were normally called principal secretaries, a term which had been used in the fifteenth century to distinguish the position from those of other household clerks, but by this time was taken to indicate a rank in the official hierarchy. The king had long had an inferior secretary 'in the French tongue', and from 1549 he also had one 'for the Latin tongue'. The latter accomplishment could no longer be taken for granted now that virtually all the officers of state were laymen. The only ordained secretary after Stephen Gardiner (1531–3) was John Boxall (1557–8). By the 1590s the office organization which Cromwell had created to carry out his manifold duties had become settled and sophisticated. When Nicholas Faunt wrote his 'Discourse touching the office of Principal Secretary of estate' in 1592, he included the keeping of a long list of 'books', or information files as we would now call them, on a huge range of subjects from foreign treaties and negotiations to 'sea causes', musters, weights and measures, the coinage and legal precedents. In 1600 as in 1540, every conceivable kind of business passed through the secretary's hands. He was not expected to make critical decisions, but he was expected to know where he could lay his hands on all the relevant information that the monarch or council might need. The secretary or secretaries still held the third royal seal, the signet, and used it fairly often for administrative instructions or for authorizing payments on the household accounts, but it never achieved the prestige of the Privy or Great Seals, and gradually fell out of use in the seventeenth century.

THE COURTS OF LAW AND EQUITY

The common law had originated in ancient custom, but from a very early date it had been the king's law in the sense that the king had the prime responsibility for administering it. It was called common because it was applied wherever the king's writ ran, and it had been

systematized, if not exactly codified, by Henry II in the later part of
the twelfth century. Only freemen might claim the benefit and protection of the common law, which in the twelfth century probably
excluded the majority of the adult population. That was a point not
commonly understood by seventeenth-century invokers of *Magna
Carta*, because by then unfree status was almost unknown, but in the
century after the Norman conquest the Common Law had by no
means been the protector of Englishmen's rights which was later
assumed. From a very early date pleadings had been classed under
two headings: pleas of the crown, which dealt with infringements of
the king's peace and broadly corresponded to modern criminal
process; and common pleas, which were between party and party, and
similar to modern civil process. All central jurisdiction had originally
been based in the king's household, but by the end of the fourteenth
century the common pleas had been taken 'out of court' and established in a court of that name which sat permanently in Westminster
Hall. This soon became by far the busiest court of common law, and
consequently the slowest and most expensive, but its decisions were
valued for their unchallengeable certainty.[64] Pleas of the crown
continued to be heard *coram rege* for some little time longer, but by
the early fifteenth century they too had moved to a stable base in
Westminster Hall, called the Court of King's Bench. By that time the
judges had long since given up touring the country, exercising their
jurisdiction *ex officio*, a practice known as the General Eyre, during
which the criminal jurisdiction of the county courts had been
suspended. Instead they toured on defined circuits twice a year,
holding sessions known as the Assizes. For this purpose they exercised
their jurisdiction by virtue of a commission of oyer and terminer, and
the Assizes had totally superseded the county courts, which carried
out only very limited functions.[65]

King's Bench was supposed to be the most distinguished and prestigious of the central courts, a position symbolized by the fact that it
had a jurisdiction in error which covered all other courts, but for most
of the fifteenth century it was in decline. This was due partly to the
fact that more relevant business was being concluded in the Assizes,
but also, particularly after 1440, to the troubled state of the country
and the difficulties faced by jurors and litigants in travelling to

64 W.S. Holdsworth, *A History of English Law*, 7th edn, ed. S.B. Chrimes
(1956), Vol. I, pp. 195ff.
65 Elton, *Tudor Constitution*, p. 463.

London. After 1485 that decline was halted and reversed. One of the problems had been that King's Bench was only to a very limited extent a court of first access. By custom, pleas of the crown were initiated in the town or county where the offence was alleged to have taken place. Consequently a court located at Westminster received only pleas originating in Middlesex. On the other hand, there were a number of technical pretexts for summoning a case from a lower court, and it was in the interests of the Assize judges to make referrals if the circumstances seemed suitable. In the Michaelmas term of 1488, for example, of fifty cases opening in the bench, forty-seven were from other courts, and of those thirty-two came from the Assizes.[66] At the same time business was increased at the expense of common pleas by the development of legal fictions. Trespass *quare clausum fregit* was a breach of the king's peace, but the trespass alleged was often purely technical, or even fictitious, and was designed not to obtain redress for a wrong sustained, but to determine the ownership of the land concerned. Clearly, no one could trespass on his or her own property, so the focus of the case became not the fact of trespass, but the issue of right – an issue properly belonging to the civil court. The attraction of King's Bench for litigants with such issues to resolve was that it was much quicker than Common Pleas, and equally secure. However, unless the alleged trespass took place in Middlesex, the same requirement for referral existed. This problem was overcome by the development of a still more blatant fiction, process by bill of Middlesex. In such cases it was mendaciously alleged that the 'offender' was in the custody of the court – that is, held in the Marshalsea prison – and could consequently be arraigned in King's Bench as a court of first instance. The court also exercised its ingenuity to create an entirely new type of action, trespass on the case (*super casu*). The common law had traditionally provided no remedy for slander or libel, but by deeming such actions to be a trespass upon the reputation of the victim, a means could be found of providing redress. Using such means, the King's Bench not merely recovered from its fifteenth-century decline, but forged ahead throughout the Tudor period, mainly at the expense of Common Pleas, which had no real means of resisting such encroachments.

Unable to defend itself against the senior bench, Common Pleas concentrated upon preventing the erosion of its business by the new and developing courts of equity. Against Chancery and Star Chamber

66   M. Blatcher, *The Court of King's Bench, 1450–1550* (1978), chs 1 and 2.

it very largely failed, but success against Requests, and later against the Ecclesiastical Commission, went some way towards compensating for that. The main trouble was that the civil jurisdiction, even more than the criminal, suffered from enormous procedural complexities. In the first instance an intending plaintiff had to obtain an 'original' writ out of Chancery, which enabled a court to take cognizance of the case. These writs followed fixed and inflexible forms which might, or might not, suit the litigant's purpose. If the only available writ did not fit the case, it might fall at the first hurdle. Once past this point, the plaintiff then had to get the defendant into court. The process for doing this was slow and frustrating, since in a civil issue no assistance could be expected from the crown's officers of the peace. Once in court every case consisted of a tangle of legal technicalities, and success depended entirely upon the skill of the plaintiff's attorney in selecting the correct issue to plead. This was more important than the question of evidence since the jury in a civil case was supposed to consist of local worthies who knew the facts, but not the law. For all these reasons, it was more difficult to summon or refer a civil case to Common Pleas than it was to bring a criminal case into King's Bench. There was never the slightest danger that the central civil court would become redundant – the sheer bulk of potential business guaranteed that – but Sir Edward Coke's anxieties in the early seventeenth century were entirely justified, even if some of his tactics were not.

Alongside these two ancient courts there was also, as we have seen, a limited common law jurisdiction in Chancery, and also the so-called Court of Exchequer Chamber. In the fifteenth century this was not properly a court at all so much as a place where the judges forgathered to resolve knotty points of law which had arisen in one or other of the established courts. The verdicts which they reached were then handed back to the relevant tribunal, but were occasionally known as decisions of Exchequer Chamber. This had nothing to do with the Exchequer proper, except the accident of location. The Upper Exchequer adjudicated disputes arising out of its own business, in which form it was known as the Court of the Exchequer, but the barons were not trained lawyers and their court did not have parity with King's Bench and Common Pleas. However, in 1579 it was decided that, in order to deal with the steadily increasing number of fiscal and commercial disputes, the barons of the Exchequer should also be appointed from among the sergeants at law. Thereafter they went on circuit as Assize judges, and in order to exercise their extended jurisdiction were constituted into the Court of Exchequer

Chamber. In 1585 this new court was given by statute the power to hear appeals of error in King's Bench, where the issue could not be covered by the existing provision in Chancery, and when parliament, to which the function properly belonged, was not in session. For this purpose the judges of Common Pleas sat with the barons. Finally in 1589 a second statute, arising out of a dispute between the Exchequer and King's Bench, conferred upon Exchequer Chamber the right to hear all complaints against the Exchequer itself, for which purpose the barons were excluded and the court consisted solely of the chief justices of King's Bench and Common Pleas.[67]

There was, strictly speaking, no central court of ecclesiastical jurisdiction, even after the establishment of the royal supremacy. Henry VIII, Edward VI and even Mary exercised ecclesiastical jurisdiction by commission, and as Mary continued to do so, even after the restoration of the papal obedience, that power was clearly not perceived to be simply a function of the supremacy. There was, however, nothing which could be described as a royal court of canon law until 1559. In that year the queen established by letters patent two Ecclesiastical Commissions, one for Canterbury and one for York. These were intended to strengthen the disciplinary machinery of the church, and were called the 'criminal courts' of the queen's ecclesiastical jurisdiction. They enjoyed wide powers, derived from their Letters Patent, and administered what was left of the canon law after all reference to the papacy had been excluded. The attempt to formulate a new canon law for the church of England was abandoned after acrimonious scenes in 1553, and was not revived until 1604.

Although there was, in theory, no connection between the two commissions, in practice the Canterbury commission was so much more powerful that it was soon known as the court of High Commission, and treated as though it had jurisdiction over the whole country. As Geoffrey Elton pointed out in his brief commentary on the commission, although it was a court, it also exercised visitational functions on behalf of the Crown. Both Wolsey, as papal legate, and Thomas Cromwell, as Vicegerent in Spirituals, had attempted that in previous generations, but only the ecclesiastical commissions put such a function upon a proper institutional basis. High Commission did not have either appellate jurisdiction or jurisdiction in error in respect of the normal ecclesiastical courts. On the other hand what it could do, and frequently did, was to deal with cases which were either *sub*

67   31 Elizabeth, c. 1; J.R. Tanner, *Constitutional Documents* (1922), pp. 345–6.

judice or had already been decided in the other courts, completely ignoring the process which had been made. In addition to disciplinary cases, it also took cognizance of all issues which were covered by the traditional moral jurisdiction of the church. However, it dealt with persons only, and not with property. Like the courts of equity, it could fine and imprison, and it could command the support of the Privy Council and the Court of Star Chamber. Its processes were swift and cheap, making it attractive to litigants. It could also, if it thought fit, wield the spiritual sanction of excommunication. However, not being a court of the common law, it had no access to the sanctions of confiscation or death. A test case in 1591 confirmed the authority of High Commission to deprive a non-conformist minister, because the court of Queen's Bench ruled that a benefice was not property in the sense which the common law recognized, but skirmishing along that jurisdictional frontier continued, the Puritans in particular making strenuous attempts to bring the commission under the supervision of the common law. Since its authority was actually derived from the royal prerogative, that became an increasingly sensitive issue as the seventeenth century opened.[68]

Because the study of the canon law was forbidden in England after 1535, the training of most practitioners in the ecclesiastical courts (including High Commission) was in the civil or Roman law. Civil law made great strides in Europe during the sixteenth century, replacing a confusion of customary codes in both France and Scotland. However, in England the common law repelled it without too much difficulty, and the only court explicitly administering the Roman code was the court of Admiralty. This had arisen from the personal jurisdiction of the lord admiral, and the court continued to be held in his name, for which reason it was also a franchise. It had authority over all cases of wreck and prize, and over a wide variety of disputes arising from loss or damage of cargoes. Until 1536 it also dealt with cases of piracy, that is to say with all felonies committed on the high seas, below the low water mark and outside the confines of creeks and estuaries. However, because the *lex maritima* followed the civil law rules of evidence, it was extremely difficult to secure convictions. In the absence of a free confession, the evidence of two witnesses was required. Given the propensity of such criminals to leave no witnesses alive, and the wandering nature of the mariner's calling, the

68   R.G. Usher, *The Rise and Fall of High Commission*, ed. P. Tyler (1968); Elton, *Tudor Constitution*, pp. 221–32.

availability of such testimony was at best highly uncertain. Consequently piracy was removed from the Admiral's jurisdiction by statute and placed under the common law. Each case was to be heard in the most convenient county, by a commission of oyer and terminer upon which the Admiral was to serve *ex officio* (see below p. 222). In spite of this, the Admiralty court remained one of the busiest, and delegated much of its work to local courts presided over by vice-admirals. Because such officials were nearly always local gentlemen unlearned in the civil law, a minor but flourishing profession of notary grew up. The Admiralty court itself had only one professional judge, but the system provided employment for a number of trained civilians, and they formed a society on the lines of the common law Inns of Court, which was incorporated as Doctors' Commons in 1565. Civilians, unlike common lawyers, received their formal training in the universities, so Doctors' Commons never acquired the educational role of the Inns of Court, remaining purely a professional association.[69]

Neither admiralty nor ecclesiastical jurisdiction remotely challenged the supremacy of the common law, but the third refuge of the civilian was eventually to cause serious disquiet in the legal establishment. As we have seen, equity was an ancient function of the royal prerogative, and had been exercised for centuries by the chancellor on the king's behalf. Chancery business had expanded in the fifteenth century, but it was a known quantity. However, the monarch could also exercise his equity jurisdiction through the council, and although there was nothing new about this either, the manner in which that jurisdiction became formalized in the early part of Henry VIII's reign sowed the seeds of future controversy. The Court of Star Chamber was created, as we have seen, out of one of the traditional functions of the council. The body which was set up by the so-called Star Chamber Act of 1487 was a distinct and special tribunal which happened to meet in the same place. In the seventeenth century it was deliberately confused with the court proper in order to make the latter accessible to statutory control. Originally the council sitting in the Star Chamber had simply signified special sessions designed to cope on a regular basis with that flood of petitions to the king which had once been addressed to the parliament. Parliaments became less frequent after 1497, but the number of petitions continued to increase, and could not simply be deferred to the next session. The procedure of the

---

69 Holdsworth, *History of English Law*, IV, pp. 235ff.

council in dealing with this business was informal, and resembled that of a tribunal of arbitration rather than a court. Sometimes the peti- tions related to issues for which the law provided no remedy, and sometimes to abuses of the normal courts, such as the intimidation of juries. In the latter cases the decisions reached were less important than the ability of the council to make its wishes respected. By 1509 defiance was a thing of the past, but evasion continued to be a problem and the council frequently found itself at loggerheads with local power structures.

It was Cardinal Wolsey who gave these sessions the degree of formality which they continued to exercise down to the civil war. He standardized the procedure into a somewhat simplified version of the civil law practice, in which cases were originated simply by written petitions of grievance in the vernacular. A fixed process of rejoinder and replication was also introduced, and formal records were kept of decrees and orders. When Sir Thomas Smith described the court in the 1560s, he considered that its main function was the curtailment of riots:

> Riot is called in our English term or speech where any number is assem-
> bled with force to do anything...If the riot be found and certified to the
> King's Council, or if otherwise it be complained of, the party is sent for
> and he must appear in this Star Chamber, where seeing (except the
> presence of the prince only) as it were the majesty of the whole realm
> before him, being never so stout he will be abashed.[70]

In other words, the court was primarily an agency of social discipline and control. Such a perception reflected Smith's own priority, which was to extol the rational structure and practical effectiveness of English government. In fact the surviving records demonstrate that in the later sixteenth century the majority of cases brought to the court had nothing to do with riots, but everything to do with civil litigants trying to sort out their disputes as quickly and cheaply as possible. Star Chamber was the most potent of the equity courts, and wielded sanctions varying from the monarch's displeasure, through fines and imprisonment, to corporal punishments. However, it could not touch life or property, and its decisions lacked the 'certainty' of the common law. Its effectiveness was a fairly accurate measure of the respect with which the authority of the crown was regarded. In a sense it succeeded

70   Smith, *De Republica Anglorum*, pp. 125–6.

too well, because by the time of the civil war it was being represented as an instrument of absolutism and a threat to those liberties which the common law was supposed to guarantee.

There was no sign of such doubts before 1603. Star Chamber sat regularly during the law terms; twice a week during the Elizabethan period, probably somewhat more frequently before that. The main doubt expressed was over its composition. In Wolsey's time any councillor could sit, which meant that the potential presence was very large, but after 1536 in principle only the twenty or so members of the Privy Council were eligible. In practice that was modified at once by the regular presence of the chief justices of the two benches, who were not privy councillors but whose professional experience was invaluable. Sir Thomas Smith believed that any peer could sit, and the opinion even existed that the monarch could afforce the court at will. Smith may have been right in a sense, because when he was writing non-councillors do seem to have sat, although not as fully participating judges. Later in the reign this practice ceased, but the theoretical uncertainty lingered. Similarly the quorum was supposed to be eight, but the attendance frequently seems to have been less, without any doubt being cast upon the legitimacy of the proceedings.[71]

The second 'conciliar' court, of lesser dignity than Star Chamber, but similar utility, was Requests. This also originated from the monarch's prerogative of justice, but specifically in respect of 'poor men's causes'. These were not necessarily trivial, but they did not involve substantial disputes over property. The great majority of petitions besought the king to redress the injustices frequently inflicted upon the poor by a judicial system designed to suit the needs of the rich. Again, this was an immemorial royal function, and Henry VII dealt with it by nominating two or more lesser councillors to hear such petitions. By 1509 this small group was meeting regularly in the White Hall at Westminster, and was sometimes known by that designation. When Wolsey was first in power he tried a number of experiments with council committees, but eventually retained only that in the White Hall, because Star Chamber was in theory a session of the full council. By 1529 the White Hall committee was a quasi-court, with its own register, but the status of its decisions is unclear. This problem was aggravated by the council reorganization of 1535–6, because none of those who made up the committee became

71 Sir Edward Coke, *The Fourth Part of the Institutes of the Laws of England* (1644), pp. 63–5. Elton; *Tudor Constitution*, pp. 163–87.

a member of the Privy Council. Cromwell resolved it in 1538–9 by formally reconstituting the committee as a court. In one sense this broke the link with the council because the two masters of Requests, as the judges of the new court were called, were not privy councillors. However, it was made clear from the start that the court took its origin in the king's prerogative of equity, and it continued to be regarded as an aspect of the council's activity. Requests sat judicially on fixed days of the week during the law terms, but the masters were prepared to receive pleas at any time, as befitted their household origin. By 1562 the business of the court had grown to such an extent that Elizabeth added two masters of Requests extraordinary to its establishment, thus enabling petitions to be received *coram rege*, even while sessions were being conducted at Westminster. Although one of the masters was always a common lawyer, and the court was scrupulously careful to make its decisions consistent with the requirements of the law, when Common Pleas was endeavouring to recover business in the late sixteenth century, it struck hard at Requests. This was partly because by that time the latter's work was almost entirely concerned with rights in property, and partly because it was the lowliest and most recently established of the 'rival' courts. In the case of *Stepney* v. *Flood* (1599) the judges of Common Pleas even went so far as to declare that Requests 'had no power of judicature', that is to say that its decisions were of no force or validity. In respect of the common law this was doing no more than stating the obvious, and in respect of the prerogative it was *ultra vires*, but the verdict seriously undermined the confidence of potential litigants. Requests began to lose business, and survived only in a smoky haze of controversy until it expired in 1643.

2

The Regions

Medieval England had no equivalent of the provinces of France, much less of the virtually autonomous principalities which constituted the Holy Roman Empire. However, the dominions of the king were by no means homogeneous. Quite apart from the deliberately created franchises, to which we shall be returning in due course, he ruled over the principality of Wales, the lordship (later kingdom) of Ireland, and the peculiars of Calais (until 1558), Man and the Channel Islands. Within England neither local identities nor local structures of government were particularly regional. The Celtic-speaking population of Cornwall felt itself to be distinct, but was neither numerous nor widely spread. The fenlands also had their own culture, but nothing to represent it at an official level. The only true region was north of the Trent, where a profound suspicion of outside interference lingered on to the middle of Elizabeth's reign, creating the perception in London of a problem which needed to be addressed specifically.

THE NORTH

England's only land frontier crossed the barren Cheviot hills between Berwick-upon-Tweed and Carlisle. Relations between England and Scotland were frequently hostile, and that fact, in conjunction with the inhospitable nature of the terrain, had formed a border society intractable to the normal disciplines of both church and state. The surnames, or clans, of Tynedale and Redesdale on the English side and of Liddesdale and Roxburgh on the Scottish side lived very largely by reiving, or cattle raiding. When there was war, or the circumstances were in other ways propitious, they raided each other in the names of their respective kings; at other times they raided the lowland communities on their own side of the border. This situation had created a number of problems both civil and military, and had given rise to the complicated system of government which appertained at the end of the fifteenth century. Berwick-upon-Tweed, the main garrison town, had only been recovered from the Scots in 1478, and although it had a normal civilian government, was not part of the county of Northumberland immediately to the south. Tynedale and Redesdale had no civilian government as such, being ruled as franchises by their respective military governors, the wardens. Norhamshire was part of the franchise of the bishop of Durham, Hexham was a liberty in the hands of the archbishop of York, while Askerton, Naworth and Greystoke, geographically within the county of Cumberland, were feudal baronies in the hands of the Dacre family. For military purposes the northern part of Northumberland and Norhamshire constituted the East March; south Northumberland, Hexham, Tynedale and Redesdale the Middle March; and Cumberland, including the aforementioned baronies, the West March. The needs of defence, and the distance from all the normal centres of royal government, had also brought into being great noble families, originally created to rule in the king's name, but by the fifteenth century enjoying extensive powers in their own right, notably the Dacres, the Percys and the Nevilles. It was famously (and accurately) stated in the middle of the century that the north east of England 'knew no prince but a Percy', and offices which were theoretically in the king's gift had long since become the monopoly of such noblemen. Although Northumberland and Cumberland were shires, on the same model as Hertforshire or Norfolk, that structure was so overlaid with others and riddled with exceptions that its offices functioned only patchily and intermittently.[1]

Further south, away from the borders, the problem was less one of structure than of tradition. The authority of great affinities, such as that of the Stanleys in Lancashire, was deeply entrenched, and that tradition had been reinforced during the reign of Edward IV by the almost viceregal powers which he had conferred upon his brother, Richard of Gloucester. In 1483 Gloucester had used his powerful northern following to secure the crown for himself, and had naturally as king done nothing to undermine the loyalty of the northern magnates with whom he had co-operated so effectively for more than ten years. Having defeated Richard, Henry was mainly concerned that

---

1   S.G. Ellis, *Tudor Frontiers and Noble Power: the making of the British state* (1995), pp. 3–17. R.L. Storey, 'The wardens of the Marches of England towards Scotland, 1377–1485', *English Historical Review*, 72, 1957.

the north should not become a disaffected area, and once it had become clear that the northern lords had accepted his rule, he was not inclined to interfere with their exercise of power. He was perhaps helped by the murder of the fourth earl of Northumberland in 1489, because the fifth earl was a minor and for almost a decade was the king's ward. It is not clear that Henry took any specific advantage of this circumstance to strengthen his own grip on the area, but at least he could be sure that he was not going to be challenged from that quarter. What he did do, and with hindsight it looks like the first stage of a carefully calculated policy, was to recruit more northern gentlemen to his own affinity. In time this was to have a profound affect upon northern politics, but it is quite possible that he intended no more than the establishment of better communications with the region. The only tangible difference which Henry VII made to the government of the northern marches was the incorporation of Tynedale into Northumberland by statute in 1494, and that was more apparent than real. Wardens continued to be appointed to police the dale, and even half a century later the sheriff seldom intervened.[2]

It was not until Wolsey came to power that any serious attempt was made to apply the king's authority directly to the far north. Wolsey was deeply suspicious of semi-autonomous noblemen, and infected the king with his fears. The fate of the duke of Buckingham, and the fact that Henry Percy, the future sixth earl of Northumberland was partly brought up in the cardinal's household, both reflect that situation. Henry VII had not only allowed noblemen like Lord Dacre to monopolize offices such as the captaincy of Carlisle, he had also farmed the shrievalties, effectively surrendering control over appointments for long periods. Henry VIII abandoned that dangerous course and resumed the normal appointment of sheriffs, but he knew perfectly well that they would be helpless without the backing of the local magnates. Wolsey's solution was not to innovate, but to return to a feature of the Yorkist strategy. Richard of Gloucester had used his own council to make his authority in the north effective, and when he ascended the throne had converted that useful instrument into a royal council under the presidency of his nephew the earl of Lincoln. The instructions issued for that council in 1484 show that it was intended to wield sufficient power to maintain the king's peace: 'Item that the said council have authority and power to order and direct all

2 11 Henry VII, c. 9; *Statutes of the Realm*, eds A. Luders et al. (1810–28), II, pp. 575-6; J. Hodgson, *A History of Northumberland* (1820–5), III, ii, pp. 222–4.

riots, forcible entries, distress takings, variances, debates and other misbehaviours against our laws and peace committed and done in the said parts'[3] After Richard's death, this council as an instrument of government was allowed to lapse. If anything survived at all it was a mere lordship council to oversee the crown lands, and even that is uncertain, as no records survive.

Neither Henry VII's uncertain relations with the Scots before the Truce of Ayton in 1497, nor the actual war of 1512–13, prompted any serious rethinking of northern security. In 1518 Wolsey warned Lord Dacre, the warden of the East and Middle Marches, that complaints were reaching him about the unsatisfactory state of justice in Northumberland, the sheriff of which had been appointed on Dacre's nomination. Cumberland was without a sheriff in 1521, and five years later was in the hands of Dacre's kinsman, Sir Christopher. However in 1525 all the wardenries were resumed into the king's hands, and conferred upon the king's 6-year-old illegitimate son, the duke of Richmond. Richmond was appointed lieutenant of the north, and endowed with large estates. He was also given a council of bureaucrats and administrators, appointed by Wolsey, both to run his estates and to control the administration of justice in the manner of Lincoln's council. Clearly nobody expected a child to impose his personality upon the government. The hope was that Richmond would symbolize Henry's personal involvement in the region, and give his council sufficient prestige to enable it to remedy some of the defects of the traditional system. The council was endowed with extensive civil and criminal jurisdiction by a standing commission of oyer and terminer, and its authority covered the counties of Yorkshire, Northumberland, Cumberland and Westmorland. Lancashire and Durham alone were exempt. However, the experiment did not work, probably because Wolsey's fall in 1529 removed the one man who was fully committed to its sucess. In 1530 Richmond was withdrawn, and his lands ceased to be one of the council's concerns. Dacre and Northumberland recovered control of the principal wardenries, and the jurisdiction of the council, now under the presidency of Cuthbert Tunstall, bishop of Durham, was restricted to Yorkshire only.[4]

The northern magnates had defeated Wolsey, but by 1532 the king

3 BL Harley MS 433, f. 264v; R. Reid, *The King's Council in the North* (1921), pp. 504–5.
4 G.R. Elton, *The Tudor Constitution*, 2nd edn (1982), p. 200; Reid, *Council in the North*, pp. 113ff. Ellis, *Tudor Frontiers*, pp. 166–7.

himself was becoming concerned, and his new chief minister, Thomas Cromwell, took up the challenge. Henry's anxiety was rooted in his Great Matter, and the entirely justifiable fear that the conservative northern lords could prove a fatal stumbling block to his ambitions. He began to apply pressure, and the first weak point proved to be the earl of Northumberland. The earl was at loggerheads with his kindred, and to some extent with his affinity, and in 1535, having no children, he made the king the heir to his vast patrimony. Ironically, however, it was the actions of the king's opponents rather than his agents which enabled a way ahead to be discovered. The Pilgrimage of Grace in the autumn of 1536 forced a number of issues. It compelled such major peers as the earls of Northumberland, Derby and Shrewsbury to choose between their traditional values and their loyalty to the king.[5] Without exception they supported Henry, although with varying degrees of enthusiasm. The fact that lesser peers, such as Darcy and Hussey, together with several of Northumberland's estranged kindred, chose the other side also assisted the process of clarification. However much dissatisfaction there may have been in the north, there was no will either to overthrow the king or to seize control of his government by force. The attainders which followed the pilgrimage, and the death of Northumberland in 1537, established the king as a northern magnate in his own right, and the policy of extending his affinity continued.

At the same time Cromwell reorganized the Council of the North on a much stronger institutional basis. Like its predecessor, it rested upon standing commissions of the peace and of oyer and terminer (see below, pp. 121–31), giving it common law jurisdiction in both party issues and pleas of the crown. Unlike its predecessor, however, it controlled the whole of the north, with the exception of Lancashire, as Durham had ceased to be an autonomous franchise in 1536. Also unlike its predecessor it consisted not of middle-ranking civil servants, but of a selection of northern peers and gentlemen, with the support of some senior administrators and lawyers. In 1544 under the archbishop of York as president, served the Earls of Westmorland and Shrewsbury, Lord Dacre, Lord Eure, Lord Wharton, Sir Marmaduke Constable, Sir Robert Bowes and Sir Henry Savile. These important men were not expected to be in 'daily attendance' to deal with routine

5   G.R. Elton, 'Politics and the Pilgrimage of Grace', in *After the Reformation*, B. Malament (1980); G.W. Bernard, *The Power of the Early Tudor Nobility* (1985), pp. 30–58. M.L. Bush, *The Pilgrimage of Grace* (1996).

administration and law enforcement, but they were expected to be present at the four major sessions each year, and they were expected to use their local prestige and influence to implement the council's decisions.[6] The council also exercised the monarch's prerogative of equity, functioning as a northern Star Chamber for the suppression of riots and other major misdemeanours, particularly on the part of the gentry. Later in the century Star Chamber and the Council of the North acted as equivalent jurisdictions, passing cases between them as circumstances dictated. The council as reconstituted in 1537 lasted until the civil war, and was an excellent example of the Tudor knack for recruiting the natural leaders of the community and harnessing them to institutions which remained under effective central control. Although the Council of the North was not an agency of the Privy Council, there was never any doubt that it was answerable to the monarch's main executive instrument.

What the Pilgrimage of Grace had begun, the rebellion of the northern earls in 1569 completed. In principle the council, presided over at that point by the earl of Sussex, should have been able to defeat that uprising by its own resources. In fact it conspicuously failed to do so, and played an altogether unheroic role. However, the collapse of that revolt, and the attainders which followed, removed any further possibility that the north as a region would seek to go its own way, or impose its priorities upon a monarchy which remained firmly rooted in the south. By the end of the century also one of the fundamental reasons for the distinctiveness of the far north was disappearing. Even before 1603 the Anglo-Scottish border had ceased to be a perennial skirmishing ground, and the pretext for its habitual lawlessness had largely disappeared. The franchises of Hexham and Norham lost virtually all their significance in 1536, and the liberty of Redesdale, already in the hands of the crown, was merged in Northumberland in 1543.[7] As the importance of the march wardens declined, that of the regular civilian jurisdiction advanced. Before 1560, and even to some extent thereafter, the preservation of order and the obtaining of any kind of redress for violent affrays depended partly upon the warden's posse, and partly upon his relations with his opposite number in Scotland. Apprehending offenders within the dales exposed the Wardens, and those who supported them, to the traditional sanction

---

6   *State Papers of Henry VIII* (1830–52), V, pp. 402–11.
7   S.J. Watts, *From Border to Middle Shire: Northumberland, 1586–1625* (1975); Hodgson, *Northumberland*, I, i, p. 371.

of the blood feud, which could be pursued in a number of ways, from arson and murder to hijacking the king's courts. In 1535 the sheriff of Cumberland found himself indicted before the Assizes by a jury composed of the kinsmen of one of the felons whom he had killed in a punitive expedition. The reconstruction of the Council of the North, by ensuring effective support to the law enforcement officers, gradually cured that problem, but the council could do little about cross-border fugitives. That issue had to be handled through the traditional system of the 'days of truce'. These were prearranged meetings, usually on the actual border, between the English and Scottish wardens or their representatives, to adjudicate disputes and to hear grievances between their respective subjects. Rough justice was the order of the day, and sometimes mutual suspicions made any progress impossible, but by and large these meetings worked. Restitutions and compensations were agreed, and occasionally offenders were handed over to justice, but the 'days of truce' were mainly a device for containing an intractable situation rather than for providing a cure. That only came with the conversion of the borders into the 'middle shires' in the seventeenth century.[8]

WALES AND THE MARCHES

The north of England, as distinct from the marches of Scotland, had a regional identity of tradition and sentiment rather than of language and government. The situation in Wales was quite different. The Welsh language was universally used, not only within what is now Wales, but in those marcher lordships which spilled over into the English counties of Worcester, Hereford, Gloucester and Shropshire. That language carried with it a culture of poetry and prophecy which was shared to some extent by all sections of society. Welsh law also survived, particularly in the marches, and carried with it distinctive social values. Land was seen as belonging to a kindred rather than an individual, so partible inheritance was the norm, and no distinction was recognized in this respect between legitimate and illegitimate offspring. Violence and even bloodshed were remedied by compensation rather than punishment, rather in the manner of the early Saxon wergild. As these laws were entirely customary, they could not be

8 D.L.W. Tough, *The Last Years of a Frontier: a history of the borders during the reign of Elizabeth* (1928).

ammended by legislation, but only interpeted by the *uchelwyr*, or wise men in the customary courts. The English believed (wrongly) that the customs of inheritance signified that the Welsh had no respect for marriage, and (rightly) that compensation, which was often evaded, made them complacent about violence. By the end of the fifteenth century the Welsh gentry were making increasing use of English law to protect the integrity of their inheritances, but showed no signs of preferring the draconian penal code of the English courts.

Wales had been subjected to the English crown since the late thirteenth century, and some parts for much longer than that. Even independent Wales had been politically fragmented, except for a few years under Llewellyn the Great, so there was little sense of what we would now call 'national identity'. What there was was a lively 'ethnic identity', focused partly on language and partly on genealogy, and this was made politically relevant by the number and scale of the English enclaves. Edward I had planted Wales with English colonies in the shape of walled towns, granting them special powers and privileges, and excluding the native Welsh from citizenship. These towns had been established partly as centres of government, and were symbols of the English ascendency. During the fourteenth century this confrontational situation had begun to erode and break down, but it was restored to full life and vigour by the revolt of Owain Glyndwr in the early fifteenth century. By assaulting the towns and by preaching racial hatred, Glyndwr ensured that his revolt was followed by a period which has been compared to modern 'ethnic cleansing', the legacy of which was still very much alive at the beginning of the Tudor period in the form of discriminatory laws and chilly hostility between the urban English and the rural Welsh.[9] There were some areas of old English settlement within what was officially Wales, in Denbighshire, Powys and south Pembrokeshire particularly, but these tended to keep themselves apart, and were not resented in the same way as the enclaves.

The political map of Wales did not change very much between 1300 and 1485. Anglesey, Caernarfon, Merionydd and Fflint formed the northern principality, administered from Caernarfon, which was equipped with its own Chancery and Exchequer. Ceredigion and Carmarthen formed the southern principality, similarly run from Carmarthen. Within the principality English law predominated, and the counties had their own sheriffs and other traditional officers, but no

9   R.R. Davies, *The Revolt of Owain Glyn Dwr* (1995), pp. 153–73, 325–42.

commissions of the peace, and no parliamentary representation. Sometimes there was a titular prince of Wales, and sometimes there was not, but it did not make much difference to the government, which was under direct royal control. It was not, however, answerable to the institutions in Westminster Hall. The remainder of the country, consisting of the later counties of Pembroke, Glamorgan, Monmouth, Brecknock, Radnor, Montgomery and Denbigh, was divided into over thirty private lordships. These were known as the marches, because they had originally been established to provide a buffer zone between lowland England and the independent highland principalities. That situation had come to an end in 1284, but the marcher lordships remained. By 1485 the majority of them had fallen to the crown by escheat, or by the attainder of their lords, but no attempt had been made to remove their autonomous structures. Within the marches the king's writ did not run, and the lords' courts administered an *ad hoc* mixture of English common law and Welsh custom. The proportion varied according to the location and the local population mix, and the redress of injustice, however manifest, presented great difficulties. Even where the king was also the lord the effectiveness of law enforcement was less than that within the principality, and much less than in the English shires. The marcher lordships acquired the reputation of being havens for criminals of all sorts, fleeing from the stricter justice of neighbouring lands on both sides, and by the 1520s the English crown had developed the will to address the problem.

Participation by the native Welsh in their own government had been slight in the immediate post-conquest period, except at the very local or commote level. That situation had begun to change by the late fourteenth century, by which time Welsh gentry were also serving with distinction in the king's armies. However, frustration with the slowness of progress in that direction had been one of the main motives for Glyndwr's actions, and one of the reasons why so many Welsh gentry who were prospering in the king's service renounced their allegiance and joined the revolt. By 1420 they were back to where they had been in 1284, and this was one of the main reasons why there were no powerful families among the native Welsh. There were English magnates, like the Fitzalans, the Staffords and the Mortimers, with lands and affinities in Wales, but no indigenous Welsh nobility. Owain Glyndwr himself had a good claim to descent from the princes of both Gwynedd and Deheubarth, but in terms of English wealth and status he was a minor esquire. The position of the Tudors was altogether exceptional, and highly significant for that reason. Although he bore an English title, and was only 25 percent Welsh by descent, Henry of Richmond was the nearest thing there was to a genuine Welsh prince in the twenty years or so before his accession. Although he had lived only briefly in Wales, and probably did not speak a word of the language, he had been identified by the bards, the main guardians of the Welsh ethnic consciousness, as the *mab darogon*, the son of prophecy. This was the messiah of Welsh expectations, who, according to an ancient prophecy of Merlin, would return to lead the British in the recovery of their realm.[10] He was not the first to be so identified, but his victory at Bosworth and subsequent accession to the throne appeared to be a full vindication of the bardic endorsement. How conscious Henry was of these expectations is unclear. His immediate family was very small, and the ramifying Tudor kindreds in north Wales seem to have derived very little benefit from the connection. A number of Welsh gentlemen and yeomen obtained posts at court, but there was nothing like the influx of Scottish favourities which was to follow the accession of James VI in 1603. Wales provided him with loyal support, both before and after his accession, and in spite of their growing disappointment with his policies the bards never entirely lost faith in Henry or his son, which is one of the reasons why the most ethnically and culturally distinctive part of the Tudor realm saw the least significant disaffection.

If Wales was troubled, it was not for political reasons. Neither Simnel nor Warbeck attracted any support there. However, the long-standing tensions within Welsh society, combined with the weakness of the marcher lordships, gave the country a reputation for lawlessness which was not entirely undeserved. Preoccupied with other issues, and seeing no major threat from that quarter, Henry merely tinkered with this problem. Within the principality he removed the legal disabilities of the Welsh, a legacy of the Glyndwr revolt, granting them equality of status. This was appreciated as a gesture, but made little practical difference because those disabilities had been largely ignored for more than a generation. The remaining marcher lords, led by the king's uncle Jasper, Duke of Bedford, were placed under heavy recognizances for the proper discharge of their judicial responsibilities, but nothing was done to curb their franchises, and the situation remained substantially unchanged. Jasper died without heirs in 1495

10 W.G. Jones, 'Welsh nationalism and Henry Tudor', *Transactions of the Honourable Society of Cymmrodorion*, 1917–18; Glanmor Williams, *Harri Tudur a Chymru/Henry Tudor and Wales* (1985).

and his lordships joined many other in the hands of the crown. However, the problem was not the identity of the lord so much as the franchisal structure itself, and no attempt was made to address that issue. Henry's main tactic in Wales was quite different from any that he employed in England, and may reflect its relatively low political priority. He placed heavy reliance upon his loyal ally Rhys ap Thomas, who became chamberlain of both Cardigan and Carmarthen within the principality, and constable of the crown lordship of Brecknock. These offices, together with a large number of lesser ones, gave Rhys magnate status in South Wales, although he was never raised to the peerage.[11] Nowhere else did Henry deliberately create a power block of this kind, and it was probably Rhys's reliability which dissuaded the king from any further attempt to reform the structure. Edward IV as earl of March had controlled an extensive border patrimony, and had established a council to administer it. When Henry VII conferred the title of prince of Wales upon his infant son Arthur in 1489 he revived that council, and gave it oversight of all the crown lands, both the principality and the lordships, but its function was purely administrative. After Arthur's death in 1501 it seems to have lapsed altogether, in spite of the fact that his younger brother Henry succeeded to the title in 1504.

By the 1520s Wolsey was as dissatisfied with the state of government in the marches as he was in the north of England, and in 1525 adopted a very similar remedy. The king's only legitimate child, the 9-year-old princess Mary, was despatched to Ludlow with a very large household under the supervision of the countess of Salisbury. Mary was not given the title of Wales, but her council was established with the same powers as that of Arthur, over thirty years before. Like the duke of Richmond, Mary herself did not remain long in her provincial posting, returning to London in 1529, but her council remained under the presidency of Bishop Veysey of Exeter. It may well have been coincidence that Rhys ap Thomas also died in 1525, at the age of 76, but it was no coincidence that he was succeeded in his important chamberlainships by Lord Ferrers, the steward of Mary's household, rather than by his grandson and heir Rhys ap Gruffydd. Rhys's discontent at this decision tempted him into treasonable conspiracy, which not only destroyed the power of his family but demonstrated convincingly why Henry VII's strategy in Wales was no longer viable. The removal of Wolsey's driving will, and the relative

11   R.A. Griffiths, *Sir Rhys ap Thomas and his Family* (1993) pp. 44–87.

weakness of Veysey, meant that the council made little progress with its disciplinary task until 1534, when Thomas Cromwell took up the neglected challenge. He replaced Veysey with Bishop Rowland Lee of Coventry, and steered a bill through parliament to remove all pleas of the crown from the marcher lordships into the nearest English shire, where they were dealt with by normal common law procedures. The council was given the responsibility for making sure that this happened.[12] Armed with this new authority, Bishop Lee conducted a judicial visitation of memorable ferocity. The Welsh chronicler Ellis Gryffydd recorded that 5,000 offenders were hanged, and although that figure is certainly a rhetorical exaggeration, the impact of such sudden severity was very great.

However, it was one thing to put the fear of God into the Welsh cattle thieves, and another to establish a system with permanent viability. The 1534 act was makeshift, and two years later it was replaced by the much more rational and draconian solution of abolishing the marcher lordships altogether.[13] This was in the context of a general reduction of franchises, but there is no doubt that the measure was primarily aimed at Wales. The distinctiveness of the principality was effectively abolished; the six existing shires were confirmed, and seven new ones created. Each county was now to be equipped with a commission of the peace on the English model, and represented in parliament by a single MP. A scattering of new parliamentary boroughs was also created. At the same time some of the land of the abolished lordships was added to the English border shires. Rowland Lee was strongly opposed to these reforms, not because they indicated any reduction in the role of the council, but because he did not believe the Welsh to be capable of even the smallest degree of self-government. Given the findings of his recent visitation, his attitude is understandable, but Cromwell's far-sighted statesmanship was soon to be totally vindicated. The 1536 Act incorporated the Welsh gentry into the English political nation on equal terms, and restored to them the governmental role that their social position indicated. The problem of lawlessness was not solved overnight, but by the later part of Elizabeth's reign the Welsh commissions were performing as well as most of their English counterparts. The language of government was English, but apart from that the features of the medieval English ascendency had largely disappeared. Seven years later, in 1543, the

12   26 Henry VIII, c. 6; *Statutes of the Realm*, III, pp. 500–3.
13   27 Henry VIII, c. 24; *Statutes of the Realm*, III, pp. 555–8.

reorganization was completed by a second act which converted the existing courts of English common law within Wales into four circuits of Great Sessions, each with professional judges. These were equivalent to the English Assize circuits, but were not answerable to the courts at Westminster. Great Sessions covered the twelve shires of Wales proper; the thirteenth, Monmouthshire, was incorporated into the Oxford circuit.

In spite of these major and generally beneficial reforms, Wales remained remote from London; an upland society with many distinctive features, and a system of local government which would take decades to settle down. The role of the council consequently became greater rather than less, and increasingly formal. The act which reorganized the Great Sessions also gave it statutory recognition:

> Item, that there shall be and remain a president and Council in the said dominion and principality of Wales and the marches of the same, with all officers, clerks and incidents to the same, in manner and form as hath heretofore been used and accustomed; which president and council shall have power and authority to hear and determine by their wisdoms and discretions such causes and matters as be or hereafter shall be assigned to them by the King's Majesty, as heretofore hath been accustomed and used.[14]

Armed with standing commissions of the peace and of oyer and terminer, it exercised both equity and common law jurisdiction over the whole of Wales, and over the English border shires of Chester, Shropshire, Hereford, Worcester and Gloucester. Principally, like the council of the north, it was a regional Star Chamber and Chancery, responsible in general to the Privy Council, but not an agency of it. Cases were referred backwards and forwards as the circumstances appeared to dictate. During the reign of Elizabeth its most effective work was done in connection with cases of riot and intimidation, enforcing respect for the relatively unfamiliar Quarter Sessions, and endeavouring to ensure the independence of juries, which were notoriously vulnerable in Wales. The one thing the council could not do – and it would have made a major difference to its authority – was to appoint or dismiss justices of the peace. Sometimes these commissions were filled in accordance with political priorities which were more evident in London than they were in the marches, and disciplin-

14   34 & 35 Henry VIII, c. 26; *Statutes of the Realm*, III, p. 926.

ing unsatisfactory justices was the necessary condition of upholding their authority. The Courts of Great Session also presented a problem, although of a quite different kind. The council had no authority to control these courts, or to hear appeals from them, and when it attempted to exercise its oyer and terminer jurisdiction, disputes were inevitable. The same was true of the Assize circuits on the English side of the border, and by the end of the century the common law jurisdiction of the council was virtually stalled.[15] It seems that Cromwell underestimated both the effectiveness and the self-confidence of the regular courts, and gave them a back-up system which they neither needed nor desired. Cheshire sought, and obtained, exemption from the jurisdiction of the Council in the Marches in 1569, but it was generally a well-respected body, and was the only agency of the Tudor prerogative to survive the civil war, being eventually abolished in 1689.

In spite of its successful integration into the English governmental system, Wales at the end of the Tudor period retained a much sharper and more durable identity than did the north of England. Although the influence of the bards had shrunk almost to vanishing point, and the remaining Welsh poets spent much time and energy lamenting the anglicization of their erstwhile patrons, in fact the language survived strongly. This was very largely the result of the Reformation. In spite of the instinctive religious conservatism of the majority of the people, there were from the start Welsh-speaking clergy of Protestant sympathies, one of whose strongest convictions was the use of the vernacular in worship. The English prayer book was first translated in 1549, the New Testament in 1568 and the whole Bible in 1584, works which had as great an influence on the Welsh language as Tyndale, Cranmer and the Authorized Version had on English. So although the language of government was English, and all justices and office holders were required to speak it, the language of the church was Welsh.[16] At the same time the language of education was good humanist Latin, and it was said of John Williams, the future archbishop of York, that when he went from Ruthin school to St John's College, Cambridge, in 1599 he spoke good Latin and Welsh, but very little English – a situation which surprised nobody. By then Welsh customary law had almost

---

15   Penry Williams, *The Council in the Marches of Wales under Elizabeth* (1958), p. 225; C. Ogilvie, *The King's Government and the Common Law, 1471–1641* (1958), pp. 126ff.
16   W.S.K. Thomas, *Tudor Wales* (1983), pp. 100–1.

entirely disappeared, and the traditional structures of Welsh society were in decline. The Welsh gentry broadened their horizons through education at Oxford or Cambridge and the Inns of Court; they found careers in central government and the church; they acquired lands in England; and they married into English families. But men like Sir John Wyn of Gwydir lost neither their sense of identity nor their influence in their home communities, and those communities offered sufficient scope for many lesser families to remain in their ancestral homes. Unlike their medieval predecessors, the Elizabethan Welsh bishops were resident, and spoke the language. Consequently, although Wales remained poor by comparison with England, much of its cultural tradition was intact, and the Elizabethan fashion for the stories of Arthur and the 'matter of Britain' gave it a role in a wider British consciousness. The Welsh and the English did not necessarily like each other very much, but both recognized the pragmatic advantages of a working relationship.

IRELAND

After 1541 Ireland was in theory a distinct kingdom, and it may therefore seem improper to describe it as a region, but in fact it enjoyed no political or cultural unity either before or after that date, and it is impossible to designate it in any other way. The Anglo-Norman invasion of Ireland had taken place in the twelfth century, and the lordship had been dependent upon the English crown since 1172, but neither the crown nor its agents ever controlled the whole island. By the early fifteenth century three types of jurisdiction were in operation. In the Pale, the area around and to the immediate south of Dublin, English control was secure and long-standing. The Pale was divided into counties, like those of the principality of Wales, the law administered was the English common law, and English was the language in normal use. Each county was divided into baronies, which were the equivalent of the English hundreds, and operated a system of barony and county courts. There were no commissions of the peace. To the west and south west of the Pale were those areas known rather misleadingly as 'the obedient lands', covering Kildare, Carlow, Tipperary, Kilkenny, Wexford, Waterford, Cork, Limerick and Kerry. Parts of this region were shired and governed in the same manner as the Pale, but most of it consisted of private lordships in the hands of the great Anglo-Irish nobles, the earls of Ormond, Desmond and Kildare. There were also isolated marcher lordships in Ulster and Connaught.[17] The marcher lords acknowledged the king's overlordship, and to that extent were part of the English realm, but the law which their courts administered was a mixture of common law and Irish custom, and they pursued their own priorities with little regard for the king's representatives in Dublin. The towns within these lordships were English colonies, like those of Wales, but much of the countryside was purely Irish, even where it was living under English law.

Within the shires, both inside and outside the Pale, the sheriff, acting in the name of the king as lord of Ireland, heard all pleas of the crown at sessions held twice a year, while the county and barony courts dealt with party issues. There were no Assize circuits, but important or difficult cases were often dealt with by special judicial commissions, resembling commissions of oyer and terminer. Cases could also be revoked to the central courts in Dublin, but because of the difficulties of travel and the frequency of special commissions, this was seldom done. The franchise courts were entirely autonomous, because the king's writ did not run in the marches. The rest of Ireland, about two thirds of the whole, was held by a confused welter of Gaelic tribes, living under their own customs and chieftains, and untouched by English influence. The relationships between the Gaelic chiefs and the marcher lords fluctuated almost from day to day, and the local balance of power swung backwards and forwards. There was, however, a certain mutual respect between the two sides. The Anglo-Irish magnates understood the Gaelic power structures, and manipulated them, while the Gaelic chiefs in turn recognized that the marcher lords were major players in their own internecine politics.

The king was represented in Ireland by a viceroy, normally known as the deputy or lord deputy, who in the late fifteenth century held most of the prerogative powers of the crown, including the right to pardon felonies and treasons, and the right to summon the Irish parliament. The lord deputy was assisted by a chancellor, and by the chief justices of the two benches, as well as by an executive council. This resembled the English Privy Council in respect of its day-by-day functioning, but, like the lord deputy himself, was ultimately answerable at Westminster. During the English civil wars in the mid-fifteenth

17 S.G. Ellis, *Tudor Ireland* (1985), pp. 19–31, 342–3; S.G. Ellis, 'Crown, community, and government in the English territories, 1450–1575', *History*, 71, 1986.

century the Anglo-Irish lords had been consistently pro-Yorkist in
their sympathies, but the relative weakness of the English crown, and
the rapid coming and going of lords deputy between 1460 and 1479,
had led to a serious weakening of the lordship, a situation only partly
redeemed by the effectiveness of Gerald FitzGerald, the eighth earl of
Kildare, who held the position from 1479 until the death of Richard
III. Henry VII was primarily concerned to secure the recognition of
his own authority in Ireland, and in the first instance that meant
coming to terms with Kildare. At that stage there was no sensible
alternative to relying upon the established Anglo-Irish magnates.
Henry appointed first his uncle the duke of Bedford and then his
infant son the duke of York as lieutenants in Ireland, but both were
figureheads. Real authority remained with Kildare, who was reappointed in the spring of 1486. In 1487 he flirted with disaster in the
person of Lambert Simnel, but the king accepted his submission,
rightly judging that he had learned his lesson.

Between 1492 and 1496 Henry's increased confidence was
reflected in the fact that he experimented with other deputies,
including his personal representative, Sir Edward Poynings. During
this period the deputy's powers were curtailed in various ways. He
could no longer summon a parliament on his own authority, and the
agenda for such assemblies was to be laid down by king's council.[18]
Pardons henceforth could be issued only on the king's personal
authority, and the deputy's right to alienate royal demesne land was
withdrawn. If the deputy needed to be absent from his post for any
length of time, he had to obtain the king's explicit consent to the
appointment of a *locum*. Having taken these modest steps to assert
himself, Henry allowed Kildare to return, and it continued to be true
as before that the earl governed Ireland through a contractual understanding with the king, which enabled him to retain most of the profits
and the patronage of his office in return for his services. Politically the
next twenty years were quiet in Ireland. Tudor authority was unchallenged, but was exercised for the most part at second or third
hand, and there was no knowing how Ireland would react if it should
be seriously challenged in England.

Wolsey showed no particular interest in Ireland, probably because
it presented no particular problem. Apart from a few months in 1515
Kildare and his son the ninth earl remained in office until 1520, and
his son was deputy again from 1524 to 1528. What prompted Henry

18   Ellis, *Tudor Ireland*, pp. 77–8.

VIII to a sudden intervention in 1529 is not quite clear. Kildare may have done something to provoke suspicion, or perhaps the king was becoming generally aware of the hostility which his treatment of Catherine was generating. For whatever reason the earl was summoned to England, and the duke of Richmond, still at that time lieutenant of the north, was named to the very occasional dignity of lieutenant of Ireland. He did not cross the sea, and the appointment seems to have been a mere pretext to overhaul the government. The chief justice, Patrick Bermingham, was appointed deputy, and a new and predominantly English council named. If this was intended to be the first phase in a new policy of direct control, it was soon aborted, and perhaps it was never anything more than a calculated reminder of political realities. Kildare was allowed to return in 1530, without office, and the deputyship was given to the English soldier Sir William Skeffington. Skeffington's brief was extremely conservative, amounting to little more than the preservation of the status quo, and the pacification of the nearest Gaelic chiefs. Kildare had undertaken to provide support, but the situation was unprecedented, and not conducive to stability.[19] In 1531 the Irish parliament, which was not normally given to obstructiveness, refused a request for a subsidy. At the same time a long running feud between the FitzGeralds and the Butler Earls of Ormonde reached a new pitch of intensity, threatening the internal stability of the Anglo-Irish community. Kildare fell out with Skeffington, and the latter was recalled, making way for the earl's reinstatement as deputy in August 1532. However the king was uneasy, with his Great Matter reaching a new climax of delicacy and controversy, and Thomas Cromwell, newly installed in Henry's confidence, was prepared to grasp the nettle. In September 1533 Kildare and a number of other Irish officials were summoned to London to give an account of themselves. The deputy declined to come on the grounds of ill health, which even if justified created a worrying situation.

Kildare was probably not engaged in political brinkmanship. There were already opponents of the Boleyns who were looking to him to raise the banner of conservative revolt in Ireland, but he was much more interested in the preservation of the FitzGerald ascendency, threatened both by the Butlers and by direct English intervention, than he was in issues of high policy. However he had already ignored warnings to desist from moving royal artillery into his private

19   Ellis, *Tudor Frontiers*, pp. 186–7.

fortresses, and should hardly have been surprised that his loyalty was being called in question. At the end of 1533 he finally responded to the royal order, persuaded apparently by being allowed to leave his son, Lord Offaly, as his *locum* during his absence. He may well have believed that his bargaining position was stronger than it was, because he can hardly have expected what actually transpired. Arraigned before the king's council for misgovernment and the abuse of his office, he was placed under arrest and detained in London.

Lord Offaly's response was radical and dramatic, so much so that it calls in question his grasp of political reality. In June 1534 he resigned his office, denounced the king as a heretic, and renounced his allegiance.[20] Whether his father had any idea of what was in his mind may be doubted, and his own purpose in choosing such a course is unclear. Probably his extreme position was taken on the assumption that Henry had so many problems nearer at home that he would be willing to make concessions, placing the FitzGerald ascendency upon a new and more secure footing. The first reactions from London also suggest that interpretation. Taken aback, the king offered negotiations with 'Silken Thomas', as he was called. However, Offaly responded not by modifying his position but by indulging in anti-English rhetoric reminiscent of the Glyndwr revolt, and stepping up his approaches to the Gaelic chieftains. Whatever his real intention, this provoked an immediate military response from England, and in October 1534 Skeffington returned to Ireland at the head of 2,000 men. Offaly's Anglo-Irish affinity promptly fell apart. However wedded the Pale gentry may have been to the status quo, they had no desire to fight against the king, and swiftly submitted.

In December 1534 Kildare died in London, and 'Silken Thomas' became the tenth earl, but his position was deteriorating rapidly. Skeffington took his stronghold at Maynooth in March 1535, and drove him to seek refuge among his Gaelic allies.[21] For a few months it seemed that he was determined to wage a war of Irish independence, because Skeffington lacked the resources to invade the tribal lands, and the racial content of the earl's propaganda increased. However, he soon realized that the chiefs had no real interest in his ideological programme, real or pretended. Their ambitions were strictly local and short term, and the concept of an independent Celtic Ireland was wasted upon them. In August 1535 Kildare decided to submit,

20 Ellis, *Tudor Ireland*, pp. 124–5.
21 Ibid., p. 128.

apparently believing that, in spite of the radical nature of his defiance, he would be protected by the unchanging realties of Irish politics. It would not have been the first time that a FitzGerald had flirted with the king's enemies, and been restored to favour by the indispensable nature of his family position. However, if the politics of Ireland had not changed, those of England had. Henry VIII was a ruthless king, fighting for the control of his realm, and unwilling to countenance any defiance or dissent. In February 1537 the earl of Kildare and his father's five brothers were arraigned for high treason, and executed. The FitzGeralds were destroyed at a stoke, and the government of Ireland would never be the same again.

Henry's decision to remove the family which had governed Ireland for most of his own reign and his father's was no mere act of casual ferocity. He may have been genuinely alarmed by the implications of Kildare's rhetoric, but there was a positive strategy behind his actions. Threatened with excommunication, and the possibility of a Franco-imperial crusade against him, he had to bring Ireland under more effective control if he did not want to find it being used against him. The policy may have been Thomas Cromwell's, but danger had also focused the king's mind. The Irish Reformation parliament had sat from 1535 to 1537, and had enacted the ecclesiastical legislation of its English counterpart without protest, but it was still necessary to make the royal supremacy effective. Neither the Anglo-Irish nor the Gaelic Irish had any particular loyalty to the papacy, and there was little opposition either to the new jurisdiction or to the dissolution of the monasteries within the Pale and the 'obedient lands'. The tribal lands, however, remained untouched, and although that presented no immediate threat, there was no means of knowing how long it would be before the king's enemies began to work upon the chiefs. It was partly for that reason that Henry elevated Ireland into a kingdom in 1541. Just as England had been technically a papal fief until 1534, so there was a general belief in Ireland that the overlordship of the country belonged to Rome, and that the king of England held the lordship as a vassal.[22] The Irish statute which enacted the change was very careful to avoid any reference to such a situation. Like the Act in Restraint of Appeals, it claimed to be declaring a situation which had long existed, blaming the disobedience of the Irish merely on the 'lack of naming the king's majesty and his noble progenitours kings of

22   B. Bradshaw, *The Irish Constitutional Revolution of the Sixteenth Century* (1979).

Ireland'.[23]Henry was thus claiming a full authority, both temporal and ecclesiastical, in Ireland, where it could not be fully sustained. The king's moves during these years also had a number of knock-on effects. The Anglo-Irish magnates, in pursuit of their own interests, had maintained a strong presence in the tribal lands and acquired a good understanding of the Gaelic culture. That understanding was not shared by the rest of the Anglo-Irish community, let alone by the 'new English', and Lord Leonard Grey, who was Deputy from 1536 to 1540, regarded the tribes as mere savages. Consequently the replacement of the FitzGerald ascendency with direct rule threatened to introduce a racial element into the endemic conflicts of the marches which had not been there before.

That threat did not develop immediately because Sir Anthony St Leger, who followed Grey as lord deputy, endeavoured to apply a more enlightened approach. In the first place he started to invite the Gaelic chieftains to attend the parliament, and some of them, notably Fitzpatrick, O'Brien, Burke of Clanrikard, MacMurrough and O'Neill, responded favourably. Some sent proctors, a few attended in person. This was altogether unprecedented because the parliament had hitherto been an exclusively Anglo-Irish institution. At the same time St Leger began to promote a policy of surrender and regrant. A chieftain who surrendered his tribal patrimony to the king would receive it back as a grant under the Great Seal, often accompanied by a baronial title on the English model. The big advantage of this from the chieftain's point of view was that it converted the land from being the communal possession of the clan into a personal estate for himself and his family, held on a notional feudal tenure and protected by English law. Henry VIII was not very happy with this strategy, perhaps out of sheer conservatism, or perhaps because he was aware of the danger of alienating an Anglo-Irish community which had so far accepted the loss of its virtual autonomy with equanimity. However, the king was deeply preoccupied with war in Scotland and in France, and after some hesitation endorsed his deputy's approach. When St Leger was reappointed by the council of Edward VI in April 1547 the prospects for success seemed reasonably good. Not only was the take-up on surrender and regrant encouraging, but Henry had also started to use Irish troops in his wars. This created administrative problems, but was a step towards integrating Ireland with the rest of his domin-

23 *The Statutes at Large passed in the Parliaments held in Ireland* (1786–1801), I, p. 176.

ions, offered prospects of reward to some Irish captains, and removed some 'turbulent spirits' from the domestic scene. There had also been a modest and uncontroversial extension of English civil government when the erstwhile lordship of West Meath, to the north west of the Pale, had been converted to shire ground in 1542.

The breakdown of St Leger's policy after 1547 is often attributed to the rise of militant Protestantism in England, and the Edwardian attempts to impose that on Ireland. In fact, as we shall see later, religious alienation followed political breakdown, and seems to have played very little part in the development of events until well into Elizabeth's reign. The true reason for the failure was impatience, and an inability to understand Gaelic customs and priorities. In the summer of 1546 there was a destructive tribal foray into Offaly, which probably had more to do with internecine strife among the tribes than it did with any hostility to English rule. However, as soon as the duke of Somerset had picked up the reins of government as lord protector in February 1547, he decided that effective counter-measures would have to be taken. In a move which anticipated his even more ill-fated policy in Scotland, he established English garrisons in all those tribal lands which were within striking distance of the Pale. The object was to deter, if not to intimidate; the effect was to provoke. The garrisons, inevitably, were attacked, and an unfocused war developed.

In April 1548 St Leger was replaced, and for the next two years the direction of policy remained principally with the council in London. By the spring of 1549 an insecure military ascendency had been established over the lands to the west of Meath, but the situation remained unstable, and after the fall of the protector in the autumn of that year it was decided to establish English civilian settlements around the garrisons.[24] This was a fateful decision, because for the first time it seemed to indicate to the Irish tribes that large-scale expropriations were in the offing, and they responded with renewed hostilities. Irish methods of warfare were violent, but unsophisticated and uncoordinated. Only relatively small numbers of experienced and well-equipped troops were needed to contain them, but even small armies cost money, and the English government of the earl of Warwick was desperately short of cash. By 1552 they were reconsidering the whole situation, and may even have been contemplating the rehabilitation of the Anglo-Irish magnates. In that year Gerald

24   D.G. White, 'The reign of Edward VI in Ireland: some political, social and economic aspects', *Irish Historical Studies*, 14, 1964–5.

FitzGerald, the heir to the earldom of Kildare, was restored in blood. Edward's death in the summer of 1553, although it removed the threat of Protestantism, made very little difference to secular policy. Mary recalled St Leger as deputy in November and restored the earldom of Kildare in 1554, but neither of these moves indicated a return to earlier priorities. Instead her council decided to press ahead with the controversial plantation of Leix-Offaly, about which the earl of Warwick had been hesitating. This was probably intended as a one-off move, rather than the inauguration of a major new policy, but unfortunately it was not so perceived by the Irish. St Leger was understandably unhappy with the direction which events were taking, and soon at loggerheads with Kildare. Early in 1556 he was recalled, and the whole conciliatory policy which he had represented since 1540 abandoned.[25]

The new lord deputy was Thomas Radcliffe, Lord FitzWalter, who succeeded to his father's earldom of Sussex in the following year. Sussex was to serve, with one short break, until October 1565, and during those nine years English policy in Ireland was committed irrevocably to the course which it was to pursue for the next century. The politics of Elizabethan Ireland were complex, reflecting not only the conflicting interests of the English, Anglo-Irish and Gaelic Irish, but also the various parties and factions which competed for favour at the English court. However, the view, first of Sussex and later of Sir Henry Sidney, that only military conquest followed by selective English colonization could stabilize and civilize the 'wild' Irish gradually prevailed. There were further plantations in Down in 1570, Antrim in 1572–3, and Munster in 1584. Provincial councils, on the lines of the Council of the North, were established in Connaught in 1569 and in Munster in 1571. Gradually between 1560 and 1585 both the remaining Anglo-Irish lordships and the tribal lands were divided into counties, with sheriffs, county courts and English law. Irish resistance was constant, and violent, but unco-ordinated.

There was no policy of universal expropriation, but after every uprising there were further confiscations, and more land to be divided between the loyal Irish and the English settlers. By the end of the century in theory the distinction between the 'obedient lands' and the Gaelic lands had disappeared, but the reality was that only constant small-scale military operations maintained even a semblance of the queen's peace in many parts of the country. In place of the constantly

25   Ellis, *Tudor Ireland*, pp. 233–5.

shifting antagonisms of chieftains and Anglo-Irish nobles, there developed a settled antagonism between the Protestant English of the ascendency and the increasingly Catholic and self-consciously Gaelic Irish. The Anglo-Irish, bereft of their former power, accommodated to this situation as best they could. Many, particularly in the long-settled parts of the the midlands and south, accepted Protestantism and identified themselves with the 'new English'. Others, however, especially of the old noble kindreds, rediscovered their loyalty to Rome and adopted Gaelic customs. The parliament represented the English ascendency, and English courtiers were given extensive grants of Irish lands, which in some cases they scarcely visited. There was no deliberate policy to dispossess the Irish landowners, but refusal to accept customary rights and tenures meant that many legitimate claims went unrecognized, and grievances festered all over the country. It is not surprising that Catholic missionaries were extremely successful, nor that the state of the Catholic faith in Ireland was very much better in 1600 than it had been in 1550.

The English military presence in Ireland fluctuated. Elizabeth was notoriously reluctant to spend money, but a few hundred men, properly equipped and competently led, were sufficient to deal with the sporadic outbreaks of violence which represented the normal expressions of Irish discontent. However, after Elizabeth's excommunication in 1570, and particularly after the outbreak of war in 1585, that situation began to change. When James FitzMaurice landed with a small band of Spanish and Italian troops at Smerwick in July 1579 and raised a papal banner, he ignited a series of revolts right across the country, and the lord deputy, Sir William Drury, discovered that he could not rely upon the Anglo-Irish community for support. In spite of the small scale of the incursion, the situation had become so alarming that Lord Arthur Grey was sent across with 6,000 men.[26] The garrison at Smerwick was destroyed and the revolts suppressed, but nothing was done to remedy the chronic social and political tensions which had created the disaffection. The only surprising thing about the revolt of Hugh O'Neill, the second earl of Tyrone, in 1593 was that it had not happened earlier. O'Neill was a man of established position, the grandson of one of the first great Irish chieftains to accept a peerage from Henry VIII, and was endowed with

26   D. Silke, *Ireland and Europe, 1559–1607* (1966), pp. 3–14. B. Bradshaw, 'Sword, word and strategy in the Reformation in Ireland', *Historical Journal*, 21, 1978, p. 484.

both charisma and military skill. For nine years he waged against the English government a genuine war of independence, and created for the first time among the disparate tribes and clans a sense of common purpose which could have sustained a successful campaign. In the context of the Anglo-Spanish war his uprising was extremely dangerous, but fortunately for Elizabeth Philip III did not take him seriously enough. The Spanish landing at Kinsale in 1601 was too little, and not designed to give Tyrone the kind of support which he needed. The invasion was defeated, and the revolt eventually suppressed at a cost of many hundreds of thousands of pounds and innumerable reputations. When Elizabeth died Ireland was subdued, but not reconciled. The policy of plantation and anglicization had not worked, because the essential ingredient for success, the co-operation of the Irish elite, had never been obtained. Until 1556 it had been possible that Tudor policy in Ireland would follow a similar course to that in Wales, but once that approach had been abandoned only complete conquest could have been effective, and that course was pursued too hesitantly and with too few resources.[27]

THE CHANNEL ISLANDS AND OTHER DEPENDENCIES

By the late fifteenth century the once extensive English provinces in France had almost entirely disappeared, and although it is artificial to describe what was left as a region, the elements are hard to classify in any other way. The Channel Islands had originally been part of Normandy, but remained in English hands when that province was recovered by the French in 1450. Whether this was the result of in-difference on the part of Charles VII or continuing English strength at sea is not clear. The language of the islands was French, and their law continued to be based upon the customs of Normandy. The English parliament had no jurisdiction, and there was no local pro-vision for legislation. Consequently the law could only be amended or extended by judicial interpretation. English justices in Eyre had originally visited the islands, and after the discontinuance of the General Eyre that practice had been continued by the judges of Assize. However, there had been no visits since the fourteenth century, and by 1500 the islands enjoyed an effective jurisdictional autonomy. The formal separation of the islands from Normandy was recognized by

27   Ellis, *Tudor Ireland*; C. Falls, *Elizabeth's Irish Wars* (1950).

Henry VII in 1495, and at the same time he issued a charter of liberties protecting the customs of the communities. In respect of their secular government, the islands were consequently in a rather similar position to Ireland, governed by the king and his personal agents, but not by the central institutions at Westminster. Ecclesiastically they were part of the Norman bishopric of Coutances until 1496, when Henry obtained a papal bull transferring them to the jurisdiction of Salisbury. In 1499 they were moved again, this time to the more logical hospitality of Winchester, which also included the isle of Wight. Unfortunately, nobody seems to have noticed. Neither the royal supremacy nor the dissolution of the monasteries provoked any recorded dissent, but after 1535 the island Deans were appointed directly by the crown, as though they had been bishops. In 1550 it was actually confirmed that the bishop of Coutances exercised his authority over the islands under the king as supreme head, which would no doubt have come as a great surprise to him, had he been aware of it. There was some enthusiasm for Protestantism in the reign of Edward VI, at least on Guernsey, where three women were burned for heresy in the reign of Mary. It was not until 1568 that a jurisdictional dispute caused someone to consult the archives, and discover the papal bull of 1499. The islands were then finally declared to be part of the diocese of Winchester, and their last notional contact with mainland France was severed.[28]

Strategically the Channel Islands were of great importance, and their French language and culture caused the English government to be constantly suspicious of fifth column activities. However, it appears that the islanders had not the slightest desire to revert to French rule, and their loyalty to the English crown was frequently commented upon. Only once, in 1549, was a French attack successful, when the island of Sark was briefly occupied. It appears that Sark was undefended, and may even have been unoccupied at the time. The incident reflects no great credit upon either country, because although Protector Somerset seems to have neglected an obvious strategic weakness, the French made no attempt to consolidate an advantage which held great potential for development. Sark was under the jurisdiction of Jersey, as Alderney was of Guernsey, but it is not clear that

---

28   A.J. Eaglestone, *The Channel Islands under Tudor Government* (1949). The term 'Channel Islands' is used in this context to mean the four inhabited islands of Jersey, Guernsey, Alderney and Sark, lying off the coast of Normandy and ruled by the English Crown.

either of the two smaller islands was fortified, or garrisoned upon a regular basis. The two main islands, however, were certainly garrisoned with English troops, and each was governed in the king's name by a captain whose responsibilities were both military and civil.[29] These captains were always English, and normally resident, although the duke of Somerset held both offices from 1546 until his death in 1552, and certainly did not reside. Relations between the captains and the island elites were potentially tense, but in practice normally amicable. This was partly because the islanders had direct access to the king's council, and later to the court of Star Chamber, guaranteed as a part of their chartered liberties, and partly because of the constraints which were built into the structures of the islands' government.

There was a bailiff on each island who acted as the captain's civilian deputy, and who was invariably a local magnate. The magistrates were called jurats, twelve in number, who were appointed for life by the captain. These were similarly local men, and the captain was required to take local advice before making the appointments. The jurats, presided over by the bailiff, constituted the principal island court, called the Chief Pleas. Chief Pleas combined the jurisdictional functions of the English Assizes and Quarter Sessions, and the only possible appeal lay to the king in council. The smaller islands also had jurats, at least in theory, and a court presided over by the prévot, who was like the bailiffs but of lesser status. Both the bailiffs and the prévots were royal officers, appointed by the crown, but the captains and the existing jurats had a voice in their selection. Each of the main islands also had a body called the Estates, but since this was neither elected nor representative the title is somewhat misleading. The Estates consisted of the bailiff and jurats, plus the rectors and constables of each of the island parishes. Its function was mainly consultative, but it could petition the crown directly if it considered that the customs and liberties of the islanders were being infringed. It could also grant taxation, if requested to do so. This was delicate ground, and the request was hardly ever made. The garrisons were paid, and the fortifications maintained, by the English crown, although the islanders might occasionally be expected to contribute to their own defence if the circumstances were sufficiently threatening. The regular expenses of government, which were not heavy, seem to have been met from regular dues and from the profits of justice. Royal commissions were

29　Ibid.

occasionally appointed, but not for judicial purposes, and were an aspect of the council's general administrative supervision. Each island was served by a number of lesser officials, procureurs generaux, receivers general, greffiers, enregistreurs des contrats, and others, who were paid modest fees and expected to make a living out of the sale of their services, like similar officers everywhere. Even in wartime the government of the islands seems to have presented few problems, and their location made them invaluable as advanced bases during the English campaigns in Normandy and Brittany in the 1590s. The failure of the French to make any serious attempt either to occupy the islands or to subvert their governments during the numerous Anglo-French conflicts of the Tudor period is a remarkable testimony to the stability of their politics.

The fate of Calais was very different. Originally, like the Channel Islands, it had been part of the extensive English possessions in France. But it had been acquired much more recently – captured by Edward III in 1347 – and had been colonized in a way which the islands had never been. Edward had expelled the French population, and both the language and the law of the town were English. It had also survived the reconquests of the fifteenth century, and its strategic importance was much more obvious. The author of the *Libel of English Policy*, a tract of the 1430s, had described Calais and Dover as 'two eyes to keep the narrow seas', but by 1510 Calais was much more of a bridgehead to give the king of England access to France whenever his belligerent instincts should so dictate. For this reason its recapture became a prime ambition of French policy. Knowing this, Henry VIII succeeded in 1543 in persuading the Emperor Charles V, who was an even more consistent opponent of the French, to guarantee its safety by treaty. When Mary went to war with France in support of her husband Philip of Spain, in 1557, there were constant rumours that the French were exploiting the anti-Spanish sentiments of the Protestant citizens in an effort to persuade them to surrender the town. In January 1558 a surprise attack by the duke of Guise was at last successful, and the 'heresy' of the lord deputy, Lord Wentworth, was blamed by both the English and imperial governments for the disaster.[30] There seems to have been no truth in the belief that the town had been betrayed; instead, penny pinching over the

---

30 'The governor of Calais was a great heretic, like all those who were with him there . . . so I am not surprised at its fall'. Sir Edward Carne to the queen, 28 January 1558, PRO SP69/11/727.

fortifications and a false sense of security in mid-winter had undermined the capacity to resist. Elizabeth made strenuous and
unsuccessful attempts to recover Calais between 1559 and 1565, but
her motive seems to have been pride rather than strategic need, as her
priorities in foreign policy were entirely defensive. The town had also
become prohibitively expensive to defend – over £20,000 a year by
1557 – and it is easy to believe that Elizabeth found that a consola-
tion for her failure. It was probably not the loss of Calais which began
to redirect English policy from its traditional preoccupations towards
overseas ambitions; that change can be detected earlier, but it was
certainly a suitable benchmark for the different priorities of the late
sixteenth century.

At the time of its loss the Calais Pale consisted of about 120 square
miles of territory, with a seacoast eighteen miles long. Its population
of about 12,000 was mostly concentrated in the town itself, although
there were villages attached to the subsidiary fortresses of Guisnes,
Hammes and Newnhambridge.[31] Security was a prime consideration
and the governor, or Lord Deputy, was both the military commander
and the civilian chief executive. He was supported by a council with
a strong military flavour, and by four principal officers: the marshall,
who was responsible for policing and discipline; the treasurer and the
controller, who between them managed the money; and the porter,
who controlled access by both land and sea. Calais was not represented in parliament until 1536, but it was subjected to English
legislation, and in that respect was unlike either the Channel Islands
or the Isle of Man.

There were three jurisdictions within the Pale. The lord deputy, or
a professional judge on his behalf, heard pleas of the crown according
to the common law, there being neither Assizes nor Quarter Sessions.
The mayor and corporation of the town heard most routine party
pleas, and managed the daily lives of their fellow citizens in much the
same way as their equivalents in mainland chartered boroughs which
were not counties in their own right. The third jurisdiction was that
of the mayor and company of the Staple. The Staplers were a monopolistic fraternity which traded in raw wool. Until the middle of the
fifteenth century they had been by far the wealthiest merchant
company, and their staple, or trading outlet, had been fixed at Calais

---

31   C.G. Cruickshank, *Army Royal: an account of Henry VIII's invasion of France,
1514* (1969), pp. 19–24; P. Morgan, 'The government of Calais, 1485–1558'
(DPhil, Oxford, 1967).

on the understanding that they would foot the bill for the royal garrison.[32] By Henry VIII's reign their trade had been greatly reduced by heavy taxation, and they could no longer sustain that burden. However, the company's court still heard all pleas relating to its members and their business, a privilege which made constant disputes with the town authorities inevitable. The Staplers still had some financial power, and that they used to persuade the crown to continue in its support, and perpetuate a situation for which there had long since ceased to be any real justification. Ecclesiastically, the Pale was an archiepiscopal peculiar of Canterbury, which probably helps to explain why Protestant ideas took root in the town so early, and how the reformer Adam Damplip could become such a thorn in flesh of the then lord deputy, Lord Lisle, in the 1530s. Calais was really a border town, like Berwick-upon-Tweed, rather than a distinct region, but while it remained in English hands its political and administrative health was never far from the council's mind, and it absorbed a disproportionate amount of time and money.

By contrast, the remote and eccentric territory of the Isle of Man scarcely ever featured in the records of the central government. By the sixteenth century the Manx language was already in decline, and the language of government was English, but neither English common law nor English legislation applied. The law was customary, and Norse in origin. It had been codified in the fifteenth century, but as there was no local provision for legislation it could be extended and adapted only by judicial interpretation. Until the middle of the thirteenth century Man had been a Norwegian dependency, but in about 1267 it had been taken by Alexander III of Scotland, and for sixty years thereafter had been contested between the English and the Scots. In 1333 Edward III finally made good his claim, and thereafter the island was a fief of the crown of England. In 1405 Henry IV conferred it upon Sir John Stanley, and it remained in the direct descent of the Stanley family (earls of Derby from 1485) until 1736. It then passed through the female line to the dukes of Atholl, and was formally repossessed by the crown in 1765.[33] In the later fourteenth and fifteenth centuries the lords of the island had occasionally styled

32 Morgan, 'Government of Calais'; E. Carus Wilson and Olive Coleman, *England's Export Trade, 1275–1547* (1963).
33 *Handbook of British Chronology*, eds E.B. Fryde, D.E. Greenway, S. Porter and I. Roy (1986), pp. 61–6. R.H. Kinvig, *The History of the Isle of Man* (1944), p. 123.

themselves kings, and claimed a right of coronation, but after the death of the second earl of Derby in 1504 these pretensions were abandoned. All the functions of government were carried out in the name of the lord, and were vested in the lord's council. The administration of justice was in the hands of the deemsters, a group of magistrates resembling the justices of the peace, who were appointed by the lord, and served for life unless disabled by criminal conviction. They convened twice a year in a high court called the Tynwald, which functioned very much like the English Quarter Sessions. There was also a representative institution of a kind, called the Keys, which consisted of twenty-four freeholders nominated by the lord. The Keys had a consultative function, but was more in the nature of a grand jury than a parliament. The island was not normally garrisoned, and seems to have been remarkably little affected either by the Anglo-Scottish wars or by the troubles of Ireland. There appears to have been no direct taxation, and the expenses of government, which were minimal, were met out of the normal and traditional dues.

Ecclesiastically Man formed a half of the Scottish see of Sodor and Man, which also covered most of the Hebrides. From 1511 to 1530 the bishop was nominally one John Campbell, but he does not appear to have been consecrated, and when Ferchar MacEachen was provided in 1530, it was in succession to George Hepburn, Campbell's predecessor. Thereafter the Scottish succession becomes confused, and it is unlikely that subsequent bishops of the Isles had any further interest in Man. However, during the Great Schism in the late fourteenth century a separate line of English bishops had been established, and by the early sixteenth century it was they who exercised effective ecclesiastical supervision. In 1542 the English parliament unilaterally declared the see of Sodor and Man to be under the jurisdiction of the province of York. Thereafter, although the diocese retained its composite title, the English bishops made no attempt to intrude into the Hebrides, and the eventual disappearance of the Scottish see in the seventeenth century was irrelevant to Man. The Reformation seems to have caused no recorded problems, probably because it was only very gradually and belatedly enforced. Henry Man was bishop from 1546 to 1556, and there was then a vacancy until John Salisbury was appointed in 1570. Thereafter the succession was continuous, but the crown seems to have had no qualms about the conformity of this northern outpost of the Church of England, and allowed it to go its own way, as in all other matters.

3

The Counties

THE ANCIENT STRUCTURE

The shires were the principal administrative divisions of England, and
were already well established by the eleventh century. By then also
each shire was divided into smaller units, normally called hundreds
although the terms 'wapentake', 'lathe' and 'rape' were also used in
some parts of the country. There were also a few subordinate divisions
known as sokes, which had originally enjoyed a degree of autonomy,
but by the fifteenth century were indistinguishable from hundreds.
The smallest administrative units were the parishes, but these were
properly ecclesiastical rather than secular divisions, and will not be
considered here. The chief executive officer of the shire was the shire
reeve, or sheriff, who represented the king and was appointed by the
lord chancellor in consultation with the judges of Assize, or other interested parties at his discretion. His Latin title, *Vicecomes*, pointed, as
Sir Thomas Smith noted, to his original status as deputy to the *comes*,
or earl. However, by the fifteenth century earls and other noblemen
had long since lost their connection with the government of any particular county, and the sheriff was answerable directly to the king.
Such an origin nevertheless explains why, with a few marginal exceptions such as Cumberland, the sheriff was always a knight or
gentleman and never a nobleman. Sheriffs were supposed to be
appointed for one year only, in order to give the king full control over
the disposal of the office, but in the early fifteenth century it was by
no means uncommon for the same man to serve for many years, and
not unknown for such positions to become hereditary. At that time the
sheriff's duties were numerous. He 'gathereth uppe and accompteth
for the profittes of the shire, which come to the exchequer', that is the
revenues of the crown lands and the profits of justice.[1] He presided

1   Sir Thomas Smith, *De Republica Anglorum*, ed. Mary Dewar (1982), p. 97.

over the county court, and twice a year conducted a tourn of the hundred courts in order to collect presentments. As the crown's chief law enforcement officer he was responsible for the execution and return of all writs directed into the county, and for the arrest and safe custody of offenders. He empanelled juries, and ensured that the county returned duly elected members when a parliament was summoned. It was also his responsibility to muster the shire regularly, to ensure that those summoned possessed adequate equipment, and to lead the levies in the king's service if called upon to do so.

Such omnicompetence created numerous problems. A strong king, such as Edward I or Edward III, when he was physically present in England, had no difficulty in keeping his agents under control. But when he was campaigning abroad, and even more when the crown was in weak hands, like those of Henry VI, abuses, and complaints of abuses, multiplied rapidly. Sheriffs could, and did, accept bribes to empanel favourable juries, or to return writs of *capias* as *non est inventus* when they knew perfectly well where the felon was lurking. Widows seeking justice for the homicide of their men often found themselves frustrated by the rich or powerful kindred of the offender, although few cases can have been as blatant as one returned from fourteenth-century Staffordshire. Felicia Pycheford had appealed Henry de Bysshebury of murder, only to be informed that the said Bysshebury, although in custody, was too ill to stand trial. Being more fortunate, or better informed, than many in such a case, Felicia was able to demonstrate that the same Bysshebury was in fact the sheriff who had made the return! Parliament complained repeatedly to the king in response to representations of such abuse; in 1340, 1368, 1404 and 1439. In 1445, when the situation had deteriorated still further as a result of the king's ineptitude, a comprehensive indictment of the sheriffs was set out in the form of a statute.[2] They were accused of taking bribes to award or refuse bail, of forestalling arrests in defiance of the king's commands, and of accepting fees for the empanelling and recording of juries. It is not surprising that the rebellious followers of Jack Cade in 1450 declared that 'The law serveth of nought else in these days but for to do wrong.'[3]

Edward IV imposed household sheriffs upon some counties, and Wolsey used Star Chamber to deal with individual complaints, but the

2   J. Bellamy, *Crime and Public Order in England in the Later Middle Ages* (1973), p. 15; *Statutes of the Realm*, eds A. Luders et al. (1810–28), II, p. 334.
3   D.M. Loades, *Politics and the Nation, 1450–1660* (1992), p. 29.

main Tudor policy was to reduce the functions of the sheriffs rather than to improve their discipline. To some extent this had already happened because of changes to the judicial structure. The replacement of occasional General Eyres with more frequent and regular Assizes had reduced the functions of the county courts, and rendered the system of frankpledge virtually redundant. Frankpledge had been a method of communal self-discipline, based upon the tithing group which exercised a corporate responsibility for the behaviour of its members. One of the sheriff's early functions had been to keep this structure in working order, a supervision known as 'view of frankpledge'. When the Assizes began to be supplemented with Quarter Sessions in the later fourteenth century, both frankpledge and the judicial functions of the county courts disappeared. The biggest changes, however, came with the expanding role of the justices of the peace under Henry VII and Henry VIII, and with the introduction of receivers of General Surveyors and Augmentations. The new revenue administration meant that lands acquired by the crown after about 1490 were no longer added to the sheriffs' farm or accounted to the Exchequer. Consequently the sheriffs responsibility steadily diminished as existing lands were alienated and not replaced on their account. Sheriffs continued to deal with the profits of justice, and with certain traditional dues, but the scale of their financial operations was greatly diminished. When the courts of Augmentations and General Surveyors were discontinued in 1554, the Exchequer continued the system of Receivers, and did not revert to the 'ancient course' in this respect. The justices of the peace not only superseded the county courts, they also took over most of the sheriff's police work. The investigation of complaints and the arrest of offenders now fell to them, as well as an increasing quantity of administrative work. Henry VII even required the justices to report to the council upon the conduct of the sheriffs, a function which Henry VIII transferred to the judges of Assize. The latter inspected both the justices and the sheriffs, a system which resulted in about 8 or 9 per cent of such officials being prosecuted for corruption every year for the remainder of the century.[4]

The obligation of all freemen to perform military service went back to the Anglo-Saxon fryd, and the Assize of Arms in 1181 had laid down what weapons every man should provide in accordance with his wealth and status. The Statute of Winchester of 1285 confirmed the

4   J.S. Cockburn, *A History of the English Assizes, 1558–1714* (1972), pp. 90–1; J.H. Gleason, *The Justices of the Peace in England, 1558-1640* (1969), pp. 1–7.

same system, and was periodically reissued down to the sixteenth century; the last time by Henry VIII in 1511. Apart from private retinues, which were mustered separately and could be quite large before Henry VII's rigorous licensing system, the general militia was assembled by townships, hundreds and counties. This normally happened about once in two or three years, but in time of war, or when invasion threatened, it might happen as often as twice a year. Until Henry VIII's reign the principal responsibility rested with the sheriff, whose servants or subordinates supervised the subdivisions of the county under his direction. For some reason the king was not satisfied with the efficiency of this system, or, more probably, Wolsey was on the lookout for another opportunity to reduce the sheriffs. By 1540 commissions were normally issued to groups of local gentlemen to conduct the musters. These commissioners were often also justices of the peace, and sometimes the sheriff was included, but this did not alter the fact that his function had been superseded. During Edward VI's reign a new type of county officer began to appear, the lord lieutenant, whose principal function was the mobilization and training of the militia. By 1580 the lord lieutenant and his deputies had superseded both the sheriff and the muster commissioners.[5]

As a result of these progressive reductions, and the loss of opportunities for supplementary income, by the late sixteenth century the office of sheriff, which had once been so sought after that John Heydon had valued it at £1,000, had become an unpopular burden. It was still important, because only the sheriff could return and execute writs, but far more judicial work was now carried out by other means, and the sheriff found himself at the beck and call of the JPs and the judges of Assize more often than he was in control. Moreover, the increasing vigilance of the Privy Council, and of the regional councils, had increased the risks involved in deploying the remaining powers of the office for its holder's gain. Sir Thomas Smith summed up the change succinctly when he wrote: 'To be short, he is as it were the generall minister and highest for execution of such commaundements according to the lawe as the Judges do ordaine, and this is ynough for the sherife.'[6] Sheriffs were selected by a process known as pricking. The rounds of consultation, including listening to the pleas

5   G.S. Thomson, *Lords Lieutenant in the Sixteenth Century* (1923); L.O. Boynton, *The Elizabethan Militia, 1558–1638* (1967), pp. 53–89. D. MacCulloch, *Suffolk and the Tudors: politics and religion in an English county, 1500–1600* (1985), pp. 258–284.
6   Smith, *De Republica Anglorum*, p. 99.

of those who either did or did not want the office, resulted in a short-list of three. The lord chancellor then literally stuck a pin in the list to indicate his choice. A serving sheriff could not also be elected as a member of parliament, but it was not until the following century that that situation was used as a technique of management. Every sheriff accounted at the Exchequer for his 'farm', which involved an annual journey to Westminster, but he did not usually take much money with him. Not only was he entitled to deduct his expenses, he was also expected to meet such assignments on his revenue as the council had chosen to make. As these revenues were also dwindling, by the later sixteenth century the sheriffs were hardly important sources of cash. The sheriff was assisted by such deputies, sergeants or other lesser officers as he might appoint, at his discretion; but these were not royal officials and the sheriff was responsible both for their conduct and for their remuneration – if any.

In addition to the sheriff, every county had two other ancient officers of lesser dignity, called the coroner and the escheator. Of the former Smith wrote: 'The Coroner is one chosen by the Prince of the meaner sort of gentlemen, and for the most part a man seen in the lawes of the Realme'[7] His duties were limited and specific, but by no means honorary. It was his responsibility to investigate every suspicious death in the county, if necessary exhuming the body of the deceased in order to do so. He proceeded by empanelling a jury of twelve or more local men, who were then given a fixed period, which might be as long as thirty days, to make their inquiries and to return with a verdict as to the cause of death. This was by no means an academic matter, because if the verdict of the inquest was *felo de se*, then all the deceased's property became forfeit to the crown. Similarly, if it was decided that another person had been responsible for the death, and that person was named, then the verdict constituted an indictment for murder which could lead directly to arrest and trial. The coroner's functions were largely unaffected by the changes which took place in local government during the Tudor period, and have continued, with some modifications, to the present day. The escheator was an officer of the same status, also appointed by the crown, for the rather similar purpose of keeping track of the monarch's feudal rights. When a tenant-in-chief died without direct heirs, his lands reverted to the crown, a process known as escheat. It was therefore the Escheator's business to locate any land within the county which was held in chief,

7   Ibid., p. 108.

no matter where the tenant actually resided, and to enforce the king's claim should the appropriate circumstances arise. This was a very much more occasional function than that of the coroner, and one which almost disappeared with the development of the Court of Wards and Liveries in the 1530s. Thereafter an official of that court, known as the feodary, was established in each county for the same purpose. As the feodaries were directly responsible to the master of the wards, who was an active political figure, and as wardships were a major source of income to the crown, the new officers carried out most of the functions, and the escheator's role became largely nominal.

The principal institution of the ancient county had been its court. This was both royal and popular; royal in the sense that it administered the common law and was presided over by the king's officer; popular in the sense that it could be attended by all freeholders, who were entitled to plead there, and later functioned as jurors and electors. Before the late thirteenth century the county court had dealt with small personal actions where the property in dispute was worth less than 40 shillings, pleas of trespass, and pleas of neglected rents and services owed by free men. Where similar rents or services were owed by villeins, they were dealt with by the manor courts. Villeins only featured in the county courts as fugitives being reclaimed by their free masters. Minor affrays, not judged to have endangered the king's peace, were also adjudicated, and missing offenders were publicly summoned to appear before the itinerant justices. If such a summons was ignored it could result in the outlawry of the party concerned, which remained a real sanction, at least down to the early fifteenth century. If it was specially authorized to do so, the county court could also deal with more serious offences, or deliver the county gaol (see below, p. 123), but it did not have these powers of itself. By the early fourteenth century, the county courts were in decline. The basic reason for this seems to have been the conservatism of their main procedure, by compurgation. This required an accused person to assemble a given number of men of good standing who were prepared to testify on oath, either to his or her innocence of the offence charged, or generally that the accused was of good character. Litigants preferred the more modern system of pleading before a petty jury, who were charged to evaluate the evidence presented to them. The greater frequency of Assizes also made the reference of any serious issues to the county court unnecessary.[8]

8 Bellamy, *Crime and Public Order*, p. 150.

By the Tudor period most of the significant business had gone elsewhere. Small property disputes and debts were still handled, but minor affrays and other misdemeanours were judged by the justices of the peace, and the recovery of fugitive villeins had long since ceased. Process of outlawry was still followed, but was largely a technicality. The distraints which followed proclamation had become so derisory that they frequently produced only a few pence, when they were enforced at all. The frankpledge system, which had been maintained by the county courts, had disappeared by the late fourteenth century, and the gaols were delivered by commissioners specially appointed for the purpose. Only in one respect had the county court actually gained in importance, because it was the venue for the election of the county members to serve in the House of Commons. As the role of parliament in central government increased, and these places became more desireable, so the possibility of contested elections increased. In the great majority of cases the members were chosen by patronage agreements of one sort or another, but the bribery or intimidation of voters was not unknown in the sixteenth century, and was to become a regular feature of later elections.[9]

HUNDREDS AND OTHER DIVISIONS

'For the shires be divided some into x, xii, xiii, xvi, xx or xxx hundreds, more or lesse, either that they were at the first C townes and villages . . . [or] did find the king to his warres an hundred able men.'[10] It seems likely that Smith's second guess was the better one, and that the origin of the hundred was military. That was certainly the case with the wapentakes of the old Danelaw, and as he rightly pointed out, the hundreds took their names from the traditional mustering places where the men of the locality had assembled when summoned in arms. The two officers of the hundred were the high constable and the bailiff. The latter was a minor crown appointment, responsible to the sheriff, whose job was to collect local dues and revenues. The former was elective, and had at one time been of considerable importance. He was the permanent captain of the hundred posse, presided at the hundred court (which elected him), enforced the Assize of Arms at

---

9   J.E. Neale, *The Elizabethan House of Commons* (1949), pp. 141ff. J. Loach, *Parliament under the Tudors* (1991), pp. 24–5, 150–1.
10   Smith, *De Republica Anglorum*, p. 100.

the local level, and ensured that the highways were kept clear, and that the hue and cry was followed when called. By the sixteenth century most of these functions had either dwindled or disappeared. His military role was taken over first by the muster commissioners and then by the deputy lieutenants. After 1573 the training of militia companies was usually entrusted to professional captains, or muster masters.[11] The high constable still had powers of arrest, and was expected to present offenders to the justices of the peace when they were called to his attention, but that was the extent of his duties. The incumbents were normally substantial yeomen, and were recognized community leaders, so that at times of civil unrest their attitudes and actions could be critical to the maintenance of order, but that authority did not owe much to the office itself.

The hundred court had gone the same way as the county court. Originally it had handled a variety of minor disputes, presented more serious offenders, and provided occasions when proclamations and other public announcements could be made. It had also provided grassroots supervision of the frankpledge system. By the sixteenth century it did little more than elect the high constable (which was not an easy task as few were willing to serve, even for one year) and provide a forum for the discussion of local grievances. Most of its work had been taken over by the justices of the peace.

These justices, as we shall see in due course, were the workhorses of Tudor local government, and so numerous had their functions become by the mid-sixteenth century that they began to adopt a number of organizational devices to streamline their operations. The one which is relevant in this context is the division of counties into what might be called 'petty session areas'. These units were never given any official name, and had no recognized structure, but they were important for the day-by-day administration of justice, and the Privy Council frequently instructed the county commissions to make use of them. Each county was so divided that every area had a group of resident justices, who would convene at their own discretion to hear minor pleas and to carry out routine investigations. This both increased the involvement of the justices with their own immediate neighbourhood and eased the crowded agendas of the regular Quarter Sessions. Ideally, each area was also to have a resident member of the quorum, but that was not always possible and he might have to be

11 Sir Clement Edwardes, *The Maner of our Modern Training* (1600); C.G. Cruickshank, *Elizabeth's Army* (1966), pp. 190–8.

imported. Because of the *ad hoc* nature of these areas, they varied greatly in extent. Normally each consisted of two or more hundreds, but a very populous hundred might be an area on its own, and an even distribution of justices throughout a county was the exception rather than the rule. When important families dropped out of the commission, either through disgrace or through the failure of heirs, it might be necessary to restructure the areas in order to suit their replacements. In many respects these divisions had taken over the local responsibilities of the hundreds by the end of the sixteenth century; but characteristically that was never formally acknowledged, and the hundreds remained the officially recognized jurisdictional units.

Like the 'petty sessions areas', the smallest administrative entities, the parishes, were not technically units of government at all. A parish was a division not of a county, but of a diocese, and some parishes lay in more than one shire. Nevertheless, unlike hundreds, parishes were real social units with which people identified, and in whose affairs they took an interest. Most of the functions of the parish community were connected, directly or indirectly, with the worship of the church. There was no court and the only secular officers were the constables. There had originally been two or three of these, but by the sixteenth century there was normally only one. He was elected annually by the householders of the parish, and his main duties were the arrest of minor offenders, the impounding of straying animals, and the report of more serious infringements to the nearest justice of the peace. It was a thankless task, and one which the more substantial parishioners strove earnestly to avoid. As a result, parish constables were often men unsuited to the task, lacking both intelligence and substance. In the literature of the Elizabethan period, they were often figures of fun. However, the parish was a very convenient unit for many administrative purposes. When Wolsey commissioned the military survey of 1522, the commissioners went round each county parish by parish to ascertain the number of able men and the state of their equipment.[12] Similarly, when Protector Somerset sent out his ill-omened enclosure commissions in 1548, they were instructed to proceed parish by parish, calling before them a jury in each place to testify to their knowledge of abuses and infringements of the law.[13] The royal supremacy also contributed to the increasing utilization of

12   R.W. Hoyle (ed.), *The Military Survey of Gloucestershire, 1522* (1993).
13   J. Strype, *Ecclesiastical Memorials* (1822), II, ii, pp. 359–65.

parishes. Incumbents were expected to be agents for the dissemination of Tudor propaganda, and not of an exclusively religious nature. The national system of poor relief, which began in 1536 and culminated in the great statute of 1601, was based upon the exhortations of the clergy, while the collection and distribution of such relief was left in the hands of churchwardens, and of overseers of the poor who were appointed for that purpose. Although they were in a sense ecclesiastical officers, these overseers were responsible to the justices of the peace and not to the bishop. Parish constables and churchwardens were in the front line in the battle against vagrancy and vagabondage:

> Item, it is ordained and enacted that . . . the churchwardens or two others of every parish of this realm shall in good and charitable wise take such good and discreet order . . . as the poor impotent lame feeble sick and diseased people, being not able to work, may be provided, holpen and relieved, so that in no wise they nor none of them be suffered to go openly in begging; and that such as be lusty or having their limbs strong enough to labour may be daily kept in continual labour, whereby everyone of them may get their own substance and living with their own hands[14]

This was no trivial responsibility, and it is not surprising that parish officers were in the habit of chivvying the rootless off their patch as quickly as possible in order to avoid having to provide for them, or their children. Because the parish was a community, it could be relied upon to act in its own collective self-interest, and this not only assisted in the control of vagrants, but also provided a means of maintaining services such as roads and bridges once the religious foundations, which had often discharged that function in the past, had been dissolved. By the end of the sixteenth century many of the functions which had once been discharged by the hundred or the tithing group had devolved upon the parish, together with a number of new responsibilities generated by that 'increase of governance' which was such a feature of the Tudor period.

14   43 Elizabeth, c. 9; *Statutes of the Realm*, IV, pp. 973–4.

COMMISSIONS

Commissions were letters patent, issued over the Great Seal of England and authorizing named individuals to carry out certain functions on the monarch's behalf. Some were of national application, such as that which investigated the state of the king's revenues in 1552 and made recommendations for action; or that which was instructed in 1549 to prepare a new code of canon law for the English church.[15] Such commissions might report to the lord chancellor, or the lord treasurer, but most frequently to the council. Sometimes their recommendations were rejected outright, as happened over the canon law, sometimes accepted and ignored, and occasionally implemented. However, the great majority of commissions were of local application – a means of bringing the authority of the crown directly to bear upon the county communities. Some of these were inquisitions, designed to obtain information. The enclosure commissions were of that kind, and so were the investigations set up after 1570 to identify religious recusants. Such commissions had no powers to act, but they might be armed with sanctions to compel those summoned to attend and give evidence.

The most regular, and perhaps the most important, commissions of this kind were those set up to assess direct taxation. From 1524 onwards, parliamentary subsidies were assessed directly upon the wealth of every individual taxpayer. This was a less monumental task than it might appear, because every subsidy act, in addition to laying down the rates on both lands and goods, also stipulated an exemption level which meant that the majority of the population paid no tax at all.[16] The commissioners were gentlemen of the county, probably the same men as the justices of the Peace, and they subdivided the county, in the same manner as for petty sessions, so that every person of substance was assessed by neighbours who could be presumed to have a shrewd idea of the accuracy of each individual's submission. The commissioners did not necessarily conduct all the enquiries themselves. They appointed assessors, who were lawyers or gentlemen of inferior

15   J.C. Spalding, *The Reformation of the Ecclesiastical Laws of England, 1552* (1992), pp. 34–5. D. Wilkins, *Concilia Magnae Britanniae et Hiberniae* (1737), IV, pp. 15ff.
16   R.S. Schofield, 'Taxation and the political limits of the Tudor state', in *Law and Government under the Tudors*, eds C. Cross, D. Loades and J. Scarisbrick (1987), pp. 227–46.

standing; but they were responsible for the accuracy of the returns made to the Exchequer. The assessors were charged on oath to 'truely inquire . . . of the best and most value and substaunce of every persone . . . wythout concelment, favor [or] affeccion', and any person dissatisfied with his or her assessment could appeal to the commissioners and be examined afresh on oath.[17] Once the certificate had been made, the nature of the commission changed. From being inquisitorial it became administrative, and collectors were appointed to bring in the money stipulated in the assessments. These were usually the same men as the assessors, and they accounted to the commissioners, who themselves accounted to the Exchequer, or the Court of Augmentations, or wherever was specified in the subsidy act.

This was not only an equitable system, it was also for a long time surprisingly efficient. Before 1558 well over 90 per cent of the money due was actually collected. The process often took longer than the council thought desirable, and distraints were sometimes issued against the collectors, but the commissioners generally knew what they were about, and sheriffs could be relied upon not to find a defaulting collector until his account was complete. By 1570, however, the system was in decline. The reason for this is unclear, but by 1576 the council was accusing subsidy commissioners in general of conniving at the underassessment of the well to do – including themselves: 'heretofore persons of very great possessions and wealthe have ben assessed at meane sommes, and persons of the meaner sort have ben enhaunced to paye after the uttermost value of their substance'[18] For the remainder of the century this was a recurrent theme in official pronouncements. By 1589 the council had given up any expectation that assessments would be realistic, and the work of the subsidy commissioners had become largely formalized. The percentage yield of taxation declined, although not dramatically. The gross yield declined in real terms because no serious attempt was made to keep assessments in line with inflation. In this respect at any rate, delegating responsibility to the local communities was not working in the late Elizabethan period, but there was no alternative because Elizabeth could no more afford a professional corps of tax collectors than her father could, and she was also desperately anxious to maintain the co-operation of the county elites.

The reason for this is easy to identify, for by the late sixteenth

17 6 Henry VIII, c. 26, s. 6; *Statutes of the Realm*, III, pp. 158–9.
18 PRO SP12/107, ff. 97–8.

century the great majority of local government functions in the counties were being carried out by commission, and although commissioners were rewarded in a number of ways, they did not expect to be paid. There were a few regular commissions of a purely administrative nature, of which the most important was the commission of sewers. This was concerned not with waste disposal, which was a matter for the earth rather than the water, but with dykes, waterways and drainage systems. The members held regular sessions to survey the functions for which they were responsible, and had the power not only to compel witnesses to give evidence before them, but also to order the necessary repairs and maintenance work to be done. The majority of commissions, however, were principally or originally judicial in nature.

The commission of gaol delivery was the simplest; a group of local gentlemen, some of them with legal training, who at regular intervals would survey the occupants of the prisons within the county, and decide on the destiny of the prisoners. Some might be dealt with summarily, others bailed to appear before another court, and other returned to custody for the same purpose. Before the rise of the commission of the peace in the late fifteenth century, the justices of gaol delivery had formed the main supplement to the Assizes. In the mid-fourteenth century it has been calculated that somewhere between 10 and 30 per cent of the indicted felons tried before the commissioners of gaol delivery were convicted and hanged. In 1348, out of 337 suspected felons held in seventeen gaols, eighty-three were convicted.[19] By the sixteenth century these commissions had a lower profile, but they remained an important part of the justice system.

The second judicial commission was that of oyer and terminer. This was the commission held by the justices of Assize, and so appeared twice a year in every county. Unlike the commissions of sewers, gaol delivery and the peace, oyer and terminer were occasional, not standing; that is, they were issued afresh for each Assize. They also consisted of outsiders, professional judges rather than local gentry, which was a valuable corrective to a system which otherwise inclined to become somewhat incestuous. Commissions of oyer and terminer were also used for non-recurring occasions; rebellion or crimes of particular significance. In earlier centuries they had been used to deal with 'crime waves' in particlular localities, but that was uncommon in the more highly governed England of the Tudors. After

19   Bellamy, *Crime and Public Order*, pp. 89–120.

1536 commissions of oyer and terminer also replaced the Admiralty Court in dealing with cases of piracy, being issued for the county which was thought to be closest to the scene of the crime, or where the suspected offenders were being held. This was the most flexible and explicit of the judicial commissions, being directed not only to a particular place, but also to particular offences or for a limited period of time. As we have seen, both the Council of the North and the council in the marches of Wales held standing commissions of oyer and terminer, but that was a special arrangement which was not repeated elsewhere. The commission of oyer and terminer had originated in the thirteenth century, and Edward IV had been particularly keen on it, but the Tudors developed and extended its use, often wishing to remind the county elites that they could, and would, use other agents when the occasion required.

In spite of this, the most important commission in regular use was undoubtedly the commission of the peace. This had originated in the fourteenth century, largely to replace the declining county and hundred courts. It seems to have been designed from the beginning to broaden the basis of royal government in the shires by involving a larger number of local gentlemen, and that was certainly its effect. The qualification for selection was 'substance', and that meant not only wealth but status and respect in the community. The original purpose of these justices was to enforce the statutes of the peace, hence their name, but their powers had soon been extended to receiving indictments on other pleas of the crown, and to conducting jury trials for an equally wide variety of offences. They were instructed to convene four times a year, and these regular features of county life soon became known as the Quarter Sessions. Originally there had been four or five commissioners per county, but either this was deemed to be insufficient, or places became sought after for social or political reasons. By the end of Edward IV's reign the average commission numbered about a dozen. In principle the commission of the peace was reissued annually, but the practice varied from reign to reign. All county commissions were issued simultaneously, and only under the most unusual circumstances would any be modified individually.

It was Henry VII who began to expand the functions of the justices of the peace by adding administrative duties to their judicial ones. He made them responsible, as we have seen, for reporting on the conduct of the sheriff. They also became collectors of information, as the king endeavoured to improve his intelligence service and recover prerogative rights which had long fallen into abeyance. As their functions expanded, the king became concerned lest the centrifugal forces of politics should reduce his control, and he began the practice of commissioning one or two councillors in every county. His intention was to ensure that their colleagues did not step out of line when royal policy differed from local feelings on any issue; but an additional effect was to increase the prestige of the commission, so that pressure to obtain membership was greatly increased. By the time that Sir Thomas Smith described its nature in 1565, the commission of the peace had expanded to thirty or forty members per county, headed by 'high nobility and chief magistrates for honours sake'.[20] Such men played no part in the routine work of Quarter Sessions, but by then the commissions had become a two-way channel of communications between the court and the county communities, both sides benefiting from the facility. They had also become the principal agencies for the policing of the countryside: 'The Justices of the Peace be those in whom at this time for the repressing of robbers theeves, and vagabunds, of privie complots and conspiracies, for riotes and violences, and all other misdemeanours in the common wealth, the prince putteth his special trust.'[21]

This expansion, and the diversification of the commission's work, required a few precautions, to prevent embarrassing mistakes, and to reduce the number of cases which required the attentions of the justices of Assize. One of these was the introduction of a professional clerk of the peace, who was legally trained and could guide the justices on technicalities. Another was the establishment of the quorum, 'in whom special trust is reposed'. These were normal justices who, because of their training or experience, were deemed to have particular expertise. At least one member of the quorum had to be present whenever a judicial session of any kind was held. They usually numbered about 10 per cent of the commission. Originally no chairman or other head of the commission had been named, but by the end of Henry VIII's reign it was normal to select a councillor or another senior justice as *custos rotulorum*. The *custos* was not only responsible for making the return of Quarter Sessions business into King's Bench, but was also the functional head of the commission.

Justices were appointed by the lord chancellor, who acted upon whatever advice he chose to take. Normally this would include the

20 Smith, *De Republica Anglorum*, p. 104; J.R. Lander, *English Justices of the Peace, 1461–1509* (1989).
21 Smith, *De Republica Anglorum*, p. 104.

opinions of the Assize judges of the relevant circuit, and of any councillors or courtiers of his acquaintance who happened to sit upon the same commission. However, as Sir Thomas Smith noted, there was by the 1560s a great increase in the 'will to manage . . . the affairs of the commonwealth', and competition for places upon the commission had become fierce. This led to intensive lobbying at court, where the good offices of kinsmen in the household or chamber were much in demand. In every county there was a handful of major families whose head could always command a place, and very often his eldest son in his lifetime. Below that level, middle-ranking families used whatever patronage or other leverage they could find, and once successful, defended their position strenuously. The politics of these appointments nevertheless changed significantly as the century advanced. In the 1520s the duke of Norfolk or the marquis of Exeter would have nominated a significant proportion of the commissions where he had a particular interest. Even in the 1560s nobody would have challenged a specific nomination by the duke of Norfolk, or by the earl of Derby in Lancashire, but by the 1580s such influences were more discreetly used, and the feuds and alliances of the gentry themselves had become proportionately more important.

The political focus was at the lower end of the commission, where the less substantial families competed for the marginal nominations. Even at this level it was difficult to get a private enemy removed, and the normal technique was to allege either seditious words or recusancy. Elizabethan Norfolk provides a number of examples of this kind of dispute. In 1595 Thomas Farmer of Barsham was in dispute with Martin Barney of Gunton over a matter of family inheritance, and Farmer accused Barney of allowing mass to be celebrated at his house. The latter was returned as a recusant, and shortly after removed from the commission. Barney, however, had the means to retaliate because Farmer was in financial difficulties, and the Assize judges had been given instructions to scrutinize the lower end of the commission with a view to removing those of 'insufficient substance'. Farmer's indigence was revealed, and he was also excluded, a disgrace from which his public credit never recovered.[22] In the same county Bassingbourne Gawdy also had his arch enemy Sir Thomas Lovell removed for inciting his fellow justices to oppose making contributions to the arming of the county levy – an offence bordering on treason in time of war.

---

22 A. Hassell Smith, *County and Court: government and politics in Norfolk, 1558–1603* (1974), pp. 243–4.

However, such removals were not common. William Lambarde commented upon the exclusion of a justice by Star Chamber as a remarkable occurrence, and John Hayward noticed only seven such cases between June 1596 and November 1607.[23] The reason for this sensitivity to the loss of face which resulted from removal was the detrimental effect which it could have upon the good order of the county. In 1623 a member of the House of Commons, who was almost certainly a justice himself, 'propownded that thowgh it were noe disgrace not to be a justice of Peace, yet to bee excluded is a disgrace'.[24]

To serve on such a commission was an honour, because it marked a man as a member of the king's affinity; to such an extent that it was illegal for a justice to wear the livery of any other lord. There were no direct financial rewards, although expenses could be claimed for attendance at Quarter Sessions. However, as the range of their activities increased, the justices became the most obvious and easily recognizable agents of royal authority. They licensed ale houses and fixed wage rates and sometimes prices in accordance with statutes for that purpose: 'Each of them hath authoritie upon complaint to him made, of any theft, robberie, manslaughter, murder, violence, riottes, complotes, unlawfull games, or any such disturbance of the peace and quiet of the Realme, to commit the persones whom he supposeth offendors, to the prison'[25] This ubiquitous jurisdiction not only gave them an unrivalled knowledge of the communities for which they were responsible, but also the power which that knowledge conferred. How was an ordinary person to know when a gentleman was speaking as a justice of the peace, and when in his private capacity as a landlord or employer? At the same time there were, in every county, scores of minor offices and sinecures in the monarch's gift: keeperships of royal parks and chases, stewardships of demesne manors, constableships of minor or decayed castles, receiverships, and a host of others. Local gentlemen had the first claim upon such morsels, and the justices were at the head of the queue. Some such positions were remunerative in themselves, but most were desirable mainly because they were 'of estimacion in the country', and rungs on the ladder of local politics. By the reign of Elizabeth the gentry of every county were bound to the crown by a steadily thickening web of such preferments. Their social

23   Gleason, *Justices of the Peace*, pp. 61–6.
24   *Commons Debates, 1621*, eds W. Notestein, F.H. Relf and H. Simpson (1935), IV, p. 284.
25   Smith, *De Republica Anglorum*, p. 104.

dominance was recognized and reinforced, and in return they governed the country in the queen's name.

The advantages of this commission were such that Sir Thomas Smith waxed lyrical: 'There never was in no commonwealth divised a more wise, a more dulce and gentle, nor a more certaine way to rule the people, whereby they are kept alwaies as it were in a bridle of good order, and sooner looked unto that they should not offend, than punished when they have offended.'[26] However, there were problems which he was reluctant to acknowledge. If the authority of the gentleman became compromised, then the government became compromised as well, and it had been Protector Somerset's failure to recognize that fact quickly enough which had made the summer of 1549 so dangerous. When Robert Ketts's followers declared that there were 'too many gentlemen in England by 500', or when the earl of Warwick feared that he could not trust his men to hold Warwick castle against the insurgents, the whole structure of authority appeared to be unravelling. The revolts of 1549 were suppressed by force, not without the assistance of foreign mercenaries, but for a decade thereafter the gentry of southern and eastern England went in fear of another 'camping summer'. That did not happen, because no subsequent council made the protector's mistake of appearing to take the protesters' side against their natural rulers. Two lessons were learned as a result of this alarming experience. The first was that there were undoubtedly justices who abused their position, and that if the council was not seen to discipline such delinquents, then the reputation and authority of the crown would suffer. Second, it was useless for parliament, or the council, or anyone else, to issue orders which the justices were not prepared to enforce. Somerset's social policy had been idealistic, and strictly in accordance with royal tradition, but it had also been directly contradictory to the interests of ther gentry as landlords and employers.

The discipline of the justices was in the hands of the council, but the old practice of notifying grievances by petition had declined in the late fifteenth century, and Henry VII needed reliable means of discovering abuses. One method which he used was the commissioning of councillors, as we have already seen; another was a form of 'fraternal self-criticism'. A statute of 1489 required that it should be proclaimed at every Quarter Sessions that the justices collectively would receive and act upon complaints against any one of their

26   Ibid.

number.[27] Whether this worked, or inspired any confidence, may well be doubted, and when the act lapsed in 1510 it was not renewed. In 1542 another statute gave the oversight to the Assize judges, and that arrangement worked reasonably well for the remainder of the century. From 1543 the clerk of the peace was required to submit transcripts of all proceedings at the Quarter Sessions to King's Bench, and although there is no evidence that the information so acquired was ever acted upon, the threat may have been salutory.

Justices might be removed from the commission for religious nonconformity; that happened under both Mary and Elizabeth, when all justices were required to take the oath of supremacy. They might also be excluded for treason, felony (even if pardoned) or lack of substance; but there was a great reluctance to remove them for misconduct or abuse of their powers. Instead, successive governments attempted to tackle the problem at source by preventing unsatisfactory men from being selected in the first place. As early as 1564 Sir William Cecil identified the source of the problem in the pressure for places on the commission which had built up in every county: 'with the increase of number of justices of peace in every shyre . . . the conservation of peace hath decreased and by multitude of an undiscret nombre of men named for justices, mayntenance, bracery, ryotts and such lyke have multiplied'[28] However, it was one thing to produce such a diagnosis, and another to do anything about it.

Elizabeth's council continued to be vigilant, as another Norfolk dispute demonstrates. Sir Arthur Heveningham, a courtier with military pretensions and an ungovernable temper, created an affray against a fellow justice, Edward Flowerdew, which landed him in Star Chamber, and resulted in both exclusion and a substantial fine; but such decisive action was rare. It was not until 1621 that a special committee of the Privy Council felt obliged to draw up some guidelines, which reveal clearly the nature of their concern. No justice was to be too young; none was to be worth less than £20 a year in 'the king's books'; no lawyer was to be admitted unless he had been a reader at one of the Inns of Court; and no clergyman unless he was a bishop, or 'of most gravyty'.[29] Like Cecil eighty years before, they had convinced themselves that the real trouble was a lack of 'substance' among the justices. However, this appears to have been a wilful

27 4 Henry VII, c. 12; *Statutes of the Realm*, II, p. 536.
28 BL Lansdowne MS 1218, ff. 99–101.
29 Gleason, *Justices of the Peace*, p. 64.

misunderstanding. There was nothing insubstantial about a man like Heveningham; he was simply unsuited by temperament to a position of responsibility, and unless the council was prepared to grasp that nettle, the problem was unlikely to be solved. By 1640 deadlock had been reached on this front. The council was committed to reducing the size of commissions, while county elites themselves had come to believe that a century and a half of effective power had made them virtually autonomous. There was bitter resentment of the council's efforts, reflected in bogus historical and legal arguments, and the resulting collapse of the long-standing *entente* between the crown and the local gentry was a major factor in the onset of the civil war.

Both the strength and the weakness of the commission of the peace lay in its resemblance to a gentleman's club. William Lambarde, a Kentish justice of the later part of Elizabeth's reign, wrote a treatise entitled *Eirenarcha* (*The Peacekeeper*), which enables us to reconstruct the full range of the commission's duties, as they were then defined. Lambarde claimed that the justices were required to enforce over 300 statutes, most of them of Tudor origin, and that these 'stacks of statutes' were in danger of breaking their backs. That, however, was the theory. Lambarde also kept a diary, unpublished in his own lifetime, which he called 'Ephemeris', and which tells a rather different story. Only about a third of the burdensome statutes are mentioned at all, most of them very rarely. The poor law duties were burdensome, and no doubt tiresome, but the great bulk of a justice's time was spent in routine police work, in petty and Quarter Sessions, and in taking sureties for good behaviour. Lambarde was sworn to the commission on 3 June 1580, and the entries in his diary over the next few months give a pretty fair idea of his preoccupations:

> The last of June 1580 and the first of July, I joined with my father-in-law, George Moulton, in the examination of Baptiste Bristow [and others] concerning a robbery. . . . The 9 of July I assisted Mr. Willoughby and Mr. Potter in the examination of Oliver Booby of Chipstead . . . All which examinations I have delivered to the Lord Chief Baron, upon his request of the same by his letters . . . The 26 August, being at Tonbridge in the execution of the commission of sewers for Medway, Sir Thomas Fane, Sir Christopher Alleyn and I, sent Thomas Chambers [and others] to the gaol for keeping ale houses obstinately and against the commandment of sundry justices.[30]

30 Conyers Read (ed.), *William Lambarde and Local Government* (1962), pp. 15–17.

These men knew each other, were often related by marriage, and regarded this kind of service as their natural prerogative. They controlled the lives of their poorer neighbours, as well as enforcing the law in the normal sense. The respect with which they were regarded was the front line of effective government in a society without either a police force or a professional bureaucracy. That was why the earthquake of 1549 had caused such profound alarm. By the time that Lambarde was writing the fences were long since back in place, but obedience could not be taken for granted. Most justices worked hard and did their job well, because it was in their interest to do so, just as it was in the council's interest to keep them happy by allowing them to cheat on their tax returns and to discharge their duties in their own way. Everybody accepted that there were rogues in the system, and that they needed to be disciplined, but a sensitive political hand was needed on the reins. That, by and large, the Tudors had, and the Stuarts did not.

TUDOR INNOVATIONS

Before 1485 there were already officials working on the king's behalf in a local context, who were not part of the county structure. Perhaps the most obvious were the general and particular receivers of the Duchy of Lancaster. The duchy was a liberty, but it also had lands scattered all over England, under its own system of management and accounting to the Duchy Chamber. These officials remained untouched by the changes of the sixteenth century, and were not answerable to either sheriffs or justices of the peace for the discharge of any of their normal duties. There were also the various surveyors and receivers of those royal lands which accounted not to the Exchequer but to the Chamber through the general surveyor. These were special acquisitions rather than ancient demesne, and were listed in 1531 as Warwick lands, Spencer lands, Buckingham lands, the lands of the Duchy of Cornwall, and the lands under the control of the chamberlain of Chester, and of the chamberlains of north and south Wales.[31] The king also had the right to the temporal profits of vacant abbeys and bishoprics, and surveyors were appointed to manage these resources as they arose. Most of these officials would have been lawyers and minor gentlemen who were resident in the

31 *State Papers of Henry VIII* (1830–52), VI, pp. 32–7.

counties where they were required to operate. In some cases they were also justices of the peace, but their functions in that capacity were completely separate. After 1531 the reorganization of the financial administration multiplied these receivers and surveyors into something like a national network. When the Court of Augmentations was established by statute in 1536, it was provided that their should be ten 'particular auditors' and sixteen 'particular receivers', answerable to the treasurer and receiver general of the court.[32] This was less than one per county, and there was no formal connection between Augmentations and the county government, except that the receivers were entitled to call the justices of the peace to their assistance if their functions were resisted or obstructed. Each of the revenue courts subsequently established – First Fruits and Tenths (1540), Wards and Liveries (also 1540) and General Surveyors (1542) – followed a similar pattern, significantly increasing the impact of the central government upon the localities. When this process was put into reverse after 1547, some of these offices disappeared again, at least temporarily. The particular receivers of General Surveyors did not survive the merger with Augmentations, but the Augmentations officials remained *in situ* after the merger with the Exchequer in 1554, becoming agents of the Augmentations Office, and continuing to function much as before. The receivers of First Fruits and Tenths disappeared with the court in 1555, only to surface again after 1559; while the agents of Wards and Liveries were unaffected, as their operation remained independent throughout.

These offices were mainly significant to the county communities for raising the profile of central government, and making its presence more intrusive. The innovation which most affected the actual government of the shires was the introduction of lieutenancies after 1550. As early as the thirteenth century the traditional feudal levies had been supplemented in times of war by commissions of array. These conferred specific powers upon trusted noblemen to raise, by empressment or otherwise, a given number of men from a named county or counties. Having assembled their men, the commissioners then commanded them for the duration of the campaign, and the regular levy, if used, would be placed under the same command. By long-standing custom the militia was not used outside England, but no such restriction applied to the commission of array, which became the normal method of raising men for overseas campaigns. The use of

32   27 Henry VIII, c. 27; *Statutes of the Realm*, III, pp. 569–74.

the term 'lieutenant' to describe this commander appears to date from 1298, when William Latimer was appointed 'notre Lieutenant e Soverein cheveteine' for the northern counties.[33] In the fourteenth century the crown endeavoured to shift the responsibility for paying these levies onto the counties, and that was fiercely resisted. Parliament also tried very hard to prevent the use of commissions of array for raising troops to serve abroad, and to insist that its own permission was required for them to be used at all. By the later fifteenth century it had failed on both counts.

Henry VIII took his prerogative for granted in respect of these commissions, using them against both the Scots and the French from 1512 onward. The first, *de arraiendo et monstrum faciendo contra Scotos*, was issued to the earl of Surrey in that year, and covered the counties of Yorkshire, Lancashire, Northumberland, Cumberland and Westmorland. The troops deployed against the Pilgrimage of Grace in 1536 were mostly raised by signet letters directed to particular gentlemen, but the duke of Suffolk, the duke of Norfolk and the earl of Shrewsbury were all given commissions of lieutenancy for different areas. In 1545 the threat of invasion from France resulted in the issuing of three commissions *de arraiatione et capitaneo generali contra francos*: to the duke of Norfolk for Essex, Suffolk, Norfolk, Hertfordshire, Cambridgeshire, Huntingdonshire, Lincolnshire, Rutland, Warwickshire, Northamptonshire, Leicestershire and Bedfordshire; to the duke of Suffolk for Kent, Sussex, Surrey, Hampshire, Wiltshire, Berkshire, Oxfordshire, Middlesex, Buckinghamshire, Worcestershire and Herefordshire; and to Lord John Russell for Dorset, Somerset, Devon, Cornwall, Gloucestershire, and south and north Wales. Russell's commission also covered the raising of men for service at sea, a task which he found particularly difficult, and which was to cause problems for the remainder of the century.[34]

Although he used them frequently, Henry did not innovate in his use of these commissions, but in the changed circumstance of a royal minority, Protector Somerset began to experiment. Faced with war in Scotland, and the threat of war from France, for the first time he created a system of lieutenancies to cover the whole country. England was divided into two military commands, with the earl of Warwick as lieutenant and captain general of the north, and Lord Seymour of

33 Thomson, *Lords Lieutenant*, p. 15n.
34 Ibid., p. 19.

Sudeley of the south. These were not traditional commissions of array, but simply of control. Under them normal commissions were issued to the earl of Shrewsbury for Yorkshire, Lancashire, Cheshire, Derbyshire, Shropshire and Nottingham; to the marquis of Northampton for Essex, Suffolk and Norfolk; to the earl of Surrey for Surrey, Hampshire and Wiltshire; and to Sir Thomas Cheney, lord warden of the Cinque Ports, for Kent.[35] Like their predecessors, these commissioners were still expected to raise men in the first instance by instructing the sheriffs of the counties for which they were responsible, but the two-tier system was a new departure, and foreshadowed the more radical changes to come.

During the 'camping summer' of 1549 drastic measures were required, and according to the eighteenth-century historian John Strype it was in July of that year that regular lieutenancy commissions were issued for the first time. No direct evidence of these commissions now survives, but a set of instructions issued to Lord John Russell, who was sent into the south west to confront the rebels there, probably represents what they were intended to achieve. Russell was to consult the justices of the peace and other local gentlemen, to defuse the discontent if possible, and to suppress any 'stirs' or seditious rumours. If persuasion failed, he was authorized 'by force of his commission' to call out the local levies and to restore order by force. Not only do these instructions make it appear that Russell had a specific commission, he also clearly had the power to overrule, if necessary, existing authorities, such as the justices and the sheriffs.[36] Similar instructions were issued early in August to the earl of Warwick, sent into East Anglia. In neither case were the local levies equal to the task in hand. Some gentlemen were able to provide useful support, but the military success of both missions rested ultimately upon the German and Italian mercenaries whom the council were able to redeploy.

Given the widespread nature of the disorders, it is very likely that commissions were also issued to other local magnates, such as Lord Rich and the earl of Arundel, who are known to have played a leading part in confronting the malcontents, but it is not possible to demonstrate that. What is clear is that something very like a general system of lieutenancy was authorized by parliament in the spring of 1550:

35   *Acts of the Privy Council*, eds J. Dasent et al. (1890–1907), II, pp. 118–19, 12–17 August 1547.
36   Strype, *Ecclesiastical Memorials*, II, i, p. 278.

Provided always, and be it enacted by the authority above said that if the king shall by his letters patent make any Lieutenant in any county or counties of this Realm, for the suppressing of any commotions, rebellions or unlawful assemblies, that then as well all Justices of Peace of every such county, and the sheriff and sheriffs of the same, as all mayors, bailiffs and other head officers and all inhabitants and subjects of any county, city, borough or town corporate within any such county shall, upon the declaration of the said letters patent and request made, be bound to give attendance upon the same Lieutenant to suppress any commotions, rebellions or unlawful assemblies.[37]

A number of such commissions were issued in April or May of 1550, not only as a precaution against rebellion but also, apparently, to superintend the musters which it was intended to hold during the summer. Very little is known about the working of these commissions, but another set was issued in the spring of 1551, and these are somewhat better documented. They covered the whole country except the jurisdictions of the Councils of the North and the Marches of Wales, which were separately provided for. Some lieutenants, such as the earl of Bedford and the marquis of Northampton, were given reponsibility for a number of counties; others, such as the earl of Warwick, for a single county. Some counties, notably Norfolk and Suffolk, also had a number of lieutenants, not all of whom were noblemen.[38] In 1552 the issue was repeated, the most noticeable difference on that occasion being that the duke of Northumberland (as he had become) had himself named for Northumberland, Cumberland, Newcastle and Berwick, while the earl of Westmorland served for the bishopric of Durham. The following year the Duke included Durham in his own commission. The system seems to have worked. There were no further large-scale uprisings, and as there was no war the musters were somewhat formal exercises and seem to have aroused little controversy. However, if Northumberland was expecting his new system of military administration to provide effective support to himself during the succession crisis of July 1553, then he was sadly disappointed.

Mary did not follow the duke's apparent intention of making commissions of lieutenancy annual, and covering the whole country. Instead, she reverted to the earlier practice of appointing lieutenants

37   3 & 4 Edward VI, c. 5; *Statutes of the Realm*, IV, pp. 104–8.
38   *Acts of the Privy Council*, III, pp. 280–1, 26 May 1551; BL Royal MS 18C xxiv, f. 89.

for particular areas at time of perceived need. Several were issued at the time of the Wyatt rebellion in February 1554, their purport being very much like those of 1549. In 1555 only the earl of Shrewsbury was commissioned, for the defence of the north against the Scots. The return of war in 1557 resulted in a number of commissions, but no attempt was made to cover the whole country. In 1558 about a dozen lieutenancies were created, with instructions resembling those of 1550, to take musters, watch the coasts, suppress all vagabonds and spreaders of seditious tales, and generally keep their countries quiet. Where there were no lieutenancies, Mary continued to use commissioners for musters, a practice in which she was to be followed by her sister. In respect of their functions, the lieutenants were entitled to override any franchisal or other privileges which might get in their way. However, in 1558 Sir Henry Jerningham, holding the commission for Kent, was challenged not only by the jurisdiction of the Cinque Ports, but also by the town of Rochester, obstructions which were specifically condemned by statute in the same year. Not wishing to offend the lord warden, the council instructed Jerningham and Sir Thomas Cheyney to resolve their difficulty by negotiation, in spite of the fact that the lieutenant clearly had the law on his side.[39]

Elizabeth followed her sister's example, rather than her brother's. Commissions of lieutenancy were issued, renewed and terminated at erratic intervals and in response to perceived needs. Before the outbreak of war in 1585 there were lieutenants in some counties of England in every year except 1561, the first being issued in May 1559. There was a tendency towards single-county commissions, and a larger proportion of the holders were commoners, rather than peers. The great majority were privy councillors, and the use of the lieutenancy as an additional system of social control and discipline, over and above its specifically military duties, becomes increasingly apparent. During the war years which followed, commissions became more numerous and more continuous, so that they began to look far more like the system pioneered by the duke of Northumberland, but they remained very much at the queen's discretion, and were more obviously instruments of the prerogative than the earlier systems of local government. Gladys Thomson described the year 1585 as a 'turning point' in the history of the lieutenancy, partly because the outbreak of war caused considerable thought to be given to the nature

39   Thomson, *Lords Lieutenant*, pp. 41–2.

of the office, and partly because the same circumstance caused a rapid development in the position of deputy lieutenant.[40] These were men appointed by the lieutenant to assist him in the discharge of his duties, and they first appear in the early part of Elizabeth's reign. Previously the lieutenant's right to call upon the sheriffs and justices for assistance had seemed to leave no need of extra help. After all, these were the same men who conducted the musters and discharged all the other relevant functions when there was no lieutenancy. However, the lord lieutenant could not afford to be isolated, and council policy during the 1560s was moving fitfully in the direction of a major reform of the musters. As early as 1560 Sir Thomas Gresham (who knew the arms market as well as he knew the exchanges) was pointing out that bows and brown bills were useless for modern warfare, and that modern weaponry required both money and training. Cavalry, too, was a major problem. It was no use assessing a man as a horseman if he was unable or unwilling to find a respectable mount. The statutes of 1558 had replaced the earlier renewals of the Assize of Arms, but had been enacted in the same spirit, based upon an undifferentiated system of mobilization, and traditional equipment.[41]

In 1573 the council at last grasped this nettle. Faced with the menacing power of the Duke of Alba in the Netherlands, civil war in France, and the mounting hostility of the Counter-Reformation, it issued instructions to upgrade the country's defences. 'a convenient and sufficient number of the most able' were to be selected at the musters, and then 'tried, armed and weaponed, and so consequently taught and trained'.[42] Both the selection and the training would require a degree of military expertise which the average sheriff or justice of the peace could not be expected to possess, and far more work than the lieutenant could carry out on his own. The deputy lieutenants had certainly originated in response to a growing awareness of this need for specialist knowledge. There may have been a few as early as 1559, and ten years later, when the earliest surviving list was compiled, every lieutenant had one or more. They numbered about two per county, and were appointed by formal letters of deputation, authorizing them to carry out all the responsibilities of the lieutenancy in the absence of the lord lieutenant. For the most part they were gentlemen of the relevant county, and were often also justices of

40   Ibid.
41   4 & 5 Philip and Mary, cs. 2, 3: *Statutes of the Realm*, IV, p. 108.
42   PRO SP12/93, f. 18.

the peace, but they were appointed to this position for their military talents, real or presumed.

After 1585 the number of deputy lieutenants significantly increased, some counties having as many as six, and counties were regularly divided into units to facilitate their work. Sometimes these corresponded to petty sessions divisions, and sometimes not. The work itself was necessary, but it could be both onerous and controversial. However much the government may have wished to improve the defence of the realm, it had no intention of paying for it; and since it was not reasonable to expect the trained bands to provide expensive equipment for themselves while their fellows paid nothing, the onus of provision fell on the county. This was one of the reasons why, in spite of the fact that those selected were exempt from the risk of being pressed to serve overseas, counties were anxious to keep their trained bands small. Following the first instruction in 1573, the lord lieutenant of Cambridgeshire, Lord North, offered 300 out of 1,000 'able men'; Sir Hugh Paulet in Somerset suggested no more than 600 out of 6,000; and the JPs of Cornwall advised only 400 out of 6,800. The county levies which were required to equip these men were fiercely resisted, even in the teeth of the Armada threat. Nevertheless a modest success was achieved. By the end of the century many counties had armouries, where arquebuses, pikes and body armour could be kept securely between training sessions, and professional muster masters, experienced captains whose job it was to try to turn raw levies into a competent home guard in a few days each year. Much of the credit for this must go to the lord lieutenants and their deputies, who not only added another dimension to county government, but also rendered the private retinue virtually obsolete. The private armouries, which had still been carefully maintained and serviced as late as 1570, had rusted or gathered dust by 1600. However fragile the achievement, the defence of the realm had by then become a public responsibility in a sense which it had not been before. Many lord lieutenants were still noblemen, but it was a significant development when their military functions came to depend upon commissions of appointment from the crown, and not upon the *manred* of themselves and their kin.

4

Towns and Cities

Like virtually every other state in Europe, sixteenth-century England
was overwhelmingly rural, and dependent upon an agrarian economy.
It was also relatively underpopulated. In the later part of the thirteenth
century something like six million people had lived in England and
Wales; by the middle of the fifteenth century there were no more than
two and a half million. The main reason for this was plague; not just
the great visitation of the Black Death in 1348–9, but its endemic
reappearance. Many consequences followed from this: late marriage,
low fertility, a free labour market, and land for which no tenants could
be found. It may have been a golden age of liberty and opportunity
for the surviving peasants, but it was a depressing one for the towns-
people. Cities like York, which had held nearly 20,000 inhabitants,
had less than half that number; and once flourishing commercial
centres such as Coventry lamented empty tenements and falling
revenues. However, by the end of the fifteenth century the corner had
been turned, for reasons which are not entirely clear. Plague
continued to recur, but probably with diminishing virulence, and the
birth-rate began to rise. By the middle of Henry VIII's reign the population had passed three million, and by the end of the century was
nearing four. All figures are imprecise because of the lack of accurate
statistical data, but the sixteenth century saw a demographic upturn
of about 25 per cent. In this recovery the towns participated fully,
although not to an equal extent. York and Coventry remained relatively depressed, while Norwich and Exeter flourished. A substantial
number of new boroughs were chartered, particularly between 1547
and 1558, and there was a spate of civic building, reflecting an
upswing of confidence and enterprise.[1]

1   A.D. Dyer, *Decline and Growth in English Towns, 1400–1640* (1991); R.Tittler,
'The incorporation of boroughs, 1540–1558', *History*, 62, 1977, pp. 24–42.
Tittler, *Architecture and Power: the town hall and the English urban community,
c. 1500–1640* (1991).

England had only one true city by European standards, and that was London. At the death of Edward IV it probably contained about 50,000 people; by 1550 it had reached 120,000; and by 1600 had probably passed 200,000, placing it in the same league as Paris, Rome and Naples. This demographic growth was out of all proportion to the rest of the country, or to any other town, and was caused by the increasing power of the capital to attract immigration, rather than by any radical change in life expectancy. Apart from the sweating sickness in 1551–2, and the influenza epidemic of 1557–8, both of which were particularly lethal to a crowded population living in insanitary conditions, there were no checks to this growth. In the early part of the century London could not compare with Antwerp or Cologne as an international trading and financial centre, but its status grew steadily, particularly as its continental rivals suffered from the effects of war and religious persecution. Antwerp never recovered from the 'Spanish fury' of 1576, and by 1600 London was probably second only to Amsterdam in wealth and influence. Situated close by the permenant centre of government at Westminster, and surrounded by the main royal residences, the city controlled about 80 per cent of England's international trade during the reign of Elizabeth, and was by far the largest contributor of men, ships and money to the war against Spain. London put out over twenty ships against the Armada, and its merchants participated regularly and extensively in the privateering operations of the 1580s and 1590s.[2] The support of London, both military and financial, had been crucial to Edward IV, and the customs of its port were second only to the royal lands as a source of ordinary revenue to Henry VIII. When Thomas Gresham began his efforts to redeem the finances of the English crown in 1552, and restore the pound sterling on the bourse, he was able to use the enormous credit facilities of the city companies, and particularly of the Merchant Adventurers. The corporation of London guaranteed the government's borrowing in Antwerp, and eventually enabled Elizabeth to buy her way out of debt. In return the council supported the political interests of the city merchants, first against foreign domination of the printing trade, and then against the Hanseatic League.[3] Relations between the court and the city were always close, and there

---

2   S. Rappaport, *Worlds within Worlds: structures of life in sixteenth century London* (1989); I.W. Archer, *The Pursuit of Stability: social relations in Elizabethan London* (1991); K.R. Andrews, *Elizabethan Privateering, 1585–1603* (1964).
3   The special privileges of the foreign printers, which had been designed to

was a substantial aristocratic investment in a number of commercial operations, starting with the Willoughby and Chancellor voyage of 1553. Within England, London was a unique phenomenon, of far greater importance than any individual county or region. The religious attitudes of its citizens and the social policies of its rulers constrained and directed the thinking of the central government to a far greater extent than did the reactions of Anglo-Irish peers or north country gentlemen.

A long way behind London came a cluster of other places, which were large enough to be of considerable weight in their areas, and were recognized as proper towns by visitors from more urbanized places, such as Flanders or Northern Italy. Norwich, Bristol and York all had between 10,000 and 12,000 inhabitants in the middle of the century, rising to 15,000 plus by the end. Newcastle upon Tyne, Salisbury, Exeter, Coventry and a few others had also topped 10,000 by 1600. Like London, these cities were counties in their own right for governmental purposes. They had their own sheriffs, and their own commissions of the peace; they conducted their own musters, and had their own deputy lieutenants. Below that level, what constituted a town depended upon what you were looking for. By 1600 there were 191 parliamentary boroughs, created by royal charter, with their privileges and their modest degree of self-government. However, some of these, like the Welsh and Cornish boroughs, were very small and their economic activity, although important locally, was little more than market level.[4] Between fifty and sixty places, apart from the major cities, were commonly described as towns by contemporaries on the basis of their population and prosperity. Most of these were chartered boroughs, but a few, like Lewes in Sussex, were still under the control of local lords. For administrative purposes, they were more like manorial villages.

A borough was not really an economic or demographic unit, but one defined by its charter. It had the right to control its own markets, and to confine to its own inhabitants the right to produce and sell

---

encourage them to work in London when native craftsworkers were very few, were withdrawn by a series of statutes in 1515, 1523, 1529 and 1534. D.M. Loades, 'The theory and practice of censorship in sixteenth century England', in *Politics, Censorship and the English Reformation* (1990), pp. 96–108. *A Treatise of Commerce . . . by John Wheeler* (1601); R.H. Tawney and Eileen Power (eds), *Tudor Economic Documents* (1924), III, pp. 299–301.

4   Joyce Youings, *Sixteenth Century England* (1984), pp. 66–87.

goods within the town, charging outsiders significant fees for permission to do the same. Its mayor, or other chief officer, held a court to which the citizens were bound to bring their disputes, but which could not touch pleas of the crown. The fact that corporate status was much sought after suggests that the advantages were clearer to contemporaries than they often are to historians. Certainly the government favoured incorporation, and the main reason for this appears to have been a consistent belief that the vested interests of urban elites were the best guarantees of order and discipline in places which were extremely difficult to police from outside. Successive councils consequently followed a policy of creating and supporting boroughs ruled by self-selecting elites in the belief that their own economic security would ensure their best endeavours against sedition and disorders of all kinds. If that was their thinking, it was certainly justified by the outcome.

In spite of their autonomy, towns were not franchises, because all writs ran in the monarchs name and because their charters were revocable at the will of the crown, without either judicial or legislative process. The Tudors did not revoke any charters, but Mary was sufficiently incensed against the city of London in August 1553 to threaten the lord mayor with the loss of his 'sword' for failing to take adequate precautions against a Protestant riot.[5] In the fifteenth century it had been laid down by statute that members serving in the House of Commons for borough constituencies had to be resident burgesses, but this law had quickly become a dead letter. Not only did some boroughs, such as Dunwich, Old Sarum and Newtown, Isle of Wight, have no resident burgesses by the sixteenth century, but a number of others were too poor to pay the necessary maintenance allowances. As we have seen, their nominations tended to be taken over by the local gentry, or by a noble patron. This was an arrangement of mutual benefit, because many small boroughs had no particular interest in being represented in a national legislature, and if they did require a spokesman, they were better served by a confident and articulate gentleman than by one of their own number. Originally private lords had chartered boroughs on their own lands, usually to encourage markets and take a share of the profits, but by the sixteenth century such grants could be obtained only from the crown, and seigneurial towns, like Lewes, were not recognized as

5   Simon Renard to the Queen Dowager, *Calendar of State Papers, Spanish*, eds Royall Tyler et al. (1862–1964), XI, p. 178, 20 August 1553.

boroughs. Boroughs were collectively assessed for taxation purposes, rather than being subject to the visitation of subsidy commissioners. In effect the municipal officers acted as *ex officio* commissioners, and were held responsible for any shortfall in the assessed yield. Towns which had been adversely affected by economic circumstances, or claimed to have been, regularly appealed for relief, and were often successful, pardons sometimes amounting to as much as £10,000 or £12,000 in a single assessment. The already noticed tendency for the yield of taxation to diminish probably owed as much to this complaisance as it did to the self-interest of the gentry, because towns which were increasing in wealth did not volunteer that information, and traditional assessments were very seldom increased. In the poll tax assessment of 1377 five towns had been rated at over £1,000, while for the subsidy of 1524 the highest, apart from London, was Norwich at £749.[6] This dramatic decline may have been partly the result of decaying urban population and prosperity, but the worst was well over by 1524, and it seems that the government of Edward III was more rigorous in its demands than that of Henry VIII.

The government needed prosperous towns and began as early as the reign of Henry VII a campaign to check urban dereliction by statute. After 1535 a number of acts were directed to specific towns, requiring householders to keep their properties in occupation and repair, and empowering the corporations to take over their responsibilities if they should be negligent or recalcitrant. By 1540 such regulations had been applied to nearly sixty towns in a concerted effort between the council and the borough representatives to check declining population. Like the rather similar campaign against the enclosure of arable land, this attempt to halt the economic clock had very little success. Decaying towns continued to decay, but urban prosperity as a whole increased. At least twenty towns showed a significant rise in population between 1500 and 1600; a few, like Exeter and Reading more than doubled; and London grew by leaps and bounds.

LONDON

In theory, London was governed by its freemen. There were three ways to become a freeman: by patrimony, by apprenticeship and by redemption. Each involved first obtaining the freedom of one of the

6 Dyer, *Decline and Growth*, p. 70.

sixty-odd guilds and livery companies which controlled the economic life of the city, and then presenting those credentials to the Court of Aldermen. Freedom of a recognized company conferred automatic freedom of the city, which could not be obtained by any other route, giving the companies a crucial, but very passive, role in the political process.

Patrimony was straightforward. The son of a citizen was entitled to membership of his father's company, whether he wished to pursue the same trade or not. Usually he did, but a younger son might well be apprenticed to a different trade, and there were many men who held citizenship by both patrimony and apprenticeship. Apprenticeship was equally simple. A young man served his training, usually for seven years, under a guild member, and on the completion of that term became a member of his master's company. It might be several years before he could afford to set up as an independent master, but that did not affect his freedom. He worked as a journeyman, just as in later years many qualified master mariners sailed as mates before obtaining their own ships. Redemption was much less straightforward, because this meant purchase. The candidate did not have to possess any skill, or even interest, in the trade which he was applying to join; he just had to convince the warden and officers of the guild of his general worthiness, a decision which could well be influenced by the depth of his purse. In fact redemption did not become an open door, because the citizens were very jealous of their privileges, and the Court of Aldermen kept a wary eye on the guilds to prevent abuse. It seems to have been used mainly by 'strangers' of recognized wealth and probity, or by political figures whose support the city wished to attract for purposes of its own. The great majority of new citizens seem to have been made by apprenticeship. Out of a sample of 1,055 new freemen created between 1551 and 1553, only 17 per cent gave London as their place of origin, indicating freedom by patrimony; 79 per cent came from other parts of England, and 4 per cent from Ireland, Wales, Scotland and Calais.[7] As we have seen, and as these figures strikingly comfirm, London grew principally by immigration.

Theory notwithstanding, by the sixteenth century the average freeman played only a very minor role in government. Originally his means of participation had been the Common Hall, an assembly of all the liverymen in the city. The Common Hall nominated two senior aldermen for the office of lord mayor, of whom the Court of Aldermen

7   Rappaport, *Worlds within Worlds*, p. 78.

chose one. In the same way they also nominated two candidates for the post of city chamberlain, and four for the positions of bridge-master, ale conner and auditor of accounts. By virtue of its charter, and unlike a normal county, the city of London chose its own sher-iffs, of whom there were two. One was selected by the lord mayor, and the other elected by the Common Hall. In the fifteenth century two of the city's four members of parliament were chosen by the mayor and the other two by the Common Hall, but this arrangement was changed in the early sixteenth century, and thereafter the whole elec-tion was conducted by the hall. This, however, was not the democratic move which it might appear, because the mayor called and dismissed the Common Hall at his discretion, and, with the Court of Aldermen, could veto any election of which he disapproved. In fact the Common Hall was not so much an institution of government as an electoral college with strictly limited powers and responsibilities. It was presided over by one of the sheriffs, who supervised its business. Much humbler means of popular participation, but perhaps in the long run more significant, were the precinct and ward motes. At the beginning of the sixteenth century there were twenty-five wards, each divided into precincts which corresponded roughly, but not exactly, to the parishes. The main function of the precinct meeting, apart from the informal exchange of ideas about city business, was to nominate ward officers for election by the ward mote. By the Elizabethan period the precincts, although they still included all freemen, had come to be dominated by the vestry meetings of the parish church, which consisted of the most substantial and active residents.

The ward motes were much more important. Originally they had consisted of all householders and other males over the age of 15, but after the early fifteenth century only the freemen had been eligible to vote. At these meetings the ward officers were elected – clerk, beadle and constable – and the members of the ward inquest or jury named, whose duty it would be to investigate complaints and present offenders. In some ways the wards were a little bit like hundreds, except that they had never had their own courts. The ward mote was linked to the constitutional structure of the city by its right to put forward names to the Court of Aldermen for the important post of ward alderman, and by the election of common councillors. It appears that there had originally been two councillors per ward, but already by 1400 the Common Council numbered 100, and thereafter it steadily increased; 187 in 1550 and 196 (with one additional ward) by 1600. The number of councillors seems to have varied with the wealth and population of the ward, and to have changed from time to time, but whether in accordance with any fixed principle is not known.[8] These elections were conducted annually, but the normal practice seems to have been to re-elect the same men, replacing them only when they wished to stand down, or died. *A Breefe Description of the famous Cittie of London*, written in 1558, declared that common councillors were liverymen who 'continue in their office as long as they shall live, except they be called to some higher office'.[9]

The Common Council was half the city's legislature, and had come into existence in 1346. In many respects it resembled the House of Commons. It could propose all manner of regulations for the good government of the city and the protection of its interests, but they only became binding regulations if they were also assented to by the Court of aldermen, which sat with the Common Council for debating purposes, but voted separately. On the other hand, no measure could become a by-law without the consent of the Common Council, and no assessment could be made for any levy imposed directly upon the wards without its approval. Where the Common Council differed from the House of Commons was in the practice of management. However strongly privy councillors may have attempted to steer it, the house retained its capacity for independent initiative, in practice as well as in theory. In London only measures proposed by the aldermen ever got onto the agenda – a much tighter control than that exercised by the speaker. The Common Council convened some five or six times a year. It was summoned by the lord mayor, and each meeting was preceded by a session of the Court of Aldermen, which, in accordance with an order of 1544, was required to prepare the business for the joint session. After 1558 all documents sealed with the common seal of the city had to be signed by common councillors as well as by aldermen, and in 1592 a Lands Committee, consisting of four aldermen and six councillors, was set up for that purpose. This subsequently became one of the city's most important bodies. The common councillors were invariably substantial and important citizens, but their power as councillors was very limited. The people who really mattered in the government of London were the aldermen.

An alderman was far more than the representative of his ward. He was not its ruler in any constitutional sense, but he was responsible

8   Valerie Pearl, *London on the outbreak of the Puritan Revolution: city government and national politics, 1625–1643* (1961), pp. 45ff.
9   Cited by Pearl, loc. cit.

for its order and good government in rather the same manner as a county JP was for the neighbourhood in which he lived. In principle he was elected, but in practice he was co-opted by his peers, because the Court of Aldermen was free to reject all the nominations made by the ward motes. He had by custom to be free of one of the twelve great livery companies,[10] and to satisfy a property qualification which by the early seventeenth century stood at £10,000. He had to be an Englishman born, but he did not have to be a resident householder, and if he was not this could somewhat undermine his effectiveness as a magistrate. Aldermen were appointed for life, and could only be removed by the decision of their peers. In spite of the forms of election, they took it in turn to be lord mayor, unless death or some extraordinary political crisis supervened, and the aldermen who had 'passed the chair' became a revered group of elder statesmen, who virtually monopolized such responsible positions as governors of hospitals and chairmen of charitable trusts.

The Court of Aldermen was the House of Lords and the Privy Council rolled into one. It appointed the recorder for life, and most of the other senior officers of the city. According to the *Reports of Speciall Cases*, written in the early seventeenth century, the aldermen:

> ...treat, determine and discuss...the pleas and matters touching Orphans, apprentices and other business of the same city. And there are redressed and corrected the faults and contempts of those which do against the custom and ordinance of the city, as well at the suit of the parties as by inquest of office...and there they do use to justify bakers, victuallers and tradesmen, and to treat and ordain for the government of the city, and for keeping the king's peace.[11]

The lord mayor conducted his own court of civil pleas, *ex officio*, as did the sheriffs, chamberlain, coroner and escheator. The mayor, recorder and senior aldermen held the commissions of peace and of gaol delivery, thus acting as magistrates for the city. There were no Assizes in the ordinary sense, the same officers also receiving the regular commissions of oyer and terminer. All the administrative duties which in the counties fell to the justices of peace were in

10 A.B. Beaven (ed.), *The aldermen of the City of London* (1908–13); Robert Ashton, *The City and the Court, 1603–1643* (1979), pp. 8–12.
11 *Reports of Speciall Cases*, p. 153, Cited in Pearl, *London on the outbreak of the Puritan Revolution*, pp. 59ff.

London the responsibility of the mayor and aldermen, who delegated many of them to the numerous inferior officers of the city and the wards.

The city was mustered by its own commissioners, and by the end of the sixteenth century the London trained bands had their own appointed officers, and constituted one of the most effective, as well as the largest, military force which could be readily available. The White Coats, as they were known, had existed for at least a generation before the general regulations of 1573, but their performace in 1554, when they had deserted in the face of the Wyatt rebellion, had not been reassuring either to the crown or to the city.[12] Nevertheless, it was London which was mustered in 1559 to put on a show for the benefit of foreign diplomats, and Elizabeth was highly delighted with the result. From 1578 onwards the city was treated separately from other counties, being ordered to train 2,000 shot and 1,000 pikes, but no cavalry. Arquebuses were expensive, but easier to afford than horses in the close confines of London. Like every other town London tried to get its quotas reduced, but pleas of poverty were unconvincing from the Court of Aldermen.

The court sat in camera, and was answerable to no one, but its power was limited in practice by the business community from which it drew its members. The livery companies were in origin private associations of tradesmen or craftsmen, partly religious fraternities, partly friendly societies, and partly monopolistic corporations. They had their own charters of incorporation, their officers, rules and resources. By the sixteenth century their primary purpose was to supervise the business activities of their members, and to ensure that no interloper practised that particular mystery within the reach of their jurisdiction. They were chartered directly by the crown, not by the city, but from 1487 onwards all their guild regulations had to be approved by the Court of Aldermen. There was consequently no straightforward chain of command, and the political life of London was a delicate balancing act.

A good, although not typical, example of this is provided by the Stationers' Company. The Stationers had originally been a humble fraternity of paper makers, but when the more exalted Scriveners refused to receive practitioners of the new art of printing in the late fifteenth century, the Stationers gave them hospitality. At first the

---

12   Loades, *Two Tudor Conspiracies* (1965), p. 60; E.H. Harbison, 'French intrigues at Queen Mary's court', *American Historical Review*, 45, 1940, p. 548.

main problem of the London printers was to organize themselves, and loosen the stranglehold which privileged foreigners had acquired over the trade after the death of William Caxton. The latter target had largely been achieved by a statute of 1534, but the sensitive nature of much of the printers' output meant that by then the crown was showing a direct interest in their operations. Proclamations and statutes imposed a licensing system, operated at first by the bishop of London, and later by the Privy Council. At the same time patents were issued by the crown, authorizing individual craftsmen, who might or might not be members of the Stationers' Company, to print particular works, such as English Bibles and prayer books. When the Stationers' Company was chartered in 1557, it was as much for the benefit of the Privy Council as of the tradesmen. The wardens of the new company were required to co-operate with, and enforce, the crown's policy of censorship, and in operating its own system of licensing, not to accept anything of which the royal censors did not approve. At the same time, the mayor and aldermen might be held responsible if the Stationers stepped out of line.[13] The patent system soon became a source of grievance, but it was difficult to oppose when the rules of the livery companies generally allowed someone who was free of one company to practise the trade of another. This originated in the system of patrimony, but had long transcended that limitation, and in fact several of the leading London printers of the mid-sixteenth century were Mercers or Drapers rather than Stationers. New books still had to be registered with the Stationers' Company, but it was difficult for the wardens to discipline people who were not members, and the patent system showed a fine disregard for all the niceties of city etiquette, because even aliens could receive them.[14]

In a sense the livery companies ran their own affairs without reference to the Court of Aldermen. There was no requirement for an alderman to be a master of a company, or vice versa, although restriction to the twelve major companies seems to have been rigidly adhered to. However, when it came to money, the companies were in the driving seat. City taxation could only be levied on the wards by vote

13   The wardens of the Stationers' Company were specifically instructed to be obedient to the ecclesiastical commissioners in 1559: *Visitation Articles and Injunctions*, eds W.H. Frere and W.M. Kennedy (1910), III, p. 25. See also *A Transcript of the Register of the Stationers' Company*, ed. E. Arber (1875–94).
14   P. Took, 'Government and the printing trade, 1540–1560' (Ph.D, London, 1978), p. 224.

of the Common Council, so that if large sums were needed quickly, perhaps in response to an appeal from the crown for a loan, only the livery companies could mobilize sufficient resources; so that it was to them rather than to the mayor and aldermen that the task fell. Paradoxically, the greatest providers in this respect, and those who most regularly gave the city its financial muscle, were not livery companies, but organizations which had no official connection with London. Both the Staplers and the Merchant Adventurers were in theory national companies, open to merchants of any town provided that they could pay the entry fine, and with headquarters outside the realm. The Staplers were based in Calais until 1558, and the Merchant Adventurers in Antwerp. However, appearances, as so often, were deceptive. The overwhelming majority of both Staplers and Adventurers were Londoners, and they conspired to retain their ascendency by fixing the entry fines at levels which hardly any provincial merchant could afford. By 1558 the Staplers, who traded in raw wool, were in full decline. In the middle of the fourteenth century they had exported 35,000 sacks a year; by 1420 that had declined to 10,000, and by 1527 to 5,000. The loss of their staple was another serious blow, and spelt the end of their involvement with public finance. By 1565 they were shipping no more than 3,500 sacks, and by the 1580s the figure was more like 200, marking the virtual end of the trade.

The Merchant Adventurers, on the other hand, were flourishing exceedingly. By 1450 they were already exporting 57,000 unfinished broadcloths a year, although at that stage less than half was passing through London. A century later the total was almost 150,000, of which 80 per cent was passing through Blackwell Hall, the company's London centre. The crisis of 1551–2 led to a reduction from that high point, but even in slack years like 1557–8, the cargo was still valued at some £300,000, which was twice the ordinary revenue of the crown. It was the enormous credit generated by this trade which enabled Thomas Gresham to solve some of the monarch's financial problems. In these transactions the company worked very closely with the city authorities, because it was actually the mayor and aldermen who had to guarantee the crown's credit, and to them that Gresham returned the bonds to Antwerp bankers as these were discharged.[15]

15   D.M. Loades, *Reign of Mary Tudor* (1991), pp. 232–8. D.R. Bisson, *The Merchant Adventurers of England; the company and the crown, 1474–1564* (1993); Eric Kerridge, *Trade and Banking in Early Modern England* (1988).

Because of the prohibitive entry fines of the Merchant Adventurers, the merchants of the outports maintained a small-scale independent trade of their own, organizing themselves into companies for the purpose. Technically they were interlopers on the Merchant Adventurers' monopoly, but the crown protected them in order to support the prosperity of the provincial towns. The Merchant Adventurers of Newcastle even obtained their own charter in 1552. The London Adventurers did not like this, but put up with it (more or less) because it did not make much difference to them, and good relations with the crown were important.

No company was ever more misnamed than the Merchant Adventurers. As long as they could ship virtually all their cloth to Antwerp in one large and securely convoyed fleet, and receive a large profit, they were not the slightest bit interested in looking further afield. Because of its value, this Low Countries trade was a major factor in Tudor foreign policy down to the 1560s; and because the London merchants were not interested, there was little long-distance voyaging or exploration before the 1550s. Early in his reign, the London merchants had driven Edward IV into war with the Hanseatic League, a confederation of north German cities which controlled the Baltic trade. At that time the league was strong, and had an ally in the king of Denmark, so the English made little progress, and the Treaty of Utrecht in 1470 confirmed the privileged status of the Hanseatic merchants in London. However, in the early sixteenth century the League became weaker and the Merchant Adventurers stronger. In 1552 the Privy Council cancelled the Hanseatic privileges, under pressure from the mayor and aldermen for some *quid pro quo* for their financial support.[16] Mary restored these privileges, which was a factor in her less than perfect relations with the city, but Elizabeth began to whittle them down again, and the Steelyard, the Hanse headquarters in London, was finally closed down in the 1580s. By that time the Merchant Adventurers had been forced to diversify. War and politics made the Low Countries outlet increasingly insecure, and starting with the Muscovy Company in 1555, the London merchants began to invest in a variety of other companies, both regulated and joint stock, set up to seek and exploit markets in other parts of the world – Levant, Barbary, Guinea, Eastland, East India, and several others. These ventures were not all successful, and most

16 *Acts of the Privy Council*, eds J. Dasent et al. (1890–1907), III, p. 489.

remained small-scale by comparison with the European trade, but they transformed the maritime scene, and began to spread London capital around the world.

The city had always been fairly cosmopolitan, another characteristic which set it apart from the rest of England. German, Flemish and Italian merchants particularly had resided, sometimes individually and sometimes in recognized groups, for centuries. There were even a few Jews who, because they were not allowed to reside in the country by English law, were compelled to masquerade as Portugese Catholics, and a number of Spaniards, some of whom later became religious dissidents. These were all excluded from the privilege of freedom, and could hold no office in the city, but were protected in other ways. The Venetians had even moved to London from Southampton in the 1480s, after being assailed by xenophobic riots. It was therefore very important, both for the city and for the king, that the 'stranger' communities in London should be protected. Consequently when a report reached Wolsey at the end of April 1517 that 'diverse younge men of the citie [had] assauted the Alyens as they passed by the stretes, and some were stricken, & some buffeted, & some throwen in the canel', he sent for John Rest, the lord mayor, and warned him to take good care that no such incident was repeated: 'This heryng the Mayre sent for al his brethren to the Guylde hall in grat hast . . . then was declared to them by Master brooke ye recorder how that the kynges counsail had reported to them yt the comminaltie that night would ryse & distresse all the Aliens & straungers yt inhabited in the citie of London'.[17] The aldermen debated the matter, agreeing that precautions should be taken, but that ' . . . it was evell to rayse men in harneys' in case they should side with the malcontents. Eventually a curfew was agreed and proclaimed. However, an alderman named John Monday, who made an ill-advised attempt to enforce the ban, was set upon to the familiar cry of 'prentyses and clubbes', and fled for his life.

The atmosphere in the city was clearly explosive, and this incident served to trigger off exactly the riot which the aldermen had intended to prevent. The houses of several merchant strangers were ransacked and a great deal of damage was done, although casualties seem to have been few. It was three o'clock the following afternoon before the lord mayor and his officers regained control of the situation, arresting

17   Edward Hall, *The Union of the Two Noble and Illustre Famelies of Lancastre and York* (edn 1809), pp. 588–9.

about 300 of the offenders. The lieutenant of the Tower, Sir Richard Cholmely, 'no greate frende to the citie' as Hall noted, added to the confusion by discharging several pieces of his ordnance, although fortunately they did no great harm to anyone. By about five in the afternoon of 1 May, when the hastily assembled retinues of the earls of Surrey and Shrewsbury, dispatched by the king, arrived on the scene, it was all over bar the recriminations. This 'Evil May Day' cast a long shadow, because it raised doubts about both the will and the capacity of the city authorities to maintain order even when, as in this case, they had been forewarned. However, it did no great damage to the economic life of London. Riots of this nature were an occupational hazard of any merchant living in a foreign city, and although this was serious by English standards, it merely served to warn everyone to take better precautions.

Apart from occasional security scares, communities of merchant strangers presented few problems, but the jurisdictional map of London was highly complex, and later alien communities were a bigger headache. From a very early date there had been religious houses within the city which formed small liberties; the Priory of St Bartholomew in Smithfield, the Austin friars, Blackfriars and Greyfriars, and a number of hospitals. In the reign of Henry II, according to the chronicler John Stow, there had been thirteen 'great conventual churches' in addition to the 126 parish churches. Most of these were suppressed by Henry VIII, and a few by Edward VI. By the reign of Elizabeth only St Catherines by the Tower remained, as the exception to prove the rule. Some of the buildings were left to fall down; some were purchased and converted to other uses, but the jurisdictional immunities remained because the process of dissolution did not, in itself, remove them. Occupants of these precincts could, and did, defy the government of the city which surrounded them, sometimes by pursuing illegal trades or offering illicit pleasures, sometimes by sheltering thieves and vagabonds. It was very hard to establish responsibility for these activities, and the Court of Aldermen, which had found the religious difficult enough to deal with, now faced an even more intractable problem. In 1550 the church and a part of the precinct of the Austin friars was granted by the crown to the Dutch community as a place of worship. This solved one problem, because the Dutch were a sober and Godly people who caused no disturbances, but it created another in that the 'stranger church', being also immune from the jurisdiction of the bishop of London, used its own rites in defiance of the Act of Uniformity, thereby setting 'an evil

ensample' of non-conformity.[18] A similar situation was created later
in the same year by the grant of the dissolved chapel of St Anthony to
the French congregation.

London was a centre for Protestant refugees from all over Western
Europe, and given their doubtful record in dealing with aliens, both
the city authorities and the business community proved surprisingly
welcoming. Despite regulations to the contrary, refugee printers, for
example, were allowed to set up their presses, and the rules governing
the number of foreign workers an English printer might employ were,
if not relaxed, then generally ignored. By 1553 the alien population
numbered many thousands, and they formed more than 10 per cent
of the adult population in five wards of the city. This number diminished rapidly after Mary's accession, but the problem returned with
Elizabeth's Protestant settlement, and niggled away for the remainder
of the century.

London was close to the centre of Royal administration in the
neighbouring city of Westminster, and was also surrounded by
suburbs, over which the city government strove to establish a measure
of control, although with varying success. Beyond Temple Bar was a
substantial liberty of the Duchy of Lancaster, which successfully
resisted encroachment, but in 1550 a major success was scored in
respect of the hitherto royal borough of Southwark, south of the river.
The king then sold 'all his lands and tenements in Southwark . . . except Southwark Place . . . and the messuage called the
Antilope' to the mayor and aldermen of London for £647. He also
gave them the lordship and manor of Southwark 'late pertaining to
the monastery of Bermondsey', and the royal manor and borough of
Southwark, and all the rights belonging to these various jurisdictions.
This was a great acquisition, because Southwark was assessed for
subsidy purposes at £800, more than any other city in England except
London itself.[19] It was promptly incorporated into the administrative
structure of the city as Bridge Ward Without, becoming the twen-
tysixth ward. As such it had an alderman, three deputies and a bailiff,
sixteen constables, a ward mote and precincts, but no common councillors. The reason for that anomaly is not clear, but it remained a
source of grievance to the freemen living there, who felt that they were

18 Andrew Pettegree, *Foreign Protestant Communities in Sixteenth Century
London* (1986), pp. 77–112.
19 John Stow, *A Survey of London* (1603), ed. H.B. Wheatley (1956), pp.
358–374.

being treated as second-class citizens. Like most wards, Southwark continued to have small liberties embedded within it, which is why the early theatres were built there, when the city government was becoming increasingly Puritanical. In the late sixteenth and early seventeenth centuries a number of brothels were located there for the same reason.

London was *sui generis* as far as England was concerned. Its lord mayor was almost invariably knighted by the monarch, and its aldermen were as rich as the richest peers. It provided the government with money, with credit, and with financial advice. Its members of parliament formed a persistent and skilful lobby, and it pioneered the provision of hospitals and workhouses in advance of national policy.[20] Both foreign and religious policies were moulded by its needs and loudly expressed opinions. The only Tudor government which did not have an obvious rapport with the city was that of Mary, which burned a large number of humble citizens at Smithfield. But even in that case the estrangement should not be exaggerated. London formed the model to which other cities aspired: rich, self-confident, and increasingly dominated by a narrow oligarchy of elite families. And when the government of Charles I began to break down, one of the most disastrous things he did was to lose control of the city when the ruling elite divided.[21]

County Boroughs: Norwich

Norwich was not the first city outside London to be granted county status. It was preceded by Bristol, York and Newcastle upon Tyne. However, by the sixteenth century it was the second largest city in England, and often the first to adopt measures of economic and social reform. It had received a new charter from Henry IV in 1404, replacing the existing four bailiffs with a mayor and two sheriffs. According to Hudson and Tingey: 'Norwich passed from the condition of a self governing community, each member of which had

---

20 W.K. Jordan, *Philanthropy in England, 1480–1640* (1959). For the petition of the City of London to Edward VI for the grant of Bridewell, see Thomas Bowen, *Extracts from the Records and Court Books of Bridewell Hospital* (1798), App., pp. 2–6.

21 Pearl, *London on the outbreak of the Puritan Revolution*, pp. 276-7. Ashton, *City and Court*, pp. 202–21.

theoretically an equal voice in the government and administration, into a community under the control of a (practically) permanent magistracy, combined for legislative purposes with a limited number of elected representatives.'[22]

The bailiffs had been directly elected by all the freemen in a Great Assembly, but the constitution introduced in 1404 and elaborated over the following decades was a good deal more complicated. As in London, freedom of the city was obtained through a chartered company or guild, which could be joined by patrimony, apprenticeship or redemption. That pattern seems to have been followed in all towns, great or small. All officers had to be freemen, but the guilds do not appear to have played any other part in the constitutional structure of the city. There were four wards, originally called leets, which were divided at first into ten and after 1447 into twelve subleets, equivalent to the London precincts. By the charter of 1404 each ward was to elect six '*probi homines*' who were to form the mayor's council, which was the governing body of the city. How the mayor was originally chosen, whether by the Great Assembly or by the '*probi homines*', is not clear, but the system obviously did not work, because in 1414 a form of electoral college was established. The mayor and his council then chose one man from each leet, or ward, who in turn nominated nineteen other freeman, and the whole eighty 'leet men' then elected the mayor. At this stage the 'leet men' also chose one of the two sheriffs, the *probi homines* selecting the other.

By 1500 a lot of this had changed. After 1417 the *probi homines* were renamed aldermen, and the indirect method of choosing the leet men was abandoned in favour of normal ward elections. The eighty were reduced to sixty common councillors, chosen by the freemen, and the mayor was elected by the aldermen and Common Council. One sheriff was chosen by the mayor and aldermen, the other by the Common Council. As in London, it appears that the Common Council, aldermen and officers all sat together when the council was convened, but voted separately, and the aldermen met much more frequently. Customs of seniority seem to have been observed in the selection of mayors, but there is no record of any formal property qualification for the status of alderman. By the original charter the mayor and four of the *probi homines* formed the commission of the peace, and that principle was adhered to although the number increased. Unlike London,

22   W. Hudson and J.C. Tingey, *The Records of the City of Norwich* (1906), p. lviii.

however, Norwich remained subject to visitation by the commissions of gaol delivery and oyer and terminer appointed for Norfolk. The city court for civil pleas was convened by the sheriffs, and there was a piepowder court for market disputes, which acted on the findings of the clerk of the market. It was this official who impinged most directly upon the daily lives of the citizens. In 1564 his inquest reported, among other things, that 'the comon berebrewers viz Thomas Narford [and eight others] brewe bere not holsome for mannes body . . . [and] the fysshemongers viz Mr. Warden Alderman [and eight others] do sell their ffysshe not well wateryd.'[23] However powerful the city elite, they were clearly not immune to criticism!

The mayor was *ex officio* escheator, and the city was additionally served by a coroner, recorder and treasurer or chamberlain. Sixteen constables served the four wards, half chosen by the mayor and aldermen, and half by the common councillors of the wards. As befitted a city of substance, the chief officers were assisted by a large number of functionaries – mayors sergeants, sheriffs' sergeants, under-sheriffs, and attornies. As in other cities, each craft or mystery had its own master and wardens, who were responsible for the discipline and economic activity of its members, and for assessing those members for purposes of national or local taxation. When necessary, Norwich was mustered by its own mayor and aldermen rather than by special commission, but this exemption did not, apparently, apply to the later jurisdiction of the lord lieutenant, and in spite of protests, the corporation was expected to pull its weight, particularly when Lord Hunsdon held the lieutenancy. In order to avoid conflict, the mayor and aldermen sometimes went out of their way to demonstrate their willingness to fulfil their military duties. In 1588 (admittedly no ordinary year) they purchased a hundred pikes, thirty-two corselets, twelve swords and an undisclosed number of muskets for £130, exclusive of the cost of carriage. They also fitted out their trained band contingent with uniforms at the city's expense. Norfolk had certified 2,096 trained men in 1584, so the city company probably numbered between 200 and 300.[24]

Just as London temporarily earned itself the royal disfavour over the Evil May Day riots, so did Norwich over its failure to stand up to Robert Kett. Kett's great camp on Mousehold Heath, which swept in

23 Ibid., pp. 181–2.
24 PRO SP12/173/99; L.O. Boynton, *The Elizabethan Militia, 1558–1638* (1967), pp. 157–8.

malcontents from all over East Anglia, attracted a good deal of sympathy among the humbler citizens, and the city authorities, which were not at all sympathetic, had no means to resist. For several weeks there was a sort of undeclared truce between the city and the camp, each hoping that time would bring a solution to the dilemma. Finally, on 21 July, negotiations having failed, the rebels took the city by force. Guns were fired and there was a considerable show of violence, but there were no recorded casualties and very little damage, so that the mayor subsequently had some difficulty in convincing the council that he had not connived at the takeover. A fortnight later, when the marquis of Northampton arrived with a small royal army, he was lured into the city, by then firmly in rebel hands, and routed. It was only the arrival of the earl of Warwick later in August, with a more substantial force, which finally defeated the rebellion. The city put on a convincing show of rejoicing, and Warwick attended a thanksgiving service at the church of St Peter Mancroft; but doubts lingered, and subsequent mayors went out of their way to be severe on those who showed any enthusiasm for the 'camping summer', or any marked animosity to the gentlemen.[25]

Norwich seems to have had an enlightened attitude, both to the problem of poor relief and to the communities of foreign craftsworkers who chose it as a refuge after 1558. In 1570 a careful census was taken of all the city's poor, listing the name, age and circumstances of those who might be considered deserving. John Hubburd of St Stephens ward was described as 'of the age of 38 years, butcher, that occupie slaughterie, and Margarit his wyfe, of the age of 30 years that sell souce, and 2 young children, and have dwelt here ever. *No alums. veri pore.*' There were forty-one such entries for St Stephens ward alone.[26] The following year a comprehensive set of regulations was drawn up by Mayor John Aldrich and his brethren. Estimating that there were upwards of 2,000 indigent people in the city, about 15 per cent of the population, they proceeded to forbid all begging, and all giving of casual alms. A Bridewell or workhouse was established 'at the Normans', where a limited number of the able-bodied could be provided with work, and careful regulations were drawn up for its government. A hospital was set up in St Giles to care for the sick, and apprenticeship schemes created for poor children. Finally deacons

25   Norwich Municipal Archives, depositions taken before the mayor and aldermen, 1549–67; Tawney and Power, *Tudor Economic Documents*, I, pp. 47–53.
26   Hudson and Tingey, *Records*, II, pp. 339–58.

were appointed for every ward, to keep a register of those deserving of relief, and to collect and distribute the alms of the citizens fairly and equitably. 'Sturdy beggars' – those unwilling to work and unworthy of relief – were inevitably to be punished, and every effort made to get them out of town.[27] This was not the first such scheme – London had already pioneered one in the 1550s – but it was in advance of government thinking, and of most other towns.

The principal 'stranger' community, of Flemish weavers, was actually invited to Norwich in 1564. Thomas Sotherton, the mayor, and his aldermen, 'by reason that the comodities of woorsted makynge is greatelye decayed', and many weavers and others in the city were out of work, took note of the fact that 'dyverse strangers of the Lowe Countryes' had arrived in London. These strangers were refugees 'ageynste the persecution then raysed agaynste them by the power of the Duke Alva', and had obtained licence from the queen to 'exercize the makynge of Flaunders comodityes made of woolle'. Sotherton, with unusually enlightened self-interest, decided that it would be in the city's interest to play host to some of these strangers, in return for instruction in the arts of making their more marketable forms of cloth. Motion was therefore made to Thomas 'then Duke of Norfolke, then lodged at his house in this citie', asking him to obtain from the queen permission for thirty master craftmen to come to Norwich for that purpose, with their families and a limited number of servants.[28] The experiment was a success. Both parties seem to have benefited, the notorious xenophobia of the English being overcome, partly by religious sympathy and partly by the obvious advantages of the arrangement. In August 1567 one of those who had come, Clais van Wervekin, a hat maker, sent for his wife and family (then in Ypres) in tones which can only be described as enthusiastic: 'You would never believe how friendly the people are together, and the English are the same and quite loving to our nation. If you come here with half our property, you would never think of going to live in Flanders. Send my money and the three children. Come at once and do not be anxious'[29] There were problems; he could not find a dough trough, and there was no fresh butter in England; but as another refugee wrote, 'it was very dear to hear the word of God peacefully'.

27 Ibid.
28 Ibid., p. 332.
29 H.Q. Janssen, *De Hervormde vlugtelingen van Ypren in Engeland* (1857), trans. W.J.C. Moens; Tawney and Power, *Tudor Economic Documents*, I, p. 299.

Like the Huguenots later, these skilled craftsmen made an economic contribution out of all proportion to their numbers, and it is unlikely that Sotherton, or any of his successors, had occasion to regret their initiative.

As in London, there were ecclesiastical enclaves in Norwich, left by the dissolution of the religious houses, but they do not seem to have caused serious problems, and with over fifty parishes in the city it was not difficult for the strangers to find a place of worship, for as long as they needed one. The main jurisdictional problem was caused by the cathedral – first the priory and after 1541 the dean and chapter. Like all ecclesiastical corporations, they were extremely jealous of their rights and privileges, and demarcation disputes with the city were endless. Norwich was not alone in this. London had similar trouble with St Paul's, and every cathedral city in England could show a complex history of disputes. Given the territoriality of the church, and the fact that the precincts were always in the heart of the towns, this was not surprising.[30] Oxford and Cambridge had the same trouble with their universities, and indeed after 1541 Oxford had both a cathedral and a university, but that was a unique arrangement.

SMALL TOWNS: RETFORD IN NOTTINGHAMSHIRE

The majority of chartered boroughs were very small. Only some seventy-five or eighty English towns had populations of more than 2,000, and there were nearly 200 boroughs, most of which would have to be classed as 'small market centres'. There were over 700 such centres, with between 1,000 and 2,000 inhabitants. They had no great merchants, and very little interest in international trade, but they enjoyed extensive powers of self-government, and collectively formed an important estate of the realm. Retford, situated near the confluence of the Idle and the Trent, and close to the Great North Road, was such a place. It consisted of two parishes, east and west, with a combined population which varied between 1,000 and 1,500 during the late sixteenth and early seventeenth centuries. Strictly

---

30   J.F. Williams and B. Cozens-Hardy, *Extracts from the Two Earliest Minute Books of the Dean and Chapter of Norwich Cathedral* (Norfolk Records Society, xxiv, 1953).

speaking, only East Retford was a borough, and burgess rights were confined to those who lived there; so during this period the borough proper seldom had more than about 800 residents, of whom some eighty were freemen, in whose hands the government of the whole town resided. The people of West Retford, like those of Southwark and with better reason, felt themselves to be second-class citizens, with little or no say in their own affairs. There were some half dozen guilds in the town, and freedom came through them, as in every other town, by patrimony, apprenticeship or redemption. However, unlike London's, the Retford authorities were anxious to encourage freedom by redemption, and in 1608 the maximum rate was fixed at £1 6s 0d. East Retford had originally been a royal manor, and its privileges had been granted piecemeal in a jigsaw of medieval charters, which were summarized and confirmed by Elizabeth in 1562. The original charter had been issued in 1279, constituting East Retford 'a free town of itself', and granting the fee farm of the borough to the bailiffs and burgesses for £10 a year, a rental which was still being scrupulously paid in the early seventeenth century.[31] As usual, the burgesses enjoyed a monopoly of trade within the town, and were also granted exemption from 'toll, pannage or murage' anywhere in England, as a sign that they had now joined the urban estate. However, it was not until 1571 that the parliamentary franchise was added, and Retford could consider itself to be a borough in the full sense.

It had been laid down in the original charter that the burgesses should assemble at the Moothall on Michaelmas Day, 29 September, to elect their bailiffs, and that practice continued throughout the Tudor period. The only formal qualification for this office was the status of freeman, but in practice candidature tended to be limited to a small number of the most prominent and wealthy families. There were normally two bailiffs, elected for a year at a time, but at times during the sixteenth century there appear to have been three. No reason for this was recorded, and the third may possibly have been a locum, to cover a period of absence or illness. Two chamberlains were elected at the same time, who also had to be burgesses, and these four officers held the keys to the town treasury. The council of the town consisted of twelve burgesses, who were also elected by the annual

31   D. Marcombe, *English Small Town Life: Retford, 1520–1642* (1993), pp. 32–40.

general assembly, in theory for one year, but in practice for as long as they were willing. The wardens of the town companies were also *ex officio* members of the council. The bailiffs, chamberlains and councillors together formed the Court of Orders, and this body was the effective government of the town. It was an open and relatively egalitarian system, and the problem seems to have been difficulty in finding enough men who were able and willing to discharge the various offices, rather than restricting access to the ruling elite. However, open systems also led to disputes, and it was as a result of one such quarrel that the twelve councillors were reclassified as aldermen in 1600, and a process set in train for the obtaining of a new charter.[32]

When it was finally sealed on 25 November 1607, this charter changed a number of traditional practices. The government was now placed in the hands of the twelve aldermen. In the first instance these were to be elected by the burgesses, but they were to retain office for life, and when replacements were needed, they would be co-opted by the existing aldermen from two nominations submitted by the assembly of freemen. This change seems to have been intended to prevent factious attempts to unseat councillors in the interests of particular interest groups. There were to be two bailiffs, as before, but the senior was now to be chosen by the aldermen, and the junior by the Common Council (which was the aldermen plus the officers) from two names submitted by the burgesses. The junior bailiff was the only member of the Common Council who could not be an Alderman. The two chamberlains were also retained, although they were now to serve for two years, and again to be chosen by the Common Council from names submitted by the freemen, whose annual assembly was renamed the Common Hall, perhaps in imitation of the metropolis. The end result of these changes was to reduce the role of the freemen, and to make the constitution much more oligarchic. This was declared to be in the interests of stability and continuity, and, given that the burgess body was so small, may have made little practical difference until the population began to grow significantly in the later seventeenth century.

The Court of Orders had met quarterly, but it seems that the Common Council under the new charter was much more frequently in session, and may have been significantly more efficient. There were also a number of permanent officials, who were servants of the town

32   Ibid., p. 38.

government rather than part of it: a high steward, a recorder, a deputy steward or town clerk, and several constables. The high steward was invariably a local gentleman, and normally one of the town's two members of parliament. His role was that of sponsor or promoter, to defend the town's interests at the county level, or in the House of Commons if necessary. The recorder was a lawyer who, under the old charter, was mainly a legal adviser because the town had no sessions of its own. The deputy steward held a leet court, which dealt with minor offences under the common law, and a baron court, which was the 'business' court of the town, dealing with commercial disputes, market rates and similar related matters under a customary code. The county Quarter Sessions met at Retford as a regular part of their itinerary, but the town had no representation upon the commission, except indirectly through the high steward. That was changed by the new charter. The leet and baron courts continued, but after 1607 each bailiff and the recorder were *ex officio* members of the commission of the peace for the duration of their tenure of office. This did not make much difference to the Quarter Sessions, but it did mean that the borough could now have its own Petty Sessions, and that eventually spelled the end of the leet court, which covered much of the same ground.

The town derived its income partly from market dues, and partly from the management of property. Its main regular expenditure was the £10 a year to the king for the fee farm, but there was a good deal of occasional spending, much of it connected with the promotion of petitions or lawsuits in which the town was involved. Litigation, in particular, was an expensive business. The Court of Orders received payments for burgess admissions, and received half of any fines levied by the town companies for misdemeanours. The profits of the leet and baron courts were also received by the town. Commercial profits were derived from the town mills, which, like the lords' mills of an earlier age, had a monopoly of local custom. There were also three annual fairs and a regular Saturday market. The fairs attracted traders from a considerable distance, and although the burgesses were entitled to one stand free, they were required to pay if they wanted more than one, an unpopular situation which several attempted to dispute. The town estate was substantial, although whether this had originated in entrepreneurial policy, or in attempts to prevent property from becoming derelict, is not clear. In 1530 the Common Council controlled thirteen houses in Retford itself, and forty-eight acres of land in the neighbouring parishes of Clarborough and Ordsall.[33] Later in the century the town's responsibilities became more complicated, if not more profitable. In 1551 a grammar school was founded in the town, and the council was given the management of the endowment. This was a fruitful source of later disputes. Their were also almshouses, again with their own charitable trust, which involved the appointment of a warden, and the allocation of the vacancies as they arose. Finally, there was the Moothall itself. This was the centre of civic life, where the rituals of local power were performed, and where the courts convened. Unlike many towns, Retford did not find the need to rebuild or extend its Moothall in this period. Although the constitution of the town changed, as we have seen, the size of the governing body remained about the same, so although the Common Hall, with 80–100 members, must have met elsewhere, the existing building remained adequate for the Common Council. Repairs and maintenance seem to have been absorbed by the ordinary budget.

There was no question of Retford being mustered separately. With under 100 freemen for most of the period, its trained band company would have numbered no more than a dozen men, which put it on a par with many rural parishes. Nonetheless, money was needed for equipment, as well as for poor relief and other social purposes for which ordinary income would not have been adequate. David Marcombe, in his study of Retford, says that the levying of borough taxes was 'very rare', and in so far as he is talking about formal assessments made by the Common Council, that is no doubt correct. However, some voluntary contributions are more voluntary than others, and the principle of local taxation was generally accepted by borough authorities. The city fathers of Oxford acknowledged this explicitly in 1608:

> We think it lawful and reasonable to use taxation of the citizens for any such purpose, if need be. And for relief of all such as are visited with the plague, and for watching to keep them in their houses or other places where they are removed, we use taxation of freemen and all inhabitants towards their relief and keeping.[34]

Retford was not particularly afflicted by plague, and unlike larger towns does not seem to have had a serious unemployment problem. As a market centre, it was not heavily dependent upon a single trade

33   Ibid., p. 39.
34   Cited in ibid., p. 37.

or craft, and was therefore protected to some extent from the trade cycle. Moreover, it was not large enough, or rich enough, to be attractive to wandering vagabonds. Unlike a city the size of Norwich, let alone London, it was relatively easy for the councillors and constables to know their own poor, and to take appropriate steps to remove those who did not belong. A good example of this survives from the neighbouring village of Southcley in the wapentake of Bassetlawe, where one Nicholas Powtrell, justice of the peace, conducted a blitz in 1571. A total of twenty-three 'valiant beggars' were detected, twelve of them women, of whom Johane Holmes may be taken as typical. She was 'taken at Normanton as a valiant beggar, examined before me and whipped, punnisshed and stocked and sent from Constable to Constable the directe waie to Faresley in the Countie of Warrwyk, where she last dwelled by the space of three yeres and more together.'[35] Some of those taken in this visitation came from as far away as Cumberland and Westmorland. Until 1607 the bailiffs of Retford would have had to get a friendly JP to perform this service for them. After 1607, they could do it for themselves.

Retford was a far more typical town than either Norwich or London. It had no wards or other subdivisions, and its guilds were on a truly domestic scale. It suffered no major catastrophe and received no large-scale immigration. The population grew somewhat erratically, with a significant setback during the hard times of the 1590s, and its constitution went through a series of developments, indicating changes in the perception of what constituted a borough. None of its burgesses had the substance to represent it in parliament, where it was regularly served by members of gentry families which had developed some connections with the town. The two parish churches, St Swithuns and St Nicholas, lost minor endowments at the time of the dissolution of the chantries in 1547, and some of that property found its way into the hands of the municipality, but as a royal borough with no priory or friary within its boundaries, it was relatively unaffected by the disappearance of the monasteries. Like every such community, it was riven with disputes and periodically divided by faction, the fortunes of which constitute most of its recorded history. It was an important place in that corner of Nottinghamshire, but almost unnoticed in the records of central government.

Individual towns were more important economically and locally than they were politically and nationally, but collectively they enjoyed

35   PRO SP12/80/27.

considerable muscle. Although government continued to be
conducted largely by the landed aristocracy, the contribution of the
urban elites to taxation, and the substantial urban representation in
the House of Commons, gave them an influence disproportionate to
their numbers.

5

The Church

There were a number of dramatic changes in the constitutional structure of the English church between 1530 and 1550. Recognition of the royal supremacy not only exposed the *sacerdotium* to parliamentary legislation in unprecedented ways, it also removed the legislative autonomy hitherto enjoyed by the provincial assemblies, or Convocations. The dissolution of the monasteries between 1536 and 1540 destroyed the whole jurisdictional estate of the regular clergy. The appointment of Thomas Cromwell as vicegerent in spirituals was not repeated, but after 1558 the crown issued ecclesiastical commissions on both a diocesan and a provincial basis, and the High Commission of the province of Canterbury became a major conciliar court by the end of the century. The creation of what was effectively a department of state for ecclesiastical affairs made the crown in parliament the ultimate arbiter of ecclesiastical discipline, liturgy and doctrine. This had the effect of making loyalty to the church and loyalty to the state indistinguishable, which was both an asset and a liability to the monarch. It was an asset in so far as orthodox clergy could be relied upon to support and promote royal policy; but a liability when conscientious objections to religious policy were perceived as political disaffection. Queen Mary's council was not alone in declaring heresy and treason to be synonymous. However, the royal supremacy also had another, and quite different, effect. Because all the Tudors, with the possible exception of Edward VI, were conservative by instinct, they preserved the provincial and diocesan structure intact. Cathedral chapters, and episcopal and archidiaconal courts – objects of strong attack by advanced reformers – were retained. The Elizabethan church was a unique hybrid; reformed in doctrine and liturgy, it retained many of its Catholic institutions, and even continued to use the remnants of the Roman canon law, because no agreement could be reached as to how to reform it.[1]

PROVINCES AND DIOCESES

Jurisdictionally speaking, there was no such thing as the *Ecclesia Anglicana*. Since the end of the ninth century there had been two archbishoprics, at Canterbury and York. For many years precedence between the two had been disputed. Canterbury had attempted to extend its jurisdiction to Ireland, and even to Scandinavia, while York sought to obtain control over Scotland, but by the fifteenth century all these expansionist ambitions had been defeated.[2] At one time the sees of Lincoln, Worcester and Lichfield had been claimed by York, but these claims had also failed by the end of the twelfth century. In 1485 the province of York consisted of the vast but thinly populated diocese of York itself, and the two much smaller border sees of Durham and Carlisle. In 1541 the new diocese of Chester was created out of parts of the existing sees of York and Coventry and Lichfield, and at first assigned to Canterbury. However, Henry VIII rapidly changed his mind, and the statute of 33 Henry VIII c.31 assigned Chester to the province of York, along with the English half of the problematic see of Sodor and Man. Canterbury was always much larger. In 1485 it controlled thirteen English bishoprics, apart from the see of Canterbury itself, and the four bishoprics of Wales.[3] The reorganization of 1541 created five new sees within the province – Peterborough, Oxford, Gloucester, Bristol and Westminster – but all these were divisions of existing dioceses, and did not result in any expansion of the archbishop's jurisdiction. Indeed, Canterbury was actually somewhat reduced by losing the former deanery of Chester.

The greater extent, and much greater population and wealth, of the southern province had led to claims of jurisdictional supremacy as

1   C. Cross, *The Royal Supremacy in the Elizabethan Church* (1969); P. Collinson, *The Religion of Protestants: the church in English society, 1559–1625* (1982); J.C. Spalding, *The Reformation of the Ecclesiastical Laws of England, 1552* (1992).
2   N. Brooks, *The Early History of the Church of Canterbury: Christ Church from 597 to 1066* (1984); Felix Makower, *The Constitutional History of the Church of England* (1895), pp. 46–7.
3   *Handbook of British Chronology*, eds E.B. Fryde, D.E. Greenway, S. Porter and I. Roy (1986), pp. 225–7.

early as the eleventh century. In 1109 Archbishop Thomas of York was constrained by Henry I to take an oath of obedience to Canterbury at his consecration, a circumstance perhaps brought about by the fact that Anselm (archbishop 1093–1109) had recently died, and the temporalities of the province were in the king's hands at the time. Subsequent archbishops of York rejected the precedent, and the dispute went backwards and forwards between England and the papal *Curia* throughout the remainder of the century.[4] By the beginning of the thirteenth century it appeared that Canterbury had won by securing regular legatine status for its incumbents. However, after the consecration of John of Thoresby to York in 1352 it became normal for the northern archbishops also to hold that rank, and in an agreement reached soon afterwards each accepted the equal jurisdictional status of the other, a precedence of honour being conceded to Canterbury which in practice meant very little.[5] In 1515 Thomas Wolsey, newly consecrated to York and not yet a cardinal, deliberately had his cross borne before him in the presence of Archbishop Warham of Canterbury, a slight which was much resented, but condoned by the king's particular favour. However, the late medieval position depended upon both archbishops holding what was in effect an *ex officio* legatine status. When Wolsey was appointed legate *a latere* in 1518 that situation was changed, and for the remainder of his incumbency the normal relationship of the two provinces was reversed. That conferred few benefits on York, which he never visited, but inhibited Canterbury's freedom of action for over a decade, when concern about heretical challenges was rising and the king's Great Matter was coming to the surface.

After 1534 legatine status of all kinds disappeared, but the preeminence of Canterbury was implicitly confirmed by the statute of 25 Henry VIII c. 21, which conferred upon that archbishop the right to issue dispensations, licences and faculties (hitherto received from the pope) for both provinces. Canterbury also continued to claim by ancient prescription the right to crown the monarchs of England, a custom of which Cranmer reminded Edward VI in 1547.[6] However, this meant very little until the following century. Mary was crowned

---

4 J.P. Migne, *Patrologia Latina*, (1841–64) vol. 150, p. 184; Makower, *Constitutional History*, pp. 284–6.
5 D. Wilkins, *Concilia Magnae Britanniae et Hiberniae*, (1737) III, p. 31.
6 'The bishops of Canterbury for the most part have crowned your predecessors, and annointed them kings of this land': J.E. Cox (ed.), *Cranmer's Miscellaneous Writings* (Parker Society, 1846), p. 126.

by Stephen Gardiner of Winchester because Cranmer was in prison on a charge of treason; and Elizabeth was crowned by Owen Oglethorpe of Carlisle, Canterbury being vacant and no other bishop willing to act. Between 1554 and 1558 the ancient constitution was briefly restored. When Reginald Pole returned to England in November 1554 Canterbury was vacant, and his authority as legate *a latere* gave him jurisdictional control over the whole English church, although he held no English benefice, and was not at that time in priest's orders. Since York was also vacant from March 1554 to June 1555, no challenge could come from that quarter, and Pole's authority was not questioned. Although Cranmer had been deprived in November 1553, Pole was extremely scrupulous about accepting appointment as his successor, and was not consecrated until the day after Cranmer's execution, on the 22 March 1556.[7] When his legatine powers were withdrawn by Pope Paul IV in June 1557, he continued to govern the English church as Archbishop of Canterbury, without challenge from the irenic Nicholas Heath of York. By dying on the same day as Mary, 11 November 1558, he saved Elizabeth the trouble of depriving him. With him died the last exercise of papal jurisdiction in England until the nineteenth century.

Apart from Pole, Cranmer was the last English archbishop to receive the pallium from Rome as the symbol of his metropolitan power, but in most respects the establishment of the royal supremacy did not greatly affect the manner in which the archbishops conducted themselves. Each had the power to visit the dioceses within his province, suspending the jurisdiction of the bishops, either generally or particularly, while he did so. Each might also have his own jurisdiction suspended for the purpose of a royal visitation, such as that conducted by Thomas Cromwell as vicegerent in 1536. This was an innovation, but not different in principle from the Legatine visitations which had been conducted in the past, and which had been carried out by Wolsey in the 1520s. The metropolitans did not appoint diocesan bishops, and never had done. In theory all bishops and arch-bishops were elected by the secular chapters or monastic bodies which served their cathedral churches. In practice they were nominated by the king and confirmed by the pope. After 1534 they were appointed by a process known as the *congé d'élire*, whereby the king directed his letters to the relevant chapter, giving them permission to elect his nominee. This rather elaborate fiction was replaced during the

7   D.M. Loades, *The Reign of Mary Tudor* (1991), p. 296.

reign of Edward VI by straightforward letters patent, but when Elizabeth restored the Edwardian settlement this sensible reform was dropped, and the *congé d'élire* was restored.[8] During the Tudor period neither archbishop had any formal right to be consulted about episcopal appointments within his province, but informal consultations appear to have been frequent, apart from the first twenty-five years of Elizabeth's reign, when neither metropolitan was a member of the Privy Council. During episcopal vacancies the crown controlled the temporalities of the vacant see, and the archbishop was responsible for exercising the spiritual jurisdiction.

Each province had a synod or assembly of clergy called the Convocation, and a number of provincial courts. The Convocations were divided into two houses, the bishops sitting in the upper, and the proctors or representatives of the other clergy in the lower. As we have seen, clergy were barred from the lower House of Parliament on the grounds that their voice should be heard here. Until 1532 each Convocation had made its own canons, or by-laws, without reference to any outside authority, but in that year the Convocations agreed to submit all future canons for the king's approval, and their legislative function thereafter declined. Apart from voting grants of clerical taxation, these assemblies achieved little after 1534. The prayer books of 1549 and 1552 were approved by parliament without reference to the convocations; and the lower house of Canterbury reaffirmed its loyalty to the mass and the papal jurisdiction only weeks before both were abolished by parliament in 1559.[9] In theory each archbishop had the power to convene his Convocation whenever he pleased, but by long-standing custom it met at the same time as the secular parliament, and that custom was respected throughout the sixteenth century. In theory too the provincial assemblies enjoyed equal status, but the reality of their relationship is reflected in the fact that, when the clergy as a whole purchased a pardon for *praemunire* in 1531, Canterbury was assessed at £100,000 and York at £18,000. By the later sixteenth century the York Convocation was little more than an echo of its southern neighbour, and neither had any influence over the ecclesiastical policy of the crown. Both in 1563 and in 1566, Puritan activists endeavoured to use the Canterbury Convocation to put pressure on

---

8 1 Elizabeth, c. 1; *Statutes of the Realm*, eds A. Luders et al. (1810–28), IV, pp. 350–55.
9 Wilkins, *Concilia*, IV, p. 179; P. Hughes, *The Reformation in England*, III (1954), pp. 22–3.

the queen over vestments and other traditional usages of which they disapproved. Their efforts were narrowly frustrated, but even if they had succeeded they had no power to make their pressure effective.[10]

In respect of pleas, the clerical estate had for a long time enjoyed special privileges. In 1136 a charter of King Stephen had decreed that any man in holy orders, no matter how humble, should be called to answer for his offences only in the ecclesiastical courts.[11] That charter was deemed to have lapsed with Stephen's death, and the degree of immunity enjoyed thereafter was uncertain in law, and fluctuated somewhat in practice. However, by the end of the twelfth century it was accepted in principle that pleas of the crown affecting the person of a man in orders could be heard only in an ecclesiastical court, although an offender might be convened before a secular court in order to establish his clerical status. In spite of considerable resentment on the part of the laity, the regular need of the crown for ecclesiastical support, especially in the fifteenth century, had ensured that these privileges tended to increase rather than diminish. Because the ecclesiastical courts administered the canon law and not the common law, they could not touch life, member or real property. Their penalties were consequently confined to imprisonment, fine or loss of preferment, even in cases of treason or felony for which a layman would die. Misdemeanours for which a layman might have been whipped or mutilated usually resulted in spiritual penalties, such as penance, or temporary residence in a selected monastery. Since from the middle of the thirteenth century it was accepted that the ability to read was an adequate test of clerical status, by 1485 there was in effect one law for the literate and another for the rest.

However, the situation was never as straightforward as this might imply. Breach of the forest laws, for example, or the witholding of feudal obligations, had never been subject to benefit of clergy, and by a statute of 1332 treason directly against the king's person was also exempt. Moreover for any capital offence, degradation from orders was automatic, and consequently anyone reoffending was treated as a layman.[12] Nor was the reading test of universal application. By the fourteenth century it was normal for both men and women of the noble and gentry class to be literate, and similarly for the growing body

10   R.W. Dixon, *History of the Church of England* (1902), V, pp. 382–4; P. Collinson, *The Elizabethan Puritan Movement* (1967), pp. 34, 65–6, 74.
11   Makower, *Constitutional History*, App. 2.
12   Ibid., pp. 399–406.

of merchants. Such people, who were notoriously not clergy, did not by custom attempt to claim the privilege. Nevertheless the growth of lay literacy after the introduction of printing in the 1470s, and the good relations which the Tudors at first enjoyed with Rome, encouraged both Henry VII and Henry VIII to commence the reduction of clerical immunities. Statutes in 1489, 1491 and 1497 sharply curtailed the privileges of those in minor orders, that is below the grade of subdeacon – a troublesome clerical proletariat who were almost as great an embarrassment to the church as they were a nuisance to the state.[13] In party pleas, by contrast, the clergy had never enjoyed any special status, in spite of repeated attempts to obtain it. The common law was never more tenacious than in its claim to unique jurisdiction over property.

Apart from dealing with pleas of the crown in respect of clerical persons, the ecclesiastical courts had proper jurisdiction over a wide range of issues. Some of these were sufficiently obvious: heresy, simony, sacrilege, *defamatio*, and the refusal to pay church dues or tithes. Others were less obvious, but of greater social importance: matrimony (including all issues of sexual morality), usury, probate of wills (including intestacy), bastardy, issues of advowson and patronage, and above all contract, where any oath had been given. It was this very high level of social usefulness which protected the ecclesiastical courts from the most disruptive effects of the Reformation. However recalcitrant the laity may have become to the whole notion of ecclesiastical discipline, society simply could not function without means to resolve disputes of this nature. Radical Protestants were openly contemptuous of such jurisdiction by the end of the sixteenth century, referring to the archidiaconal tribunals as the 'bawdy courts', but as the crown would never permit the introduction of congregational self-discipline on the reformed model, and refused to assume responsibility for routine ecclesiastical jurisdiction, the traditional courts continued to be indispensable.

Apart from a few years under Edward VI when they operated in the name of the king, the ecclesiastical courts continued to function in the name of the relevant archbishop or bishop, suggesting an autonomy of jurisdiction which in fact had long since departed. After 1534 parliament assumed the right to legislate on all eccelesiastical affairs, and the church courts enforced relevant statutes in addition to

13   4 Henry VII, c. 13; 7 Henry VII, c. 1; 12 Henry VII, c. 7; S.B. Chrimes, *Henry VII* (1972), pp. 243–4.

the traditional canon law. The main problem with these courts was that their teeth had become very blunt. They could fine or imprison laymen, as they could clergy, but imprisonment was not a realistic option in the face of widespread defiance, and enforcing fines could be a matter of great difficulty. The spiritual penalties of penance and excommunication, which had been reasonably effective in enforcing compliance before 1500, lost most of their force during the Reformation. The former disappeared with the Catholic sacramental system, and the latter was no longer taken seriously by lay society. Exclusion from the sacrament itself might trouble individual consciences, but it did not affect the salvation of a conscientious Protestant, and the social ostracism which was supposed to accompany it very seldom did. Excommunication, like outlawry, had become a paper tiger. This problem was partly answered during the reign of Elizabeth by the establishment of the ecclesiastical commissions, which carried rather larger guns, but the main function of all such courts after the Reformation was the resolution of party disputes rather than the imposition of discipline.[14]

Apart from the overriding jurisdiction of the crown, the archbishops were the summit of this pyramid. Each province had an appeal court, presided over by an official principal, which heard cases appealed from the episcopal courts, or occasionally from other courts within the province. It was also possible for these courts to take original cognizance, in cases where the judge of a lower court referred it by letters of request. In the province of York this institution was called the Chancery Court, and was presided over by the archbishop's auditor; in Canterbury it was called the Court of Arches, and was conducted by the dean of the arches. The Arches Court was so called because it originally sat in the church of *Sancta Maria de arcubus* (St Mary-at-Bowe), which was a Canterbury peculiar within the diocese of London. Canterbury (but not York) also had from 1534 a Court of Faculties, established to exercise the powers conferred upon the archbishop by the Act 25 Henry VIII, c.21: 'to grant to the king or to his subjects, all such licences, dispensations, compositions, faculties, grants, rescripts, delegacies, or any other instruments or writings, as before had been obtained by the king or his subjects from [Rome]'.[15]

14   R.A. Houlbrooke, *Church Courts and the People during the English Reformation, 1520–1570* (1979); M.J. Ingram, *Church Courts, Sex and Marriage in England, 1570–1640* (1987).
15   *Statutes of the Realm*, eds A. Luders et al. (1810–28) III, pp. 464–71.

This function, which was withdrawn by Mary and restored by Elizabeth, covered such matters as licences to marry without banns, or to hold benefices in plurality. The jurisdiction of this court, which could be extended to new licences by the authority of the Privy Council, covered, as we have seen, the whole country.

Each archbishop could exercise his jurisdiction in certain matters personally, without institutional assistance, and this (somewhat paradoxically) was known as his Court of Audience. According to Edward Coke:

> This court is kept by the archbishop in his palace, and medleth not with any matter between party and party of contentious jurisdiction, but dealeth with matters *pro forma*, as confirmations of bishops elections, consecrations and the like, and with matters of voluntary jurisdiction, as the granting of the guardianship of the spiritualities *sede vacante* of bishops, admission and institution to benefices.'[16]

In theory the competence of the Court of Audience was the same as that of the Appeal Court, but the practice appears to have been rather different. Each province also held a Prerogative court to deal with exceptional testamentary and probate cases. These were usually cases where the testator had left property worth more than £5 in a diocese, or dioceses, other than that in which death had taken place. By the mid-sixteenth century this limit was fairly low and, in spite of the fact that the minimum for the diocese of London was £10, probably brought the majority of gentry wills out of the diocesan and into the provincial jurisdiction. The other category of testator dealt with at that level was the bishops themselves.

In addition to his metropolitan functions, each archbishop was also a diocesan, although in this respect the responsibilities of York far exceeded those of Canterbury. Diocesan bishops were by ancient custom known as ordinaries, a title which signified that the main management functions of the church were normally in their hands. Traditionally, ordinary jurisdiction was both spiritual and temporal, and was consequently conferred by both appointment and consecration. However, in February 1547, following the first demise of the crown since the recognition of the royal supremacy, it was proposed to issue to the bishops fresh commissions in the name of King Edward VI, which clearly implied that their whole authority depended upon

16 Sir Edward Coke, *The Fourth Part of the Institutes* (1644), p. 337.

appointment only. In objecting to the proposed form of words, Stephen Gardiner wrote to Sir William Paget:

> And soo it wold be a marvelous matier, if, after my long service and the losse of my master, I shuld lose that he gave me by construction of a commission; and that I shuld offende in going aboute to doo wel, to see thinges wel by visitacion, and receyving of convictes to my charge as ordinarye, and am but a delegate.'[17]

His objection was ignored at the time, because neither Cranmer nor Somerset believed that consecration was essential to the exercise of episcopal jurisdiction. However, when the Edwardian settlement was restored by Elizabeth, no fresh commissions were issued, and in practice no bishop of the Anglican church, either then or subsequently, exercised his authority without consecration.

A bishop's functions were (and are) of two kinds. On the one hand, he had the same pastoral responsibility as all beneficed clergy to preach and teach, to administer the sacraments and generally to minister to the Christian souls under his care. In addition he had those spiritual functions peculiar to his office: to examine and ordain priests and deacons, and to administer the rite of confirmation. On the other hand, he had what might be broadly called the duties of management in respect of his diocese. One of these was discharged by the process of visitation, which might be conducted either personally or by delegate. In the course of a visitation both the behaviour and the effectiveness of the clergy were assessed, as well as the behaviour of the laity, and the physical condition of churches and precincts. Originally visitations had been intended to be annual, but that had long since proved to be too ambitious, and by the sixteenth century they were normally triennial, often in association with the convening of a diocesan synod. A bishop was also expected to ensure that all the benefices in his diocese were adequately served. If a vacancy occurred in a living which was in his own gift, then he was supposed to proceed at once to collate a new incumbent; if the living was in the hands of a patron, he had to endeavour to ensure that the patron presented promptly, and to institute the person presented without delay. Unsuitable presentations were a constant headache, and might require considerable tact on the bishop's part if the patron was

17   Gardiner to Paget, 1 March 1547; *The Letters of Stephen Gardiner*, ed. J.A. Muller (1933), pp. 268–72.

powerful and opinionated. The bishop also issued licences to incumbents to be absent from their cures for good reason, and ensured that adequate cover had been provided during their absence.

At the same time, every bishop was also a temporal lord, with a substantial estate to administer, and very often a secular position to sustain. In the fifteenth century many bishops controlled large affinities of local gentry, and acted as councillors and officers of state, in addition to serving in the House of Lords.[18] This position changed somewhat after the Reformation, because most episcopal estates were considerably reduced, first by Edward VI and later by Elizabeth. Elizabethan bishops were still peers of the parliament, but their wealth and social status were those of major gentry. With a handful of exceptions they did not hold any secular offices higher than that of justice of the peace, and were in consequence much more likely to reside on their cures. At the time of the *valor ecclesiasticus* in 1535, episcopal revenues had ranged from £3,000 a year at Winchester to £135 a year at Bangor. Seventy years later most of these had been more than halved in real terms, and the late medieval traditions of hospitality and social leadership had been seriously undermined.[19] The reformed church of England had retained its episcopal structure, but the bishops had been 'unlorded', and become in effect ecclesiastical civil servants.

Every diocese had a consistory court, conducted in the bishop's name, although not by himself in person. It was presided over by a judge who normally combined the offices of vicar general and chancellor of the diocese, and who was the bishop's normal agent in daily business and administration. The consistory court was both a court of first instance and a court of appeal from the consistory courts of the archdeaconries, but there was no clear distinction between the types of business which originated at the different levels. It seems to have been largely a matter of local convenience. Unusually, the diocese of Canterbury had no consistory court, but there was a special branch of the Court of Arches, called the Court of Peculiars, to deal with business arising from those parishes within the province which were exempt from normal episcopal jurisdiction. In the early sixteenth century, when many bishops were regularly absent from their sees on public business, the role of the diocesan chancellor was one of power,

---

18 Felicity Heal, *Of Prelates and Princes* (1980), pp. 1–49.
19 *Valor Ecclesiasticus*, eds J.Caley and J. Hunter (1810–34); Heal, *Of Prelates and Princes*, passim.

particularly in the exercise of patronage. However, he was not the bishop's only agent, because an ordinary had the authority *ex officio* to issue commissions to deal with any business, judicial or otherwise, which fell within his own competence. Such commissions had to be specific rather than general, and were usually issued to a single officer. A bishop's spiritual functions were supplemented in his presence, and replaced in his absence, by other men who held episcopal orders, but not episcopal appointments. These assistants had first appeared in the thirteenth century, and usually held notional titles derived from Asiatic or African provinces of the Roman empire, for which reason they were known as bishops *in partibus infidelibus*. By the sixteenth century they were called suffragan bishops, and derived their titles from towns within the dioceses which they served – Berwick, Dover and Thetford, for example. Sixteen or seventeen men served in eleven different sees during the century, so they were an occasional rather than a regular feature of the church.[20] Suffragans, unlike diocesan bishops, were not subject to the *congé d'élire*. By the statute of 26 Henry VIII c. 14 it was laid down that a bishop wishing to appoint a suffragan had to submit two names to the king, who selected one. The successful candidate was then presented to the appropriate archbishop for consecration. Because he held no recognized office his powers were defined by the commission with which his diocesan issued him, and his income consisted of whatever revenues might be assigned for his support (usually a rectory and a prebendal stall in the cathedral of the see). As the public role of the episcopate declined, the need for suffragan assistance also declined, and no further appointments were made after 1592.

CHAPTERS, ARCHDEACONRIES AND DEANERIES

Every diocesan bishop was based at a cathedral church, which had originally been served by a group of priests living collegially as a part of his familia. However, by the tenth century the discipline of these houses was widely believed to have become unsatisfactory, and may in some cases have been so. Reform-minded bishops, such as Oswald of Worcester, began a campaign to replace the secular canons with monks. This pressure was maintained after the conquest by Lanfranc and his successors, and by the time that the monastic movement

20 *Handbook of British Chronology*, pp. 287–8.

began to lose momentum at the end of the twelfth century about half of the nineteen English cathedrals had monastic chapters.[21] In these institutions the bishop was also the abbot, but the effective head of the house was the prior, and the properties and jurisdictions of the bishop and the monastery were distinct. In those cathedrals which retained a secular establishment, however, the situation was more complicated. The head of such a chapter was the dean, who was elected by the members on the king's *congé d'élire* and confirmed by the bishop. The dean was supported by various other officers, such as subdean, treasurer and precentor, who were appointed in theory by the chapter, but in practice usually by the dean. The property of such chapters had originally been held corporately, in accordance with the terms of their charters of foundation. However, these charters were renewed and modified from time to time, and were by no means uniform. By the sixteenth century secular foundations normally held part of their property corporately, while part was allocated individually to the support of the officers and members. These portions were known as prebends and were identified by the parishes in which the lands were situated. Sometimes the prebendary was also the incumbent of the parish, but the revenues of the two positions were distinct. Prebends were usually in the gift of the bishop, but royal or lay patronage was also exercised in some cases. It was normal for the officers of the chapter to reside in the precinct, but collegiate life was minimal by the early sixteenth century. Other prebendaries were not usually resident, and pluralism in such positions was the norm rather than the exception. Each chapter existed to support its bishop, and to provide a modified version of the monastic opus dei (see below, pp. 191–2) as a spiritual focus for the diocese.

Secular chapters, like monasteries, were jurisdictional peculiars, outside the normal structure of deaneries and parishes, and answerable in ecclesiastical matters to the bishop only. In secular matters also they enjoyed certain privileges, and the precincts were normally exempt from the local jurisdiction of the mayor and corporation of the towns in which they were situated. These privileges did not affect pleas of the crown, but they did protect lay servants living in the precinct from controls to which they would otherwise have been subjected, and they formed a regular source of friction with the local community. In addition to the prebendaries, secular cathedrals were also served by clerks, usually in minor orders, whose job it was to sing

21   Makower, *Constitutional History*, pp. 299–300.

the daily offices, and who were called the minor or petty canons. Collegiate institutions of a similar nature also existed in many other churches apart from the secular cathedrals, where the dean, prebendaries and lay clerks were established to sing masses for the souls of deceased patrons.[22] This became a fashionable form of spiritual insurance after the decline of monastic endowments in the early thirteenth century, and cathedral chapters also received some of their revenues in return for performing the same service, but in the latter case such endowments were specifically identified. Colleges were separate from the parishes in which they were situated even when, as often happened, the dean was also the incumbent and they shared the same building.

The Reformation led to many changes. All the cathedral monasteries were dissolved between 1538 and 1540, including the house of regular canons which uniquely served Carlisle. The double sees of Bath and Wells and of Coventry and Lichfield, which had had both secular and monastic cathedrals, lost the latter, at Bath and Coventry. In their place new secular chapters were created, in accordance with the terms of the statute 31 Henry VIII c. 9,[23] and endowed with the property of the dissolved monasteries. Bath and Coventry were not so restored, but six new cathedrals were established at Chester, Peterborough, Gloucester, Oxford, Bristol and Westminster to serve the new sees, and in each case utilizing the revenue of the former monastery. The eight refounded cathedrals, together with these six, became known as the 'new foundation', while the surviving secular chapters were called the 'old foundation'. The charters of the new foundation were distinguished by their emphasis upon clearer and tighter structures. The establishment of officers was decreed, and the number of prebends in each case laid down, together with much stricter rules of residence. The number and function of the minor canons was also specified, and provision made for schools, almshouses and other ancilliary functions which had previously evolved over a period of time.[24] A typical cathedral of the new foundation would have a dean and eight or ten prebendaries, the former required to reside permanently and the latter for a given portion of each year; while a

---

22   S.E. Lehmberg, *The Reformation of Cathedrals* (1988); K.L. Wood-Legh, *Perpetual Chantries in Britain* (1965).

23   *Statutes of the Realm*, III, pp. 278–80; Makower, *Constitutional History*, pp. 302–3.

24   Lehmberg, *Reformation of Cathedrals*.

similar establishment of the old foundation might have a dean and forty or fifty prebendaries with no residence requirement whatsoever.[25] Naturally, the prebends of the new foundations were not only much more uniform in their income, but also much more substantial, and in most cases remained in the king's gift.

The church which these cathedrals were designed to serve when they were established in 1541 and 1542 was still largely traditional in doctrine and worship. Ten years later that was no longer the case, and Protestant leaders, even those like Hugh Latimer who were quite happy with espiscopal government, were questioning the usefulness of such institutions. However, apart from Westminster they all survived, and as the first generation of prebends (who were nearly all monks of the former monasteries) and deans (former priors) died, the opportunity was taken to replace them with known reformers. This process had not advanced far by the time that Edward VI died in 1553, and was abruptly halted by Mary's accession. The catholic Restoration breathed new life into the cathedrals, but it did not greatly affect their constitutions. Mary did not revive any of the monastic cathedrals, because the major new Benedictine house at Westminster had already ceased to have that status. Instead the queen recognized her father's creations, and gave new statutes to Durham, which seems to indicate that she had no intention of returning to monastic chapters, even if the length of her reign had permitted it. On the other hand, she did restore the patronage of several chapters to the bishops, as a part of her general policy of strengthening the episcopate after the severe mauling it had received from her brother's regents.[26] Mary and Pole, aware of the weakness of the English clergy as agents of a new Catholicism, endeavoured to use the cathedrals as exemplars of good practice and centres of orthodox spiritual life. Protestant prebendaries who had been introduced under Edward were weeded out and replaced with good Catholics, but time would have been required for such a policy to have borne fruit, and time was denied.

All intercessory foundations had been dissolved by statute in 1547, on the grounds that prayers for the dead were superstitious, and with that act the cathedrals had lost their supplementary chantry revenues. The canons had also lost one of their regular functions, and since most

25 *A History of York Minster*, eds, G.E. Aylmer and R. Cant (1977); D. Marcombe, 'The dean and chapter of Durham, 1558–1603' (PhD, Durham, 1973).
26 Loades, *Reign of Mary*, pp. 375–6.

of them were not qualified preachers, concern over their usefulness was increased. Mary restored none of the chantries and only a handful of the collegiate churches, which had gone down at the same time. However, she did encourage new foundations, and set a personal example in that direction. Rather surprisingly the great shrines, such as St Cuthbert at Durham and St Thomas at Canterbury, which had drawn crowds of the devout for centuries, and which had made their host churches major centres of pilgrimage, were not restored either. The spiritual power of the Marian cathedrals was to be based not upon relics and miracles, but upon the sacraments and teachings of the church.[27]

After Mary's death, and the new settlement of religion which followed it, the future of such institutions was again called in question. To leaders whose vision of a pastoral ministry was exclusively parochial, they could have no function except as parish churches, and their considerable revenues would be much better deployed in education or charity. However, Elizabeth liked cathedrals and found the patronage which they exercised useful. The more the puritans denounced them as 'dens of loitering lubbers', the more determined the queen was to preserve them. Apart from the chapel royal they provided the last significant support for church music, and it was from their choirs that the queen's own choristers were recruited.[28] Eventually her policy was justified, even by rigorous Protestant standards, because cathedrals such as Durham, set in conservative parts of the country, where local patrons were unsympathetic to the established faith, became powerful centres of reformed practice, from which preachers unawed by gentry disapproval could spread the evangelical message. The Elizabethan church was pragmatic about its infrastructure, and found uses for what was there.

Although a cathedral was in most respects subject to the authority of its bishop, there were also areas in which the dean and chapter were autonomous. The same applied to archdeacons. This was an office of considerable antiquity, being first mentioned in the early ninth century. For about two hundred years it was normal for each bishop to be assisted by a single archdeacon, who acted as his representative and principal man of business. However, by the twelfth century the situation had changed. Archdeacons had become exclusively ecclesi-

27 E. Duffy, *The Stripping of the Altars* (1993), pp. 524–64.
28 Lehmberg, *Reformation of Cathedrals*.

astical agents, in charge of subdivisions of a diocese. These divisions usually, but not invariably, coincided with the secular counties, making the archdeacon the ecclesiastical equivalent of the sheriff. He held his consistory court *ex officio* rather than as the bishop's delegate, and exercised the full range of first instance jurisdiction which came within the competence of the canon law. He held powers of visitation in his own right, and referred cases to the bishop at his discretion. Archdeacons were normally episcopal appointments, but occasionally the position was in the gift of the king, or of some other lay lord. The office carried no emoluments of its own, and was usually associated with a prebend in the parent cathedral, although other arrangements could be made in exceptional cases. Cathedral chapters were exempt from archidiaconal jurisdiction, the dean performing the same office within his precinct. Archdeacons, because of their key role in the pursuit of offenders, acquired an early reputation for ruthlessness and insensitivity; hence the tongue-in-cheek question much favoured in rhetorical exercises as to whether an archdeacon could be saved. He was called the *oculus episcopus*, and during the Reformation period was the most active official in the punishment of heresy, religious dissent, or vandalism against church property. Far from undermining his authority, the establishment of Protestantism if anything augmented it, if only because the need for constant vigilance against recusancy and other subversive activities showed no sign of diminishing, and ideological tests of loyalty to the regime became more rather than less important.[29] However the rural chapters, or assemblies of clergy, over which the archdeacons had presided in earlier times had become obsolete by the sixteenth century.

From about the twelfth century each archdeaconry had been divided into rural deaneries, and it is possible that these units had originally been subdivisions of the diocese, antedating the archdeaconries. They consisted of convenient groups of parishes, and were approximately equivalent to the secular hundreds, although not always co-extensive with them. Rural deans were appointed by the bishop, and were answerable to him. They were responsible for the general supervision of the clergy, in respect of their behaviour and professional competence, and of the behaviour of the laity in so far as that might

29 G.J.R. Parry, *A Protestant Vision: William Harrison and the Reformation of Elizabethan England* (1987); Peter Holmes, *Resistance and Compromise: the political thought of the Elizabethan Catholics* (1982).

interest the ecclesiastical courts. They administered benefices within
their deaneries during vacancies, and investigated complaints or alle-
gations. They had no jurisdiction, either of their own or by delegation,
and consequently no courts. Probably for this reason their importance
had declined in the pre-Reformation period, and they usually acted
only as commissaries for the bishop, or on the instructions of the
archdeacon. By 1535 many bishops no longer appointed them, and
where they still existed it was often in a purely honorary capacity.[30] In
1571 the province of Canterbury made an attempt to revive the office,
when a provincial council resolved that each archdeacon, during his
annual visitation, should propose names to the bishop for appointment. It was apparently envisaged that the position would be held for
only one year at a time, which would have meant most of the incumbents in the deanery taking it in turn. No significant change resulted
from this resolution, and rural deans virtually disappeared in the early
seventeenth century, squeezed out by the increasing importance of
both the archdeacons and the parishes.

PARISHES

The parish was the basic unit of ecclesiastical government; it was also
a worshipping community in a sense that no other unit was, except a
monastery. Originally parishes had been large and somewhat amorphous, served by teams of clergy operating from important central
churches. These 'old minsters' had resembled cathedrals, except that
they were not the seats of bishops, and their clergy had no defined
collegiality. However, between the tenth and the twelfth centuries
there had been a major development of church building, mostly by lay
patrons, and the old parishes had been divided into smaller units
dependent upon these new foundations.[31] The patrons not only
provided the buildings, but also the glebe land to support the priest,
and usually retained the right of presentation to the living thus
created. There is no evidence that this development was planned, or
depended in any way upon ecclesiastical initiative, but the bishops
accepted it, and established a measure of control over appointments.

30 Their position had been undermined as early as the Council of Oxford in
1222; Wilkins, *Concilia*, I, p. 585; Makower, *Constitutional History*, pp. 322–4.
31 Beat Kumin, *The Shaping of a Community; the rise and Reformation of the
English parish, 1400–1560* (1996), p. 13.

Once appointed, there was no doubt that a parish priest was answerable to the bishop as his ordinary, but the influence of his patron over his behaviour frequently continued. By the end of the thirteenth century this development was virtually complete, and the tithes which the canon law decreed for the upkeep of the parochial ministry were due to these parish priests. Originally each parish so founded had been a rectory, and the incumbent a rector who received the full tithe. However, long before the sixteenth century many rectories had been granted by their patrons, or their patrons' successors, to monasteries or other religious corporations, who both collected the tithe and held the advowson. In such cases – about a third of all parishes by the sixteenth century – the cure might be served by a vicar, who held the 'petty tithes' of minor produce, or by a stipendiary priest appointed by the rector.[32] A duly appointed vicar had security of tenure, but a stipendiary curate could in theory be removed at any time.

By the Tudor period many of the wealthier livings had been impropriated, and absentee incumbents were numerous, often because of pluralism. Consequently the actual cure of souls was frequently in the hands of a resident curate, and these curates often remained in a single parish for their entire working lives. The parish has been somewhat optimistically defined as 'a township or cluster of townships having its own church, and ministered to by its own priest . . . to whom its tithes and ecclesiastical dues are paid'.[33] A more accurate description might be that of a community defined by dependence upon a particular church, and living within the boundary of that church's jurisdiction. Tithes and dues were often paid to distant parties who had little or no share in the life of the parish, and this was a frequent source of grievance and complaint.

The unplanned, even random, ways in which parishes had come into existence had also left major inequalities. The *Valor Ecclesiasticus* of 1534 listed 8,838 benefices, some of which were as small as a few streets of a crowded town, and some as large as seventy square miles. Some had the cure of 3,000 or more souls, some fewer than ten. Some were worth less than £5 a year, some as much as £500. These problems were well recognized, but the dead hand of custom prevented any serious attempt at reform. The parochial map had been 'frozen' in about 1300, and the vested interests which had grown up since then

32   Makower, *Constitutional History*, pp. 338–40.
33   D.M. Palliser, 'The parish in perspective', in *Parish, Church and People: local studies in lay religion*, ed. S.J. Wright (1988), p. 7.

made it almost impossible to create new parishes, or to discontinue existing ones. Parish churches remained in almost uninhabited locations, thanks to the movement of population, while growing towns like Liverpool or Hull had no parishes of their own.[34] One of the reasons why so many senior clergy accepted the dissolution of the monasteries was in the hope that some of the wealth so released would be redeployed in support of the parochial ministry, and Cardinal Pole also made that one of his priorities between 1555 and 1558; however, virtually nothing was achieved. Where parishes were very extensive, particularly in the north of England, they were frequently equipped with one or more 'chapels of ease', which were technically chantries, and such chapels were usually continued by the chantry commissioners after 1547 for parochial purposes. Later in the century the Puritans also became exercised about the deficiencies of the parochial system, and in many places established 'lectureships', which were intended principally to provide the sermons which poorly paid incumbents lacked the education to supply.

The dissolution of the monasteries had also meant that large numbers of impropriated livings came into the hands of the crown between 1540 and 1560. However, this opportunity for reform was also neglected, most advowsons simply being sold with the estates to which they were attached, to lay purchasers. The early medieval situation, where a large proportion of benefices was controlled by lay patrons, was thus recreated, and although many gentry strove to exercise their patronage rights responsibly, that could not be guaranteed. It was for this reason that a lay Puritan group was established early in the seventeenth century to purchase advowsons, and thus ensure the appointment of sympathetic clergy.[35] However, during the Tudor period it remained broadly true that wealthy livings attracted nonresident and pluralist clergy, while poor livings, upon which the incumbents very often resided, did not attract those who were sufficiently educated to provide a parochial ministry appropriate to a religion of the word.

Nevertheless it would be a serious mistake to define a parish, or its religious life, simply in terms of its incumbent. By the middle of the thirteenth century, if not before, it had become customary for the laity

34   Kumin, *Shaping of a Community*, pp. 16–17.
35   The feofees for impropriations: C. Hill, *The Economic Problems of the Church* (1956), pp. 258–63. E.W. Kirby, 'The lay feofees: a study in militant puritanism', *Journal of Modern History*, XIV, 1942, pp. 1–25.

to share in the management of parochial resources. The maintenance of the nave of the church, and the provision of liturgical books and ornaments, had become the responsibility of the whole community. At first there seems to have been no established method of conducting this business, which varied from parish to parish, but by the mid-thirteenth century references begin to appear to *procuratores parochiae*. At first these were clearly occasional officers, appointed as needed, but the tendency of testators to bequeath property to parish churches, which remained distinct from the endowment of the benefice, created the need for a corporate identity, and consequently for regular officials. By the mid-fifteenth century this requirement had been institutionalized by the normal appointment of churchwardens, who exercised their responsibilities on behalf of the whole community of the parish. By this means, and in the face of a good deal of clerical opposition, parishes became 'virtual' corporations, able to hold property, and to sue and be sued in the king's courts. In theory the common law did not recognize this situation, but in practice it was achieved by utilizing the enfeoffment to use, a device originally developed to avoid feudal incidents, whereby an owner of property enfeoffed a group of trustees (who could be replaced as necessary) 'to the use' of the intended beneficiary. In 1497 a judgement of Common Pleas explicitly forbade churchwardens to act as feoffees to use, but that proved to be no obstacle. Thereafter, if the warden (or the parish) was the intended beneficiary, other individuals in the parish were named as the feoffees, and that arrangement was, and remained, legally acceptable.[36]

By the end of Henry VIII's reign churchwardens can be found administering, buying and selling property, organizing collections for a variety of parish purposes, lending out parish money at interest, receiving testamentary gifts, arranging entertainments, and spending large sums on the ornamentation, enlargement or even rebuilding of the parish church. By 1560 they normally attended ecclesiastical visitations, and one of their main responsibilities had become the presentation of offenders against the canon law. After 1571 this attendance was cumpulsory, and the churchwardens were also expected to report on the diligence and competence of the incumbent, or whoever actually exercised the cure of souls. By the end of the century churchwardens were additionally responsible for the collection of the poor rate, for its distribution to the deserving, and for the management of

36   Kumin, *Shaping of a Community*, pp. 25–6, 207–9.

whatever facilities the community might chose to establish for caring
for its sick, or setting the idle to work. In fact churchwardens were
extremely useful local officers, who discharged a variety of public
duties, and it may well have been for that reason that the equity jurisdiction of the crown was so frequently exercised in their defence. Both
Requests and Chancery regularly assisted wardens to overcome problems created by a mixture of recalcitrant parishoners and legal
ambiguities.[37]

Churchwardens were appointed in a variety of ways. The
commonest, and the most appropriate to their function, was election
at Easter by a general parish meeting. But in some parishes the patron
controlled one or both appointments, and in others the incumbent
had a say; the variety of practice seems to have been infinite. Wardens
frequently emphasized that they were the 'servants' of the parish, and
that was stressed in the manner in which they presented their
accounts. In one London parish they were required by local ordinances: 'at the yeres ende [to] geve and make accomptes of their
Receytes paymentes and dettes for the same yere to the person and to
the most parte of the most honest men of the same parisshe for the
tyme beyng',[38] and that seems to have been typical. There were usually
two wardens per parish, but three or even four was not uncommon,
and the same parish sometimes varied from year to year for no obvious
reason.

The churchwardens were drawn from the most substantial families
in the parish, and the office consequently resembled that of justice of
the peace, rather than that of constable. Although the duties might be
onerous, it carried status in the community, and was therefore not
difficult to fill. A recent study of English parishes by Beat Kumin has
shown that, from a sample of some seventy parishes in one year
(1524), the great majority of wardens were craftsmen or tradesmen
assessed at between £1 and £15 in goods for taxation purposes.
Occasionally minor gentry were elected, and even a small number of
women, this being virtually the only public office with which they were
entrusted. The same individuals were often elected for years on end,
and it is not surprising that the same family names also recur regularly.[39] Except in the very poorest parishes, the wardens were assisted

---

37   I.S. Leadam (ed.), *Select Cases in the Court of Requests* (1898), pp. 196–8. J.L.
Barton, 'The medieval use', *Law Quarterly Review*, 81, 1965, p. 576.
38   Lambeth, 19 May 1505; C. Drew, *Lambeth Churchwardens' Accounts and
Vestry Book* (Surrey Records Society, XVIII, 1941), pp. xii–xiii.
39   Kumin, *Shaping of a Community*, pp. 22–42.

by a professional clerk. Before the Reformation he was called the 'holy water clerk' and performed a variety of functions from serving at mass to cleaning the church. After the abolition of minor orders he was usually a layman, whose main function was to keep detailed accounts and minutes of parochial meetings, particularly those of the select vestry. The select vestry was a semi-official Elizabethan development which institutionalized the controlling role of the elite families of the parish by guiding, and eventually replacing, the general meeting. Wealthy parishes might also have a plethora of other officers; sextons, bedesmen, alewardens, clock keepers, organ keepers and scavangers are all recorded, although not necessarily in the same place. Such officers were employed upon a casual basis, and might be paid wages or 'rewards' according to the nature and extent of what they were called upon to do. Sidesmen assisted the churchwardens at visitations, and by keeping order in the church during service time, but like the wardens themselves, these were not usually paid. Before the Reformation, where there were choirs, these consisted of lay clerks who were employed by a chantry foundation of some kind attached to the church. After 1558 choirs and musicians were either voluntary or paid out of the parish funds.

The Reformation altered the nature of parochial life in a number of ways. The Chantries Act of 1547 put an abrupt end to a rich seam of local piety by confiscating the endowments and other possessions of huge numbers of parish guilds and lay fraternities. These were associations which might be devoted to the practice of a cult, the maintenance of a particular image or altar, or prayer for the souls of members living and dead. Such arrangements were not 'perpetual', like the more substantial chantries. Their endowments might consist of no more than a single beast, and their revenues were often counted in pennies. Managing such fraternities and arranging their devotions formed an important element of lay participation in the spiritual life of the community; so much so that several scholars have recently argued that far from increasing the lay part in public worship, the advent of the prayer book and the outlawing of 'superstitious practices' actually diminished it.[40]

Most contributions to the liturgical or material well-being of the church were probably voluntary, but parish rates were also levied for a wide variety of purposes. In addition, income was received from

40   J.J. Scarisbrick, *The Reformation and the English People* (1984); C. Haigh, *English Reformations: religion, politics and society under the Tudors* (1993).

property held in trust for the parish, and from pew rents, which were a very visible expression of communal status. The legal status, particularly of the rates, was uncertain, but before the Reformation defiance and neglect were alike uncommon, each community having its own ways of forcing the dissident into line. The Reformation, however, saw a collapse of both confidence and solidarity, at least for a generation or so. Bequests and voluntary contributions virtually dried up, sometimes because of disapproval of the new order, and sometimes simply because of confusion and uncertainty. Both the physical destruction of the traditional apparatus under Edward VI and Elizabeth, and its restoration under Mary, cost the parishes large sums of money, and it is not surprising that compliance was sometimes slow or reluctant.[41]

On the other hand, it would be a mistake to see the changes in too negative a light. When collegiate foundations were dissolved, prebendaries who had no parish responsibilities, and were frequently absentees, were replaced by a smaller number of curates who were required to be present and assist the incumbent. Visitations became far more frequent, and government concern about the health of parochial worship had some beneficial effects. After about 1580 the money began to come back, in the form of endowments for schools, charities or sermons. Before 1540 the conformist pressures of most parishes had militated against the spread of Protestant ideas, but after 1580 those same pressures supported the reformed establishment and encouraged obedience to public authority. By 1600 parishes were less autonomous than they had been a century before, and their liturgical life was less rich and diverse, but they had acquired new functions, both religious and secular. Like other developments of the period, these changes had tended to polarize local communities. Parish elites became stronger, and the poorer elements increasingly marginalized, a division symbolized both by the establishment of select vestries and by the growth of poor relief. However, the ascendency of the 'better sort' was a fundamental characteristic of Tudor government, and one of its great sources of strength.

41   R.H. Pogson, 'Revival and reform in Mary Tudor's church', *Journal of Ecclesiastical History*, 25, 1974, pp. 249–65.

THE RELIGIOUS ORDERS

The whole essence of the monastic life as it had originally been conceived had been withdrawal from the world – the repudiation of secular concerns and responsibilities. Monks were supposed to devote themselves to the *opus dei*, the maintenance of a perpetual fountain of prayer and praise to God, which was deemed to represent the highest form of human existence. However, that was never the whole truth about real monasticism, even in its earliest and most uncontaminated form. Even the most ascetic had to live somewhere, and eat something. Consequently monasteries were founded by lay patrons, who gave them land, building materials, and sometimes income of various kinds. Until the late twelfth century such endowments were a common and fashionable expression of lay piety, which not only demonstrated the wealth and status of the donors, but also ensured valuable spiritual merit for both themselves and their descendants. Wealth created temptations, and landholding created temporal obligations. Property granted to a monastery might be held in perpetuity, but it was not held in full ownership, and whatever rights the king had in respect of such property before it was granted, he had still. Moreover, such communities had to be ruled, both for the sake of their own members and also for the sake of such dependents as might come with the lands which had been granted. Consequently by the twelfth century we find great Benedictine houses such as St Albans and Glastonbury, with an income equivalent to that of a major peer, and ruled by an abbot who owed the king the feudal service of many knights. The abbey estates might be run by stewards, or they might be leased, or they might be sub-infeudated, in exactly the same way as the estates of a temporal lordship. There was, however, one major difference. Because a monastery did not die, knight its sons or marry its daughters, a whole range of feudal rights was lost to the crown. For this reason, from an early date the permission of the king, and of any other mesne lord who might be involved, was required before land could be so granted *in mortuam manum*, and this requirement was given statutory force in 1279.[42] By that time the fashion for great monastic endowments was past, but there were already in existence some fifty houses, mostly Benedictine, whose revenues qualified their heads to sit with the temporal and spiritual peers in the House of Lords, if the king so called them.

---

42 7 Edward I, *Statutis de Religiosis*: Makower, *Constitutional History*, p. 30.

This situation caused great unease, not least among the more zealous religious themselves, and a number of new and more rigorous orders were founded between the tenth and the twelfth centuries, notably those of Cluny and Citeaux. However, success brought its own nemesis, as the prestige of these orders attracted benefactions which had previously gone to the Benedictines. Indeed the Cistercians inadvertently encouraged this process by insisting upon a regime of physical work for the monks, which may well have been good for their spiritual discipline, but was also good for the revenues of their houses. By the thirteenth century the Cluniac priory of Lewes and the Cistercian abbey of Fountains were among the richest foundations in the country.

Jurisdictionally, Benedictine abbeys were independent entities. A General Chapter of the order met every three years, and legislated when necessary for the better observance of the rule, but the chapter did not exercise routine supervision, and Benedictine houses were subject to normal episcopal visitation. The Cistercian General Chapter, on the other hand, did exercise regular jurisdiction. All abbots were supposed in theory to attend, and Cistercian houses were subject to visitation by commissaries of the abbot of Citeaux. They were consequently exempt from episcopal oversight. This was even more true of the Cluniacs, because the order had but one abbot, at Cluny, all other houses being priories subject to his jurisdiction only. As a temporal lord, an abbot or prior held whatever honour and manor courts were appropriate for his properties, although as a spiritual person he did not conduct them himself. Each monastic precinct was also privileged in respect of normal secular jurisdiction. Monks were clergy, although many of them were not in major orders, and they were not supposed to leave their cloisters, so in theory they did not come within the reach of the secular courts. The situation in practice was not so simple, because monks did travel on business, and sometimes exercised cure of souls in parishes at some distance from their houses. However a monk charged with a crime outside his precinct would invariably be handed over to his own abbot for punishment, just as a secular priest would be surrendered to his ordinary. For any offence committed within the precinct, the abbot's control was unchallenged. Lay dependents of an abbey might, however, cause difficulties, especially if they could not claim orders of any kind. If such a person committed a crime within the precinct, it would be at the abbot's discretion whether he dealt with the offence himself or handed the offender over to the sheriff, but if the crime was extramural, then the question of privilege did not normally arise.

All monasteries were also sanctuaries where fugitives, not so much from justice as from the fury of their enemies, could find refuge. All churches and consecrated buildings shared this characteristic to some extent, but monasteries had the infrastructure to enable them to accommodate fugitives, and were consequently often appealed to. Some houses, notably Durham and Westminster, had chartered sanctuaries of considerable extent and power, where many people could live unmolested for long periods. Sanctuary was a constant source of grievance, and the right to claim it was gradually whittled down. Notorious offenders, or those already convicted, could not be sheltered; nor could heretics, traitors, or those guilty of only minor offences.[43] Abbots and priors normally exercised jurisdictional rights of sanctuary with great discretion, because it was important to maintain good relations with the neighbouring community, and with the relevant royal officers. Legislative attacks on sanctuary began in 1376, and a judicial decision of 1399 laid down that no new refuges were to be created. Henry VII reduced the number of 'sanctuary offences' considerably, and Henry VIII excluded a further range of crimes, including murder, burglary, arson and rape. Before the monasteries themselves came under attack, this aspect of their traditional functions had already virtually disappeared.

Not all monasteries, of course, were rich and powerful; and not all the regular religious were monks. In this context the houses of female religious are not particularly important, except that they provide examples of women exercising jurisdiction in their own right. The abbesses of large houses such as Barking or Wilton had the same authority within their precincts as their male counterparts, and the same immunities. In the unlikely event of a nun committing an offence outside her cloister, she would normally be surrendered to the jurisdiction of her superior. Where nunneries held lands on feudal tenure, the abbess or prioress owed the relevant military service, and was in the same position as any other woman, or cleric, holding such lands. The services were performed by proxy. On the eve of the Reformation only one female house, that of the Bridgettines at Syon, ranked in the top thirty in terms of wealth.[44]

By the end of the thirteenth century the monastic ideal had lost a

43 *State Trials and Proceedings for High Treason*, eds T.B. Howell et al. (1816–98), I, pp. 965–7.
44 D. Knowles, *The Religious Orders in England*, III (1959), p. 473.

lot of its attractiveness. Recruitment was already declining before the shattering blows of the Black Death, and patrons were looking elsewhere. The main beneficiaries of this change of fashion were the new mendicant orders, the Dominicans and Franciscans. Dedicated to learning, and to a pastoral ministry, they regularly provided the preaching which poorly supported parochial clergy lacked the education to supply. They became chaplains and confessors to the powerful, and their houses became regular features of the urban scene. Although spread over the whole country, they were particularly active, and particularly well supported, in the towns. Unlike the monks, they did not seek, or receive, large landed endowments, and consequently avoided the litigious conflicts with neighbouring estates which were such a feature of monastic management. Friars were subject to the discipline of their order, exercised by a provincial, rather than to the head of a particular house, and the provincial was the ordinary to whose jurisdiction they would be referred in the event of any crime or misdemeanour. Like every order, the friars lost their initial integrity and underwent a process of reform, which divided them into observants and conventuals. The former continued to enjoy the more active lay support, but the latter were the more numerous. The precincts of mendicant houses enjoyed the same privileged status as those of the monastic orders, but were much more limited in their extent, and did not contain significant numbers of lay dependents.

At the end of the fifteenth century the regular orders were in difficulties throughout western Europe. The English friars had maintained their numbers well. They had fully recovered from the plague losses of the late fourteenth and early fifteenth centuries, and were about 3,000 strong in 1485. However, with the exception of the Carmelites and the observant Franciscans, they had lost the respect of the more earnest laity, and no longer provided the spiritual leadership which had once been their characteristic. Dom David Knowles described the seventy years from 1430 to 1500 as 'the darkest period in the history of the English friars'.[45] It was not so much that they were positively disgraceful as that they were inactive, both intellectually and pastorally. Lay enthusiasm had largely transferred itself, first to the establishment of perpetual chantries, and more recently to the endowment of schools and university colleges. John Colet, the dean of St Paul's, was a pioneer when he entrusted the management of his new school to lay trustees, but he provided a pointer to the direction of

45   Ibid., p. 52.

future reform. The new intellectual currents first of humanism and then of doctrinal challenge, which somewhat belatedly struck England between 1490 and 1520, had a stimulating effect upon the friars, but not quite in the way which their superiors might have wished. Exposed in the front line of controversy, particularly in the university of Cambridge, several of them became leading exponents of the doctrinal Reformation soon to be known as Protestantism. Robert Barnes and Miles Coverdale were Austin friars, and John Bale was a Carmelite. A number of other friars became leading supporters of Henry VIII's campaign between 1529 and 1534. The disciplinary state of the mendicants during this period is unclear. A rare letter to William Wetherall, the provincial of the Austin friars in England, presents a gloomy picture of laxity and carelessness at the Augustinian house in Canterbury, but to what extent these accusations were true, and if so whether they were typical, is not known. What is clear is that the friars in general had somewhat recovered their energy by 1530, but were not in good estate to offer any determined defence of the traditional ecclesiastical order.[46]

The state of the monasteries is a subject of vigorous controversy. Numbers had certainly declined, not only since the mid-fourteenth century, but even since the mid-fifteenth. Great houses like Leicester and Westminster, which in their heyday had housed almost a hundred monks, now had no more than twenty-five or twenty-six. Recruits were still there, and their quality was no worse than before, but they were too thinly spread. At the beginning of the sixteenth century 120 of the richer abbeys, with incomes of over £200 a year, held about 2,500 religious, while some 260 poorer establishments contained approximately another 2,000; an average community therefore numbered about twelve. Discipline was probably not as good as it should have been, but the real argument against the English monasteries on the eve of the Reformation was that they occupied a capital endowment approaching £2 million in value for the sake of what had become a minor element in the religious life of the country. The monks were not providing spiritual leadership, and their contribution to the theological debates of the day was minimal. However, there were exceptions. The Carthusians, the most zealous of the reformed orders, had retained both their integrity and the respect of lay society. Their London house at Sheen, in particular, provided instruction and inspiration for men as different and significant as Thomas More and

46   Ibid, pp. 53–5.

Reginald Pole. Moreover, they provided the most principled and intransigent opposition to the recognition of the royal supremacy.

Henry seems to have feared that the regular religious in general would prove recalcitrant to his claims, and there were grounds for that fear. A previous quarrel between the English crown and the papacy at the end of the fourteenth century had seen the dissolution of the 'alien priories' – that is, cells dependent upon continental houses – for a rather similar reason.[47] Most of the regular orders had an international organization of some kind, and might be presumed to be more aware than their secular counterparts of their place in the universal church. However, the vast majority of them took the oath of supremacy when the visiting commissioners required it – with the notable exception of a group of London Carthusians led by their prior, John Houghton, and some of the observant Franciscans from Greenwich who had been particularly active on behalf of Queen Catherine. The king's savage treatment of the Carthusians reflected his fear lest their prestige should disrupt the fragile fabric of obedience upon which so much depended. Their defiance also prompted thoughts of a 'final solution' to the problem presented by the orders. In 1535, the same year that the Carthusians suffered, Thomas Cromwell sent out two sets of commissioners, one to prepare a *valor* of the whole church and the other to commence a general visitation of religious houses, using his power as vicegerent in spirituals.

In spite of some appearances to the contrary, the king's thinking at this point was not entirely political. For a number of years he had been aware of reforming voices declaring that the huge resources of the regular orders constituted an affront to society and a threat to his own jurisdiction. In 1529 Simon Fish had declared that the monks and friars had 'gotten ynto theyre hondes more then a therd part of all youre Realme', and speculated rather wildly that the begging friars were taking over £43,000 a year.[48] 'And what', he asked rhetorically, 'do al these gredy sort of sturdy idell holy theves . . . Truely nothing', save impugn the king's authority and make a nuisance of themselves. Fish's attempt to argue that the bishops and abbots were 'stronger in your owne parliament house then youre selfe' was hardly supported by the events of 1532–4, but Henry took Fish's *A Supplicacyon for the Beggers* seriously, and not only out of fear or avarice. In 1533 Eustace

---

47   D. Matthew, *The Norman Monasteries and their English Possessions* (1962).
48   Simon Fish, *A Supplicacyon for the Beggers* (1528), ed.F.J. Furnivall (EETS extra series, 13,1871), p.8.

Chapuys, the imperial ambassador, reported apprehensively that the king appeared to believe that his coronation oath bound him to recover the goods which his predecessors had alienated to the church, and rumours were circulating in Brussels as early as January 1534 that Henry had distributed the property of the monasteries to his nobles.[49] In fact the king was nowhere near such a decision. Even as late as 1536 he seems to have been thinking of pruning the regular establishment rather than destroying it. Precedents were not lacking for the dissolution of small houses which had ceased to be viable, and the diversion of their resources to other purposes. The priory of Luffield in Northamptonshire was virtually uninhabited when it was finally closed in 1494; the small nunnery of St Rhadegund (Cambridge) was suppressed to become Jesus College in 1496; and the inhabitants of nine houses of Austin canons were relocated to other establishments in the course of the fifteenth century. More recently, Wolsey had suppressed no fewer than thirty small houses, and the not-so-small St Frideswide's in Oxford in favour of his colleges there and at Ipswich.[50] Neither a religious order, nor the descendants of the founder, if any such still existed, had any legal claim upon the property of a house dissolved by lawful authority.

How Henry arrived at the policy which he eventually implemented is not clear. It has been noticed that the tone of the visitation returns became increasingly hostile. The same vistors, reporting both good and bad in the early stages, could later find no good to say, and the implication is that their instructions had changed.[51] Cromwell seems to have wished to proceed gradually, using his powers of visitation, but either he changed his mind or the king decided otherwise. The statute of 27 Henry VIII c. 28 simply dissolved all houses with an income of less than £200 a year, and vested the property in the king and his heirs. The preamble spoke of 'manifest sin, vicious, carnal and abominable living . . . daily used and committed amongst the little and small abbeys, priories and other religious houses', commending by contrast the virtuous proceedings of the major houses, but the whole impression is contrived. To suggest that £200 a year marked a borderline between vice and virtue was ridiculous, and to make no

---

49 *Letters and Papers of the Reign of Henry VIII*, eds J.S. Brewer et al. (1862–1932), VI, no. 235.

50 Knowles, *Religious Orders*, p. 470. St Frideswide's had an income of £220 a year and (probably) twenty inmates.

51 Knowles, *Religious Orders*, pp. 268–70.

stipulation as to how the property was to be used indicated the true nature of the operation. Any religious wishing to transfer to a larger house were to be permitted to do so, but the widespread contemporary belief that the act signalled a wholesale attack upon the orders seems to have been justified.[52] In the event the major houses were not dissolved by statute, but surrendered in response to a variety of pressures between 1538 and 1540. The friars, untouched by either the 1535 visitation or the 1536 act, were suppressed piecemeal by visiting commissioners in the course of 1538. In terms of their property it was hardly worth the effort, but the mendicants had stronger links to Rome than any of the monastic orders, and although few had refused the oath of supremacy, the suspicion which attached to them was somewhat greater.

By 1540 the king had completed his answer to the problem posed by his own earlier statement that the clergy were 'but half our subjects, yea, and scarcely our subjects'. The jurisdictions of the secular clergy were firmly under royal control, and those of the regulars had disappeared. Land to the value of at least £1.5 million, producing an annual income of some £75,000, had come into the possession of the crown. This constituted the largest single shift in the property market since the conquest of 1066, and an enormous vested interest in the royal supremacy. Cromwell had at one time declared that he would make his master the richest prince in Christendom, and with the benefit of hindsight it appears that the dissolution offered him a unique opportunity to free the crown from the need for direct taxation, with all that that implied. However, sales began almost at once, and within a decade the bulk of the land had been dispersed. Most of the proceeds went to fund Henry's wars, between 1542 and 1546, but those wars were not even in prospect when the sales began, and the policy was certainly not adopted for that purpose. Perhaps Cromwell realized that the petitions and requests which began to land on his desk as soon as large-scale dissolutions were in prospect indicated an opportunity to consolidate aristocratic support for the king's revolutionary proceedings. There was undoubtedly a large demand: noble families anxious to round out their holdings in key areas; former monastic stewards trying to capitalize on the new situation; brokers setting up profitable deals on behalf of gentry clients; and aspiring yeomen trying to gain a footing in the county elite. It is possible that sales began

52   27 Henry VIII, c. 28; *Statutes of the Realm,* III, pp. 575–8; J. Youings, *The Dissolution of the Monasteries* (1971).

almost accidentally in response to the great demand, and continued after Cromwell's fall because the king was anxious to capitalize upon the new patronage opportunities which were being created. Some grants were preferential, and a few were outright gifts, but the great majority were sales at a standard rate of twenty years' purchase. By the end of the reign over £800,000 had been received by the Court of Augmentations, and it remains an interesting and unanswered question how a few hundred customers managed to find such a very large sum of money, especially when it is remembered that war taxation was making unprecedented demands at the same time. At his death in 1547, Henry was no better off financially than he had been before, but he had made it extraordinarily difficult to unscramble the Reformation omelette which he had created.

Just how difficult became apparent when his elder daughter Mary succeeded to the throne in 1553. Mary was determined to restore both traditional religion and the papal authority. The former presented few difficulties, because Protestantism had struck root only in London and parts of the Home Counties; however, the latter involved a long political battle. It required the powerful intervention of Philip in the autumn of 1554 to persuade Pope Julius III that he would have to write off the property of the English monasteries if reconciliation was to be secured.[53] By an agreement finally reached in January 1555 the 'possessioners', as Cardinal Pole significantly called them, were allowed to retain the land for which they had, after all, paid a fair market price. However their title was recognized only by English law, and not by the church. When Paul IV was persuaded to take the logical step of canonically ending the dissolved houses in the summer of 1555[54] the situation was eased, but Pole continued to make it clear that in his view voluntary restitution was necessary for true absolution. Very few responded to his pressure. There were some half dozen new foundations during the reign, largely as a result of pressure from surviving ex-religious. Mary endowed all of them herself, but the total landed capital committed was no more than £40,000, or about 5 per cent of what the crown had originally received. Her father had dispensed far more in the endowment of new dioceses and cathedrals.

53 D.M. Loades, 'Philip II as king of England', in *Law and Government under the Tudors,* eds C. Cross, D. Loades and J. Scarisbrick (1987), pp. 177–94.
54 By the Bull *Praeclara*; Knowles, *Religious Orders,* p. 423; *Documenta ad Legationem Cardinalis Poli spectantia (Documents Relating to the Legatine Missions of Cardinal Pole),* eds J. Moyes, F.A. Gasquet, and D. Fleming (1896), pp. 31–4.

Only Westminster, with an income of £1400 a year and about thirty monks, was a significant foundation, and the reappearance of Abbot Feckenham in the House of Lords was no more than a gesture.[55] Mary certainly did not resurrect the regular clergy as a significant aspect of the religious or political life of the country, and with the return of Protestantism under Elizabeth the whole of her modest endowment was resumed by the crown.

Sanctuaries did not entirely disappear, even after 1558, but they became residual. Benefit of clergy, sanctuary and abjuration could still be referred to in legislation as late as 1601, but the last serious quarrel on the subject resulted from the attempt to revive the monastic sanctuary at Westminster in Mary's reign.[56] By the time of Elizabeth the church presented no obstacles to the omnicompetence of royal jurisdiction, and no body of clergy remained who owed any allegiance outside the realm. The Society of Jesus, which began to send missionaries into England after 1580, was a proscribed organization, and such English people as entered the regular religious life after 1558 did so abroad and in defiance of their allegiance. Meanwhile the diaspora of monastic property had strengthened the pre-existing elite of English society. Conservative commentators noted that gentlemen had become 'good cheap' in England, and it was on the back of this rising prosperity that the College of Arms did such a flourishing trade, and the commissions of the peace came under the pressure which we have already noticed. If one of the major achievements of the Tudors was to transform England from a feudal society into a gentry commonwealth, then the dissolution of the monasteries was an important step along the way.

55   *Calendar of the Patent Rolls, Philip and Mary* (1936–9), III, pp. 546, 354; PRO SP12/1/64; Loades, *Reign of Mary*, p. 300.
56   *Acts of the Privy Council*, VI, p. 135, 28 July 1557; Loades, *Reign of Mary*, pp. 385–6.

6

Franchises and Lordships

Because of the peculiar circumstances of the Norman conquest, the pattern of both landholding and jurisdiction in England was very simple. All land belonged in principle to the crown, and all jurisdiction of a public nature was derived from that source. Franchises were areas where the king had granted jurisdiction to the territorial lord, who might be either lay or ecclesiastical. In such liberties the king's writ did not run, but the lord remained the king's subject and answerable to him for the manner of his government. The effectiveness of such control depended very largely upon the personalities involved. Once a franchise had been created there was no obvious way of removing it, because it became settled in law and custom, and was not revokable at the king's will. When a franchise reverted to the crown through default of heirs, it might remain in the king's hands, or it might be regranted. By the late fifteenth century most of the great secular franchises – the Duchy of Lancaster, the Earldom of Chester and the Duchy of Cornwall, for example – were vested in the crown, but they continued to be governed by their own machinery and in accordance with their own customs. These liberties had usually originated in response to the problems of governing remote parts of the kingdom, but by the early sixteenth century they were a handicap rather than a help to the royal power.

In a similar manner William I had taken all the land to which his jurisdiction extended into his own hands. There was consequently no such thing as allodial land in medieval England. Some of that land was retained under royal control, and became the king's demesne. The demesne fluctuated considerably in extent and profitability from one generation to another, as it was depleted by grants and replenished by escheats and forfeitures. Towards the end of Henry VI's reign it was very low, no more than 1 or 2 per cent in some counties and probably about 2 per cent overall. The deliberate policies of Edward IV and Henry VII recovered that position, and by the 1520s the comparable figure was about 5 per cent, producing an income which had by then reached about £40,000 a year.[1] The improvement of income was not only the result of increased stock. Henry VII in particular had been at considerable pains to improve the management of his estate, some of which was administered directly by stewards and bailiffs on the king's behalf, and some leased for a term of years or lives. However, the great bulk of the landstock had originally been distributed by William to his followers, or to such of the original holders as succeeded in making their peace with him, on feudal tenure. Land held directly of the king by this means was said to be in chief by knight service; that is, the holder swore homage and fealty, acknowledging a duty to support the king in arms with a given number of men when called upon to do so. He also owed his overlord counsel, and customary fees for the knighting of his eldest son and the marriage of his eldest daughter. Such a fief was hereditary, again upon the payment of a fee, and if the holder died leaving an heir under age, then the custody and wardship of that heir belonged to the crown until the heir achieved the age of majority. This was the prevailing form of landholding in western Europe, and had been widespread in England before the conquest, but by the end of the eleventh century it was universal.

At first most fiefs were sub-infeudated, that is to say the mesne lord created fiefs of his own, which he granted to his followers and supporters on the same terms. This system had created considerable problems in France, because many sub-vassals believed that their primary allegiance was to their lord, who could consequently lead his following against the king if he chose to do so. William endeavoured to prevent that situation from arising in England by requiring all sub-vassals also to swear an oath of allegiance directly to the king – the so-called 'oath of Salisbury'. The result was never entirely satisfactory, and sub-infeudation was eventually abolished by the statute of *Quia emptores* in 1290. This confirmed instead the system of alienation, which had been growing for a number of years. Alienation was simply sale, whereby the vendor transferred land, and a proportion of the feudal obligations appropriate to its extent, to a purchaser in perpetuity. The land thus alienated ceased to be a part of the vendor's fief, and became, in effect, a separate tenancy in chief, the dues of which were owed directly to the crown. By this time military service

---

1   S.J. Gunn, *Early Tudor Government, 1485–1558* (1995), pp. 24–8; B.P. Wolffe, *The Crown Lands, 1461–1536: an aspect of Yorkist and early Tudor government* (1970); B.P. Wolffe, *The Royal Demesne in English History* (1971).

had been widely commuted to cash payments, so the inconvenience of holding by the fortieth part of a knight's fee was not apparent.[2] The king obviously gained by this change, but it appears that the mesne lords also welcomed it, because the loss of feudal service was more than compensated by the opportunity to raise cash when it was needed. Sub-infeudation could only be used after 1290 in respect of temporary grants, which resembled leases for a period of years. Alienation continued to require a royal licence, for which a fee had to be paid, but that was less a system of control than a means of raising revenue. Licences were scarcely ever refused.

There was, however, rather more to feudal tenure than a custom of landholding. It also involved a contractual political culture. Neither the grant of land nor the oath of allegiance was unconditional. Both sides agreed to abide by the rules which governed their relationship. Tenants in chief had originally been the king's companions in arms, and latterly his nobles. They expected to be consulted over decisions of public policy, to have their own disputes fairly adjudicated, to be the beneficiaries of the king's patronage, and to have their local interests and authority respected. Originally, if a tenant broke his feudal contract, his lord could annul it and confiscate his fief; by the same terms if the lord was at fault, his tenant was entitled to 'defy' him. It was this culture, as much as the realities of political power, which led to the noble revolts against John, Henry III, Edward II and Richard II. By the fifteenth century English kings had been made well aware of the realities of contractual authority. However, by then the simplicities of early feudalism had long since departed. *Quia emptores* was a symptom of change. By the end of the thirteenth century many tenants in chief were comparatively humble men, and great lords were creating affinities, no longer bound by feudal laws but by subtler and more flexible bonds of dependency. The Hundred Years War had hastened this tendency. Traditional feudal levies were of little use for fighting protracted campaigns in France, while straightforward mercenaries were expensive and unreliable. Much the most satisfactory method was to authorize a nobleman to raise a given number of men, initially at his own expense, and then to reimburse him for his outlay. Most of the troops who served in France between 1340 and 1450 were raised by variants of that method, and by the middle of the fifteenth century noble affinities were well established, a situation

2   J.M.W. Bean, *The Decline of English Feudalism, 1215–1540* (1968), pp. 7–39.

sometimes known as 'bastard feudalism'. A nobleman supported by a powerful affinity was in a strong position to demand the king's 'good lordship', and if a number of noblemen felt that they were being deprived of that commodity, the crown could be in danger. That is essentially what happened between 1450 and 1460. In fact the decay of traditional feudal tenure had done little to change the relationship between the king and his nobles.[3]

By the middle of the fifteenth century the church in one way or another held about 35 per cent of the tenancies in England, the gentry about 40 per cent, and the nobility about 18 per cent. In one sense these are misleading figures, because the political realities of the period grouped many of the gentry into the noble affinities. The real resources at the command of the earl of Northumberland or the duke of Somerset were much greater than the scale of his own landholding might suggest. However, in another sense they are highly significant. It did not require a major shift of resources as between the gentry and the nobility to alter the balance of power between them, so much as a change of political culture. By the 1520s the balance of landholding had shifted only a little, the nobility's share having been reduced somewhat by the growth of the royal demesne. After 1540, with the church's holdings more than halved, the nobility had about 10 per cent, the gentry about 50 per cent and the crown about 25 per cent. Thereafter the crown share began to fall again as fiscal pressures enforced sales, but the gentry benefited somewhat more than the nobility, which is an indicator of the truth of the early seventeenth century boast about the Commons' ability to 'buy out' the Lords.[4] There is no need to believe that the Tudors made any deliberate attempt to reduce the landed wealth of the nobility, and indeed the numerous peerage creations of Henry VIII are evidence to the contrary, but by changing the nature of 'good lordship' they changed the rules of the political game. The landed basis for a gentry common-wealth was already in place by the time that Edward IV took the throne. By the late sixteenth century feudal tenure survived primarily as a source of income to the crown. Whenever the heirs to a tenancy in chief failed, the land escheated to the queen, who might regrant it,

3   J.R. Lander, *Crown and Nobility, 1450–1509* (1976; K.B. McFarlane, *The Nobility of Later Medieval England* (1973); J. Gillingham, *The Wars of the Roses* (1981).
4   Felicity Heal and Clive Holmes, *The Gentry in England and Wales, 1500–1700* (1994), pp. 97–135.

or add it to the demesne at pleasure. The wide diffusion of such tenancies also created a large number of wardships, which were normally sold to interested parties at rates which became standard.[5] Sometimes, however, such wardships were kept in the hands of the crown, or granted for reasons other than profit. When the earl of Cumberland died in 1570, for example, the wardship of his son George was granted to the master of the Court of Wards, Sir William Cecil, who brought the boy up as a Protestant and far away from his northern estates. When military tenure was eventually abolished by the Long Parliament, it was to prevent that kind of manipulation rather than because the system had become obsolete.

MANORS AND HONOURS

The commonest unit of land management was the manor. A manor, however, was a legal definition, not a topographical one. The fields of a single village might be divided between several manors, or one manor might embrace a number of villages. Manors varied enormously in size, in value and in population. The one characteristic which they all had in common was a court, which consisted of the homage or tenants of the manor, presided over by the bailiff or steward in the name of the lord. If for any reason the homage disappeared, then the court disappeared with them, and what remained was a seigneury, not a manor. By the sixteenth century it was almost as difficult to create a new manor as a new parish, although it could sometimes be accomplished by dividing an existing manor. Manors might be discontinued by the removal of the homage, or by conversion into a corporate town. In the latter case the tenures became burgages and the court changed its nature in accordance with the terms of the charter.[6] No manor could be destroyed except by the will of its lord, because even if the entire homage died of the plague, their places could be supplied from outside if so desired. On the other hand, manors were not suitable to every kind of land use. One of the main points of having tenants, and consequently a court, was to agree procedures for crop rotation and shared responsibilities, and to reduce

5   S.L. Waugh, *The Lordship: royal wardship and marriages in English society and politics, 1217–1327* (1988); Joel Hurstfield, *The Queen's Wards: wardship and marriage under Elizabeth I* (1958).
6   Eric Kerridge, *The Agrarian Problem in the Sixteenth Century and After* (1969).

the land to workable units. This was most appropriate to open-field arable farming, and the 'classic' manor, as it used to be perceived by economic historians, was of that nature. Manorial organization was certainly used in areas of 'old enclosure', such as Devon, where arable and dairy farming was mixed, but it was not appropriate to large-scale sheep ranching of the kind practised in some upland areas.

Declining population in the early fifteenth century put pressure on the manorial system, not only because it became harder to find suitable tenants, but also because a declining food market made arable farming less profitable. Sheep required less labour and produced a higher return. Consequently many lords, even in old arable areas, began to seek unity of possession in order to convert their lands to this new use. As long as the population remained low this caused few problems, because even if tenants had to be removed, they would experience no difficulty in finding another tenement nearby. At the same time prices remained low, entry fines and other dues remained depressed, and traditional labour services virtually disappeared because they were impossible to enforce. The rising population of the late fifteenth and early sixteenth centuries brought this situation to an end. By 1520 enclosure was an issue of bitter controversy, and Sir Thomas More could write of sheep 'eating up men'. The manorial system was at the heart of this controversy for two reasons. On the one hand it was alleged that unscrupulous lords were evicting their tenants, either directly or by extortionately raising rents and fines; and on the other hand that they were abusing their rights of common and making it impossible for their tenants to secure redress by controlling the processes of their manor courts. These disputes came to a general and violent head in 1548 and 1549, when riots and rebellions spread across the Midlands and the south of England, causing the greatest social crisis of the century.[7]

There is no denying the strength of feeling about these issues, but the causes were not as straightforward as some contemporaries believed. Manorial tenures were much more secure than they were represented to be, but it was possible to be deceived by appearances. Like England itself, every manor was divided into tenurial land and demesne land. The tenurial land had originally been unfree, because the early homage would have have been villeins, but by the sixteenth

7   J. Cornwall, *The Revolt of the Peasantry, 1549* (1977); D.M. Loades, *Essays in the Reign of Edward VI* (1994), pp. 65–72. J. Cornwall and D. MacCulloch, 'Debate: Kett's rebellion in context', *Past and Present*, 93, 1981.

century that had long ceased to be the case. As Sir Thomas Smith said of bondmen *adscripti glebae*, 'so fewe there be that it is not almost worth the speaking'.[8] Nevertheless, in spite of being held by freemen and freewomen, the tenures remained bond, or customary. The tenancy was recorded in the court roll of the manor, of which the tenant was given a copy, and land so held was termed 'copyhold'. Copyhold might be for life only, but was normally heritable upon the payment of a fee. Copyhold could not be pleaded in the courts of common law, which recognized only freehold tenure; but custom of the manor in respect of tenancies could not be violated by the lord or anyone else. Although it was only pleadable in the manor court, appeal lay to the crown in Chancery, because custom was equally under the crown's protection. Demesne land, on the other hand, could be dispensed at the will of the lord. He might keep it in his own hand, to be farmed by a bailiff or steward, he might lease it as freehold, he might grant it on a tenancy at will for short periods at a time, or he might grant it on what was known as a 'demesne copyhold'. This last was deceptive, and the cause of much trouble, because the instrument of grant appeared to be identical to a normal copy, but it was not protected by the custom of the manor because the land was deemed to be in the lord's hand. Demesne copyhold was in fact no more than tenancy at will, and could be revoked at any time, but it appears that many who received it believed otherwise. It was therefore possible for a manorial lord to cause a great deal of grievance without in any way breaking the law.[9]

Very often, however, the problem was not one of tenure at all. It was normal for the custom of the manor to allocate shares in the use of the common land and the woodland, to correspond with the shares which each tenant held in the arable fields. These shares usually took the form of quotas; so many loads of timber might be removed, so many beasts pastured. Such quotas were much harder to protect than tenures, and encroachment by the lord, who was much the most powerful man in the community, was hard to resist. Even more seriously, a lord who was unable to obtain unity of possession might decide to enclose his demesne land. This he was entitled to do, although it disrupted the agricultural pattern of the manor. It was when he decided to commute his common quotas for additional land that the trouble really began. Even if he was trying to be fair, the

8   Thomas Smith, *De Republica Anglorum*, ed. Mary Dewar (1982), p. 135.
9   Kerridge, *Agrarian Problems*, pp. 17–31.

homage would be likely to consider his claims excessive, and it was not unknown for a lord, disgruntled by the attitude of his tenants, to enclose the whole common and convert it to his own use. It was this type of enclosure which caused so much of the anger which exploded in Norfolk in the summer of 1549.[10] Other aspects of custom were controversial in a different way, because it decreed not only terms of tenancy and quotas of use, but also scales of fees for regular actions, such as renewing a lease, agreeing an inheritance or commuting a service. These scales had often been fixed generations earlier, because for at least a hundred years before 1530 there had been stable or declining prices. When prices began to rise thereafter, there was anger and incomprehension. At first many lords suffered a serious loss of income in real terms, and their natural reaction was to increase the level of fees. This the homage in most cases flatly refused to accept, demanding that the customary rates only be used. Lords often considered themselves justified in ignoring this obstructiveness, and an additional and powerful sense of grievance was thus created.

There were consequently rights and wrongs on both sides in this developing confrontation, and the inflexibility of manorial custom was directly responsible for the crisis. Unfortunately the sanctity of such custom also turned what was really an economic issue into a moral one. The crusade launched by the so-called 'commonwealth men' in defence of the traditional Christian concept of the stewardship of wealth is beyond the proper scope of this study, but it is important to understand its persuasive force. The first argument was that farming 'in severalty' was causing unemployment and driving men off the land; 'the decaye of England only by the great multitude of sheep, to the utter decaye of household keeping, mayntenance of men, dearthe of corne, and other notable dyscommodityes'[11] Circumstantial arguments were adduced declaring, for example, that there were forty fewer plough-teams in Oxfordshire in 1550 than there had been in 1500, and consequently that some 250 ploughmen had been forced into vagrancy. Denunciations, both moral and religious, were heaped upon those deemed to be responsible: 'the great farmers, the graziers, the rich butchers, the men of law, the merchants, the gentlemen, the

10　S.K. Land, *Kett's Rebellion* (1977); Ballad, 'Vox populi, vox dei' (1547–8), in F.J. Furnivall, *Ballads from Manuscript*, I (1868–72), pp. 126–46. Depositions taken before the mayor and aldermen of Norwich, 1549–67, ff. 1–125.
11　*Four Supplications, 1529–1553*, eds F.J. Furnivall and J. Meadows Cowper (EETS, 1871), pp. 93–102.

knights, the lords and I cannot tell who';[12] In other words, those men of substance upon whom the king and his council depended for the effective application of government. To denounce the political nation collectively as 'Men utterly void of God's fear. Yea, men that live as though there were no God at all' was to apply an extremely dangerous solvent to a society heavily dependent upon deference and obedience. In this campaign traditional thinkers like Sir Thomas More were at one with the Protestant preachers of the next generation: 'O wycked servauntes of Mammon' thundered Thomas Lever in 1550, 'always bothe ennemyes and traytours to God and the king'. Successive Tudor governments from Henry VII to Edward VI took this rhetoric seriously, and endeavoured by both statute and proclamation to protect an economic order which was being inexorably destroyed by demographic expansion and inflation. This was dangerous in two ways. In the first place, laws which were so directly contrary to the economic interests of the governing class were not going to be enforced. 'It boots not how laws be made', as one contemporary observed, 'for we see few or none put into effect.' Second, the paralysis produced by this conflict of interests encouraged the aggrieved to take the law into their own hands, secure in the conviction that their cause was not only just, but in line with the king's intentions.

If 'commonwealth' thinking was based upon a static view of the agrarian economy, it was also based upon ignorance of the money market. The moral theory of the 'just price' had no foundations in economic reality, and a conviction that the price of a chicken, which had been 4d in 1500 should still have been 4d in 1560 inevitably led to pointless rage and frustration. For this attitude the Protestant preachers were much to blame. Not only did they brand as extortion any attempt to respond to the pressures of inflation, they condemned usury out of hand, denouncing the compromises which traditional theology had made with market forces. Moreover the growing complexities of the market eluded them: 'I have heard howe that even this last yere [1549], ther was certayn Acres of corne growyng on the ground bought for viii poundes: he that bought it for viii sold it for x. He that gave x pounds, sold it to another above xii poundes'.[13] Neither

---

12   Robert Crowley on the causes of Kett's rebellion, from 'The Way to Wealth' in *Select Works of Robert Crowley*, ed. J.M. Cowper (EETS, 1872), pp. 132–3.
13   Thomas Lever's sermon at Paul's Cross, 14 December 1550, in R.H. Tawney and Eileen Power (eds), *Tudor Economic Documents* (1924), III, pp. 47–50.

the preachers nor the earlier 'commonwealth' intellectuals intended
to stir up a hornets' nest in the countryside. Belatedly, in the summer
of 1549, they strove to support the council's insistence that redress
could only come from the king. However, by then the damage had
been done. The minority of Edward VI, and Protector Somerset's
unwillingness to heed the warning signs, resulted in a 'camping
summer' which appeared to shake the social and political order to its
roots.

This crisis has been extensively studied, but it is worth noting some
of the ways in which manorial customs contributed to the tension.
When Somerset's commissioners visited the town of Cambridge in
1548 they were told (among many other things): 'that Andrew
Lambes close is crofte lande and ought to lye open with the fylde at
lamas as common' and 'that Mr.Hynde unlawfully dothe bringe into
Cambridge felde a flock of shepe to the number of vi or vii C, to the
undoinge of the farmers'.[14] The customs of the manor of Aldeburgh
in Suffolk a few years earlier also illustrate the wide range of traditional fees which could become items of controversy:

> Item every Tenant paieth for a Cotage ground not buylded if it
>   conteyne iii xx fote every way   id
> Item every Tenant paieth for halfe a Cotage which is xl fote every
>   way   0b
> Item for every Curtilage conteyning xl ffote or under   0b
> Item for the ffyne of every Cotage buylded   iis
> Item for the ffyne of every Cotage ground unbuylded xiid.[15]

The fact that disputes over manorial tenures, rents and fees festered
and became excuses for riots and other forms of protest reflected not
only the pressures which circumstances were putting on the system,
but also the failures of the last major area of private jurisdiction.

Customary law had originally been created by the communities
themselves. No royal decree or Act of Parliament had instructed the
homage of Aldeburgh that two shillings was the proper fee for a
'Cotage buylded'. Nor had this been imposed by the lord of the manor;
it had been agreed. However, there was a fundamental flaw in this kind
of custom. Although made by the community, it had to be enforced
by the lord's court, and that could only mean by continued co-opera-

14   C.H. Cooper, *Annals of Cambridge* (1842–1908), II, pp. 38–40.
15   Tawney and Power, *Tudor Economic Documents*, I, pp. 9–10.

tion between the homage and the lord, or his steward. If that co-operation had broken down, leaving either party aggrieved, the next level of appeal should have been to the court of the honour of which the manor was a part. However, the disintegration of traditional feudalism since the thirteenth century had left the links between manors and honours extremely tenuous in many cases. Once upon a time the lord of the honour would either have been the same person as the lord of the manor, or his immediate overlord. By the sixteenth century there was usually no connection, and many honour courts had either disappeared or become purely notional. The same was even more true of the next level, the barony. Baronies, honours and manors had originally corresponded roughly with levels of sub-infeudation, but by the fifteenth century had become mainly units of financial management. The Percy honour of Cockermouth in Cumberland, or the nearby baronies of Egremont and Gilsland, were still meaningful units in the early sixteenth century, not least in terms of patronage and *manred*, but that had long ceased to be the case in most of lowland England.[16]

Consequently it was no longer natural to appeal to a superior court of the customary law, and there would not have been much expectation of redress in doing so. Only the king was now seen as providing justice, either via Chancery or by one of the more recently developed equity courts. So although in one sense a loss of confidence in the custom of the manor, and in the structure of the customary courts, was a symptom of a radical social malaise, at the same time it contributed significantly to the unification of jurisdiction in the hands of the crown. By the same token it began to be recognized after 1560 that enclosure was not a form of moral delinquency, and that statutes and edicts insisting upon the maintenance of 'husbandrie' were a waste of effort. When William Box endeavoured to persuade Lord Burghley of the need to grow more corn in 1576, he suggested legislation to enclose all remaining common land, and put it under the plough.[17] In 1573 Thomas Tusser was prepared to admit that some land was more suitable for enclosure than for traditional farming, and that 'severalty' encouraged farmers to invest in improving their land: 'Example (if doubt ye do make), by Suffolk and Essex go take.'[18]

---

16   S.G. Ellis, *Tudor Frontiers and Noble Power: the making of the British state* (1995), pp. 35, 41, 81, 242.
17   BL Lansdowne MS 121, f. 173r.
18   Thomas Tusser, *Five Hundred Points of Good Husbandrie* (1580), eds W. Payne and S.J. Herrtage (1878), pp. 140–6.

Enclosure by agreement became increasingly common, and the universal role of customary law in regulating farming practices and land use declined in proportion. Open field manors did not disappear until the Enclosure Acts of the early eighteenth century, but by 1600 a mixture of economic circumstances and the increasing omnicompetence of royal government had relegated the traditional machinery of barony, honour and manor to the sidelines of jurisdiction.

FRANCHISES IN THE KING'S HANDS

A franchise was a jurisdiction within which the monarch's writ did not run, and all government was conducted in the name of the lord, or other holder. The Principality of Wales, which was by far the largest, we have already considered in another context, along with the marcher lordships which fringed it. Both the principality itself and the majority of the marcher lordships had remained in the king's hands after 1509, and their distinctiveness was that of form rather than substance. The same was also true of a number of other major liberties which were wholly within England. The most important of these, although in rather different ways, were the Earldom of Chester and the Duchy of Lancaster. The Earldom was an indirect consequence of the Welsh wars of Edward I, having been created in its palatinate form for the king's son, Edward of Caernarfon, in 1301.[19] From 1398 it became permanently linked to the Principality of Wales, but the institutions of the two franchises remained entirely separate. The close involvement of the crown produced occasional anomalies. For example, in 1506 when letters patent extended the privileges of the town of Chester, which was parcel of the earldom, they were issued from the Chester Exchequer but in the king's name, in spite of the fact that his son Henry was earl of Chester at the time. Cheshire, which constituted the territorial extent of the palatinate, was not represented in parliament until 1543, and claimed exemption from parliamentary taxation, which it lost in 1540, before its first members had actually been elected!

The earldom was governed as a part of England in the sense that only English common law and local custom were recognized. Welsh custom, which still survived in some places, had status only at manorial level, and was not pleadable in any of the Earl's courts. English

19 *Victoria County History, Cheshire,* II, ed. B.E. Harris (1979) p. 9.

statute also applied, even before 1540. Cheshire had a number of the familiar English shire officers, such as sheriff and escheator, although they were appointed by the earl and not by the monarch. However, the palatinate also had distinctive officers and institutions, and all offices were terminated when the earldom changed hands, as happened in 1502 on the death of Prince Arthur. Normally the existing officers were reappointed, but that was not necessarily the case as most earls were minors on their creation, and the positions were effectively in the gift of the crown. The most important offices were those of justice, deputy justice and chamberlain. Originally the justice had both presided at the County Court and exercised such regalian rights as appointing to the constableships of castles and making grants of demesne land. However, by 1350 his administrative responsibilities were already diminishing, and the justice was commonly a nobleman who left the performance of his duties to his deputy. After the death of the earl of Derby in 1504 the justice was normally a gentleman with some legal experience, but most of the work continued to be done by the deputy. In Chester the County Court continued to be the supreme tribunal, as it had been originally in all counties, and was untroubled by the visitations of the Assizes. There was no commission of the peace, and the duties of gaol delivery were discharged by the County Court itself. Because there were neither Quarter Sessions nor Assizes, the court convened some eight or nine times a year, and had cognizance of all issues, both pleas of the crown and party pleas. It heard appeals from all other courts within the palatinate, including the Pentice Court of Chester, but was itself subject to procedure by writ of error from the monarch. Process followed the normal course by grand and petty jury, but as there were no justices of the peace, indictments came mainly from the traditional sheriff's tourn or judicial perambulation. The justice was also supposed to conduct an eyre once a year for the same purpose, but practice in this respect seems to have become somewhat lax.[20]

The chamberlain presided over the Exchequer, which was not only the principal fiscal court, but also acted as a Chancery for the franchise and conducted general administrative business. By the sixteenth century it was the chamberlain who exercised the royal prerogative of equity. The Exchequer issued commissions, including judicial commissions *pro hac vice,* which were occasionally used to supplement the efforts of the County Court. It was also the chamberlain who

20   Ibid.

convened the unique county assembly later known as the 'Chester parliament'. In theory this consisted of all the freemen in the county, and was called to vote the local taxes which took the place of tenths, fifteenths and parliamentary subsidies. The 'community of the county' not only voted taxes, it was also responsible for assessing them, and must have been the nearest thing to a democratic assembly anywhere in late medieval England.

Cheshire was divided into hundreds, and each hundred had its court. These courts retained their vitality long after similar assemblies in other counties had become moribund, because of the absence of justices of the peace. They were presided over not by high constables but by officers called bailiffs, who had originally been elected but were latterly appointed by the chamberlain. There were a number of other hundred officers, and the impression is that hundreds remained a more important elenent of government in Cheshire than elsewhere. In the early fourteeth century there had also been an experiment with officers called sergeants of the peace, who were substantial gentlemen appointed by the earl as local law enforcement officers. Their relationship to the sheriff is obscure, and the experiment does not seem to have succeeded, because they had disappeared by the fifteenth century. By the reign of Henry VII Cheshire shared the unhappy reputation of Wales for lawlessness, and the king began to intrude upon the privileges of the palatinate by including it in occasional commissions of oyer and terminer which were issued for groups of counties. Henry VIII, or possibly Wolsey, followed for a while a policy of building up the power of the courtier duke of Suffolk just over the border in Flint and Denbigh, in the hope of improving the state of public order in the whole area, but this seems not to have worked,[21] and when the Council in the Marches was resurrected, as we have seen, in 1525, it was also given oversight of the earldom. That seems not to have worked either, and when Cromwell finally decided to deal with Wales in 1535, Chester was included in his brief.

The statute of 27 Henry VIII c. 24 revolutionized the government of the palatinate no less than that of the principality. Thereafter all writs ran in the name of the king, but much more important, the functions of the County Court were drastically reduced by the intro-

---

21   S.J. Gunn, 'The regime of Charles Brandon, Duke of Suffolk, in north Wales, and the reform of Welsh government, 1509–1525', *Welsh History Review*, 12, 1985; P. Williams, *The Council in the Marches of Wales under Elizabeth* (1958), which also covers the earlier period.

duction of a commission of the peace. Quarter Sessions were held, as in all other counties, and the County Court convened only once a year. Instead of being included in one of the English Assize circuits, however, Chester was added to the Great Session circuit of Flint, Denbigh and Montgomery. Removal of exemption from parliamentary taxes spelled not only representation at Westminster, but also the end of local taxes, and with them of the 'community of the county'. Thereafter local rates, when needed for such purposes as militia training, were raised by the justices of the peace, as they were elsewhere. In most respects, however, the framework of the palatine government was preserved, as a kind of antiquarian shell, and the personal position of Sir Thomas Englefield, the justice of Chester, was protected by a clause of the act itself.[22] The county court dwindled, and the Exchequer lost most of its functions, but both continued to exist, and justices and chamberlains for Chester continued to be appointed. In 1569, in response to its own petition, Chester was removed from the jurisdiction of the Council in the Marches, and it seems that there was no longer considered to be any particular disciplinary problem.

The other major royal palatinate was the Duchy of Lancaster. Like Chester, this had been specifically created for a prince of the blood, in this case John of Gaunt, the fourth son of King Edward III. He succeeded to the earldom of Lancaster in the right of his wife, Blanche, the daughter of Henry of Grosmont, when the latter died in March 1361. The dukedom was revived for him in November 1362, and converted into a palatinate in 1377. At first this was for the life of the existing duke, but in 1396, three years before he died, it was settled in perpetuity upon his heirs, presumably with no intention of the eventual outcome. It was the return of Gaunt's exiled son, Henry of Bolingbroke, to claim the Lancaster inheritance which triggered the events leading to Richard II's deposition later in 1399. The duchy was then merged with the crown when Bolingbroke became king as Henry IV. Henry, however, was careful to preserve the autonomous jurisdiction of the duchy, granting in parliament a charter which declared its lands and possessions to be separate and distinct from those of the crown.[23] The Royal prerogatives within the palatinate were then vested in an establishment called the chancellor and Council of the

22 *Statutes of the Realm*, III, p. 558.
23 *Victoria County History, Lancashire*, I, eds W. Farrer and J. Brownhill (1906) p. 296.

duchy. When Henry VII secured the throne in 1485, there seems to have been some doubt about the nature of the connection between the duchy and the crown, because it was vested in him and the heirs of his body by a statute separate from that which recognized his title to the throne. Like Chester, Lancaster had its own Exchequer, over which the chamberlain presided, but unlike Chester it also had a separate Chancery. The chancellor was the senior officer, and there was no office of justice. The duke appointed the sheriff, and the king's writ did not run, but since the king was *ipso facto* also the duke the point of the distinction is even harder to see than in the case of Chester. The duke issued commissions of oyer and terminer, and also of the peace, so the administration of justice in the franchise was, to all intents and purposes, the same as within a normal county, access to the king's courts via a writ of error lying in the same way as for other franchises. The statute of 1536 consequently made very little difference to the way in which Lancashire was run; a clause in the act even providing that commissions to justices there should continue to be issued over the duchy seal, although in the king's name. Unlike Chester, Lancashire had been represented in parliament almost from the inception of the palatinate, and had never enjoyed exemption from parliamentary taxation. The special commissions of oyer and terminer were replaced by membership of a normal Assize circuit, but the same justices continued to act, and the distinction must have been hard to discern.

However, in one respect Lancaster was unique. The palatinate proper covered only the county of Lancashire, but the duchy was much more extensive. It held lands all over England, and when the monasteries were dissolved, the property of all those houses which had been founded by former dukes of Lancaster were added to the duchy estate, not coming under the control of the Court of Augmentations.[24] Moreover, in place of a normal barony court, the Duchy of Lancaster continued to have a chancellor and a chancery court, which became known as the Court of Duchy Chamber. This court not only managed the estate, and provided a model of administration and accountancy upon which the procedures of Augmentations were based, it also continued to exercise Chancery jurisdiction in respect of the tenants

---

24   R. Somerville, *A History of the Duchy of Lancaster* (1953), Vol.I: 1265–1603; G.R. Elton, *The Tudor Revolution in Government* (1953), pp. 203ff, 208. Duchy of Lancaster Entry Books of Orders, vol. VI, ff. 204v–205; G.R. Elton, *The Tudor Constitution*, 2nd edn (1982), pp. 387–8.

of that estate. As Sir Edward Coke wrote in the early seventeenth century, 'The proceeding in this Court of the Duchy Chamber at Westminster is as in a Court of Chancery for lands, etc. within the survey of that Court, by English bill etc., and decree; but this Chancery Court is not a mixed Court as the Chancery of England is, partly of the common law and partly of equity.'[25] Duchy Chamber had no common law jurisdiction, because it was not by then any part of a true franchise. Other extensive baronies were also vested in the crown, notably the Duchy of Cornwall, but Cornwall had never been a palatinate in the same manner as Chester and Lancaster, and never had a court of such peculiar jurisdiction. Duchy Chamber remained independent when all the other financial courts were merged into the Exchequer in 1554, and by Coke's time was a curiosity worthy of comment.

FRANCHISES HELD BY PRIVATE LORDS

By the early sixteenth century the Regality of Durham was the only full palatine jurisdiction still in the hands of a subject. Older than either Chester or Lancaster, it traced its origins to the need for defence against the Scots, and the king's desire to have an agent of his own in the far north, as a counterweight to the necessary power of the major northern nobility.[26] The regality was co-extensive with the bishopric of Durham, and included the county proper, the wapentake of Sadberge in North Yorkshire, and the 'shires' of Bedlington and Norham within Northumberland. Within these lands all writs ran in the name of the bishop rather than the king, but the structure of government was not particularly distinctive. The common law was administered by justices of the peace and justices of Assize, in the same manner as in other counties. The commissions, whether of the peace, gaol delivery or oyer and terminer, were issued by the bishop, but as in Lancaster the justices of Assize were the king's judges of the northern circuit. The bishop's chief executive officer was his chancellor, who was invariably a cleric, and who presided over the Chancery court, which dealt with administrative business and equity jurisdiction. Durham was not represented in parliament, and in theory

25   Sir Edward Coke, *The Fourth Part of the Institutes* (1644), p. 206.
26   Robert Surtees, *The History and Antiquities of the County Palatine of Durham* (1816–40).

should have been exempt from national taxation. In practice the regality paid normal taxes, unless, as sometimes happened, it was exempted by the terms of the subsidy act in acknowledgement of its contribution to the defence of the border. The bishop's officers assessed such taxes when they fell due, and statute was administered as in the other franchises.

Politically, the bishop's position was unique, because in both Chester and Lancaster the local nobility and gentry were dealing, directly or indirectly, with the king. The bishop of Durham had to work out a set of viable political relationships for himself. Traditionally this involved conferring major offices, such as that of steward, upon sympathetic nobles. In 1569 the earl of Westmorland complained bitterly that Bishop Pilkington had deprived him of the right to lead the bishopric men in the queen's service, a role which he claimed his family had discharged for generations.[27] At a slightly lower level there were offices such as that of sheriff and escheator, which were bestowed upon gentry whose families made up the bishop's affinity. When the crown was weak, the bishop's position could be exposed, so it was necessary for him to have resources and *manred* with which to sustain himself. His income, at about £2,800 a year, was certainly adequate for that purpose, but he normally lacked the kindred which was so necessary for power in the region. However, the late medieval bishops were magnates in fact as well as name, and in the sixteenth century such men as Sir Robert Bowes, Sir Thomas Tempest and Sir William Eure rose in the bishop's service before establishing themselves in the confidence of the crown.[28]

The statute of 1536, which formally ended the autonomy of the regality, consequently made little real difference. It was provided in the act that the bishop himself and his chancellor should be *ex officio* commissioners of the peace, which ensured that the commission could not be 'captured' against him, but the political situation remained unchanged. Cuthbert Tunstall was a royal servant first and foremost, more skilled in diplomacy and administration than in government. For a short time after his enthronement in 1530 he was president of the Council of the North, but he was not a success in that office, and may well have been appointed mainly to get around the problem presented by the regality to the jurisdiction of that body.

27   PRO SP12/48/155, 159; M.E. James, *Family, Lineage and Civil Society* (1974), p. 43.
28   James, *Family, Lineage and Civil Society*, p. 45.

Once the palatinate status of the regality had been removed, the authority of the council could be extended to the whole region, and that was done after the defeat of the Pilgrimage of Grace in 1537. Tunstall's extremely reluctant conformity to the religious changes of Edward VI's reign prompted a radical plan for his removal. In 1551 he was arrested upon a flimsy charge of misprision of treason, and deprived by a royal commission in the following year. The bishopric was then abolished by statute. It was alleged, both at the time and since, that the motive for the duke of Northumberland's initiative in this matter was to create a new palatinate for himself, and to seize the extensive endowments of the see.[29] However, this appears not to have been the case. A new 'palatinate' was indeed created, but it was left in the king's hands and the provisions of 1536 were not repealed. Northumberland became steward, with the leading of the bishopric men, but obtained no lands. Instead it was proposed to create two new sees, one in Durham and the other in Newcastle, which would have absorbed almost the whole endowment of the old see. Probably the main reason for the attack, apart from the desire to be rid of Tunstall, was the need to increase the number of senior ecclesiastical posts in the north to which reliable Protestants could be appointed.[30] Edward VI's death put an end to these plans, and in 1554 the traditional see was restored, with all its surviving prerogatives. At the time of the Catholic rising in 1569, Durham cathedral and its clergy were prime targets, and a succession of strongly Protestant bishops throughout Elizabeth's reign more or less fulfilled the Edwardian intention. For some unexplained reason Durham County remained unrepresented in the House of Commons until the late seventeenth century. Both the see and the cathedral were abolished in 1647, but restored in 1660. The bishopric remained extremely wealthy until Bishop Van Mildert wisely divested himself of much of his income to found the university in 1832, and the remnants of the palatinate administration survived into the present century, the Chancery Court being finally discontinued in 1978.

There were a great many less important franchises in the early sixteenth century, but none of them had full palatinate status. The Isle of Ely was a franchise in the hands of the bishop, where the royal writ

29   D.M. Loades, 'The last years of Cuthbert Tunstall, Bishop of Durham, 1547–1559', *Durham University Journal*, 66, 1973; Charles Sturge, *Cuthbert Tunstall* (1938), pp. 281–96.
30   PRO Parliament Roll, 7 Edward VI; C65/161, item 12.

did not run, but all that meant was that the justices of the peace and Assize operated there by virtue of an episcopal commission, as they did in Durham. The bishop also appointed his own officers, but there was no question of exemption from taxation, and for most purposes, including parliamentary representation, the Isle of Ely was a part of Cambridgeshire. In 1536 it was provided that the bishop and his chancellor should be justices of the peace, but there was no separate commission for the isle. The same applied in the archbishop of York's peculiar at Hexham, although that was not finally incorporated into Northumberland until 1572. The other border liberties, Tynedale and Redesdale, had been created for military purposes, and were run by their wardens without much reference to the niceties of government in lowland England. The wardens administered both common law and march custom, and both were subjected to statute law, although normally exempt from regular taxation. Tynedale was already in the hands of the crown when it was discontinued by statute in 1494, and merged into Northumberland. Redesdale seems not to have been encompassed by the 1494 act, and therefore presumably fell in 1536, by which time it too was in royal hands. As so often, practice and theory appear to have been at variance, because although by 1550 both Tynedale and Redesdale had been part of Northumberland for some time, Sir Robert Bowes reported in that year that the keepers exercised all public authority in the king's name, and the sheriff very seldom intervened.[31]

At the opposite end of England a rather similar situation appertained in the Cinque Ports. This franchise, originally comprising the five towns of Hastings, Dover, Hythe, Romney and Sandwich, had expanded by the late thirteenth century to embrace nearly forty towns and villages around the south east coast, from Seaford in Sussex to Brightlingsea in Essex. It had been created to provide ship service for the crown, and was therefore a variant of military tenure. In their heyday the towns sent as many as fifty ships in response to the king's demand, which was by far the largest contingent in any navy royal. In return the crown granted the towns extensive commercial privileges, and virtual jurisdictional autonomy. The situation was complex, because each town had its own charter, in addition to the collective grants of 1204, 1252 and 1260.[32] The Cinque Ports were not a

31   John Hodgson, *A History of Northumberland* (1820–5), III, ii, pp. 222–24.
32   K.M.E. Murray, *The Constitutional History of the Cinque Ports* (1935); F.W. Brooks, 'The Cinque Ports', *Mariners' Mirror*, 15, 1929.

palatinate, in the sense that the monarch's writ ran there, but the return of writs belonged exclusively to the officers of the franchise, and the sheriffs of Kent, Sussex and Essex did not interfere. The court of the Cinque Ports was called the Shepway, and functioned in much the same way as the County Court of Chester, administering the common law. Already by the fourteenth century it was convened by the lord warden, who was an officer of the crown and who appointed the judges, rather misleadingly known as the barons. Consequently, although it was not served by normal judicial commissions, and acted as both Assize and Quarter Sessions, it was not in any meaningful sense autonomous. Although by the sixteenth century the Cinque Ports had ceased to perform any useful ship service, they clung to their privileges tenaciously, particularly the exclusive right to plead in the Shepway. By the late sixteenth century seven of the Cinque Ports were represented in the House of Commons, but they were still listed under the title of the liberty, and not of their counties. The Cinque Ports were not touched by the statute of 1536, and although they had enjoyed a reputation for lawlessness (particularly at sea) in the thirteenth century, by the reign of Elizabeth their jurisdictional status was little more than an antiquarian curiosity.

Sixteenth-century England was littered with jurisdictional exemptions of various kinds, which fell far short of palatinate status, but which conferred jealously guarded privileges. One such was the Stannaries, the corporation of Cornish tin miners. Because of the special skills, and risks, which were involved, these miners had been granted a monopoly to extract and refine the ore. By the nature of their occupation they could hardly be inhabitants of any particular corporate town, so that status was conferred upon the company itself, which was given the right to hold its own court. To that extent it did not differ from many other commercial companies, but the Stannary court, which imposed strict controls upon the processing and marketing of tin, was also granted the right to hear pleas of the crown. Consequently the tinners could plead, and be impleaded, only in that court. Stannary jurisdiction was personal rather than territorial, resembling in that respect the authority of an ecclesiastical court over a clerk in holy orders. The Stannary court was conducted by a single judge, and administered both the common law and stannary custom. This judge was appointed by the warden, in whose name the court was also held, but by the sixteenth century the warden, like the lord warden of the Cinque Ports, had long since been a crown appointment, so the franchise involved almost no degree of genuine autonomy. In the 1590s this position was held by the courtier Sir Walter Raleigh.

The jurisdiction of the lord admiral was also, somewhat paradoxically, a franchise. The admiral was a major officer of state, appointed by the crown, but because his jurisdiction was exercised *ex officio* without commission, and the profits were not accounted to the Exchequer, it had many of the characteristics of a liberty. The office of lord admiral had originated in the thirteenth century as a military command, and his court had developed its procedures and jurisdiction slowly over a long period. By the late fifteenth century the admiral had lost all contact with active sea service, but his court had established a wide-ranging jurisdiction.[33] The law which it administered was not the common law but, as we have seen, a mixture of civil law and custom called the *lex maritima*, which was the nearest thing to international law which then existed. Because these procedures were deemed to be ineffective, however, it was determined to transfer criminal pleadings to the ordinary courts. Consequently the statute of 28 Henry VIII c. 15 decreed:

> For Reformation whereof be it enacted . . . that all treasons, felonies, robberies, murders and confederacies hereafter to be committed in or upon the sea, or in any other haven, river, creek or place where the Admiral or admirals have or pretend to have power authority or jurisdiction, shall be enquired, tried, heard, determined and judged in such shires and places in the realm as shall be limited by the king's commission or commissions to be directed for the same, in like form and condition as if such offence or offences had been committed or done in or upon the land.'[34]

In other words such cases were to be heard by commissions of oyer and terminer under the common law. The lord admiral and the admiralty judge were to serve on such commissions *ex officio*, but the jurisdiction had been resumed by the crown.

The situation seems to have improved temporarily, but after Cromwell's fall the statute was allowed to lapse, and the admiralty court resumed its sway. By the 1570s piracy was again at the top of

---

33   R.G. Marsden, *Select Pleas in the Court of Admiralty* (Selden Society, 1892–7); Sir Travers Twiss, *The Black Book of the Admiralty* (Rolls Series, 1871–6).
34   *Statutes of the Realm*, III, p. 671.

the international agenda, and complaints against the extreme tardiness of the Admiralty Court could be heard from all quarters. The problem was eventually brought under control, not by hanging more pirates but by proceeding effectively against their sponsors and backers ashore, a campaign in which the Admiralty Court played only a minor part. The admiral received all fines, confiscations and amercements levied, and 20 per cent of all lawful prizes, out of which he paid the expenses of the court. After the death of the earl of Oxford in 1514, Tudor admirals were normally again active sea commanders, so the exercise of admiralty jurisdiction became increasingly a matter for the judge or commissary, and for those who acted locally in his name. Wherever there was sea coast there was matter for the Admiralty Court, and by the later fifteenth century it was normal to appoint vice-admirals of the coasts.[35] These officers conducted their own courts, and received an agreed proportion of the profits, while appeal could lie to the lord admiral himself. Vice-admirals were appointed by the admiral, and not by the monarch, but they had something of the nature of justices of the peace. Not only were they supposed to hear pleas and try offenders, they were also supposed to catch them, and police work became a large part of their function. It was extremely rare for a justice of the peace to be accused of accepting bribes or conspiring with criminals, but such charges were often made against vice-admirals, and often, it would seem, with justice. Piracy was in the blood of such coastal gentry families as the Killigrews in Cornwall or the Bulkeleys of Anglesea, and successive lord admirals were insufficiently vigilant in that respect. One, Lord Thomas Seymour in 1549, was actually accused of conducting such unlawful practices himself, and executed for that reason – among others.

The admiralty is a perfect example of the kind of ambiguity which could exist between public and private authority in the Tudor period. Numerous port towns and other jurisdictions claimed exemption from the admiral's control, and thus became franchises within a franchise. The Cinque Ports were naturally exempt, having their own Admiralty Court, which proved particularly difficult to pressurize when the crown was endeavouring to improve the behaviour of English seamen. However, towns like Great Yarmouth, which had conducted a long-standing feud with the Cinque Ports, appointed their own vice-admirals, without reference to either the lord admiral

---

35   R.G. Marsden, 'The vice admirals of the coasts', *English Historical Review*, 22, 1907.

or the crown, and were entitled to do so by their charters. Even more uncontrollable were those coastal manors and honours where the lord claimed admiralty jurisdiction as part of his customary rights. Such claims were often substantiated, and meant that lords who might control no more than a few hundred yards of foreshore were entitled to hold their own Admiralty Courts. This not only made the coast extremely difficult to police, it also meant that the vice-admiral's control was very patchy. The monarch might be able to exercise effective control over the lord admiral, who was a crown servant, and through him over the vice-admirals, but there was no way in which central government could discipline these innumerable petty liberties without resorting to legislation. The act of 1536 did not touch them, because they did not impinge directly upon a regalian right. In fact the act for the resumption of franchises removed only the tip of the iceberg. The intention expressed in the preamble was comprehensive:

> Where divers of the most ancient prerogatives and authorities of justice appertaining to the Imperial crown of this Realme have been severed and taken from the same by sundry gifts of the king's most noble progenitours, kings of this realm, to the great diminution and detriment of the royal estate of the same, and to the hindrance and great delay of justice;[36]

but the effect was much less so.

The real hindrance to unity of control in the hands of the monarch was not the major franchises, most of which had been neutralized by one means or another long since, but the innumerable minor liberties, many of them offering no more than a single exemption. Some of these had been granted by the crown, directly or indirectly; others by mesne lords. They belonged to a distributive concept of authority, of which the feudal system itself had been the greatest example. What the Henrician statute did do was to signal a major change of attitude. The frontier between public and private jurisdiction was being moved. The crown was encroaching, and would continue to encroach, upon any autonomous authority which affected the common weal. The church, the nobility, ancient and privileged corporations – all were equally subjects, and in so far as privileges continued to be enjoyed, they were enjoyed by the monarch's sufferance.

---

36   27 Henry VIII, c. 24; *Statutes of the Realm*, III, pp. 555–8.

7

Informal Structures

No description of formal structures can express the whole truth about the way in which authority was exercised and transmitted in early modern England. The political nation was extremely small by modern standards: between 1,200 and 1,500 families of gentry status and above; some 10,000 individuals in a population of between two and a half and three million. The peerage averaged about fifty families through the sixteenth century, and an average county elite perhaps a little more. The Merchant Adventurers Company had about 100 members. Within these groups the members knew each other well, married into each other's families, and shared common elements of culture and education. The clergy were rather more numerous, at least in the early part of the sixteenth century. In 1500, between the regulars and the seculars in major orders, they may well have numbered 17,000 or 18,000, but they cannot really be counted as a single interest group. The divisions between the clerical leadership and the rank and file were notorious, and only the former, perhaps 10 per cent of the total, could be counted as part of the governing class. By 1600 the clerical population had declined by some 40 per cent, but the increasing incidence of graduate clergy meant that about a quarter of that total would have ranked as gentlemen in the new dispensation. There was no equivalent of the old school tie, but the shared experience of training in the Inns of Court increased the corporate identity of the common lawyers as a profession, and increasing resort to the universities by both clergy and lay gentry in the latter part of the century laid the foundations for an elite of education. By contrast the older affinities, linked by service to a noble house and shared interests in regional affairs, were losing their earlier strength. Only the royal court retained its attractiveness unimpaired. Not only did it become by far the most important centre of patronage, draining the support away from noble households, it also benefited from the increasing institutional strength of the crown to draw in clients and dependents from the elite of every county. The English sense of identity was changing. Kindred and county meant less in 1600 than they had a century earlier, while professional and crown service meant more.

THE COMMON LAWYERS

The Inns of Court in their sixteenth-century form were of comparatively recent origin. Traditionally, aspiring lawyers had trained simply by attending the courts in session, where places were reserved for them and judicial comment was largely designed for their enlightenment. As Sir John Fortescue put it, 'the laws of England . . . are read and taught in these courts, as if in public schools, to which students of the law flock every day in term time'.[1] No fees appear to have been charged for this instruction, but of course the student was earning nothing, and having to support himself. As there were no formal qualifications, the student must have turned himself into a practitioner by trial and error, and probably by attracting a patron to inspire confidence in potential clients. There were inns in London for 'apprentice lawyers' from at least 1329, but these seem to have been simply hostels to accommodate those coming from the provinces to sit at the feet of the justices of King's Bench and Common Pleas. Very little is known about either the locations of these inns or their internal economy, but as training must have lasted for several years, it is likely that they developed into student communities where professional friendships and associations could be formed as they were in the inns of a later period.

Legal education in the later sense was developed first in the Inns of Chancery, as a side line to their main business of training Chancery clerks.[2] The connections between the business of that department and the courts of common law were sufficiently close to make this a natural development. From about 1370 senior Chancery clerks were giving instruction in such basic matters as the processing of writs, fitting their lectures into the vacations between law terms. So successful, and presumably profitable, was this operation that within a generation the Inns of Chancery were being devoted mainly to the training of common lawyers, the demand for the latter being far greater than that for Chancery clerks. Very little is known about the manner of this

---

1   Sir John Fortescue, *The Praise of the Laws of England,* ed. S.B. Chrimes (1942), p. 117.
2   J.P. Dawson, *Oracles of the Law* (1968), p. 36n.

instruction; there are references to both 'readings' and 'moots' in the early fifteenth century, but it is not known whether these were similar to the later exercises of the same name. At the same time the Inns of Court were essentially clubs or company halls for established lawyers, rather similar to the company halls which served the merchant community of London. Law readings, moots and other exercises were held, but these were voluntary practices for established lawyers rather than instruction for beginners.

Lincoln's Inn began to change that pattern in about 1436, when nineteen of the fellows undertook what was clearly a programme of training for intensified readings and lectures, presumably in response to a new policy of admission. By 1460 a regular syllabus of instruction was in place, and participation was made mandatory for the junior members, or 'clerks'. A few years later it was noted that Lincoln's Inn was too expensive for anyone but the son of a gentleman to enrol at, so presumably substantial fees were already being charged, and that may well have been the main reason for the change of direction. Between 1460 and 1495 a full *cursus honorem* was developed, which amounted to a graded system of professional qualification. 'Fellows of the bench' first appear in 1441, and a few years later 'bencher' had replaced 'Master' as the normal term for a senior member, reflecting the greater importance of formal instruction, because the bench was the chairman's seat for training disputations. After a period of experience in this occupation, usually four or five terms, a bencher would normally be elected to read an exercise, which might be specified, or might be of his own choice, at which point he became a reader. As early as 1455 the general body of the members were being referred to as 'barristers', from the bar which separated the participants from the bench during formal exercises. The most junior, the students proper, sat in front of the bench, below the bar, and for that reason were known as 'inner barristers'. The more senior sat at the sides of the room, outside the bar, and were known as 'utter barristers'. Formal transfer from one status to the other, as a result of the successful completion of a set number of disputes, existed by 1494, and soon after was known as the call to the bar.[3]

Lincoln's Inn was the pioneer. The other inns – Gray's, Inner Temple and Middle Temple followed a similar process of development over the following half century. By about 1550 it was normal for

3   On the *cursus honorem,* and other particulars of the Inns of Court, see E.W. Ives, *The Common Lawyers of Pre-Reformation England* (1983), pp. 36–42.

a young man to spend four or five years as an inner barrister, followed by a further two or three as an utter barrister, before being allowed to practise in the courts. To a large extent progress in the profession was related to progress at the inn. A bencher would have begun to practise, and election as a reader signified a successful professional start. Lawyers remained members of their inns for life, whether they were practising in the capital or not, and this created permanent links between them, binding the provincial practitioners to London. However, not all members of the inns were professional lawyers. By the reign of Elizabeth, just as it was becoming normal for a young gentleman to spend a year or two at university, in order to acquire a fashionable smattering of classical learning, so it was customary to sit for a few terms as an inner barrister. Such a young man left the university without a degree, and left his inn without ever being called to the bar. Nevertheless the importance of this 'third university' in shaping the attitudes and administrative skills of the gentry class would be hard to overestimate. The law was immensely important. Its rules governed the acquisition and transmission of property, laid down codes of political conduct, and safeguarded the rich against the depredations of the poor. As E.W. Ives wrote a few years ago:

> The same concurrence of law and administration is seen in county government. The most powerful officer was the justice of the peace, and the most important organ the court of quarter sessions. Crime and county business were dealt with side by side; a rogue might be bound over to keep the peace, or a householder to replace a ruinous public bridge on his property, while a respectable yeoman who forgot his share of road repairs might find himself prosecuted along with a pickpocket.[4]

It was not only the justice of the peace and the sheriff who needed a knowledge of the law. Every steward, surveyor and indeed householder, was better equipped to face the realities of life with such a knowledge. Agnes Paston had advised her son Edmund in the 1460s 'to thynkke onis of the daie of yowre fadris counseyle to lerne the lawe, for he seyde manie tymis that ho so ever shulde dwelle at Paston schulde have nede to conne defende hymselfe'.[5] That situation did not change, and the increasing demands made upon the gentry by the crown emphasized the importance of such skill for respect and

4 Ives, *Common Lawyers*, p. 9.
5 *Paston Letters and Papers*, ed. N. Davis (1971), I, p. 27.

substance in the local community. The law was also the only professional management training then available. When John Fairechild applied to Wolsey for the post of clerk of the works at Tournai in 1513, he claimed to be qualified to work as a clerk in a common law court, as an attorney, or a solicitor, a court keeper or an auditor, qualifications which had already earned him the position of clerk controller to the duchess of Norfolk. Lawyers were prominent in the House of Commons, and in business affairs at all levels. The law was by far the largest secular profession and, as the clergy lost status after 1535, the most influential profession in all aspects of public life.

The leaders of the profession were the eight or nine judges who made up the two benches at Westminster. They not only exercised a general oversight over all those pleading before the courts, they were also responsible for the discipline of the Inns of Court. Immediately below the judges in status were the half dozen or so sergeants at law. These were selected by the lord chancellor from among those perceived to be the ablest barristers pleading before the courts, and have been described as the 'reserve judges'. Judges and sergeants together formed the order of the coif, and vacancies of the benches were filled from their ranks. A call to the bar did not constitute an automatic right to plead, nor did the status of bencher, because ranks were only relevant to the inns themselves. It was the judges who decided when a man should be allowed to appear in court, and although they commonly observed the customs outlined above, they were not bound by them. A barrister with access to the court was rather misleadingly called an 'apprentice at law', and it was from among these apprentices (in fact senior lawyers) that the sergeants were chosen. There were about a hundred of them at any given time, and they did most of the advocacy work at Westminster, as well as acting as recorders for the most important towns, and taking retainers as legal advisers from the members of the nobility. Together with the judges and sergeants they formed a closely knit and cohesive group, well known to each other personally, and jealous of their collective identity. The remainder of the legal profession, ten or twenty times as numerous, operating as attorneys, solicitors, clerks, land agents, legal advisers and men of affairs, were bound together much more loosely by a common *esprit de corps*, by membership of the inns, and by mutual interest.

As Ives has shown in tracing the career of Thomas Kebell, their commonest social origin was among the minor gentry. Thomas was the third son of Walter Kebell of Rearsby, near Leicester, himself a man of obscure origin who had become the steward of the honour of Burgavenny. By about 1430 Walter had become a man of some substance, and Thomas was born in or about 1439 to Walter's second wife, Agnes. Between them his father and his mother had a ramifying kindred among the parish gentry of that part of Leicestershire, but could claim no importance at county level. When John Kebell succeeded his father in about 1463 the estate was worth some £85 a year. Thomas, with no prospect of support from his father's lands, enrolled at the Inner Temple in about 1454. Very little is known about his progress over the next few years. He married at some unknown date, and probably gave his first reading in about 1465. By then he had almost certainly been admitted as an advocate, but it took him nearly twenty years of successful practice to achieve distinction. In 1486 he became a sergeant at law, and it was probably in that year that he gave the reading on the statute of Westminster I, which subsequently became celebrated.[6] Thomas Kebell's practice can be only very patchily reconstructed. He first appears in the records as one of the sureties for a royal grant in 1470, and thereafter references to him multiply steadily. In 1474 he surpassed both his father and his elder brother by becoming a justice of the peace for Leicestershire, and he served on a number of royal commissions over the next decade. At about the same time he attracted the attention of the king's chamberlain, William, Lord Hastings, who became his patron and for whom he undertook a variety of legal work. It was almost certainly this patronage which marked him out for preferment. Hasting's fall in 1483 put him in no particular danger because he was not a political figure of any significance, and he continued to undertake legal commissions for former members of the Hastings retinue who had attached themselves to other patrons – including Henry VII.

Kebell served as a sergeant until his death in 1500, and the records of his practice during that period are rich and varied. His income probably reached about £300 a year during this period. He married twice more after the death of his first wife, and left a son, Walter, by his second marriage. He built up a substantial estate in Leicestershire, centred on the manor of Humberstone, where he lived in considerable luxury. Both his will and his inventory survive, showing that he died possessed of goods worth nearly £800.[7] He was a far richer man,

6 Ives, *Common Lawyers*, p. 64. For a full account of Kebell's career, see Ives, *passim*.
7 PRO PROB12 ff. 22v–23v; Wiltshire Record Office 88: 5/17a; Ives, *Common Lawyers*, pp. 425–47.

and a much more important man in Leicestershire, than either his brother or his nephew. Many of his business transactions also remain, showing him to have been as effective in this capacity as in his legal practice. Success on this scale did not make a lawyer popular. As William Harrison somewhat sourly remarked: 'as after the coming of the Normans the nobility had the start, and after them the clergy; so now all the wealth of the land doth flow unto our common lawyers.'[8] In a sense Kebell was a representative figure. His career demonstrates not only what was possible for a common lawyer, but also what was achieved by a number of men in each generation – dozens, or even scores, in the course of the sixteenth century, making them an important presence on the social and political scene. But he was not typical, because of the 145 lawyers who were assessed in goods for the 1523 subsidy ninety-eight – the overwhelming majority – were rated at between £40 and £100. Only eleven came into Kebell's bracket of £300+. Nevertheless an average assessment of about £60 made the lawyers a very substantial group, and a significant presence within the political nation.

A century later both the size and the wealth of the profession had increased. Between 1510 and 1560, 109 men were called to the bar at Lincoln's Inn. Between 1560 and 1600 the comparable figure is 346, with a marked leap in the 1560s and another in the 1580s.[9] Altogether in the four inns 1,063 men were called to the bar in the course of Elizabeth's reign, and the total number of barristers in practice at any given time must have been approaching that figure; an increase of some 70–80 per cent from 1523, a period during which the increase in the population at large was about 25 per cent. By the early seventeenth century professional lawyers made up a significant proportion of the gentry class, somewhere between 5 and 10 per cent, and a very much larger proportion of that class had undertaken some legal training. Any figure would be a guess, but it could have been as high as 40 per cent. The educational pattern had also changed. Hardly any lawyers of Thomas Kebell's generation had been anywhere near a university, for the simple reason that the universities did not teach English law, and were still primarily institutions for aspiring clergy. Between 1590 and 1640 about 60 per cent of those who were called

8   William Harrison, 'The description of England', in Raphael Holinshed, *Chronicles etc.* (1807–8), I, p. 304.
9   W.R. Prest, *The Rise of the Barristers: a social history of the English bar, 1590–1640* (1986), p. 7.

to the bar had matriculated at either Oxford or Cambridge, and many had proceeded to degrees.[10] In terms of wealth and political power, although not of numbers, lawyers had overtaken the clergy before the end of the sixteenth century, and constituted the strongest professional interest group. It was the common law, rather than theology or contractual custom, which dominated the constitutional thought of the mid-seventeenth century, and has remained stronger than any ideological abstractions to the present day.

It is, however, important to remember that although the common lawyers formed much the largest group, they were not the only lawyers in sixteenth-century England. Before 1535 canon lawyers held many of the senior benefices of the church. They were few in number, but were all university graduates on the fast track to ecclesiastical promotion. After 1535 the study of canon law was banned from the English universities, and the skill gradually died out. The practitioners of Roman law, the civil lawyers, however, survived as a professional group. These were also university graduates, and a number of them held degrees from continental academies. They functioned particularly in the equity courts, and in the Court of Admiralty. By the late fifteenth century they were numerous enough, and influential enough, to have their own inn, the Doctors' Commons, and after 1535 they took over the business of the ecclesiastical courts. Individually a number of civilians were wealthy and influential, but they were small as a profession by comparison with their common law colleagues, and cannot be compared to them as a pressure group.

THE MERCHANTS

Merchants were not a profession in the same sense as lawyers or clergy. The interests of different trades and manufactures frequently conflicted, and the legislation of the middle and later years of the sixteenth century is littered with their attempts to score points off each other. However, the nature of their calling gave them wider horizons than their farming or artificer neighbours. England was covered with a close network of market towns, and a farmer in, say, Leicestershire might be within reach of a dozen markets on different days of the week. There were also numerous fairs which acted as centres for a larger area, and to which merchants might bring their goods from the

10   Ibid., App. D.

length and breadth of England. In spite of the poor roads, England's internal communications, thanks to navigable rivers and the paucity of natural obstacles, were reasonably good. Bridge and ferry tolls, although a nuisance, were not seriously obstructive; and highway robbery was a good deal less common than piracy at sea. One of the consequences of this was the development between 1550 and 1650 of what Eric Kerridge has called a 'metropolitan economy'.[11] Factors and agents of London merchants travelled to local fairs and markets, buying produce, which might then be redistributed either through London or directly. By this means a uniform system of weights and measures, based on those of London, gradually became accepted, and was eventually imposed by law. A metropolitan market for woollen cloth was already established by the middle years of Henry VIII's reign, when London controlled over 80 per cent of the export trade. This did not mean that 80 per cent of the cloth produced was sold through London, but it did mean that the London factors set the price levels. Such practices were not necessarily detrimental to the interests of provincial merchants. The hostmen of Newcastle upon Tyne based their prosperity upon selling their coal to the capital, a trade which was little hampered by piracy because of its high bulk-to-value ratio, and unsuitability for surreptitious disposal. Merchants trading in any particular commodity would tend to know their colleagues in other towns, and probably the London merchants whose factors they met week by week.

London was also the centre for those credit transactions which eventually became banking. A provincial merchant or landowner would have an account with a London merchant, who would advance him money for his purchases and be repaid, plus a commission, out of the profits of his sales. For example, in 1603 Sir Thomas Temple of Stowe in Gloucestershire had a London account with Thomas Farringdon. Farringdon paid bills in accordance with Temple's written and verbal instructions, and received payments from his tenants, and from graziers, woolmen and other to whom he had sold produce.[12] Farringdon was a merchant, but he was also a banker, lending out money from the credit balances in his possession to other London businessmen. By that time this sort of brokerage

11   Eric Kerridge, *Trade and Banking in Early Modern England* (1988).
12   E.F. Gay, 'The Temples of Stowe and their debts: Sir Thomas Temple and Sir Peter Temple, 1603–1653', *Huntington Library Quarterly*, II, 1938–9, pp. 425–8.

had been going on for at least a quarter of a century, and helped to knit the whole commercial community together in a bond of common interest.

The best example of a group with a high profile and considerable political power is the Company of the Merchant Adventurers. These were the merchants trading abroad in unfinished woollen cloth. We have already looked at them as an aspect of the power of London, but they were in theory a national company, and they certainly ran a nationwide network of agents. Their great advantage, both in dealing with the government and in dealing with potential rivals, was the scale of their capital resources. The company was not a joint stock operation, but it maintained permanent factors, not only at Antwerp but also at other ports of regular resort. This enabled individual members to unload their cloth and wait for the right market conditions before selling, instead of having to shift their goods at short notice in order to turn the ship around.[13] Contemporaries complained with justice that the Merchant Adventurers stifled the export trade of outports such as Southampton and King's Lynn, and drove out the Hanseatic merchants who had played such a large part in developing the economies of the east coast ports between 1470 and 1530.[14] However, because their resources enabled them to act as bankers to the crown, they forced successive Tudor councils to take commercial priorities seriously, and in the long run that did England a major service. As one contemporary observed:

> all experience of tymes have proved that thincorporated fellowshipp of merchants have alwaies kept best traffique for the common weale of their contry and that particular trades of sole persones not putt under orderly governement have bene to the decaye of those persones and to the common losse of theyre wholle natyon.[15]

The numerous companies which sprang up during Elizabeth's reign followed the same principle, which was the conventional wisdom of the time. As a result it is very difficult to see merchants simply in the context of their own urban community, even if that was London. It

---

13   R. Davis, *English Overseas Trade, 1500–1700* (1973); G.D. Ramsey, *John Isham, Mercer and Merchant Adventurer* (Northamptonshire Record Society, 21, 1962).
14   J.D. Fudge, *Cargoes, Embargoes and Emissaries: the commercial and political interaction of England and the German Hanse, 1450–1510* (1995), pp. 207–12.
15   PRO SP15/11, f. 222.

would be a long time before England became a nation of shopkeepers, but there is a good case for arguing that these companies exercised a degree of influence, and even political power, at least comparable with that of the lawyers, and by 1600 greater than that of the church.

Nor was the dependence of government upon commercial operations simply a question of underwriting loans, or contributing towards taxation. As public expenditure increased, the crown's need for services of all kinds increased. The navy provides some very good examples of this. In spite of importing as many as fifty French and Flemish gun founders, Henry VII bought most of his guns in Mechlin, but by 1543 his son was able to order no fewer than 200 cast iron cannon from workshops in England. By the reign of Elizabeth English guns, both iron and bronze, were among the best and most sought after in Europe. In 1500 the king had six or seven ships, and one dry dock at Portsmouth. When Henry VIII died in 1547 he left a fleet of over fifty ships, and dockyards at Portsmouth, Gillingham, Woolwich and Erith. Henry VII spent about £1,500 a year on his navy; by the reign of Edward VI it was costing £20,000 a year in peacetime, and three times as much in war.[16] Inflation over the same period was 100–150 per cent. Even the parsimonious Elizabeth was spending over £20,000 a year, but that represented a fall in real terms, as inflation continued to rise. Nevertheless ship building and armaments represent areas of the economy where the increased activity of the crown, and the technological advances which had to be pursued, provided a significant stimulus to industrial development. Elizabeth also invested in commercial expansion in a way which none of her predecessors had attempted, supplying both ships and money to such adventurers as William Hawkins and Francis Drake. As we have seen, courtiers, royal servants and city merchants were equally involved in supporting voyages, from Willoughby and Chancellor to Frobisher, Davies and Hudson. In this process the networks of the court and the city became extensively interwoven, to the benefit of both.

The mercantile community is extremely hard to quantify in social or political terms. Outside London the number of men whose wealth would have qualified them as gentlemen should probably be counted in hundreds rather than thousands. Within the capital the richest aldermen were the equals of peers, but it is doubtful whether those worth more than £50 a year would have numbered more than 1,000 – less than 1 per cent of the population. The commonwealth men

16   D. Loades, *The Tudor Navy* (1992), pp. 38, 101–2, 153–4.

blamed merchants, and particularly bankers, almost as vehemently as they blamed covetous landlords for the decay of what they saw as the traditional virtues of rural life. Twentieth-century historians who took such accusations at their face value have spoken of the 'rise of capitalism', and suggested that the merchant community was leading an entrepreneurial revolution in sixteenth-century England. The truth was a great deal less dramatic. Merchants had power and social influence in direct proportion to their wealth, which meant quite a lot in London, and a little in major provincial cities like Bristol and Norwich. They were more successful than their predecessors of a century before, and operated upon a wider stage, but they were in no position to set new agendas. Indeed the most successful of them hastened to invest their wealth in land, and their grandsons were indistinguishable from the traditional gentry. In rethinking political priorities they were less important than the lawyers. It would be almost another century before the financial power of the city of London was sufficient to alter the course of government, and the mercantile community could rival the landed interest in political power.

HOUSEHOLDS AND AFFINITIES

Aristocratic households were traditional centres of power, patronage and conspicuous consumption. The English Crown had succeeded in preventing the worst excesses of centrifugal feudalism, and had by the fifteenth century created a more centralized system of government than existed anywhere else in Europe, but it had not even attempted to alter the culture of personal loyalty. The concepts of public authority and the common good certainly existed, particularly among the clerical intelligentsia, but political and social discipline were usually seen in terms of obedience to a lord or other officer. Officers representing the monarch, such as judges of Assize or sheriffs, held the larger structure together, as we have seen, but the authority of the lord in his 'country' was natural rather than delegated, and was exercised through his household. Early medieval society had been organized for war, and the aristocracy were the men who fought, as distinct from the men who prayed and the men who worked. Even in the Tudor period the majority of the nobility and gentry still thought of service to the crown in arms as their proper vocation, although Lord Wharton was being a conservative northerner when he inscribed

'Pleasure in acts d'armys' over the door of Wharton Hall in 1559.[17] The circumstance of the Hundred Years War had given this culture a powerful new life. Traditional feudal levies were useless for prolonged campaigns, and the normal shire musters were for home defence only. Mercenaries were available, but hugely expensive in large numbers, so as we have seen aristocratic retinues became the mainstay of the royal armies. Regularly called upon over a long period of time, such retinues acquired a semi-permanent nature, and their value in domestic politics was soon appreciated. A nobleman's retinue would consist partly of his able-bodied male tenants, partly of an inflated number of yeomen servants, and partly of knights and gentlemen from his 'country'. These latter might be engaged through formal indentures of loyalty and service, or through verbal contracts of a similar nature, possibly confirmed with oaths.

The existence of such retinues, so well adapted to the pursuit of feuds, had always been a potential threat to the peace of the countryside. Henry V had busied 'giddy minds' with foreign wars – giving the private armies their proper occupation – but by the middle of the fifteenth century the ending of the French war, combined with the weakness of Henry VI, had brought about a major crisis. The yeomen servants quickly became professional bullies, used to fight enemies and intimidate victims. Independent gentry were forced to seek from a patron the protection which the king's courts and officers could no longer afford, and the dependency networks continued to grow, sucking in a larger and larger proportion of the ruling class. This created not only a situation of chronic political instability, but also a new variant of the traditional culture of personal loyalty. The household yeomen, who might number as many as 200 in the service of a great magnate such as the duke of York or the earl of Northumberland, wore their master's livery and badge, and recognized no authority but his. Even important gentlemen who had retinues of their own, like Sir Thomas Tempest, were proud to wear the badge of a lord, to be identified as his men, and to uphold him in his quarrels. Great houses, like Thornbury and Brancepeth, were not only fortesses with well-equipped armouries, they were also centres of aristocratic breeding and culture. A nobleman's gentle retainers would send their sons and daughters to be reared in their lord's house, to learn the skills appropriate to their status in life, and to absorb the atmosphere of obedience and deference with which they were surrounded.

17 Lawrence Stone, *The Crisis of the Aristocracy, 1558–1640* (1965), p. 200.

Edward IV had turned this situation to his advantage by establishing some controls over it. He focused the loyalty of the nobility upon himself, and built up his own and his brother Richard's personal followings. Although he caused Acts of Parliament to be passed against abuses of livery and maintenance, he made no serious attempt to reduce the system itself, largely because he had been brought up in it, and shared its values. Henry VII had a different background, and took a very different view. He could no more abolish the private retinue than he could abolish the aristocracy itself. Nor did he wish to do so, because the need of the crown for military service remained, even if it was seldom called upon. Instead he revived Edward's statute of 1468 against retaining, restricting the issue of private liveries to household servants, and imposing a system of royal licences.[18] It was this last clause which was seriously insisted upon, and provoked the celebrated (if largely formal) fine of £70,000 on Lord Abergavenny for retaining 471 men in Kent. At the same time Lord Brooke served the king in Brittany in 1489 with a personal following of almost a thousand men, and Lord Daubeney raised a similar number for the intended Scottish campaign of 1497.[19] Like Edward, Henry also sought to build up his own following, particularly in areas where the crown had little traditonal presence, like the far north. He did this by retaining important gentlemen himself, at first on a small scale. The death of the fourth earl of Northumberland in 1489 enabled him to chip away at the Percy following, and put a few 'fee'd men' into his own livery. Once retained, they were not allowed to accept the badge of any other lord, and in this way the king began to become a presence in the borders, as distinct from a distant overlord who could usually be ignored.

Henry VIII and Wolsey continued with the same policy. The great households created for Princess Mary at Ludlow and for Henry Fitzroy at Middleham in 1525 have to be seen as part of this programme.[20] Neither of these ventures was particularly successful, and Wolsey's fall in 1529 prevented further initiatives of the same kind; but the king did not give up the intention, and the failure of the

18   19 Henry VII, c. 14; *Statutes of the Realm*, eds A. Luders et al. (1810–28) II, pp. 658–60; S.B. Chrimes, *Henry VII* (1972), pp. 188–90.
19   Stone, *Crisis of the Aristocracy*, p. 203.
20   Loades, *Mary Tudor: a life* (1989), pp. 36–8. Much new work on FitzRoy's household is presently being done by Beverly Murphy, to whom I am grateful for information.

Pilgrimage of Grace in 1536 gave him a fresh opportunity. Being more warlike than his father, however, Henry was forced to give hostages to fortune. The earl of Wiltshire (admittedly a peer of his own creation) led 1,500 men to France in 1514, and in 1523 it was estimated that at least a third of the duke of Suffolk's army had been provided by his fellow peers.[21] Domestic upheavals had to be encountered in the same way, because the only military force directly at the king's disposal was the 200 yeomen of the guard. Until 1536 there had been little cause for anxiety on that front, but when Sir John Thimbleby 'assembled all his tenauntes frendes and servauntes together under the colour to do the Kinges service' and then joined the rebels at Pontefract, the old alarm bells began to ring again. A way out of this dilemma was clearly essential if all the effort which had gone into strengthening the royal power over the previous fifty years was not to be wasted, and in 1544 it was found. Quite illegally, and without any precedent, Henry sent militia conscripts out of the country to reinforce the garrison of Boulogne. There was no resistance and, apparently, no complaint.[22]

This coup did not transform the situation overnight. Edward VI used mercenaries, both at home and abroad, and both he and Mary used selective retaining to support their respective regimes.[23] Mary also used traditional methods to raise the force which went to the Low Countries with the earl of Pembroke in 1557, and in her abortive attempt to recover Calais in January 1558. On the latter occasion Lord Mountjoy remembered that he had been summoned 'with all my menn, frindes, and all the power I was able to make for her highnes service in the warrs',[24] but the summons had been cancelled before he had any chance to act. Even as late as the Armada campaign of 1588 there was a role, albeit a minor one, for aristocratic retinues. However, the corner had clearly been turned by 1558. Mary used her lord lieutenants as well as her nobles to raise Pembroke's force, and in 1573 Elizabeth regularized the new system by creating the trained bands. It was now these select men who were exempt from service overseas, it

21 Stone, *Crisis of the Aristocracy*, p. 203. S.J. Gunn, 'The French wars of Henry VIII', in *The Origins of War in Early Modern Europe*, ed. J. Black (1987).
22 Stone, *Crisis of the Aristocracy*, p. 205; J.J. Goring, 'Social change and military decline in mid-Tudor England', *History*, 60, 1975; J.J. Goring, 'Military obligations of the English people, 1511–1558' (PhD, London, 1955).
23 W.K. Jordan, *Edward VI: the threshold of power* (1970), pp. 57–69; D.M. Loades, *The Reign of Mary Tudor* (1991), pp. 194–231.
24 *Memoirs of Sir Hugh Cholmley* (1787), pp. 5–6.

being generally accepted that the remainder were liable to be pressed. With a shift of emphasis characteristic of Tudor methods, the same men were left in charge, but with a different title. The lord lieutenants were noblemen, for the most part, but they now led the trained bands by virtue of that office rather than as lords in their countries. 'Ancient Pistol and his forced levies', who were now sent abroad, were much more likely to be led by professional captains and commanded by career soldiers. This change did nothing for the quality of the expeditionary forces sent to the Low Countries or Brittany later in Elizabeth's reign, and Sir John Norris raged about the feeble and disaffected men who were swept off the streets of London or Bristol to make up his army. However, by 1600 the military necessity which had created the aristocratic retinue in the first place, and sustained it through centuries of political evolution, had finally been brought to an end.

In the last phase of its existence the quasi-military retinue began to change its nature. Between 1550 and 1553 the Duke of Northumberland licensed his friends to retain men in order to protect his own position, a manoeuvre which conspicuously failed. In 1554 the imperial ambassador, Simon Renard, urged his master to pay substantial inducements to the leading nobles, because the number of their retainers made them potentially dangerous opponents of Mary's marriage to Philip.[25] However, if that was their intention they were no more successful than Northumberland. The duke of Suffolk could raise no more than a handful of men in 1554. Both these examples serve to demonstrate that *manred* was not what it had been, a conclusion reinforced by the events of 1569. In that year the earl of Cumberland was still thought to be strong enough for his slowness in declaring his hand against the rebels to cause anxiety. However, the earls of Northumberland and Westmorland, who did try to bring out their followers against the crown, had only very limited success. Even in the far north, which was probably the most conservative part of England, the days when a great nobleman could raise a private army to trouble the king had passed. The deputy lieutenants of Cheshire reported during the same crisis that they were having difficulty mustering the county because so many men claimed to be retainers of the earl of Derby, but this may have been a technical pretext to avoid the inconveniences of service, because there was no doubt of Derby's loyalty. Even when she was in need of military support, Elizabeth

25   Renard to the Emperor, 3 September 1554. *Calendar of State Papers, Spanish*, eds Royall Tyler et al. (1862–1954), XIII, p. 45.

avoided the noble retinue as an option. In 1588 the earl of Pembroke volunteered to raise 300 horsemen and 500 footmen from west Wales at his own expense for the defence of the realm, but his offer was not taken up. What remained was shadow rather than substance, as courtiers jostled and competed to wear the colours of the leading favourites; Dudley or Cecil in the 1560s, Essex or Cecil in the 1590s. Sir Richard Molyneux was typical of this genre when he told Lord Burghley 'during my life I am only yours to be disposed on'. He did not have military service in mind, and in spite of the earl of Essex's tendency to collect bravos, these latter day affinities were closer to the political 'connections' of the eighteenth century than to the armed retinues of the fifteenth. The language of deference and dependence was misleading, because the gentry had been shaking themselves free from private lordship for over a century. In the words of Lawrence Stone, they had discovered that 'the king was a better Lord than the earl of Derby'. Essex looked briefly dangerous in 1601, because he acted in London and because the queen was old, but the fate which rapidly overtook him merely served to confirm that the crown could no longer be threatened by maverick peers, however many men they appeared to have in their service.

The gradual decay of traditional loyalties altered the nature of the great households, and reduced their political and social significance. Edward, earl of Derby, who died in 1572, was an old-fashioned peer who had 'bredd up many youths of noblemen, knights and esquires sonns' in his house. Twenty years earlier it had been noted that Princess Mary provided the best upbringing in piety and virtue for the daughters of noblemen and gentlemen.[26] Even as late as 1596 Sir Horatio Palavicino, who was certainly no backwoodsman, placed his eldest son in the household of the earl of Shrewsbury. However, the idea that it was no disparagement for a gentleman with an inheritance of £700 or £800 a year to be dependent upon a nobleman was rapidly becoming outmoded. By 1624, when Gervase Markham recalled the style of the Elizabethan second earl of Southampton, it was an elegy for a lost ideal. He had gone 'bravely attended and served by the best gentlemen of those countries where he lived; his muster role never consisted of four lackeys and a coachman, but of a whole troupe of at least an hundred well mounted gentlemen and yeomen'[27] By the time

---

26   Henry Clifford, *The Life of Jane Dormer, Duchess of Feria*, ed. J. Stevenson (1887), p. 63.
27   Gervase Markham, *Honour in his perfection* (1624), p. 20.

that Markham wrote, fashion had followed the departure of the military role. Gentlemen sent their sons to the universities and the Inns of Court, while those with military ambitions took service with a professional commander, probably abroad. There was little prospect for an aspiring soldier in the household of the third earl of Bedford. The noble household had become domesticated, and careers in the public life of the realm could only be found in the service of the crown. In 1572 the queen issued a fresh proclamation insisting that the wearing of livery must be confined to household servants, and in 1595 Lord Burghley finally prohibited any gentleman retained by a private lord from sitting as a justice of the peace.

While the gentleman servant withdrew to mind his own affairs with increased attention, the yeoman retainer dwindled into the footman and the butler. Cardinal Wolsey had kept over 400 servants in his houses in the 1520s; the duke of Northumberland over 200 in the early 1550s. The fourth earl of Derby had a staff of 118 at Knowsley in the 1580s, but a hundred years later the ninth earl needed only thirty-eight. The earl of Oxford had kept 100 men in his livery in the 1570s, but after the civil war even the duke of Albemarle had only six footmen.[28] As the noble households were reduced, the gentry followed suit, impelled partly by the need for economy, but much more by the sheer redundancy of such a method of display. The increasing effectiveness of royal government meant not only that they no longer needed the protection of their social superiors, but also that it was far too risky to pursue their own quarrels by force. Aristocratic brawling had not disappeared by 1603. Courtiers and their servants fought pitched battles on the streets of Westminster, and feuds in the countryside could still result in sieges and violent death as late as 1589. However, by that time such behaviour was not tolerated by the council, and the perpetrators were appropriately punished. The chances of a gentleman being involved in violent conflict of some kind during his adult life declined from about 60 per cent in the middle years of Elizabeth to about 20 per cent on the eve of the civil war. Although the disappearance of 'tall fellows', whether for protection or for display, was a gain to public order, there was also another side to the change.

One of the functions of a great household had been to maintain the honour of the householder, and that was achieved by generosity as much as by power. By 1600 the decline of hospitality was a pervasive

28   Stone, *Crisis of the Aristocracy*, pp. 212–13.

theme with the successors of the 'commonwealth men'.[29] However, as with earlier denunciations of aristocratic covetousness, it would be unwise to take these lamentations at their face value. Late Elizabethan bishops, with seriously depleted resources and reduced social status, certainly did not keep the lavish tables which Longland or Tunstall had kept in the earlier part of the century. Moreover, Calvinist ethics discouraged indiscriminate charity, on the grounds partly that the poor were the authors of their own misfortunes, and partly that organized giving was more effective.[30] Some Puritanically minded gentlemen preferred to be remembered for their frugality and good husbandry rather than for their generosity, but that did not become the prevailing attitude. What seems to have happened is that the diminishing scale of housekeeping which accompanied the declining retinues of the early seventeenth century led to the disappearance of the 'open house' type of hospitality which had caused Thomas Cromwell to feed 200 people twice a day at his London house in the 1530s, or the earl of Derby to entertain all comers on three days every week in the 1560s. In 1629 it was noted to his credit that Lord Petre gave alms to 105 poor people at Christmas and Easter.[31] It was all very well for Sir John Oglander to say 'I scorn base getting and unworthy penurious saving', but those who followed his advice, and neglected the skills of estate management for the pleasures of conspicuous consumption, faced bankruptcy. By 1586 the reckless behaviour of the earl of Oxford had cost him his entire estate.

By 1600 the economic situation had changed considerably from that of the early sixteenth century. Stable prices, long leases and predictable rents were things of the past. An estate, large or small, needed attentive management if real levels of income were to be maintained, and those families which prospered, both noble and gentle, were those which gave that attention. Opportunities for investment were far more varied, and potentially profitable, but were not for those who could not be bothered to husband their resources. It had been the dawning awareness of the need for such care which had caused gentlemen to be denounced for covetousness in the 1540s, and lingering reluctance to face the facts of economic life which led to the lamentations over the demise of hospitality. Those who took care of their income could afford to indulge in traditional generosity, up to a

29 Felicity Heal, *Hospitality in Early Modern England* (1990), p. 93.
30 Heal, *Hospitality*, pp.133–38.
31 Stone, *Crisis of the Aristocracy*, p. 48.

point, and could be sure of lavish praise for doing so. When Sir Ralph Delaval's son praised his late father for having kept 'an open, great and plentifull' house in the early years of the seventeenth century, it is reasonable to assume that he had not left him an incumbered inheritance. There was also an element of deception, even of self-deception, in conventional attitudes. When Francis Osborne told his son 'Covetousnesse . . . like a candle ill made, smothers the splendour of an happy Fortune in its own grease', he did not define covetousness.[32] Gentlemen who proclaimed this doctrine were a little like students who dissemble their industry in order to maintain credit with their peers.

A gentleman's influence did not necessarily decline with the scale of his housekeeping, but it did somewhat change its nature. The pejorative way of looking at this was to say that a man who had his tenants' money in his coffers did not have their hearts in his keeping. However, *manred* had started as a means of discharging tenurial obligations, become a system of physical self-defence, and ended as a mere status symbol. By 1600 a peer did not need *manred* to maintain a political connection, and a gentleman did not need it to support his authority as a justice of the peace. Wealth, office and education had become the indicators of substance. By 1620, and earlier in some places, a public spirited man would leave money to found an almshouse or a school, endow a scholarship to one of the universities, or establish a parish charity. A hundred years earlier he would have endowed a fraternity, or given 'a great dole'. The mid-sixteenth century was a period of economic and social disruption for a number of reasons, and it would be wrong to suppose that it permanently affected the political order. It was, however, a warning sign of the decline of the traditional affinity. The earl of Warwick expressed serious doubts as to whether his men would hold Warwick castle against the insurgents.[33] In Norfolk bemused gentlemen were rounded up and placed in Norwich gaol. Such events cast a long shadow, and made the Elizabethan gentleman more grateful for his commission of the peace and his deputy lieutenancy. The ancient virtue of generosity, promoted alike by Welsh bards and English moralists, gradually gave way to a more measured set of social relationships.

32   F. Bamford, *A Royalist's Notebook* (1936), p. 230.
33   *Historical Manuscripts Commission Reports* (1980); Bath MSS at Longleat, vol. IV, Seymour Papers, ed. M. Blatcher (1968), pp. 115ff; vol. V, De Lisle and Dudley Papers, ed. G. Dyfnallt Owen (1980), pp.139ff.

Aristocratic families, however, remained important social units. Children were a resource, for a nobleman or a gentleman, no less than for a king, and the management of their marriages could have important consequences for the family fortunes. In the early sixteenth century, as we have seen, it was normal to place the eldest son, and probably the eldest daughter, in the household of a patron. Some great households held a number of such charges, who would receive a basic academic training, along with instruction in the arts of arms, courtesy and household management, according to sex. When he married, assuming that his father was still alive, the heir would return with his bride to the parental home, where they would pass the first few years of their married life, before being set up on their own. The placing of an eldest son was, however, not a universal practice, and very often all the children of the house were brought up together, first in the nursery and then in the schoolroom. This tended to improve relations between parents and children, and certainly ensured that the latter were taught in accordance with their father's wishes. Relations were also improved as the aristocracy gradually abandoned the practice of wet-nursing, thereby improving the bonding between the infants and their mothers. It is often assumed that close kinship implied good working relationships in later life, but this frequently depended upon how a child's upbringing and marriage were handled. Eldest sons, and daughters generally, were not allowed much freedom of action, a father's authority to control such matters never being called in question. Indulgence tended to increase with the passage of time, and lower down the social scale. The children of a minor seventeenth-century gentleman had a much better chance of pleasing themselves than those of an early sixteenth-century nobleman. Consequently it was generally believed that domestic relationships had improved, and John Aubrey, the author of *Brief Lives*, looking back, compared the present favourably with the past: 'then . . . sonnes must not be company for their father . . . [the] child perfectly loathed the sight of his parents as the slave his torture'. Even if this was a gross exaggeration, it serves as a warning against assuming that different generations of the same family were natural allies.

Except for the heir, children of both sexes normally left home on marriage, and dowagers were customarily provided for separately, even at the level of the minor gentry. So a household did not normally contain three, let alone four, generations of the same family. It might, however, contain other kindred; the husband's unmarried sister, for example, or less well-to-do cousins who served as stewards or other superior servants. In the early sixteenth century a nobleman's house might well contain a dozen of more members of his kindred, in addition to his officers and councillors; perhaps as many as forty 'above the salt'. These numbers diminished somewhat with the changes which we have already noticed, but not in the same proportion. Men of substance continued to accept the traditional responsibility to care for their kindred, even if they were less concerned to relieve the poor at large. The houses of the aristocracy continued to be major social centres, providers of employment and consumers of services, long after medieval affinities had disappeared. A country house like Theobalds, or Hardwick Hall, was no longer a fortress or a place of refuge in time of trouble, but it was a great support to the building trade. It could almost be said that tall fellows were replaced by tall chimneys as status symbols during the reign of Elizabeth. As W.G. Hoskins pointed out some years ago, there was a great rebuilding across the whole of southern England between 1520 and 1620, and across the north of England half a century later.[34] The houses which resulted were more comfortable, better designed for privacy, and better constructed, than those which they replaced, but they also had a degree of built in obsolescence which required the frequent attentions of skilled craftsmen. Once the English country house had shed its political and military functions, it still had a great future ahead of it.

THE ROYAL COURT

In the sixteenth century the court was the theatre and focus of a personal monarchy. It had always been the context within which the monarchs lived both their private and their public lives, but its significance had changed with the passage of time. Earlier rulers had often been 'saddle kings' who spent most of their time on the move, even when there was no war to drag them into campaigning. They travelled with their household knights and clerks, accompanied by menial servants, and often with an escort of archers or men-at-arms. The king used his own demesne manors, consuming their produce as he went, or enjoyed the hospitality of the major religious houses along his route. His writing office and his treasury travelled with him, and the func-

34 W.G. Hoskins, 'The re-building of rural England, 1570–1640', *Past and Present*, 4, 1953, pp. 44–56.

tions of government could be performed wherever he happened to be. There was little that was hieratic or formal about this procedure, which took its origins from the lifestyle of early Germanic chieftains. The king was a great lord, but he was different in degree rather than kind from other lords. Although a ruler like Henry II or Edward I was capable of celebrating a major feast with great pomp, it is hard to define an image of kingship.[35] European courts in general lacked institutional structure, apart from the papal *Curia*, which was essentially civilian and not peripatetic. However, by the fifteenth century much of this had changed.

A household book of Edward III, the earliest to give relevant information, lists some 245 servants and officers, as distinct from the military presence,[36] but gives only a rudimentary idea of the structure. The first full account of the late medieval household is the *Liber Niger Domus Regis (Black Book of the King's Household)* of Edward IV, compiled in the 1470s, where it is described as: 'the new house of householdes, principall of England in tymes of peace, bylded upon these kinges foundations, precedents, and upon other more notable and husbandlye householdes, by the greate counsayll of lordes spirituall and temporall'.[37] The *Liber Niger* makes clear the division of the court into two distinct functions, the *domus providencie*, or service departments, providing everything from meals and cleaning to transport and firewood, and the *domus regie magnificencie*, where the king kept his state, held his council and received ambassadors. The former – the household proper – was under the control of the lord steward, and the latter, the chamber, under the lord chamberlain. The schedule of the latter included 172 offices, from the knights of the body to the pages and minstrels, and that of the former 15 departments, with some 25 chief officers and about 200 others.[38]

This basic structure continued throughout the Tudor period, with one very important exception. After 1495 Henry VII increasingly withdrew from the public life of the chamber, where his chief officers kept their tables, and where he was expected to dine in state. The time so gained he spent in his private apartments, attended only by a handful of yeomen servants, and this intimate establishment became

35   Sydney Anglo, *Images of Tudor Kingship* (1992), pp. 10–15.
36   *A Collection of ordinances and Regulations for the . . . Royal Household* (1790), pp. 1–12.
37   Ibid., p. 20.
38   Ibid., pp. 135–240.

known as the privy chamber. His son, who had no particular need for privacy, developed the privy chamber into the centre of the court, on the principle that everything of importance happened in the king's presence. For a time the gentlemen of the privy chamber appeared to rival the king's council in influence over their master, but the succession of a minor, followed by two women, reduced it again to a domestic status. Both Mary and Elizabeth perforce chose female attendants for the intimate access which the privy chamber required, and the connection with the council was broken.

The household was hierarchic and stable. Under the lord steward it was supervised by a controller and a treasurer, who ran the financial office, known as the Board of Greencloth. Every department was run by a sergeant, assisted by anything from two to over twenty yeomen, grooms and other menials. In theory the gift of these offices was in the hands of the steward or the controller, but in practice the sergeant usually made his own arrangements without interference. Places were much sought after, and there was a regular career structure. However, it was a rather closed world, recruiting narrowly from families with established court connections, and made little impact outside.[39] With a few exceptions the staff of the household had little contact with the glittering world of the court proper, although they were well paid and enjoyed a number of perquisites. Apart from a few laundresses it was an entirely male world, which created disciplinary problems and provided regular custom for the Westminster brothels. However, the court was also a jurisdictional peculiar, normally defined by the limits of the palace of Westminster, but defined *ad hoc* when the court was elsewhere. The jurisdiction belonged to the lord steward *ex officio*, and he administered the common law in sessions which were held as often as was deemed necessary. The problems of the household therefore very seldom impinged upon the ordinary courts. The senior officers were usually married and lived away from the court, but as a group they had little impact or influence.

The chamber and privy chamber were totally different, and much harder to define, both in terms of their regular members and in terms of attendance. The monarchs chose the members of their Privy Chamber to suit themselves, and such positions were subject to formal appointment and the payment of an annual wage, which was usually £40. Under Henry VIII the privy chamber was run by a principal gentleman who was called the groom of the stool, and he appointed

39   D. Loades, *The Tudor Court* (1986), pp. 59–72.

the menial servants. At its greatest extent the privy chamber numbered about forty, half of them gentlemen, and those positions were fiercely competed for. Mary and Elizabeth similarly chose their ladies, who were also formally appointed, and male courtiers intrigued and conspired to have their wives and daughters called to such positions of influence. After 1553 the privy chamber had no power as such, but it was generally believed that both queens listened to their chosen companions – probably wrongly, except on personal issues. However, it was the chamber which was the most amorphous part of the court, and the one which made by far the greatest impact on aristocratic society. At the time of the Eltham Ordinances in 1526, seventy-three gentlemen officers of the chamber were entitled to bouge of court, and 273 were paid wages without entitlement to bouge.[40] Of these, about half were gentlemen or above, and there was a similar, but smaller, establishment for the queen's side, with about sixty places 'worth a gentleman's having'. Not all these served all the time. Some were 'quarter waiters', which meant that they worked 'shifts' of three months. Faced with a huge demand for places at court, Henry shared them around in an attempt to secure maximum participation and magnificence at a manageable cost. This policy meant that gentry families from every county were represented, and on a major court occasion, like the visit to the Field of Cloth of Gold in 1520, the whole of England and most of Wales counted gentlemen in the king's train.

This was the most comprehensive, and by far the most important, of the court networks. By this means patronage, and indeed knowledge of what was happening, were fed out into the county communities. As we have seen, families with court connections, like the Bacons of Stiffkey in Norfolk, had a head start on their rivals in the competitions of local politics. One of the most striking political successes of the Tudors was the extent to which they succeeded in making their court the centre of the aristocratic world. By 1558 office was as essential to the authority and self-esteem of a nobleman as military command had once been. Castiglione's *Il Cortegiano* (*The Courtier*) was translated into English in 1561, and the enormous success of Henry Peacham's *The Compleat Gentleman* in 1622, reflecting the same renaissance ideal, showed how deeply that culture had penetrated the English aristocracy. There were still country peers, like Lord Berkeley, who attended court only on special occasions, or when summoned; but by the 1530s absence from the court was

40 *Household Ordinances*, pp. 163–70.

beginning to be looked upon as a sign of disaffection. To ignore or reject a summons, as the earls of Westmorland and Northumberland did in 1569, was tantamount to treason; and to leave without licence, as the duke of Norfolk did in 1572, was almost as bad.

Lord Burghley expressed the prevailing attitude when he compared a man without a friend at court to 'a hop without a pole' (that is, a climber without assistance): 'all such as aspire and thirst after offices and honours run thither amaine with emulation and disdaine of others; thither are revenewes brought that appertaine unto the state, & there they are disposed out againe'.[41] This was not quite accurate, as the institutions of central government had gone 'out of court' long before, but as an assessment of the rewards expected, it was symptomatic. Such rewards took a huge variety of forms. Peerage titles and great estates were not usually on offer, although Charles Brandon became duke of Suffolk essentially for being Henry VIII's favourite jousting companion.[42] More usually gains took the form of annuities, opportunities to make preferential purchases of various kinds (particularly monastic lands), and later trading privileges and manufacturing monopolies. Such gains could make a major difference to a gentleman's fortunes. The virtually landless Sir Walter Raleigh survived on them, and even the earl of Essex depended upon his sweet wine monopoly in the 1590s.

Fashions in clothes, food and manners were also transmitted from the chamber to the county elites. Music, entertainment, piety and above all education were emulated in the same way. The late medieval aristocracy had scorned book learning as fit only for clerks, and the instruction to the master of the king's henchmen in the *Liber Niger* had required him to: 'show the scoolz of urbanitie and nourture of Inglond, to lern them to ride clenely and surely, to drawe them also to justes, to lern hem were theyre harneys; to have all curtsey in wordez, dedes and degrees'.[43] The first two Tudors turned this around completely. The future Henry VIII was given the best renaissance education available, and by 1520 John Skelton was mocking the backwoodsmen for the king's amusement: 'noble men borne, to lerne they have scorne' ('Colin Clout' l. 621). Henry needed servants who could maintain his honour by meeting sophisticated Italians and Frenchmen on their own ground, and as early as 1531 Sir John Elyot was warning

41 Loades, *Tudor Court*, p. 133.
42 S.J. Gunn, *Charles Brandon, Duke of Suffolk, 1484–1545* (1988).
43 A.R. Myers, *The Household of Edward IV* (1959), pp. 126–7.

the English nobility that if their sons were not trained for this kind of service, then the sons of commoners would be preferred before them. They got the message, and humanist scholars of distinction (or at least ability) appear as tutors in innumerable noble and gentle households by the middle of the century. By the end of the century a few books in the library and a decent smattering of classical learning were a part of every gentleman's social credibility: 'Alasse you will be ungentle gentlemen if you bee no schollers; you will do your prince but simple service, you will stand your countrie in but slender stead, you will bring yourselves but to small preferment, if you bee no schollers.'[44] In this enduring social revolution, the Tudor court played a fundamental role.

There was, of course, also a negative side to this hypnotic attractiveness. Alongside the ambassadors, scholars and musicians, the court swarmed with mountebanks, quacks and parasites of every description, who might prey upon gullible fortune seekers to their total destruction. Courtiers were notoriously underemployed, spending much of their time waiting for an opportunity to put in a purely cosmetic appearance. This encouraged a gambling habit which could easily get out of control, and it was not unknown for gentlemen, and even peers, to be forced to withdraw, having accumulated debts which they could not sustain. The lifestyle also was expensive, even when not aggravated by compulsive gambling. In 1537 the earl of Cumberland found his marriage to the king's niece, Lady Eleanor Brandon brought with it a 'train of expenses' which forced him to alienate one of his richest manors, and it was only when he was able to withdraw after Eleanor's death ten years later that he could repair his fortune.[45] No doubt many unsuccessful courtiers would have echoed the words of Shakespeare:

'I have been begging sixteen years in court,
Am yet a courtier beggarly, nor could
Come pat betwixt too early and too late;
For any suit of pounds.'[46]

There were also moral dangers, and not only of pride and covetousness. The court was a man's world, but it was also a world where

---

44   G. Pettie, *The Civile Conversation of S.Guazzo* (1586), sig. Av.
45   Stone, *Crisis of the Aristocracy*, p. 451.
46   *Henry VIII*, act II, scene 3, ll. 82–5.

women had an important role and presence, particularly when the ruler was herself a woman, or when the king had a forceful consort. Both Henry VIII and Elizabeth encouraged the game of courtly love, for different reasons; the former because he enjoyed it, and the latter because it enhanced her image. Most of the relationships developed in this way were platonic, and innocuous enough, but not all. Passionate love affairs could bring disgrace on both parties, particularly under the eagle eye of the Virgin Queen. Sexual licence was an accusation constantly made by anti-court propagandists, and had been since the early Middle Ages. There was some substance in the charge, as the sad story of the unsupervised upbringing and calamitous fall of Catherine Howard makes clear. However, before 1603 such an attitude can not unfairly be dismissed as sour grapes, as can disillusioned comments like that of Raleigh when he complained that the court of Elizabeth (out of which he had done pretty well) glowed 'like rotten wood'. Perhaps the dangers of the court made it more exciting; they certainly do not seem to have checked the growth of its appeal. There was, after all, both honour and reward in being one of those 'about the king', to whom your neighbours and friends from the country appealed for intercession and favours. If the perches proved slippery and falls not infrequent, it was a game well worth the risks.

Most people in Tudor England never saw their monarch. Mobility varied a good deal from one reign to another, but with very few exceptions was confined to a fifty-mile radius around London. Henry VII had commenced his reign by making a grand tour, reaching York in March 1486, and returning through the marches of Wales, going as far south as Bristol. The circumstances of that progress were unique, however, because he needed to show himself to his new subjects, and particularly to secure the submission of those northerners who had been so loyal to Richard. Henry VIII only once went north of the Trent, when he also visited York in 1541. He went to Portsmouth on a number of occasions, and was four times at Calais, but for the most part his restless wanderings were within the Home Counties. Edward VI made only one progress during his short reign, and Mary made none at all, although she did travel to Winchester for her wedding in July 1554, and to Dover in August 1555 when Philip returned to the Low Countries. Elizabeth's progresses are well known, but she actually went less far afield than her father. Like Mary (and Edward) she never left England, and her most distant destinations were Kenilworth in 1575 and Norwich in 1578. Both these progresses are fully recorded, and we can trace every step through Suffolk and Norfolk on the latter occasion. When the queen entered Suffolk she was greeted by the sheriff, Sir William Spring, accompanied by 500 mounted gentlemen and 1,500 serving men on horseback, 'which surely was a comely troop, and a noble sight to behold'.[47] This escort, riding in shifts, stayed with her right across the county, which took three days, when a similar escort from Norfolk took over. Elizabeth loved these occasions, just as her father had done, for the demonstrations of loyal enthusiasm which they provoked, and which were an important part of the Tudor political armoury.

By comparison with the peregrinations of Francis I or Charles V, Tudor progresses were small affairs. The travelling household numbered only a few score, because the departmental sergeants hired local help as they went, rather than taking their regular staff with them, and the chamber servants worked in shifts. In 1592 it was reckoned that the progress of that year required 300 carts and some 1,800 horses. Nevertheless these progresses required a great deal of planning, and were expensive. The benefit is hard to calculate. Thomas Churchyard's description of the celebrations at Norwich suggest that the occasion was remembered there with gratitude long afterwards, and may finally have eradicated the bitter legacy of 1549.[48] Men and women travelled long distances to see the queen, even if it was only to stand by the roadside as she went by, and no doubt passed on the experience to anyone who was willing to listen to them. There was actually a good deal more physical mobility among ordinary people in the period than is sometimes realized, but unless you were a gentleman who occasionally (or frequently) travelled to London on business, your chances of seeing even the more mobile Tudors would probably have been no more than about 25 per cent.

Consequently, royal appearances had to be supplemented by the promotion of a royal image – *maiestas*. Understandably this did not concentrate upon the monarch as chief executive. The oldest image was that of the warrior, and it was still used if it was remotely plausible. Edward IV had been a successful soldier in his youth, and so had Henry VII, although he studiously avoided that role in later life. Henry VIII delighted in warlike symbolism, and used both real

47   Thomas Churchyard, 'The Queenes Majesties entertaynement in Norfolk and Suffolk', cited by Zillah Dovey, *An Elizabethan Progress* (1996), p. 40.
48   Churchyard, 'The Queenes Majesties entertaynement', in John Nichols, *The Progresses and Public Processions of Queen Elizabeth* (1787–1805), III.

campaigns and war games in the form of jousts to promote himself as a warrior. However, Henry VI did not lend himself to similar propaganda, and neither did Edward VI, for a different reason. Henry had no image worth speaking of, and that became a serious disadvantage to him, but young Edward's piety and intellectual tastes lent themselves to exploitation, and he became the 'young Josias' and the 'Godly Imp'. A renaissance prince, even if he could be presented as a soldier, was also expected to be much more. He could be extolled as the wise and magnanimous hero – a new Alexander – with the moral qualities of the chivalric *prud'homme*, but he also needed *gravitas*, wisdom and even intelligence. Henry VII succeeded on *gravitas*, and on wisdom, but not on much else. In spite of keeping a lavish court and patronizing scholars and artists with generosity, he acquired the reputation of a miser, even in his own lifetime. As more than one contemporary explained, he was respected, and even feared, but not loved.

His son was far more successful. Starting with the advantages of an imposing physique, a lively mind, and well-trained skills in both tilting and tennis, he quickly became the most successful image builder of his generation. In spite of Henry's bellicosity, Erasmus (who hated war) could write of him in 1519: 'Learning would triumph if we had such a prince at home [in the Low Countries] as England hath . . . he openly shows himself a patron of good letters.'[49] Fastidious Italians praised his court as the centre of all civility, and Dominico Memmo allowed himself to be tempted from St Mark's, Venice, to be his organist. The king's 'musicke' became the envy of Europe, and he spent far more than he could afford on lavish entertainment, and on building. In Hans Holbein he found a court artist who was not only the finest portrait painter of his generation, but the creator of that unique visual image of kingship will still survives in the popular imagination.[50] Henry needed all of this promotion to overcome the unpopularity of his 'proceedings' with his first queen, and later with his daughter Mary; but although he was cordially hated in some quarters by the end of his life, he never lost his grip upon the loyalty of his subjects. Most of them may never have seen him, but his larger-than-life image bestrode the realm.

His son's regents made some attempt to fashion young Edward in

49   P.S. Allen and H.M. Allen, *Opus Epistolarum Des. Erasmi Roterdami* (1906–58), 5, p. 241.
50   Roy Strong, *Holbein and Henry* VIII (1967).

his father's mould, but it did not work. The boy was robust enough, and keen on sport, but lacked both the stature and the physical skills to be imposing. Nor was 'Josias' an image which appealed to all. Had he lived, he would no doubt have found a persona for himself, but it was not to be, and for the remainder of the century the Tudor image makers had to struggle with a quite different problem. What symbols of power could be used for a woman? Mary hardly seems to have noticed the difficulty at all. She saw herself as the restorer of normality – of all that was decent and upright in the old order – but that was very hard to translate into visual terms. Writers spoke of the queen's 'Godly proceedings', but she did not even have herself painted surrounded by the trappings of the old faith. As has often been noted, her approved portraits were extremely realistic, but lacking any particular iconographic significance.[51] Philip's problem was different. He knew the importance of imagery, and wished to present himself as a soldier and a Catholic, but his heart was never in the business of being king of England, and he completely failed to capture the imagination of his island subjects.

By contrast, Elizabeth inherited her father's priorities, and his skill. For obvious reasons she could not use his essentially masculine image, and for both personal and political reasons had no desire to play the Amazon. At first she seems to have had images wished upon her by Protestants like John Foxe, gratified by her religious settlement. To them she was Deborah, the judge of Israel, one of the few women of power and virtue recognized by the Old Testament, or the new Constantine, a concept which ducked the issue of gender altogether. Elizabeth seems to have accepted and used both these images, but the one which she developed for herself was rather different. Courtly love had been invented by the troubadors, but it had the immense advantage of offering women an honourable, even a dominant role, which was why it had originally been encouraged by powerful women like Eleanor of Aquitaine. The knight's lady, whose favour he wore on his helmet and in whose service he performed his deeds of valour, was an object of desire, but also of great respect. Convention required that she should be unattainable, either because of her superior status or because she was married to another. No one could be more unattainable than the queen, and Elizabeth naturally found the prospect of receiving devoted service for no more reward than a smile or a perfumed favour irresistibly attractive. So she became Gloriana,

51   Loades, *Mary Tudor*, pp. 331–2.

Belphoebe or Astrea, drawing alike on courtly love and classical mythology.

This image did not appear at once, but developed over a number of years, particularly after Sir Henry Lee began the Accession Day tilts in 1578. Virginity was originally no part of this propaganda, because in spite of hyperbolic remarks about being wedded to her realm, Elizabeth probably never made a conscious decision not to marry. When time had foreclosed the option, or at least the prospect of an heir, she was content to allow others to present her as a Virgin Queen – 'the imperial votaress passed on / In maiden meditation, fancy-free'.[52] Elizabeth's portraits tell the same story. After her smallpox attack in 1562 only images taken from an approved original by Nicholas Hilliard could be lawfully reproduced, and all the well known paintings of her show the same formality, the same devices, and the same mask-like countenance. They are icons, not portraits.[53] Elizabeth used her sex as a weapon with which to baffle and subdue the men who, although technically her servants, would otherwise have dominated her. They found it an infuriating and fascinating experience, but they quickly learned that success depended upon playing the game of politics according to the rules which she laid down. As Sir John Davies commented at the end of the reign:

> All parliaments of peace and warlike fights,
> All learned arts and every great affair,
> A lively shape of dancing seems to bear.[54]

Long before she died, the dance of state had lost its appeal to those forced to perform it, but it left behind one of the most potent historical myths to bedevil the curriculum of public education.

However, if the court was the theatre, access to it was in theory tightly controlled. The porters who manned the gates were given strict instructions to exclude all vagabonds and other undesirables, and no doubt did so. However, it was only necessary to appear respectably dressed, with a plausible pretext of business, to gain admittance. The public rooms of whichever palace was in use were thronged with petitioners and spectators, in addition to those who

52　*A Midsummer Night's Dream*, act II, scene 2, ll. 163–4.
53　Roy Strong, *The Portraits of Queen Elizabeth* (1963); J.L. Hughes and P.F. Larkin, *Tudor Royal Proclamations*, II (1969), pp. 240–1.
54　*The Works in Verse and Prose of Sir John Davies*, ed. A.B. Grosart (1869–76), I, p.189; Roy Strong, *The Cult of Elizabeth* (1977), pp. 46ff.

were, in some sense, on duty. There were recognized opportunities to present pleas to the monarch without going through the expensive procedure of bribing the ushers. Henry VIII was vulnerable when he was about to go hunting, Mary on her way to mass, and so on. Security was, by modern standards, almost non-existent, because although the monarch needed physical protection, all the Tudors preferred to run the risk of being accessible to their subjects. Even Elizabeth, upon whose life several attempts were made, shrugged off the dangers and welcomed direct contact with ordinary people. There were safeguards. The privy chamber was off limits to everyone except its own staff, unless the monarch commanded the contrary, and the wearing of weapons in the royal presence was a serious offence. So too was the offering of any kind of violence, as a number of short-tempered courtiers discovered to their cost. Even Lord Lisle, in high favour at the time, was rusticated for throwing a punch at the bishop of Winchester in 1545. Consequently, although most court masques and other indoor entertainments were theoretically private, in fact quite a lot of people got to see them, and stories about their magnificence spread widely. Tournaments were fully public, and in Elizabeth's reign grandstands were erected and charges were made for admission. Henry VIII had no objection at all to his people knowing that he had broken the most spears, when a joust was held to welcome some visiting dignitary; and Elizabeth encouraged her courtiers to stage elaborate conceits in her honour before getting down to the serious business of knocking each other off their horses.[55]

Henry VIII insisted in playing in the first division of the European league, and his court was completely out of proportion with both the population and the resources of his kingdom. Towards the end of his reign it was costing some £40,000 a year, about 35 per cent of his ordinary revenue. He also owned an enormous number of houses. Nineteen were inherited from his father, some large and much frequented palaces like Richmond and Westminster, others small and unvisited, like Langley and Minster Lovell in Oxfordshire. Only one, Baynard's Castle, was in London; the others were scattered across nine counties from Kent to Worcestershire. Henry VII had used no more than five or six of these residences, and some were leased out, but his son was a restless mover, and visited almost all at one time or another, very often on hunting trips. Henry VIII retained all his

---

55 Alan Young, *Tudor and Jacobean Tournaments* (1987); Strong, *Cult of Elizabeth*, pp. 129–63.

father's properties, and built five more from scratch. Two of these, St James and Nonsuch, were palaces, although neither matched Westminster in size. Nonsuch was the king's absorbing hobby over a number of years. He imported Italian sculptors and plaster workers to supply the decoration, and designed its internal layout for his own convenience.[56] Several representations of it survive, although the house itself was pulled down in the late seventeenth century, and it seems to have been a rather crude imitation of Francis I's chateau of Chambord. Bridewell, which was somewhat smaller, was constructed in 1515 as a new London residence, and it was there that Henry entertained the emperor Charles V on his visit in 1522. The king also acquired no fewer than twenty-six properties by purchase, exchange or forfeiture. Many of these were small, like Enfield in Middlesex, and the reason for Henry's interest cannot now be recovered; but others were prime residences which rapidly became favourites, such as Whitehall and Hampton Court, both acquired from Wolsey. A dozen further houses were retained after the dissolution of the monasteries, and two of these became the king's manors in York and Newcastle, later used by the Council of the North.

The great majority of these properties were kept in regular use, although not necessarily by the king himself, and were maintained by the office of the King's Works, which underwent a major expansion during this period. Henry made a habit of using his own houses when on progress, especially after he had dissolved the monasteries which had served him in the early years of his reign. He no longer used Westminster as a residence, leaving it to the permanent institutions of government, and his favourites (apart from Nonsuch, which was never really finished) were Whitehall, Greenwich and Hampton Court. Some, like Hanworth in Middlesex, were used by his consorts, and others, such as Hatfield, by his children. Virtually all were used regularly, and kept by a skeleton staff when not in use, so Henry had almost sixty houses, from Canterbury to Newcastle, providing household employment, and demands for goods and services from the communities in which they were situated.

After 1547 the level of activity and expenditure was sharply curtailed. Edward alienated thirteen of his father's houses, five of which subsequently reverted to the crown. During his brief reign he

---

56   On the royal residences generally, see H.M. Colvin (ed), *The History of the King's Works*, IV: 1485–1660 (1982), ii, pp. 1–367. On Nonsuch specifically, see J. Dent, *The Quest for Nonsuch* (1962).

used only a few residences himself, and acquired but one – Somerset House in the Strand, on the attainder of the former protector in 1551.[57] Relatively little building work was done at this time, but that does not necessarily mean neglect, as there was no backlog of repairs. However, two minor properties, Mortlake in Surrey and the More in Hertfordshire, seem to have fallen into disrepair, and were not subsequently used. Mary sold, granted or otherwise disposed of eleven houses, including Nonsuch, which was granted to the earl of Arundel in 1556, and Bridewell, which was made over to the City of London as a workhouse in the same year. Two houses were returned to the bishops who had earlier forfeited them, and two, Dartford and Syon, were temporarily restored to religious use. Mary did not retain any of the houses which came to her by forfeiture, or make any purchases. Apart from resuming Dartford and Syon, Elizabeth continued to deplete the stock. Four properties were alienated, two, Clarendon and Enfield, allowed to decay, and Ampthill was partly demolished in 1567.[58] Elizabeth left it to her subjects to build great houses, and neither purchased nor retained any for herself. The Works accounts, however, show a recovery of expenditure from the middle years of the century and it seems that, with the exception of those mentioned, the queen maintained her properties in good repair. Of course the absence of either consort or family for over forty years considerably reduced the need for housing. From its peak in 1547, the list of houses in the care of the Office of Works had dropped by about 25 per cent at the end of the century, but it was still long and well scattered, marking a royal presence, of a sort, in a number of places where the people never saw their monarch in the flesh.

Wherever it was, and particularly at Westminster or Hampton Court, the royal household was a major employer. Apart from the noble officers and gentle ushers, sewers, carvers and cup bearers, there were between two and four hundred yeomen, grooms, scullions, pages and other menials. This made the court a major consumer, particularly of foodstuffs. Repeated attempts were made, first by Wolsey, then by Cromwell, and finally by William Cecil, to keep the 'ordinary' within bounds, but they never enjoyed more than short-term success. Economy was simply not consistent with the ideal of magnificence which inspired the whole ethos of the court.[59] In 1547 about three

57 Loades, *Tudor Court*, p. 200.
58 Ibid., pp. 193–202.
59 *Household Ordinances*, pp. 281–2; ibid., pp. 251–2; Loades, *Tudor Court*, pp. 60–4.

hundred people were entitled to bouge of court, that is the right to be fed at the royal tables, either in the hall or in the chamber. That included some officers, such as the master of the horse, whose departments were not part of the household at all, and the whole of the Privy Council. However, the actual number of meals provided was very much greater. This was partly because the duty of hospitality was interpreted very loosely, and partly because of the chronic waste and inefficiency which were encouraged by the perquisite system of reward. By the 1560s, and probably earlier, it was normal for the meals supplied to the public tables in the chamber to be returned almost untouched. This was because there were at least two kitchens functioning, one for the household, and one for the queen herself.[60] Both the hall and the chamber were fed from the household kitchen, but the food provided by the privy kitchen was of superior quality. Noble and gentle servants consequently clamoured and intrigued to receive their meals from the latter, delivered direct to their private apartments, instead of attending their proper places in the chamber. This was strictly against the rules, and successive lord chamberlains struggled to prevent it, but to no avail. The kitchen servants connived at this and other irregularities, because the unused food was theirs, to dispose of as they thought fit. If they moved quickly they could sell it in good condition to the licensed victuallers of London and Westminster, and many a venison pie or roast chine of beef found its way down that route. It is therefore not surprising that the household consumed many times the quantity of food which should have been required for those entitled. The lord chamberlain also controlled the guest list, and was supposed to know what visitors and guests 'of honour and repute' were to be entertained on any given day; but that also was a custom more honoured in the breach than the observance. The monarch's pleasure was unpredictable. Not only was Elizabeth known to defer the start of a progress from day to day without warning, but there was no knowing whom she would summon at short notice, how long they would be in attendance, or how many servants they would bring with them. Consequently the entitlement on any given day was little more than guesswork, even before the question of abuse arose.

60 'Item the taking of dysshes from her majesties borde is one of the greatest occasions of ther keping of ther servauntes for almost few or none in this hows that likes of ther ordinarye diet for that they ar growen in such delicacy that no meates will serve them but that which comes from her majesties table': BL MS Lansdowne 21, 67, f. 120.

The system of supply for this rambling and voracious establishment was a network in itself. Originally, as we have seen, the court had moved far more extensively, consuming the produce of royal manors as it went. However, this was soon recognized to be far too haphazard, and unsuited to the reduced mobility of the thirteenth or fourteenth century. Consequently a system of purveyance was developed, which was a tax in kind. Those officers of the household whose business it was to take up provisions were entitled by commission to requisition whatever they required, and to pay for it at a rate which they could determine themselves, and which was always well below the market value. By the fifteenth century purveyance had been restricted to basic commodities, such as meat, fish, grain and cheese. Fresh fruit, milk, cream, salad vegetables, eggs and other similar items had to be purchased in the normal way. On the one hand this helped to encourage the growth of market gardening in the London area, a development for which the huge population of the capital was mainly responsible. On the other hand the depredations of the purveyors were becoming increasingly restricted to the Home Counties, and were provoking vigorous and repeated complaints. By the early sixteenth century the system was in obvious and urgent need of reform. Not only was purveyance itself a burden which was very unequally distributed, but the procedures of the Board of Greencloth were so ponderous that suppliers of all kinds had to wait months, and sometimes years, for their money.[61]

In 1536 Cromwell set out to deal with these problems by introducing county composition agreements. By the terms of these, the justices of the peace in each county would contract with the purveyors of the household to supply given quantities of specified commodities at the 'king's price'. The justices' own agents would then purchase the produce at the full market price, the shortfall being made up by a county levy, collected on the basis of the subsidy assessments. This scheme had, or should have had, two great advantages. It spread the burden geographically, because all counties were included in its scope unless they had been exempted for some specific reason. Hampshire, for example, was often called upon to victual the fleet. Second, it made the requirement predictable from year to year, so that suitable

---

61 Theoretically the cofferer should have issued prest money to all purveyors on the basis of their estimated needs, and should have taken monthly accounts of their expenditure; however, it seems clear that that did not actually happen. *Household Ordinances*, p. 228; Loades, *Tudor Court*, pp. 70–2.

arrangements could be made well in advance. However, the scheme was not imposed, and was taken up only slowly; partly because it involved a burden upon counties which had hitherto contributed very little, and partly because of a general reluctance to pay any tax which had not been voted by parliament. By 1558 about a dozen such agreements were in place, all relating to grain. A statute of 1555 had also tightened up the administration of the older system. All commissions to purveyors were to be limited to six months, and were to specify the county or counties to which they applied.[62] Every commission was also to specify the nature and quantity of the provisions to be received. On making his purchase, the purveyor was to give the supplier a written receipt, which then had to be presented to the Board of Greencloth for payment. It is not clear that this led to any major improvement either, because no timetable was specified and such receipts may well have been discounted.

William Cecil tried again where Cromwell had left off. In 1561 a book of composition rates was drawn up to be kept in the counting house for the benefit of future negotiations, and by the following year at least three counties had compounded for a variety of produce. However, it was very slow work and some agreements entered into were not honoured. Meanwhile the number of purveyors operating outside the composition system had grown dramatically. By 1575, fifty-six purveyors held between them 111 commissions.[63] Perhaps this uncontrolled growth helped to persuade the counties of the advantages of composition, because by 1578 twelve counties had general agreements in place. By 1591 Burghley clearly felt that the situation had reached a point at which pressure could be applied, and a commission 'for household causes' was established, which summoned representatives of all counties to come to London in October 1592 'for some composition to be made for Her Majesty's household'. By 1600 the new system was complete and in place. A long list of commodities was separately rated, provision made for annual adjustments, and careful arrangements laid down for getting the provisions to the relevant household department in a fit state to eat. Cattle arrived on the hoof, sometimes after a long journey from Cornwall or Cumberland. Poultry was also delivered alive, and sometimes from a distance; but fresh fish had to be obtained close at hand,

---

62   2 & 3 Philip and Mary, c. 6; *Statutes of the Realm*, IV, i, p. 282.
63   Allegra Woodworth, *Purveyance for the Royal Household in the Reign of Elizabeth* (Transactions of the American Philosophical Society, 1945).

and moved with expedition. Although the purveyors' functions were drastically reduced by the end of the Tudor period, the network of contacts and transactions involved in supplying the royal household had, if anything, become wider. From Launceston to Berwick and from Caernarfon to Great Yarmouth, contributions were being made to keep the queen's meals on her table, and to feed that ravenous horde of officers, servants, visitors and parasites which made up the Tudor court.

Because of its nature, the court provided not only a means of communication between the monarch and his or her subjects, but also a vehicle for similar communication among the subjects themselves. Many families served for generations, and made their marriages and their property deals as well as their political careers in that context. It was in many respects like a great academy, whose alumni remain in contact with each other throughout their lives, and whose alliances, feuds, achievements and failures were alike conditioned by the experience.

Epilogue:

A Unitary State?

England was undoubtedly more unified in 1600 than it had been a century before. Virtually all the exempt jurisdictions had disappeared: the church, the religious houses, the marcher lordships, the secular franchises, all had either been abolished or brought under royal control. The privileges which remained, such as those of the major towns and chartered companies, had been granted by the crown, and were revocable in the same way. The common law was received without competition, and the monarch's writ ran uniformly through the realm. At the same time, the sense of national identity had also grown. This was not a Tudor invention. It had grown out of the Hundred Years' War, and as early as 1377 Edward III's last Chancellor, ironically Adam Houghton, bishop of St Davids, could tell the parliament: 'Israel is understood to be the heritage of God as is England. For I truly think that God would never have honoured this land in the same way as he did Israel through great victories over their enemies, if it were not that He had chosen it as His heritage.'[1] Even the end of the war in defeat and humiliation did not check this manner of thinking: 'Regnum Anglorum regnum Dei est' ('The realm of England is the kingdom of God') one poet wrote in the unpromising year of 1460, and by 1520 an English nobleman attending the king at the Field of Cloth of Gold could declare that if he found he had one drop of French blood in his veins, he would cut it out with a knife. The idea that God was an Englishman was adopted later by the Protestants, and became a hallmark of the anti-Catholic propaganda of the Spanish war, but a sense of Englishness did not depend upon the reformers. An Italian observer in about 1500 had written: 'The English are great lovers of themselves, and of everything belonging to

1 *Rotuli Parliamentorum* (1810–28), II, p. 362, translated and cited in J.W. McKenna, 'How God became an Englishman', in *Tudor Rule and Revolution*, eds DeLloyd J. Guth and J.W. McKenna (1982), pp. 25–43.

them; they think there are no other men than themselves, and no other world but England.'[2]

Loyalty to the crown played a part in this, and the progress which medieval kings had made towards establishing a uniform system of law and administration. The growth of English as a literary language had also helped, because by the end of the fifteenth century a standard written form had developed. It may well have been difficult for a Yorkshire man to understand the speech of an East Anglian, but those who came to London on business, or in search of apprenticeships, never seem to have had any problems about being accepted. Many people disliked the prayer book when it was introduced in 1549, but no one from a place where English was normally spoken complained that he or she could not understand it. It could even be argued that the introduction of Protestantism damaged the sense of national identity, rather than enhancing it. The English had no particular enthusiasm for the pope, and regarded his jurisdiction as foreign, but the Reformation was associated with Germany and Switzerland, an image intensified by the role of refugee theologians and congregations during the reign of Edward VI. Ironically it was Mary, who had never left England and whose religious ideals were distinctly insular, who started to make Catholicism look foreign through her marriage to Philip, and his role in the reconciliation. It was Elizabeth who made Protestantism English, and the pope, through the bull *Regnans in excelsis* of 1570, who finally made the old religion something threatening and alien.[3]

Consequently there was no straightforward causal relationship between the growth of English national identity and the growing unity of jurisdiction; each influenced the other. Moreover, both national identity and administrative unity transcended Englishness, because both embraced Wales. The way in which Wales was incorporated into the English system, its ruling class integrated and aspects of its culture adopted, represents one of the major success stories of the Tudor period. The Welsh origin of the dynasty helped, but is by no means the whole explanation. By contrast, similar aims but different methods failed disastrously in Ireland. As England and Wales grew together,

2   *A Relation of the Island of England . . . about the year 1500*, ed. C.A. Sneyd (Camden Society, 32, 1847), pp. 53–4.
3   D. Loades, 'Relations between the Anglican and Roman Catholic churches in the sixteenth and seventeenth century', in *Rome and the Anglicans*, ed. W. Haase (1982), pp. 1–53.

England and Ireland grew apart. However, it was politics rather than culture which determined that failure, and the survival of Celtic language, dress and customs was a symptom of alienation rather than a cause.

England became more united, more prosperous and more populous during the sixteenth century, but it did not become very much more centralized. There was no network of *intendants* in England, and full-time professional servants of the crown were few, and relatively humble. The House of Commons and the commission of the peace together symbolize the style of Tudor government. The first brought the localities to the centre, and the second took the centre out to the localities. Both legislation and taxation were actions of central government, but neither could be implemented without the co-operation of the gentlemen in the shires. When the opportunity arose to bring the Welsh courts under Westminster control, it was not taken, and the courts of Great Session were re-established instead. The Tudors never intended, and could not have achieved, the bureaucratic centralization of a modern state. What they did do was to create a gentry commonwealth under the crown, with a church made in its own image. As long as the monarch continued to recognize the intangible limitations which this imposed, the system continued to work. Sir Thomas Smith could praise the absolute power of the English crown, because he was using the term within a context which he then went on to explain:

> Although in times past there were certaine countie Palatines, as Chester, Durham, Elie, which were *hault* justicers, and writtes went in their name and some Lorde marchers of Wales, which claymed like priviledge. Alle these are nowe worne away. The supreme justice is done in the kinges name, and by his authoritie onely.[4]

This political culture came from the centre. Wales and the marches adapted to an order which was formed by the court and the common law. Wales influenced that order to some extent, both through the 'matter of Britain' and through the official sanctioning of the Welsh bible and prayer book, but it was overwhelmingly lowland English. England's own highland zone influenced it hardly at all. The question was always how the lowlands would impact upon the highlands, never the other way round, except in the purely local matter of cattle raiding.

4 Thomas Smith, *De Republica Anglorum*, ed. Mary Dewar (1982) p. 87.

It was the twin magnets of London and the court which drew in the gentlemen, the lawyers and the merchants from distant parts of the realm and acclimatized them to the required identity and priorities.

The gentry commonwealth thus formed broke down in 1640, because Charles I took his monarchical power too much at its face value, and did not read the small print in his contract. It also failed because it did not at first succeed in embracing Scotland. However, that is another story, and eventually the ethos of that commonwealth prevailed also north of the border. Both in 1660 and in 1689 it determined the nature of the constitutional settlement. Only gradually did it change into a form of democracy between 1830 and 1930.

Glossary

adscripti glebae: literally 'bound to the soil'; a state of personal unfreedom, in which the people were legally a part of the land upon which they lived.

a latere: a special commission which enabled the holder to act on the pope's behalf in all but the most sensitive cases.

arcana imperii: mysteries of state, or political secrets.

auditorship of the prests: the office responsible for authorizing, and keeping track of, advance payments made out of the Exchequer to royal officers for specific purposes.

bourse: the Antwerp Exchange, the main centre for financial transactions in Europe, opened in 1536.

butlerage: the revenues of the chief butler of England, originally an important court office, but by this time a sinecure.

capias: a writ instructing a sheriff or other officer to make an arrest.

centuriatis comitiis or tributis: a reference to the ancient Roman practice of assembling and voting by hundreds and by tribes.

Code of Justinian: A formulation of Roman Imperial Law issued by the emperor Justinian (527–565). It was the standard reference text of the civil law throughout the medieval and early modern periods.

commote: the smallest unit of local government in Wales; roughly equivalent to the English hundred.

consulta: an advisory document or memorandum, usually produced by the council.

coram rege: in the king's court; used by this time of a court of law rather than of the monarch's actual presence.

Curia: the administrative and jurisdictional machinery in Rome which supported the pope.

cursus honorem: a curriculum, or succession of qualifications of increasing distinction.

custos rotulorum: literally 'the keeper of the rolls'; the officer responsible for making returns of Quarter Sessions business into King's Bench, and chairman of the commission of the peace.

de arraiatione et capitaneo generali contra francos: literally 'of array and captaincy against the French'.

de arraiendo et monstrum faciendo contra Scotos: literally 'to muster and show a deed against the Scots'; that is, to prepare aggressive as well as defensive action.

defamatio: slander; the damaging of another's reputation without just cause.

dominium politicum et regale: a royal and constitutional regime; meaning a government where the chief executive power was in the hands of a prince, but subject to limitations imposed not only by laws and customs but also by institutions.

ex aequo and ***bono***: literally 'out of equality and good'; equitably and justly.

familia: literally 'household'; all those who lived under the bishop's roof and were dependent upon him – not necessarily his family in the modern sense.

first fruits and tenths: clerical taxation, constituting the first year's revenue of any benefice, and an annual payment thereafter.

frankpledge: an oath to keep the peace, guaranteed by membership of a group of about ten men (tithing) with mutual responsibility.

fyrd: the Old English militia. All men between 16 and 60 were required to possess weapons, and to appear when summoned to the king's service.

gravitas: literally 'gravity' or 'weight'; a combination of experience and seriousness of purpose.

in mortuam manum: literally 'into the dead hand', meaning that ecclesiastical corporations did not have a human life cycle.

in partibus infidelibus: literally 'in infidel places'; the towns and provinces used for these titles had been in Muslim hands for centuries.

intendants: professional provincial administrators, much used by Cardinal Richelieu in France during the reign of Louis XIV.

judices fiscales: literally 'fiscal judges'; judicial officers who had the duty of collecting money from fines and amercements.

Laws of Oleron: a primitve code of customary origin, intended to maintain discipline on shipboard; first recorded in the twelfth century, and named from an island off the Biscay coast of France.

legislator humanus: the human legislator; meaning those members of the society referred to who took part in the law-making process.

maiestas: literally 'majesty' or 'magnificence'; the whole of the monarch's honour or prestige.

manred: the commandment of personal service, usually of a military nature.

mero moto suo: by one's own sole authority; that is, without consultation or consent.

nobilitas major: the titled nobility, subject to creation by patent; that is, barons and above.

nobilitas minor: the untitled nobility, not subject to creation by patent; that is, knights, esquires and gentleman.

non est inventus: literally, 'he (or she) cannot be found'; a formal return, often a euphemism for 'I cannot be bothered to look'.

oculus episcopus: literally 'the bishop's eye', because of his role in detecting and prosecuting offences *ex officio*.

pleas of the crown: criminal offences of a serious nature (treasons and felonies), which were reserved for trial in the king's courts of common law.

probi homines: literally 'honest men'; that is, men of substance and good repute.

prud'homme: a man, particularly a soldier, of honour and reputation, especially one who observed the formal rules of courtesy.

populus: those who had some stake in the community, including peasant farmers, craftsmen and merchants as well as the gentry and aristocracy.

potestas jurisdictionis: jurisdictional authority; as distinct from spiritual authority.

praemunire: the offence of exercising ecclesiastical jurisdiction without the king's consent, or exceeding the proper limits of that jurisdiction; formalized by statute in 1393.

pro hac vice: 'one-off'; commissions and other instruments issued for a single, specific occasion.

quare clausum fregit: the breaking of a 'close' or enclosed property; used mainly of land rather than premises.

quorum: the core of the commission of the peace, consisting of those justices who had legal qualifications or other special training.

sacerdotium: literally 'the priesthood', but used to include all those in major orders. In some circumstances it also included those in minor orders.

Salic Law: the customary law of the French succession, which banned women from possessing the crown, or transmitting a claim to it.

sede vacante: literally 'with the seat vacant'; used to describe an episcopal interregnum.

Staple of Calais: the sole licensed export outlet for raw wool; operated by the Company of the Staple, or Staplers.

ultra vires: beyond the proper competence of the officer or institution concerned.

valor ecclesiasticus: a census of ecclesiastical wealth, taken by commission in 1535.

Wards and Liveries: the office (later court) responsible for administering the estates of minors who had inherited tenancies held in chief from the crown.

Select Bibliography of Secondary Works

Adams, S., 'Eliza enthroned', in *The Reign of Elizabeth I*, ed. C. Haigh (London, 1984).

Adams, S., 'Faction, clientage and party in English politics, 1550–1603', *History Today*, 32, 1982.

Alsop, J.D., 'Innovation in Tudor Taxation', *English Historical Review*, 99, 1984.

Alsop, J.D., 'The Revenue Commission of 1552', *Historical Journal*, 22, 1979.

Anglo, S., *Images of Tudor Kingship* (London, 1992).

Anglo, S., *Spectacle, Pageantry and Early Tudor Policy* (Oxford, 1965).

Archer, I.W., 'The London lobbies in the late sixteenth century', *Historical Journal*, 31, 1988.

Archer, I.W., *The Pursuit of Stability: social relations in Elizabethan London* (London, 1991)

Ashton, R., *The City and the Court, 1603–1643* (Oxford, 1979).

Axton, M., *The Queen's Two Bodies* (London, 1977).

Baldwin, J.F., *The King's Council in the Middle Ages* (London, 1913).

Bean, J.M.W., *The Decline of English Feudalism, 1215–1540* (Manchester, 1968).

Beck, J., *Tudor Cheshire* (London, 1968).

Beer, B.L., *Northumberland* (Kent State, 1973).

Beer, B.L., *Rebellion and Riot: popular disorders in England in the reign of Edward VI* (Kent State, 1982).

Bellamy, J.G., *Bastard Feudalism and the Law* (London, 1989).

Bellamy, J.G., *Crime and Public Order in England in the Later Middle Ages* (London, 1973).

Bernard, G.W., *War, Taxation and Rebellion in Early Tudor England* (Brighton, 1986).

Bernard, G.W., *The power of the Early Tudor Nobility: a study of the fourth and fifth Earls of Shrewsbury* (Brighton, 1985).

Bernard, G.W. (ed.), *The Tudor Nobility* (Manchester, 1992).

Blatcher, M., *The Court of King's Bench, 1450–1550* (London, 1978).

Bossy J., 'The Counter Reformation and the people of Catholic Ireland,

1596–1641', *Historical Studies*, 8, 1971.

Boynton, L.O., *The Elizabethan Militia, 1558–1638* (London, 1967).

Bradshaw, B., 'The Edwardian reformation in Ireland', *Archivum Hibernicum*, 24, 1976–7.

Bradshaw, B., *The Irish Constitutional Revolution of the Sixteenth Century* (Cambridge, 1979).

Bradshaw, B., 'Native reaction to the Westward enterprise: a case study in Gaelic ideology' in *The Westward Enterprise*, eds K.R. Andrews, N. Canny and P.E.H. Hair (London, 1978).

Bradshaw, B., 'Sword, word and strategy in the Reformation in Ireland', *Historical Journal*, 21, 1978.

Brigden, S.E., *London and the Reformation* (Oxford, 1989).

Brisson, D.R., *The Merchant Adventurers of England: the company and the crown, 1474–1564* (London, 1993).

Brooks, F.W., 'The Cinque Ports', *Mariners' Mirror*, 15, 1929.

Brooks, F.W., *The Council of the North* (London, 1953).

Brown, A.L., 'The King's councillors in fifteenth century England', *Transactions of the Royal Historical Society*, 5th series, 19, 1969.

Burns, J.H., *Lordship, Kingship and Empire: the idea of monarchy, 1400–1525* (London, 1992).

Burwash, D., *English Merchant Shipping, 1460–1540* (Toronto, 1947).

Bush, M.L., *The Government Policy of Protector Somerset* (Manchester, 1975).

Bush, M.L., *The Pilgrimage of Grace* (Manchester, 1996).

Bush, M.L., 'The problem of the far north: a study in the crisis of 1537 and its consequennces', *Northern History*, 6, 1971.

Byrne, M. St C., *Elizabethan Life in Town and Country* (London, 1961).

Canny, N.P., *The Elizabethan Conquest of Ireland: a pattern established, 1565–1576* (London, 1976).

Canny, N.P., *The Formation of an Old English Elite in Ireland* (London, 1975).

Carpenter, C., *Locality and Polity: a study of Warwickshire landed society, 1401–1499* (Cambridge, 1992).

Caspari, F., *Humanism and the Social Order in Tudor England* (Chicago, 1954).

Challis, C.E., *The Tudor Coinage* (Manchester, 1978).

Chrimes, S.B., *English Constitutional Ideas in the Fifteenth Century* (New York, 1965).

Chrimes, S.B., *Henry VII* (London, 1972).

Clark P., *English Provincial Society from the Reformation to the Revolution* (Brighton, 1977).

Clark, P., and Slack P., (eds) *English Towns in Transition, 1500–1700* (London, 1976).

Clayton, D.J., *The Administration of the County Palatine of Chester, 1442–1485* (Chetham Society, 3rd series, 35, 1990).

Clough, C.H. (ed.), *Profession, Vocation and Culture in later Medieval England* (Liverpool, 1982).

Cockburn, J.S., *A History of the English Assizes, 1558–1714* (Cambridge, 1972).

Collinson, P. , *The Elizabethan Puritan Movement* (London, 1967).

Collinson, P., 'The monarchical republic of Queen Elizabeth I', *Bulletin of the John Rylands Library*, 69, 1986–7.

Collinson, P., *The Religion of Protestants: the church in English society, 1559–1625* (Cambridge, 1982).

Colvin H.M. (ed.), *The History of the King's Works*, IV: 1485–1660, pt 2 (London, 1982).

Condon, M.M., 'Ruling elites in the reign of Henry VII', in *Patronage, Pedigree and Power in Late Medieval England*, ed. C. Ross (London, 1979).

Cornwall, J., *The Revolt of the Peasantry, 1549* (London, 1977).

Cornwall, J., *Wealth and Society in Early Sixteenth Century England* (London, 1988).

Coward, B., *The Stanleys: Lords Stanley and Earls of Derby, 1385–1672* (London, 1983).

Cross, C., *The Royal Supremacy in the Elizabethan Church* (London, 1969).

Cruickshank, C.G., *Army Royal: an account of Henry VIII's invasion of France, 1514* (Oxford, 1969).

Cruickshank, C.G., *Elizabeth's Army* (Oxford, 1966).

Davies, C.S.L., *Peace, Print and Protestantism, 1450–1558* (London, 1976).

Davies, C.S.L., 'Provisions for armies, 1509–1550: a study in the effectiveness of early Tudor government', *Economic History Review*, 2nd series, 17, 1964–5.

Davies, R.R., *The Revolt of Owain Glyn Dwr* (Oxford, 1995).

Davis, R., *English Overseas Trade, 1500–1700* (London, 1970).

Dawson, J.P., *Oracles of the Law* (London, 1968).

Dean, D.M., and Jones, N.L., (eds) *The Parliaments of Elizabethan England* (London, 1990).

Dent, J., *The Quest for Nonsuch* (London, 1962).

Dietz, F.C., *English Government Finance, 1485–1558* (Champagne/Urbana, Ill., 1921)

Doran, S., *Monarchy and Matrimony* (Stroud, 1996).

Dovey, Z., *An Elizabethan Progress* (Stroud, 1996).

Dowling, M., 'The gospel and the court: reformation under Henry VIII', in *Protestantism and the National Church in Sixteenth Century England*, eds P. Lake and M. Dowling (London, 1987).

Dowling, M., *Humanism in the Age of Henry VIII* (London, 1986).

Duffy, E., *The Stripping of the Altars* (Yale, 1993).

Dunlop, I., *Palaces and Progresses of Elizabeth I* (London, 1962).

Dunne, T.J., 'The Gaelic response to conquest and colonisation: the evidence of the poetry', *Studia Hibernica*, 20, 1980.

Dyer, A.D., *Decline and Growth in English Towns, 1400–1640* (London, 1991).

Eaglestone, A.J., *The Channel Islands under Tudor Government* (Oxford, 1949).

Edwards, J.G., *The Principality of Wales, 1267–1969* (Cardiff, 1969).

Ellis, S.G., 'A border baron: the rise and fall of Lord Dacre of the North', *Historical Journal*, 35, 1992.

Ellis, S.G., 'Crown, community and government in the English territories, 1450–1575', *History*, 71, 1986.

Ellis, S.G., *Reform and Revival: English government in Ireland, 1470–1534* (London, 1986).

Ellis, S.G., *Tudor Frontiers and Noble Power: the making of the British state* (Oxford, 1995).

Ellis, S.G., *Tudor Ireland* (London, 1985).

Ellis, S.G., 'Tudor policy and the Kildare ascendency in the Lordship of Ireland, 1496–1534', *Irish Historical Studies*, 20, 1977.

Elton, G.R., "The body of the whole realm": parliament and representation in Medieval and Tudor England, in *Studies in Tudor and Stuart Government and Politics II* (Cambridge, 1974).

Elton, G.R., *England under the Tudors* (3rd edn, London, 1993).

Elton, G.R., *The Parliament of England, 1559–81* (Cambridge, 1986).

Elton, G.R., 'Politics and the Pilgrimage of Grace', in *After the Reformation* ed. B. Malament (London, 1980).

Elton, G.R., *Reform and Reformation, 1485–1558* (Cambridge, 1977).

Elton, G.R., *Reform and Renewal* (Cambridge, 1973).

Elton, G.R., *The Tudor Constitution* (2nd edn, Cambridge, 1982).

Elton, G.R., 'Tudor government: points of contact; the Council' in *Studies in Tudor and Stuart Government and Politics*, III (Cambridge, 1983).

Elton, G.R., 'Tudor Government; points of contact; the court', in *Studies in Tudor and Stuart Government and Politics*, III (Cambridge, 1983).

Elton, G.R., 'Tudor government: points of contact; the Parliament', in Studies in *Tudor and Stuart Government and Politics*, III (Cambridge, 1983).

Elton, G.R., *The Tudor Revolution in Government* (Cambridge, 1953).

Everitt, A., 'Social mobility in early modern England', *Past and Present*, 33, 1966.

Falls, C., *Elizabeth's Irish Wars* (London, 1950).

Ferguson, A.B., *The Indian Summer of English Chivalry* (Durham, N.C., 1949).

Fox, A., and Guy, J.A., *Reassessing the Henrician Age* (Oxford, 1986).

Fudge, J.D., *Cargoes, Embargoes and Emissaries: the commercial and political interaction of England and the German Hanse, 1450–1510* (Toronto, 1995).

Gillingham, J., *The Wars of the Roses* (London, 1981).

Gleason, J.H., *The Justices of the Peace in England, 1558–1640* (Oxford, 1969).

Goring, J.J., 'Social change and military decline in mid-Tudor England', *History*, 60, 1975.

Graves, M.A.R., *Early Tudor Parliaments, 1485–1558* (London, 1990).

Graves, M.A.R., *Elizabethan Parliaments, 1559–1601* (London, 1987).

Graves, M.A.R., *The House of Lords in the Parliaments of Edward VI and Mary* (Cambridge, 1981).

Graves, M.A.R., *Thomas Norton, the Parliament Man* (Oxford, 1994).

Graves, M.A.R., *The Tudor Parliaments: crown, lords and commons, 1485–1603* (London, 1985).

Griffiths, R.A., *The Reign of Henry VI* (London, 1981).

Griffiths, R.A., *Sir Rhys ap Thomas and his Family* (Cardiff, 1993).

Griffiths, R.A., and Thomas, R.S., *The Making of the Tudor Dynasty* (Cardiff, 1985).

Gunn, S.J., *Charles Brandon, Duke of Suffolk, 1484–1545* (Oxford, 1988).

Gunn, S.J., *Early Tudor Government, 1485–1558* (London, 1995).

Gunn, S.J., 'The French wars of Henry VIII', in *The Origins of War in Early Modern Europe*, ed. J. Black (London, 1987).

Gunn, S.J., 'The regime of Charles Brandon, duke of Suffolk, in north Wales, and the reform of Welsh government, 1509–1525', *Welsh History Review*, 12, 1985.

Gunn, S.J., and Lindley, P., *Cardinal Wolsey: church, state and art* (London, 1991).

Guy, J.A., *The Cardinal's Court* (Brighton, 1977).

Guy, J.A., 'The King's Council and political participation' in *Reassessing the Henrician Age*.

Guy, J.A., 'The Privy Council: revolution or evolution' in *Revolution Reassessed*, ed. D. Starkey and C. Coleman (London, 1986)

Guy, J.A., 'Thomas Cromwell and the intellectual origins of the Henrician revolution' in *Reassessing the Henrician Age*.

Guy, J.A., *Tudor England* (Oxford, 1988).

Gwyn, P.J., *The King's Cardinal: the rise and fall of Thomas Wolsey* (London, 1990).

Haigh, C., *Elizabeth I* (London, 1988).

Haigh, C., *English Reformations: religion, politics and society under the Tudors* (Oxford, 1993).

Haigh, C., *Reformation and Resistance in Tudor Lancashire* (Manchester, 1975).

Haigh, C., *The Reign of Elizabeth* I (London, 1984).

Harbison, E.H., 'French intrigues at Queen Mary's court', *American Historical Review*, 45, 1940.

Harbison, E.H., *Rival Ambassadors at the Court of Queen Mary* (Princeton, N.J., 1940).

Harriss, G.L., 'Medieval government and statecraft', *Past and Present*, 24, 1963.

Hassell Smith, A., *County and Court: government and politics in Norfolk, 1558–1603* (Oxford, 1974).

Hawkwood, A.D.K., 'The enfranchisement of constituencies, 1509–1558', *Parliamentary History*, 10, 1991.

Hayes-McCoy, G.A., 'Gaelic society in Ireland in the late sixteenth century', *Historical Studies*, 4, 1963.

Heal, F., *Hospitality in Early Modern England* (Oxford, 1990).

Heal, F., *Of Prelates and Princes* (London, 1980).

Heal F., and Holmes, C., *The Gentry in England and Wales, 1500–1700* (London, 1994).

Helmholtz, R.H., *Canon Law and the Church of England* (Cambridge, 1987).

Hill, C., *The Economic Problems of the Church* (Oxford, 1956).

Hoak, D.E., *The King's Council in the Reign of Edward VI* (Cambridge, 1976).

Hoak, D.E., 'The King's privy Chamber, 1547–1553', in *Tudor Rule and Revolution*, eds D. Guth and J.W. MacKenna (Cambridge, 1982).

Hoak, D.E., 'The secret history of the Tudor Court: the King's Coffers and the king's purse, 1542–1553', *Journal of British Studies*, 26, 1987.

Hoak, D.E., 'Two revolutions in Tudor Government: the formation and organisation of Mary I's privy Council', in *Revolution Reassessed*, eds D. Starkey and C. Coleman (London, 1986).

Hodgett, G.A.J., *Tudor Lincolnshire* (London, 1975).

Hodgson, J., *A History of Northumberland* (Newcastle, 1820–5).

Holdsworth, W.S., *A History of English Law*, 7th edn, ed. S.B. Chrimes (London, 1956).

Holmes, P., *Resistance and Compromise: the political thought of the Elizabethan Catholics* (Cambridge, 1982).

Holmes, P.J., 'The Great Council in the reign of Henry VII', *English Historical Review*, 101, 1986.

Holmes, P.J., 'The last Tudor Great Councils', *Historical Journal*, 33, 1990.

Hoskins, W.G., 'The re-building of rural England, 1570–1640', *Past and Present*, IV, 1953.

Houlbrooke, R.A., *Church Courts and the People during the English Reformation, 1520–1570* (Oxford, 1979).

Houlbrooke, R.A., *The English Family, 1450–1700* (London, 1984).

Howard, M., *The Early Tudor Country House: architecture and politics, 1490–1550* (London, 1987).

Hoyle, R.W., 'Henry Percy sixth Earl of Northumberland and the fall of the House of Percy', in *The Tudor Nobility*, ed. G.W. Bernard (Manchester, 1992).

Hughes, P., *The Reformation in England* (London, 1950–4).

Hurstfield, J., *The Queen's Wards: wardship and marriage under Elizabeth I* (London, 1958).

Ingram, M.J., *Church Courts, Sex and Marriage in England, 1570–1640* (London, 1987).

Ingram, M.J., 'Communities and courts: law and disorder in early seventeenth century Wiltshire', in *Crime in England, 1550–1800*, ed. J.S. Cockburn (London, 1977).

Irwin, L., 'The Irish Presidency Courts, 1569–1672', *Irish Jurist*, new series, 12, 1977.

Ives, E.W., *The Common Lawyers of Pre-Reformation England* (Cambridge, 1983).

Ives, E.W., 'Court and county palatine in the reign of Henry VIII: the career of William Brereton of Malpas', *Transactions of the Historical Society of Lancashire and Cheshire*, 123, 1971.

James, M.E., *Change and Continuity in the Tudor North: the rise of Thomas, first Lord Wharton* (York, 1965).

James, M.E., *English Politics and the Concept of Honour, 1485–1642* (Past and Present, supplement 3, 1978).

James, M.E., *Family, Lineage and Civil Society* (Oxford, 1974).

James, M.E., 'The murder at Cocklodge, 28th April, 1489', *Durham University Journal*, 57, 1964–5.

James, M.E., *Society, Politics and Culture: studies in early modern England* (London, 1986).

Jansen, S.L., *Political Protest and Prophecy under Henry VIII* (London, 1991).

Jenkins, G.H., *Hanes Cymru yn y Cyfnod Modern Cynnar, 1536–1760* (Cardiff, 1983).

Jones, M.K. and Underwood, M.G., *The King's Mother: Margaret Beaufort, Countess of Richmond and Derby* (Cambridge, 1992).

Jones, N.L., *Faith by Statute* (London, 1982).

Jones, W.J., *The Elizabethan Court of Chancery* (Cambridge, 1967).

Jordan, W.K., *Edward VI: the threshold of power* (London, 1970).

Jordan, W.K., *Edward VI: the young king* (London, 1968).

Jordan, W.K., *Philanthropy in England, 1480–1640* (London, 1959).

Kerridge, E., *The Agrarian Problem in the Ssixteenth Century and After* (London, 1969).

Kerridge, E., *Trade and Banking in Early Modern England* (Manchester, 1988).

King, J.N., *English Reformation Literature* (Cambridge, 1982).

Kinvig, R.H., *The History of the Isle of Man* (Oxford, 1944).

Kipling, G., *The Triumph of Honour* (London, 1977).

Knighton, C.S., 'The principal secretaries in the reign of Edward VI: reflections on their office and archives', in *Law and Government under the Tudors*, eds C.Cross, D. Loades and J. Scarisbrick (Cambridge, 1987).

Knowles, D., *The Religious Orders in England*, III (Cambridge, 1959).

Koebner, R., 'The imperial crown of this realm: Henry VIII, Constantine the Great and Polydore Vergil', *Bulletin of the Institute of Historical Research*, 26, 1953.

Kumin, B., *The Shaping of a Community: the rise and reformation of the English parish, 1400–1560* (Andover, 1996).

Lambert, S., 'Procedure in the House of Commons in the Early Stuart period', *English Historical Review*, 95, 1980.

Land, S.K., *Kett's Rebellion* (Norwich, 1977).

Lander, J.R., 'Council, administration and councillors, 1461–1485', *Bulletin of the Institute of Historical Research*, 32, 1959.

Lander, J.R., *Crown and Nobility, 1450–1509* (London, 1976).
Lander, J.R., *English Justices of the Peace, 1461–1509* (Stroud, 1989).
Lehmberg, S.E., *The Later Parliaments of Henry VIII, 1536–1545* (Cambridge, 1977)
Lehmberg, S.E., *The Reformation of Cathedrals* (Cambridge, 1988).
Lehmberg, S.E., *The Reformation Parliament, 1529–1536* (Cambridge, 1970).
Lloyd, C. and Thurley, S., *Henry VIII: images of a Tudor king* (London, 1990).
Loach, J., *Parliament and the Crown in the reign of Mary Tudor* (Oxford, 1986).
Loach, J., *Parliament under the Tudors* (Oxford, 1991).
Loach, J., *Protector Somerset* (Bangor, 1994).
Loades, D.M., *Essays in the Reign of Edward VI* (Bangor, 1994).
Loades, D.M., *John Dudley, Duke of Northumberland* (Oxford, 1996).
Loades, D.M., 'The last years of Cuthbert Tunstall, Bishop of Durham, 1547–1559', *Durham University Journal*, 66, 1973.
Loades, D.M., *Mary Tudor: a life* (Oxford, 1989).
Loades, D.M., 'Philip II as king of England', in *Law and government under the Tudors*, eds C. Cross, D. Loades and J. Scarisbrick (Cambridge, 1987).
Loades, D.M., *Politics and the Nation, 1450–1660* (4th edn, London, 1992).
Loades, D.M., *The Reign of Mary Tudor* (London, 1991).
Loades, D.M., 'Relations between the Anglican and Roman Catholic churches in the sixteenth and seventeenth century', in *Rome and the Anglicans*, ed. W. Haase (Berlin, 1982).
Loades, D.M., *The Tudor Court* (London, 1986).
Loades, D.M., *The Tudor Navy* (Andover, 1992).
Lockwood, S., 'Marsilius of Padua and the case for the royal ecclesiastical supremacy', *Transactions of the Royal Historical Society*, 6th series, 1, 1991.
Lowe, D.E., 'The Council of the Prince of Wales and the decline of the Herbert family during the second reign of Edward IV (1471–1483)', *Bulletin of the Board of Celtic Studies*, 27, 1977.
MacCaffrey, W., *Elizabeth I* (London, 1993).
MacCaffrey, W., *The Shaping of the Elizabethan Regime: Elizabethan Politics, 1558–1572* (Princeton, N.J., 1969).
McCoy, R.C., 'From the tower to the tiltyard: Robert Dudley's return to glory', *Historical Journal*, 27, 1984.
MacCulloch, D.N.J., *Suffolk and the Tudors: politics and religion in an English county, 1500–1600* (Oxford, 1986).
MacCulloch, D.N.J., *Thomas Cranmer* (Yale, 1996).
McFarlane, K.B., *The Nobility of Later Medieval England* (Oxford, 1973).
McKenna, J.W., 'How God became an Englishman' in *Tudor Rule and Revolution*, eds De Lloyd, J. Guth and J.W. McKenna (Cambridge, 1982).
McKenna, J.W., 'The myth of parliamentary sovereignty in late medieval England', *English Historical Review*, 94, 1979.
Makower, F., *The Constitutional History of the Church of England* (London, 1895).

Marcombe, D., *English Small Town Life: Retford, 1520–1642* (Leicester, 1993).

Marcombe, D. (ed.), *The Last Palatinate* (Leicester, 1987).

Marsden, R.G., 'The vice admirals of the coasts', *English Historical Review*, 22, 1907.

Mayer, T.F., *Thomas Starkey and the Common Weal: humanist politics and religion in the reign of Henry VIII* (Cambridge, 1989)

Mertes, K., *The English Noble Household, 1250–1600* (Cambridge, 1988).

Miller, H., *Henry VIII and the English Nobility* (Oxford, 1986).

Miller, H., 'London and parliament in the reign of Henry VIII', *Bulletin of the Institute of Historical Research*, 35, 1962.

Miller, H., 'Lords and Commons: relations between the two Houses of Parliament, 1509–1558,' *Parliamentary History*, I, 1982.

Morgan, D.A.L., 'The king's affinity in the politics of Yorkist England', *Transactions of the Royal Historical Society*, 5th series, 23, 1973.

Murray, K.M.E., *The Constitutional History of the Cinque Ports* (Manchester, 1935).

Myers, A.R., 'Parliament 1422–1509', in *The English Parliament in the Middle Ages*, eds R.G. Davies and J.H. Denton, (London, 1981).

Myers, A.R., *The Household of Edward IV* (Liverpool, 1959).

Neale, J.E., *Queen Elizabeth and her Parliaments* (London, 1953–7).

Nichols, J., *The Progresses and Public Processions of Queen Elizabeth* (London, 1823)

Nicholson, G., 'The Act of Appeals and the English Reformation', in *Law and Government under the Tudors*, eds C. Cross, D. Loades and J. Scarisbrick (Cambridge, 1987).

Notestein, W., 'The winning of the initiative by the House of Commons', *Proceedings of the British Academy*, 11, 1926.

Ogilvie, C., *The King's Government and the Common Law, 1471–1641* (London, 1958).

Palliser, D.M., 'The parish in perspective', in *Parish, Church and People: local studies in lay religion*, ed. S.J. Wright (London, 1988).

Parry, G.J.R., *A Protestant Vision: William Harrison and the Reformation of Elizabethan England* (Cambridge, 1987).

Pearl, V., *London on the Outbreak of the Puritan Revolution: city government and national politics, 1625–1643* (Oxford, 1961).

Pettegree, A., *Foreign Protestant Communities in Sixteenth Century London* (Oxford, 1986).

Pogson, R.H., 'Revival and reform in Mary Tudor's church', *Journal of Ecclesiastical History*, 25, 1974.

Prest, W.R., *The Rise of the Barristers: a social history of the English bar, 1590–1640* (Oxford, 1986).

Prestwich, M., *Cranfield: politics and profit under the early Stuarts* (Oxford, 1966).

Pulman, W.B., *The Elizabethan Privy Council in the 1570s* (Berkeley, Calif., 1971)

Putnam, B.H., (ed.) *Early Treatises on the Practice of Justices of the Peace in the Fifteenth and Sixteenth Centuries* (Oxford, 1926).

Quinn, D.B., *The Elizabethans and the Irish* (Ithaca, N.Y., 1966).

Rappaport, S., *Worlds within Worlds: structures of life in sixteenth century London* (Oxford, 1989).

Rawcliffe, C., 'The great lords as peace keepers: arbitration by English noblemen and their councils in the late middle ages', in *Law and Social Change in British History,* eds J.A. Guy and H.G. Beale (London, 1984).

Read, C., *William Lambarde and Local Government* (London, 1962).

Redworth, G., *In Defence of the Church Catholic: the life of Stephen Gardiner* (Oxford, 1990).

Reid, R.R., *The King's Council in the North* (London, 1921).

Reid, R.R., 'The rebellion of the northern Earls, 1569', *Transactions of the Royal Historical Society,* new series, 20, 1906.

Rex, R., *Henry VIII and the English Reformation* (London, 1993).

Richardson, W.C., *A History of the Court of Augmentations* (Baton Rouge, 1961).

Richardson, W.C., *The Report of the Royal Commission of 1552* (London, 1974).

Richardson, W.C., *Tudor Chamber Administration* (Baton Rouge, 1952).

Robinson, W.R.B., 'Early Tudor policy towards Wales: the acquisition of lands and offices within Wales by Charles Somerset, Earl of Worcester', *Bulletin of the Board of Celtic Studies,* 20, 1962–4: and 21, 1964–6.

Rose Troup, F., *The Western Rebellion of 1549* (London, 1913).

Ross, C.D., *Edward IV* (London, 1974).

Ross, C.D., *Richard III* (London, 1981).

Rowse, A.L., *Tudor Cornwall* (2nd edn, London, 1969).

Russell, J.G., *The Field of Cloth of Gold* (London, 1969).

Samaha, J., *Law and Order in Historical Perspective: the case of Elizabethan Essex* (London, 1974).

Scarisbrick, J.J., *Henry VIII* (London, 1968).

Scarisbrick, J.J., *The Reformation and the English People* (Oxford, 1984).

Schofield, R.S., 'Taxation and the political limits of the Tudor state', in *Law and Government under the Tudors,* eds C. Cross, D. Loades and J. Scarisbrick (Cambridge, 1987).

Silke, J., *Ireland and Europe, 1559–1607* (Dublin, 1966).

Silke, J., *Kinsale: the Spanish intervention in Ireland at the end of the sixteenth century* (Liverpool, 1970).

Skinner, Q., *The Foundations of Modern Political Thought* (Cambridge, 1978).

Slavin, A.J., 'The Tudor state, reformation and understanding change', in *Political Thought and the Tudor Commonwealth: deep structure, discourse and disguise,* eds P.A. Fideler and T.F. Mayer (London, 1992).

Smith, A.G.R., *The Emergence of a Nation State: 1529–1660* (London, 1984).

Smith, R.B., *Land and Politics in the England of Henry VIII: the West Riding of Yorkshire 1530–1546* (Oxford, 1970)

Somerville, R., 'The Duchy of Lancaster Council and the Court of Duchy Chamber', *Transactions of the Royal Historical Society*, 23, 1941.

Somerville, R., 'Henry VII's Council Learned in the Law', *English Historical Review*, 54, 1939.

Somerville, R., *A History of the Duchy of Lancaster* (London, 1953).

Somerville, R., 'The Palatinate Courts in Lancashire', in *Law Making and Law Makers in British History*, ed. A. Harding (London, 1980).

Starkey, D., 'Court, council and nobility in Tudor England', in *Princes, Patronage and the Nobility: the court at the beginning of the modern age*, eds R.G. Asch and A.M. Birke (London, 1991).

Starkey, D., *The Reign of Henry VIII: politics and personalities* (London, 1985).

Starkey, D., (ed.) *Henry VIII: a European court in England* (London, 1991).

Starkey, D., *The English Court from the Wars of the Roses to the Civil War* (London, 1987) .

Stone, L., *The Crisis of the Aristocracy,1558–1640* (Oxford, 1965).

Stone, L., *The Family, Sex and Marriage in England, 1500–1800* (Oxford, 1977).

Strong, R., *The Cult of Elizabeth* (London, 1977).

Strong, R., *Holbein and Henry VIII* (London, 1967).

Strong, R., *The Portraits of Queen Elizabeth* (London, 1963).

Strong, R., *Splendour at Court* (London, 1973).

Sturge, C., *Cuthbert Tunstall* (London, 1938).

Surtees, R., *The History and Antiquities of the County Palatine of Durham* (London, 1816–40).

Surtz, E. and Murphy, V., *The Divorce Tracts of Henry VIII* (Angers, 1988).

Thomas, K., *Religion and the Decline of Magic* (London, 1971).

Thomas, W.S.K., *Tudor Wales* (Llandysul, 1983).

Thompson, J.A.F., *The Early Tudor Church and Society, 1485–1529* (London, 1993).

Thompson, J.A.F., *The Transformation of Medieval England, 1370–1529* (London, 1983).

Thompson, G.S., *Lords lieutenants in the Sixteenth Century* (London, 1923).

Tittler, R., *Architecture and Power: the town hall and the English urban community, c.1500–1640* (Oxford, 1991).

Tittler, R., 'The incorporation of boroughs, 1549–1558', *History*, 62, 1977.

Tough, D.L.W., *The Last Years of a Frontier: a history of the borders during the reign of Elizabeth* (Oxford, 1928).

Ullman, W., 'This realm of England is an Empire', *Journal of Ecclesiastical History*, 30, 1979.

Usher, R.G., *The Rise and Fall of High Commission*, ed. P. Tyler (London, 1968).

Virgoe, R., 'The composition of the King's Council, 1437–1461', *Bulletin of the Institute of Historical Research*, 43, 1970.

Wall, A., 'Patterns of politics in England, 1558–1628', *Historical Journal*, 31, 1988.

Watts, S.J., *From Border to Middle Shire: Northumberland, 1586–1625* (London, 1975).

Weikel, A., 'The Marian Council revisited', in *The Mid-Tudor Polity, 1540–1560*, eds J. Loach and R. Tittler (London, 1980).

White, D.G., 'The reign of Edward VI in Ireland: some political, social and economic aspects', *Irish Historical Studies*, 14, 1964–5.

Whiting, R., *The Blind Devotion of the People* (Cambridge, 1989).

Williams, G., *Harri Tudur a Chymru/Henry Tudor and Wales* (Cardiff, 1985).

Williams, G., *Recovery, Reorientation and Reformation: Wales 1415–1642* (Cardiff, 1987).

Williams, G., *Wales and the Acts of Union* (Bangor, 1992).

Williams, G., *Welsh Reformation Essays* (Cardiff, 1967).

Williams, P., *The Council in the Marches of Wales under Elizabeth* (London, 1958).

Williams, P., *The Later Tudors: England 1547–1603* (Oxford, 1995).

Williams, P., *The Tudor Regime* (Oxford, 1979).

Williams, W.O., 'The survival of the Welsh language after the union of England and Wales: the first phase, 1536–1642', *Welsh History Review*, 2, 1964.

Wilson, E. Carus and Coleman, O., *England's Export Trade, 1275–1547* (London, 1963).

Wolffe, B.P., *The Crown Lands, 1461–1536: an aspect of Yorkist and early Tudor government* (London, 1970).

Wolffe, B.P., *The Royal Demesne in English History* (London, 1971).

Wood Legh, K.L., *Perpetual Chantries in Britain* (Cambridge, 1965).

Woodworth, A., *Purveyance for the Royal Household in the Reign of Elizabeth* (New York, 1945).

Youings, J., 'The Council of the West', *Transactions of the Royal Historical Society*, 5th series, 10, 1960.

Youings, J., *The Dissolution of the Monasteries* (London, 1971).

Youings, J., *Sixteenth Century England* (London, 1984).

Young, A., *Tudor and Jacobean Tournaments* (London, 1987).

Youngs, F.A., 'Towards petty sessions: Tudor JPs and the division of counties' in *Tudor Rule and Revolution*, eds De Lloyd J. Guth and J.W. McKenna (Cambridge, 1982).

Zell, M., 'Early Tudor JPs at work', *Archaeologia Cantiana*, 93, 1977.

Index

GENERAL THEOLOGICAL SEMINARY
NEW YORK